The English Language Arts
in the
Secondary School

Prepared by

THE COMMISSION ON THE ENGLISH CURRICULUM

The English Language Arts

in the Secondary School

Prepared by

THE COMMISSION ON THE ENGLISH CURRICULUM

of the

NATIONAL COUNCIL OF TEACHERS OF ENGLISH

New York

APPLETON-CENTURY-CROFTS, INC.

Preface

The English Language Arts in the Secondary School is the result of several years of curriculum study by the National Council of Teachers of English Curriculum Commission and the members of the Production Committee. This volume applies at the secondary level the principles of curriculum development established by research findings and by the tested experience of the Commission, the Committee, and teachers throughout the country.

Scope of the Volume. Part I—The Adolescent and the World Today—expresses the Commission's conviction that any curriculum in the language arts must be based upon an understanding of the adolescent and the world in which he lives. It sets the stage for what follows.

Part II—The Language Arts Program—offers specific guidance in curriculum development with profuse illustrations from individual schools and classrooms and from city and state programs now in operation. Assistance is given in designing the program as a whole and in building instructional units involving all four of the language arts and teaching skills in use. Separate chapters present in detail helps for meeting youth's needs through literature and developing competence in reading, speaking, listening, and writing. Another on the teaching of grammar, usage, and spelling attempts to bring order out of the many viewpoints expressed in these fields today and to give the teacher concrete help for classroom practice. In addition to the treatment of each of the language arts in turn, relationships among them are clearly indicated throughout the chapters.

"Making Communication Arts and Skills Reinforce Each Other" assembles experiences in the use of symbols in read-

v

ing and in writing and in the related graphic and speech arts in many schools throughout the country. "Meeting College Entrance Requirements in English" traces recent changes in emphasis from specific ground to be covered to the development of mature powers of thinking and expression through constant use of language in reading, writing, speaking, and listening in purposeful situations under expert direction. It brings the teacher up to date on what colleges actually expect of high school graduates and presents promising local practices in bridging the gap between secondary schools and colleges.

Preparation of the Volume. Hundreds of teachers conducted inquiries for the Production Committee through English Clubs affiliated with the National Council of Teachers of English, contributed curriculum materials developed in their local communities, participated in workshops and institutes co-sponsored by the Council and colleges and universities, and reacted orally or in writing to phases of the program when presented by members of the Production Committee and others at the Council's annual national conventions.

All members of the Production Committee were members of the committees which produced Volume I. As a result, Volume III has had full benefit of those earlier years of cooperative planning and discussions of the language arts curriculum in the entire range from nursery school through graduate study.

As early as 1947, the Production Committee discussed the implications of Volume I for the secondary school. When the writing was completed for the first volume, the Committee for Volume III held planning sessions to establish the scope of this volume, to prepare a working outline, and to select writers, some of whom were not members of the committee, to produce first drafts of chapters.

These drafts were duplicated and shared first among members of the Production Committee and, after revision,

with the Curriculum Commission. Annually at Commission
meetings, sections of the volume were discussed and successive revisions were prepared. Further changes were made to
incorporate materials developed by curriculum workers who
were using Volumes I and II and to give recognition to the
work of national organizations which were studying America's stake in a literate society.

Acknowledgments. The Commission is grateful for the
many examples of good practices presented throughout this
volume and acknowledged in footnotes.

Appreciation is also extended to the public schools in the
following localities from which photographs were received:
Atlanta, Georgia; Baltimore, Maryland; Berkeley, California;
Bountiful, Utah; Dallas, Texas; Denver, Colorado; Detroit,
Michigan; Ellenville, New York; Indianapolis, Indiana; Jef-
ferson, Arkansas; Kingston, New York; La Grange, Georgia;
Bloomfield School District and Duarte School District, Los
Angeles County, California; New York City, New York; Oak-
land, California; Pasadena, California; Peekskill, New York;
Richmond, Virginia; Rockville, Maryland; Sacramento, Cali-
fornia; San Carlos, California; San Francisco, California;
Vancouver, Washington; and Washington, D.C. Photographs
were also loaned by the Messmer High School, Milwaukee,
Wisconsin; Lake Forest Academy, Lake Forest, Illinois; The
Summer Demonstration Secondary School of the University
of California; The Laboratory School, Wisconsin State College, Platteville, Wisconsin.

To the National Council of Teachers of English Executive
Committees (1945–1956), the Director and the other members of the Curriculum Commission, the Director of Publications, the Production Committee and all other contributors
to Volume III, as well as to Appleton-Century-Crofts, Inc.,
publishers, and the staff in the Bureau of Publications of the
Baltimore Public Schools, the chairman is personally and
professionally grateful.

A. M. B.

THE COMMISSION ON THE
ENGLISH CURRICULUM

NATIONAL COUNCIL OF TEACHERS OF ENGLISH

704 S. Sixth St., Champaign, Illinois

DIRECTOR

Dora V. Smith, Professor of Education
University of Minnesota, Minneapolis
Minnesota

ASSOCIATE DIRECTORS

Angela M. Broening, Director of Publications,
formerly Head of the English Department
of the Forest Park High School and
Supervisor of English in Junior High Schools,
Baltimore Public Schools, Baltimore 18,
Maryland, Chairman, Production Committee,
Vol. III

Alfred H. Grommon, Associate Professor of
Education and English, Stanford University
Stanford, California

Helen K. Mackintosh, Chief, Elementary
Schools Section, Division of State
and Local School Systems, U. S. Office
of Education, Department of Health,
Education, and Welfare, Washington, D. C.

Porter G. Perrin, Professor of English
University of Washington, Seattle
Washington

MEMBERS OF THE COMMISSION

Harlen M. Adams, Executive Dean, Chico State College, Chico, California

Harold A. Anderson, Department of Education, University of Chicago, Chicago, Illinois

Roy P. Basler, Associate Director Reference Department, Library of Congress, Washington, D. C.

Dwight L. Burton, Associate Professor of English Education, Florida State University, Tallahassee, Florida; Editor, *The English Journal*

Simon Certner, Department of English, DeWitt Clinton High School, New York City, New York

Herbert L. Creek, Professor Emeritus, Department of English, Purdue University, Lafayette, Indiana

Muriel Crosby, Assistant Superintendent, Director of Elementary Education, Wilmington Public Schools, Wilmington, Delaware

MEMBERS OF THE COMMISSION

Carter Davidson, President and Professor of English, Union College and University, Schenectady-Albany, New York

John J. DeBoer, Professor of Education, University of Illinois, Urbana, Illinois; Editor, *Elementary English*

John C. Gerber, Professor of English and Co-ordinator of Communication Skills, State University of Iowa, Iowa City, Iowa

Margaret R. Greer, formerly Consultant in Library Service and Textbook Selection, Board of Education, Minneapolis, Minnesota

Helene W. Hartley, Professor of Education, Syracuse University, Syracuse, New York

W. Wilbur Hatfield, Secretary-Treasurer Emeritus of the National Council of Teachers of English, and formerly Editor of *The English Journal* and of *College English;* 10631 Seeley Avenue, Chicago 43, Illinois ·

Max J. Herzberg, Director of Publications, National Council of Teachers of English; Literary Editor, *Newark News,* South Orange, New Jersey

John C. Hodges, Professor of English, University of Tennessee, Knoxville, Tennessee

J. N. Hook, Professor of English, University of Illinois; Urbana, Illinois; Executive Secretary, National Council of Teachers of English

Charlton G. Laird, Professor of English, University of Nevada, Reno, Nevada

Dorothea McCarthy, Professor of Psychology, Fordham University, New York City, New York

Lucia B. Mirrielees, formerly Professor of English, Montana State University; Box 926, Stanford 1, California

E. Louise Noyes, formerly Head of the English Department, Santa Barbara High School, California; 425 Stanley Drive, Santa Barbara, California

Thomas C. Pollock, Dean and Professor of English, Washington Square College of Arts and Science, New York University, New York City, New York

Robert C. Pooley, Professor of English and Chairman, Department of Integrated Liberal Studies, University of Wisconsin, Madison, Wisconsin

* Grace Rawlings, Principal, Liberty School, Baltimore, Maryland

Marion C. Sheridan, Head, Department of English, James Hillhouse High School, New Haven, Connecticut

Edna L. Sterling, Director of the Language Arts, Seattle Public Schools, Seattle, Washington

Marion R. Trabue, Dean, School of Education, Pennsylvania State College, University Park, Pennsylvania

Blanche Trezevant, Assistant Professor of Education, Florida State University, Tallahassee, Florida; formerly Supervisor of English, Louisiana State Department of Education

* Kate V. Wofford, Head, Department of Elementary Education, University of Florida, Gainesville, Florida

J. Wayne Wrightstone, Director, Bureau of Educational Research, New York City Schools, Brooklyn, New York

* deceased

PRODUCTION COMMITTEE FOR VOLUME III

Angela M. Broening, Director of Publications, formerly Head of English Department of the Forest Park High School and Supervisor of English in Junior High Schools, Baltimore, Maryland, Public Schools, *Chairman*

Dorothea Fry, John Muir High School, Pasadena, California

Laurence B. Goodrich, Professor of English and Head of Department of English and Speech, State University Teachers College, Oneonta, New York

Lennox Grey, Professor of English and Head of the Department of the Teaching of English and Foreign Languages, Teachers College, Columbia University, New York, New York

Helene W. Hartley, Professor of Education, Syracuse University, Syracuse, New York

Lou LaBrant, University of Kansas

City, Kansas City, Missouri, formerly of New York University and Ohio State University

Mark Neville, Headmaster, The Latin School of Chicago, Chicago, Illinois

Helen F. Olson, Head of the Department of English, Queen Anne High School, Seattle, Washington

Marion C. Sheridan, Head of the Department of English, James Hillhouse High School, New Haven, Connecticut

Dora V. Smith, Professor of Education, University of Minnesota, Minneapolis, Minnesota, and Director of NCTE Curriculum Commission

W. Wilbur Hatfield, Secretary-Treasurer Emeritus of the National Council of Teachers of English, and formerly Editor, *The English Journal* and *College English*

ADDITIONAL CONTRIBUTING AUTHORS

Virginia Alwin, Associate Professor of English, Arizona State College, Flagstaff, Arizona

Harold R. W. Benjamin, Professor of Education, George Peabody College for Teachers, Nashville, Tennessee

Dwight L. Burton, Associate Professor of English Education, Florida State University, Tallahassee, Florida; Editor, *The English Journal*

Luella B. Cook, formerly Consultant in Curriculum Development, Minneapolis Public Schools, Minneapolis, Minnesota

Adelaide Cunningham, Roosevelt High School, Atlanta, Georgia

Lawrence K. Frank, Author and Lecturer, and formerly Director, Caroline Zachary Institute, Human Development, 25 Clark Street, Belmont 78, Massachusetts

Virginia Belle Lowers, Supervisor

of Senior High School English and Foreign Adjustment, Curriculum Branch, Los Angeles City Schools, Los Angeles, California

Constance McCullough, Professor of Education, San Francisco State Teachers College, San Francisco, California

Thomas C. Pollock, New York University, New York, New York

Robert C. Pooley, University of Wisconsin, Madison, Wisconsin

Francis Shoemaker, Professor of English, Teachers College, Columbia University, New York, New York

Dora S. Skipper, Florida State University, formerly Curriculum Coordinator, Florida State Department of Education, Tallahassee, Florida

Blanche Trezevant, Assistant Professor of Education, Florida State University, Tallahassee, Florida

Contents

Contents

PART I

PART I

The Adolescent and the World Today

PREVIEW OF CHAPTER 1

The Promise of Today's World

The Demand for Increased Intellectual Power

The Need for Ability to Communicate

The Effect of Speed

The Tensions Caused by Submergence of the Individual

The Need for Resolution of Conflicting Purposes and Traditions

The Function of the Language Arts Program in the World the Adolescent Faces

The World the Adolescent Faces

THE WORLD confronting the adolescent today is both promising and threatening. The boy and girl growing up nowadays are privileged to live in one of the most exciting, dynamic periods in the history of Western civilization, but they face all the confusions, uncertainties, and hazards that accompany a period of rapid and almost overwhelming change.

The Promise of Today's World

The world is promising, especially to energetic young men and women, because of the immense potentialities it offers them for attaining cherished aspirations. Never before have there been available such resources of new knowledge and understanding, of new tools and techniques, and of trained professional personnel for meeting the needs of living. Never before could people look forward with such confidence to the progressive improvement of health and the extension of the span of life; to the provision of housing that will foster healthier, wiser, happier family living; to the reduction of mental illness and emotional disorders and, more important, to the development of healthy personalities.

Indeed, in almost every aspect of living there now exist the means to achieve what in earlier generations were hardly-dreamed-of goals. Americans have a clearer understanding of what the democratic aspiration means, not only in terms of political organization but in terms of recognizing and respecting the worth and dignity of the individual personality. Born, in part, of similar aspirations among other peoples toward a better way of life are world-wide unrest and upheavals.

The means are available to achieve goals. Resources are actually in hand or potentially available for truly astonishing advances in making living more secure, more effective, more fulfilling of the individual's goals and values.[1]

Demand for Increased Intellectual Power

Automation, which is contributing to these material benefits, will require "trained and educated people in unprecedented numbers," according to Peter F. Drucker.[2] "Even in routine jobs automation will require ability to think, a trained imagination, and good judgment plus some skill in logical methods, some mathematical understanding, and some ability well above the elementary level to read and write."

As reported by John Fischer,[3] Mr. Drucker cited the example of one large manufacturing company employing 150,000 people, which now hires 300 college graduates annually. When its automation program is completed, a few years from now, it will need to hire 7,000 college graduates each year. Every one of them will be a leader of small group specialists, working with vastly complicated machines and procedures; and ideally each of them should have the kind of education and ability which now are required only on the upper levels of management.

And John Fischer further observed:

The same process seems to be operating in public affairs at least as rapidly as it is in industry. A generation ago, any reasonably intel-

---

[1] "Big Changes in Your Life—Just 5 or 10 Years Ahead," *Changing Times—The Kiplinger Magazine,* Vol. 9, No. 10 (October, 1955), pp. 41–48; "Automation," *Time,* Vol. LXVII, No. 12 (March 19, 1956), pp. 98–106.

[2] Peter F. Drucker, "America's Next Twenty Years," *Harper's,* Vol. 210 (1955): March, pp. 27–32; April, pp. 41–47; May, pp. 39–44; June, pp. 52–59.

[3] John Fischer, "The New Demand for Leaders" (paper delivered on Friday afternoon, February 24, 1956, at the Third Annual Editor-Educator Conference co-sponsored by the Magazine Publishers Association and the National Education Association).

ligent and honest man could hope to fill almost any governmental post—from the local school board to an ambassadorship—with a fair prospect of success. The problems were comparatively straightforward; most of them could be handled by the exercise of common sense. Alas, today, government isn't that simple. Even an alderman is now expected to be expert in race relations, sewage disposal, traffic regulation, municipal finance, the social services, television techniques, personnel management, juvenile delinquency, housing codes, campaign oratory, and the prescribed etiquette for welcoming visiting firemen from Moscow, Pakistan, and Siam.

Need for Ability to Communicate

Although specialized training is an obvious necessity for the new army of leaders needed in every field—from engineering to school teaching, from politics to the electronics industry—there is one qualification common to all of them. This is the basic requirement for leadership everywhere and in all periods of history. *It is the ability to communicate*. The one essential tool for every sort of leader is skill in the use of words. Indeed, his job—always and without exception—primarily is to explain, to persuade, to give clear directions, to encourage and console; in sum, to convey ideas to other people.

The Effect of Speed

Another significant characteristic of the world the adolescent faces is speed. When an airplane can streak from California to New York in less time than it took an express rider to travel twenty-five miles from Washington's headquarters, it is easy to repeat the cliché of a shrinking country. When a president of the United States can speak directly to millions of listeners in both hemispheres before the sound of his voice travels to the back of the room in which he is sitting, it is simple to claim that time and distance are somehow being annihilated.

It is too simple. Time and distance are the same today as they ever were. They just look different with man moving faster than sound and his words moving 186,000 miles per second. In this connection, it has been suggested that the world is getting larger rather than smaller.[4] Certainly it is getting larger in the number of people crowded onto its lim-

[4] Cf. John H. Lounsburg, "The World Is Growing Larger," *Peabody Journal of Education*, Vol. 31, No. 5 (March, 1954), pp. 278–279.

ited land surface. Certainly the complexity of problems arising from the steady increase of interdependency among these people grows greater year by year. Certainly the area, physical or cultural, that any one man or group of men can at least see, if not understand, becomes more comprehensive and more detailed as a consequence of daily technological advances.

Such widenings of horizons are all tied to *accelerating speed and range of communication.* Not only are there more people in the world decade by decade, but they talk more to one another, see more of one another, and do both more rapidly than would have seemed possible only yesterday. They depend upon one another more and more as they share more and more of their ideas, goods, and services.

Tensions Caused by Submergence of the Individual

The world the adolescent faces today is one of growing anonymity as well as of increased speed. He goes somewhere, anywhere, rapidly; and when he gets there he is likely to be one of a crowd. He is more important as an element of the large, faceless group than was his father or grandfather, and far less important as a well-recognized individual with unique traits and tendencies.

Paradoxically, however, the adolescent of today is kept very conscious of himself as an individual because of the many tensions that pull him in opposing directions. *He lives in a society beset by tensions.* He grows up in a community, a nation, and a world in which he is aware of more conflicting and severe strains than were readily apparent to most of his ancestors at a comparable age. Whether there are actually more of such tensions today than there were in certain earlier troubled times is, of course, an open question. It is probable that the men of every era tend to exaggerate the difficulties faced by their own generation and to minimize those faced by their ancestors. Certainly the current decade is at least as well supplied with tough, tension-producing problems as have been most periods of American history, and the adolescent of today has means of seeing and hearing about these problems almost as fast as they occur and wherever they occur. He faces these problems as a member of several groups, moreover, and his loyalty to each of the groups is likely to produce individual tensions.

As an Eagle Scout, a church member, or a high school student of social problems, he learns to think of the welfare of others, to put the country and the community ahead of selfish interests, and to honor his conscience as his king. As an after-hours and summer businessman, a member of the hot-rod set, or a participant in family quarrels, he may learn to think first of his own welfare, to regard individual profit as he observes many "successful" men view it, and to avoid at all costs the reputation of being a "square." Thus equipped, he is tortured by doubt of himself every hour of the day. If he shows his girl a degree of courtesy his mother and her mother regard as a minimum standard of manners for a decent boy, he may be falling so far below the movie idol in his girl's fancy as to bring upon himself her contempt. If he drives safely, he is "chicken." If he studies his lessons too intently, he may grow up to be an "egghead."

Under such pressures, he may hide in the crowd and grow more and more confused and ill at ease. No matter which way he turns, he may feel guilty according to some mass standard.

For adolescents or their parents and teachers, it is not easy to keep a balanced, long-term view of the present situation, realizing the promise as well as the threats of this contemporary world. It is especially difficult for young people to gain perspective on these broader problems when they are confused and perplexed about their own development. Physically they are themselves changing and attaining consciousness of sex. They are substituting dependence on their own powers and reliance on their fellows for dependence upon the family. While looking askance at the conflict between tradition and current patterns of thought and behavior, they are facing at the same time the revision of their own childish beliefs and expectations in the course of their growing maturity. They are concerned about their own personal competence to meet the demands of adult life both in earning a living and in becoming participating and respected members of society.[5]

What makes these preoccupations, which adolescents have always had, so acutely disturbing today is that there are so few dependable patterns for them to follow, so few guides to consult. The very process of social and cultural change has made the old certainties and many of the long-accepted goals and patterns increasingly incongruous with the kind of life young people must learn to carry on today.

They cannot live according to the standards and patterns of the former agricultural, handicraft life. They are no longer able to *make* a living, exercising their strength, fortitude, skill, and courage to wrest a livelihood from the soil or by simple home craft. Today they must learn to live in cities, in multifamily dwellings with neighbors from different backgrounds and traditions; they (including wives who go out of the home to earn) must learn to *earn* a living by money wages; they must try to create and maintain a home and family life despite many obstacles and conflicting demands and the innumerable choices confronting them. Also, they must try to accept and put into practice an amazing array of new ideas and new assumptions, new techniques, and new ways of living, necessary for health, welfare, mental hygiene, occupational competence, and national security.

But the situation is further complicated by the continual impact of newspapers, magazines, radio, television, movies, and the variety of advertisements where all the conflicts and confusions of the contemporary world are portrayed.

Adults are accustomed to think of these problems and diffi-

[5] Cf. Robert J. Havighurst, *Human Development and Education* (New York, Longmans, Green & Company, 1952), p. 352.

culties as "out there" in space, speaking of them as social problems. The locus of every social problem, however, is in individual personalities, each of whom is striving to maintain some order and to find some security in his "private world" because as a personality he lives by and for ideas in the symbolic world of his cultural traditions.

Need for Resolution of Conflicting Purposes and Traditions

These goals and purposes are defined by traditions which are transmitted or translated by parents and teachers to children and youth who are thereby inducted into the cultural world of their people. The persistence of traditions and the continuity of culture are dependent upon communication, chiefly by language in and through which individuals talk not only to others but to themselves. And probably the bulk of this talk is to reassert, to reaffirm, to clarify, and to apply these ideas and expectations by and for which they live.

The increasing divergence of the emerging new conceptions and dynamic ways of thinking from the centuries-old assumptions and expectations of a static world is the source of many perplexities today. It is not merely a question of using language with more care and precision, with well-defined referents and all the other important criteria of semantics. It is a question of developing a new frame of reference, reflecting the dynamic conceptual organization and new ways of thinking now being developed by science, medicine, psychiatry and the arts, with terms and expressions that will be more expressive of what must be communicated.[6]

The Function of the Language Arts Program in the World the Adolescent Faces

A world of change, of speed, of massed groups, of heightened tensions, and of gravely conflicting views—this, in general terms, is the world the adolescent faces today. To meet

[6] Cf. Lawrence K. Frank, *Nature and Human Nature—Man's New Image of Himself* (New Brunswick, N. J., Rutgers University Press, 1951).

such a world with equanimity and intelligence, the adolescent needs an education of great scope and power. In communication skills, he needs particularly an education at once more comprehensive and more exact than his forefathers required.

He must develop for himself powers of expression commensurate with the requirements of an enlarged and interrelated world. He must have skill in intelligent reading and listening that he may broaden the background of his knowledge and increase his powers of judgment and imagination, upon which the adequate use of language depends. Through a persisting habit of reading and of listening to radio, television, and public addresses, he must keep abreast of the world today and increase his appreciation of the contribution of times past. He must know from personal contact with the literature of his own country and that of other nations what men have thought and felt and lived for in days gone by and have bequeathed to him as a part of his cultural tradition. These thoughts and attitudes, together with those of his own day, he must be able to stack up against some standard of reference resulting from his own thinking and judgment.

To achieve this power, he must practice the skills of logic required to resolve conflicts. The quality of his own thinking will be the measure of his power to analyze and to evaluate. The breadth and precision of his use of language will determine the extent of his ability to influence others. He must understand, also, the social and psychological factors which influence men's attitudes and points of view. He must learn not to be disturbed by these differences, but to accept them and respond to their challenge.

Adolescents increasingly depend upon newspapers and magazines, upon motion pictures, and upon radio and television for their information and ideas. They find in them also a source of great personal enjoyment. Habits of choice and of careful assessing of values are crucial to the turning of these influences into constructive channels, stimulating, not blunting, to the imagination and sense of moral values.

Special emphasis should be given in the program of the language arts to the fact that the locus of every social problem is in an individual personality, striving to find some security within himself through which he may hope to be equal to the conflicting demands of the life about him. Later chapters in this volume will illustrate from the classrooms of the country what the teaching of literature and of imaginative expression in both speech and writing can do to foster this security and the individuality of which it is a part. These chapters demonstrate also that the problems of communication, both intimately personal and set in the framework of social conflict, are a major concern of the program in the language arts today.

Tarkington, Thou Should'st Be Living in This Hour *

OGDEN NASH

O Adolescence, O Adolescence,
I wince before thine incandescence.
Thy constitution young and hearty
Is too much for this aged party.
Thou standest with loafer-flattened feet
Where bras and funny papers meet.
When anxious elders swarm about
Crying "Where are you going?" thou answerest "Out,"
Leaving thy parents swamped in debts
For bubble gum and cigarettes.

Thou spurnest in no uncertain tone
The sirloin for the ice-cream cone;
Not milk, but cola, is thy potion;
Thou wearest earrings in the ocean,
Blue jeans at dinner, or maybe shorts,
And lipstick on the tennis courts.

Forever thou whisperest, two by two,
Of who is madly in love with who.
The car thou needest every day,
Let hub caps scatter where they may.
For it would start unfriendly talk
If friends should chance to see thee walk.

Friends! Heavens, how they come and go!
Best pal today, tomorrow foe,
Since to distinguish thou dost fail
Twixt confidante and tattletale,
And blanchest to find the beach at noon
With sacred midnight secrets strewn.

Strewn! All is lost and nothing found.
Lord, how thou leavest things around!
Sweaters and rackets in the stable,
And purse upon the drugstore table,
And cameras rusting in the rain,
And Daddy's patience down the drain.

Ah, well, I must not carp and cavil,
I'll chew the spinach, spit out the gravel,
Remembering how my heart has leapt
At times when me thou didst accept.
Still, I'd like to be present, I must confess,
When thine own adolescents adolesce.

CHAPTER 2

The Adolescent the Teacher Faces

NO SECONDARY SCHOOL TEACHER and his students need to meet as strangers on the first day of the school year. It is inconceivable that any teacher can be completely unaware of what adolescents are like. Such a wealth of material is available on adolescents that even the inexperienced teacher knows, theoretically at least, the characteristics of twelve- to eighteen-year-olds. Headlines in newspapers, feature articles in popular magazines, serious studies in the general magazines, and scientific reports in educational periodicals, pamphlets, and books—all these are reminders to teachers that adolescence is a period of storm and stress, of conflict of loyalties, and of eagerness for security, for recognition, and for an opportunity to become increasingly independent of adult direction and supervision.

A knowledge of adolescents as a total group is important as a backdrop against which the teacher views *his own* adolescents in action. Unless the teacher is informed concerning the physical, mental, and emotional characteristics of twelve- to eighteen-year-olds and the language characteristics which become evident during these years, he may be alarmed or disappointed by his day-to-day experiences with individual members of his classes.

The secondary school teacher need not meet a *specific* group of adolescents as strangers if he has had access, before the opening day of school, to the cumulative records of the individuals whom he is to teach. These records usually include the individual's health history, family data, mental test

13

data, scholastic achievements, special talents, emotional adjustment, out-of-school experiences, values and ambitions, vocational interests, and avocational interests.

Varied Approaches to Understanding the Adolescent

To facilitate interpretation of these records and as an aid to understanding the flesh and blood individuals within a class, this chapter gives in outline form the characteristics— mental, physical, emotional, and linguistic—of twelve- to eighteen-year-olds; an annotated list of books that show teen-agers through the eyes of highly creative writers; and a bibliography of educational books, periodicals, and pamphlets that report the findings of research concerning adolescence.

In addition, this chapter presents a picture story—actual photographs of teen-agers in situations, both in and out of school, which reveal their intellectual, social, and emotional interests, their relations with each other, and their response to the curricular offerings of the total secondary school program (between pages 20 and 21).

But no story of adolescents in general, or of some other person's students, takes the place of a teacher's intimate study of *his own* students. Instead of being a burden to the teacher of language arts, this kind of approach toward getting to know teen-agers is for him a natural adventure. The communication arts of reading, writing, speaking, and listening reveal so much about the inner thoughts, feelings, desires, and values of each person that the teacher of English inescapably comes to know his students as individuals.

In Chapters 4–7, illustration after illustration reveals what a young person reads and how he reacts to it and shows the importance of this kind of information to the teacher in coming to know individuals.

So, too, does what he writes, if the teacher has the imagination and the insight to create writing opportunities in which boys and girls feel free to use language to help them understand themselves and the world around them.

In speech—conversation, informal discussion, role-playing,

dramatizations, concert reading of parts of a book, choral reading of poetry—no matter what kind of oral communication is engaged in, the teen-ager is revealing to the sensitive teacher not only what he needs in terms of training in the speech arts, but also what he must have to help him mature in his sense of values, his sense of humor, his sense of beauty, and his sense of what is appropriate to do in order that other teen-agers may enjoy his company and that he may learn from sharing experiences.

Chapter 8 is rich in illustrations of how the listening environment which the teacher creates can influence the ways in which young people relate themselves to one another within the classroom, in the auditorium, in clubs, in out-of-school teen-age groups, and in their response to the mass appeals of radio, television, movies, and magazines.

The Contribution of the Language Arts to Healthy Personality

One of the joys of teaching is the opportunity to influence the development and the growth of the young student. There are few experiences that evoke the glow the teacher feels in seeing a young person mature in language power, in human relations, in the personal satisfactions which may be derived from increased good taste in reading and listening, and in the power to use words orally and in writing so as to achieve adequate adjustment for himself and his teen-age friends.

If the goal of healthy personality is to be attained, the secondary schools have a great obligation during the adolescent years to provide through literature, dramatic performances, and artistic explorations, opportunities for boys and girls to discover themselves—their own personal values and feelings —and to develop the insights and understandings for all their human relationships.[1] At no other time in life are individuals more in need of such help or more ready and capable of learning, because they have so many curiosities, such acute perplexities, and such high aspirations.

[1] Lawrence K. Frank, "Ways of Studying Personality," *Baltimore Bulletin of Education*, Vol. XXVIII, No. 1 (January, 1951), pp. 1–15.

CHARACTERISTICS OF 12—18-YEAR-OLDS

The listing of the characteristics of young people and their manifestations in language, which follows, is the work of a curriculum group wishing to base its program securely on the psychology of adolescents.

Physical, Mental, and Emotional Characteristics	Language Characteristics

Level: 12–15 Years

STUDENTS	STUDENTS
1. Go through a period of rapid growth and development, making many new adjustments necessary (many girls are approximately a year ahead of boys in physical and organic maturity).	1. Desire to have fun, a fact which manifests itself in language expression related to sports, amusements, and humorous situations; develop increased maturity in interests through clubs and teamwork; show interest in language activities related to animals, adventure, mystery, collections, and explorations, but resist tasks requiring lengthy application; girls show interest in sentiment and romance.
2. Undergo internal changes involving heart, gland, and bone structure; the heart grows faster than do the arteries, thus causing a strain on the heart and often conflicts and emotional upsets.	2. Desire to be interesting is manifested in the individual's pursuit of his own welfare, and in human relationships, with increasing social sensitivity to reaction of individuals and group in language situations.
3. Need emphasis on good posture; possess relatively poor coordination; often feel they do	3. Desire to understand and express themselves through dramatization and imaginative

STUDENTS

STUDENTS

not "belong"; evidence marked concern and interest in their accelerated growth and changing bodies, and take increasing pride in personal appearance.

thinking; show wide variation in educational attainment; desire to realize their capacities as shown in their attempts to understand personal abilities and to seek interests that will fulfill their recognized language needs.

4. Have wide intellectual interests as a group but growing specializations of interest on the part of the individual; are more capable of intellectualizing their own experiences than at earlier levels but often are hampered by their emotions; are alert, active, and curious about everything; want facts; are still interested in first-hand experiences but are increasingly capable of learning vicariously.

4. Desire to become informed and to discuss ideals by which men live (manifested in hero worship); and express a challenging mental attitude toward social problems, and a concern about right and wrong.

5. Often feel socially insecure and may compensate by making themselves conspicuous in one way or another hoping for group approval; are more interested in approval, but need and desire adult support at times; desire to understand themselves, to be interesting, and to have freedom with security; experience anxiety over financial, social, and family insecurity; desire satisfying vocational experiences for immediate needs and for building for the future.

5. May display marked aggressiveness in speech and a tendency toward constant argumentation; show a liking for parliamentary procedures; enjoy hobbies involving use of much technical knowledge and skill and employ a more logical approach to solving problems; establish habit of reading periodicals and books related to interests; experience a need to express a new awakening to beauty.

Level: 15–18 Years

STUDENTS

STUDENTS

1. Reveal great individual differences in intelligence, scholastic achievement, background, and interests; increasingly wide variations in groups of older children because of the additional years of living and differing experiences.

1. Reveal great variations in degrees of development in the various language arts; a small percentage have developed the ability to write creatively, but a greater number probably have powers that are undeveloped; often show reluctance in sharing their production; manifest far less difference in reading interests between sexes than between individuals; exhibit a wide range in ability in various aspects of language power; an individual may be skillful in one or more abilities (as reading or speaking) and immature in aspects of others (as skill in spelling or punctuation in writing); range from almost total inadequacy to a successful degree of fluency in oral expression; increase in writing skills as their thinking becomes more clarified; acquire skill in discriminative use of many types of instructional materials.

2. Complete their physical changes and have grown-up-looking bodies; require adequate food, sleep, and precaution against fatigue; are aware of physical characteristics of themselves and others; admire physical vigor and courage; tend toward awkwardness; become concerned about sex, pair with the opposite sex, as well as go in crowds.

2. Extend language experiences in the treatment of mature problems, including relationships among persons, sexes, economic classes, races, political parties, nations, and periods of history; boys seek fiction and talk about physically vigorous and morally courageous heroes; girls enjoy romantic stories.

STUDENTS

STUDENTS

3. Have strong feelings for their group; are extremely sensitive to the opinion of the group; give importance to the gang and seek its approval and acceptance; remain inherently conservative as to group pattern; become increasingly aware of the importance of cooperation with others in classroom and school activities; have strong feelings of loyalty.

3. Increase in power to think together in large groups (whole classes), to share opinions, and to reach a common feeling and understanding; are so preoccupied with radio and television programs popular with the group, and with activities, pleasures, and friends that it is necessary that all reading and expression suggested by the school be meaningful to them in order to compete successfully for their out of school time; are willing to use their specific talents for the group (e.g., poster-making, lettering, running machinery, writing verses, planning programs); co-operate because of group loyalty.

4. Have considerable feeling of insecurity; may replace lack of assurance and security by rowdyism; often cover shyness and sensitivity by apparent indifference; often indulge in conspicuous behavior and employ various other devices for gaining attention.

4. Make considerable use of slang and swearing in their speech since it serves not only to furnish a form of expression for their emotions, but also to attract attention of adults and to show belongingness in their own group; are interested in dramatics for personal satisfaction and to gain status within the group.

5. Are growing increasingly independent of parents and other adults; resent domination; respect adults without feeling dependence on them; are curious about people in the adult world and seek vocational guidance.

5. Desire intensely to gain information on their special interests, so are easily led toward becoming good readers; appreciate the importance of vocational success and are willing to master necessary language skills and adult standards;

STUDENTS

STUDENTS

many delight in expressing opinions, very often in a critical way; are willing to "sharpen" their powers of discrimination to select from many sources those literary experiences including books, periodicals, music, radio programs, plays, etc., which best fill their needs.

6. Have intense emotions and sensory impressions; subordinate intellectual drives to emotional and social needs; are uncertain or questioning with regard to values, particularly in respect to such areas as meaning of life and nature of success; desire insight into themselves; seek understanding of self, asking: "What am I like as an individual? Why am I as I am? Why do I do as I do?", frequently alternating between self-reliance and self-distrust.

6. Have begun to see remote goals and are willing to go through experiences and practices in language even though tedious, because of the values anticipated in successful accomplishments; develop interest in becoming informed as to human relationships and issues; enjoy the beautiful in nature, literature, and human beings; strive to acquire beauty for themselves as a means of securing favorable reaction, as expressed in words, from the group.

WHAT TEEN-AGERS ARE LIKE

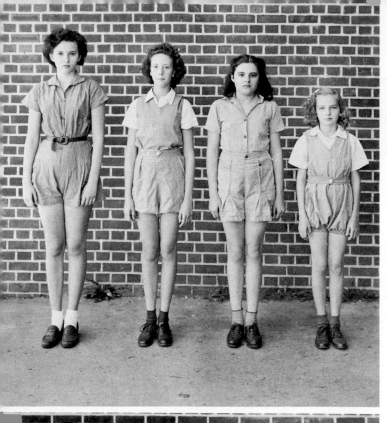

How they diffe

physically

emotionally

intellectually

These seventh-grade boy
and girls who are within
a month of the same
chronological age show
marked differences in
height and weight. The
are differences, too, in
rate and pattern of the
emotional and intellectu
growth.

Dramatic talent

Music ability

Physical skills

Science

Photography as hobby

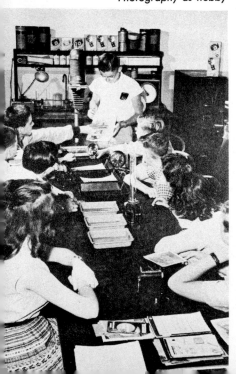

Physical handicap

Physical handicap

Talent in art

Skill in the graphic arts

What they enjoy

Public speaking

World affairs

Hearing test

Sports news

Producing school paper

Mechanical skills

Role as cheer leader

Swimming

Lacrosse

Broad jump

Basketball

Dancing after lunch

Basketball

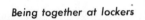

Being together at lockers

After school

At lunch

Between classes

At formal parties

On the farm

Down the bay

At a pet show

Hiking through the woods

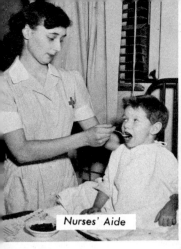

Nurses' Aide

Students help in library

Summer workshop for Red Cross student leaders

Safety patrol

Bike inspectors

FTA senior substitutes for elementary teacher

Decorators of school display cases

Senior volunteer for library storyteller

Co-operative planning

Checking sources of information

Using library resources

Recording talk
for self-evaluation

Listening to a recorded play

Considering a career

Seeking advice from the school counselor

Listening partners

Participating in forum on the air

Newspaper reporting

Reporting to a group

Recording committee reports to improve delivery

Creative expression
through dramatics

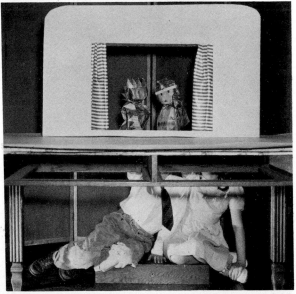

Creative expression through
preparing stage properties
and miniature stage sets

Business machines

Non-verbal experiences
enrich language

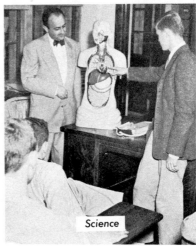

Science

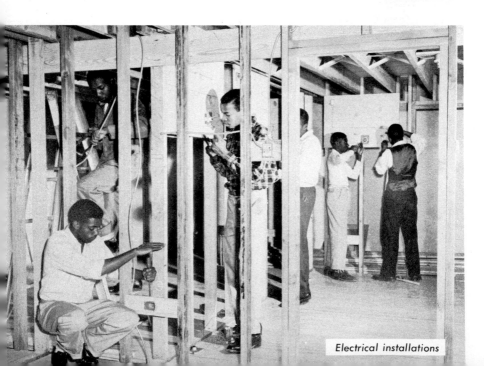

Electrical installations

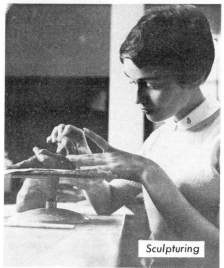

Sculpturing

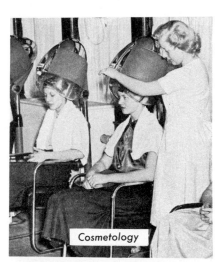

Cosmetology

Designing signs and showcards

How they earn

Food checker

Messenger

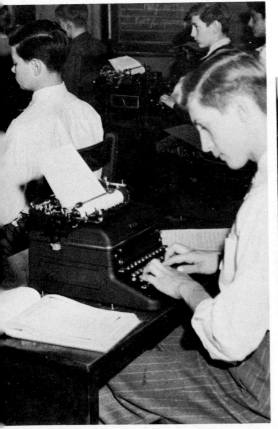

Junior typist

Waitress

Mail clerk

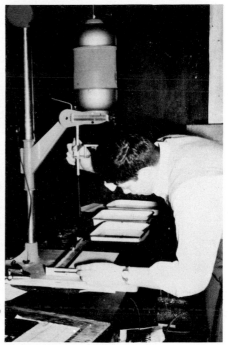

Photographer's assistant

Boy assistant in library

Girl assistant in library

BOOKS WHICH PORTRAY TEEN-AGERS [2]

Adolescents take particular delight in reading fiction about other young people like themselves who succeed and fail in their aspirations. Recent years have brought to the shelves of libraries many such books for young people, but they never stay there long. Mrs. Margaret Alexander Edwards, who has spent years in observing and evaluating the reading choices of high school boys and girls in the Young People's Room of the Enoch Pratt Free Library in Baltimore, has prepared a list of the best of these books which reveal young people to themselves. The particular way in which they "hold the mirror up to Nature" is indicated in the annotations. The list is useful in guiding the reading of adolescents. It is equally so in helping the teacher who reads the books to understand and appreciate the problems of individual students in his own classes.

BRO, Marguerite, *Sarah* (New York, Doubleday & Company, Inc., 1949).
    Love and sorrow, friends, work—all the experience of living through the years—change a sensitive child into a mature artist.

CAVANNA, Betty, *Going on Sixteen* (Philadelphia, Westminster Press, 1946).
    From the Freshman Frolic on, Julie felt left out of things until a poster contest, a collie dog, and her friend Dick helped her to gain confidence and popularity.

DALY, Maureen, *Seventeenth Summer* (New York, Dodd, Mead & Company, Inc., 1942).
    Angie Morrow boarded the train for college at the end of her seventeenth summer, saying goodbye to Jack Duluth and hoping with all her heart that their poignant first love would endure.

DAVIS, Clyde B., *The Newcomer* (Philadelphia, J. B. Lippincott Company, 1954).
    As a newcomer to town, Henry Trotter tried too hard to impress the gang, only to find himself attached to two misfits—poor, rich Christopher and the young Amazon, Opal Mackenzie—until, after some hilarious but humiliating experiences, he learned to relax.

[2] Selected and annotated by Margaret A. Edwards, Enoch Pratt Free Library, Baltimore.

DAVIS, Clyde B., ed., *Eyes of Boyhood* (Philadelphia, J. B. Lippincott Company, 1953).

The indestructible American boy as real as Clarence Day, Jr., as immortal as Huck Finn, has been depicted with humor and understanding by John Steinbeck, Ernest Hemingway, O. Henry, and other distinguished authors.

FORBES, Kathryn, *Mama's Bank Account* (New York, Harcourt, Brace & Company, Inc., 1943).

Short scenes from the life of a Norwegian carpenter's family in San Francisco centering about Mama, a woman of "infinite resource and sagacity" who despite scanty material resources passed on to her children the largesse of her spirit.

FRANK, Anne, *Anne Frank: The Diary of a Young Girl* (New York, Doubleday & Company, Inc., 1952).

For two years, this fifteen-year-old girl hid with her family and four friends in the abandoned half of an old office building in Amsterdam where she experienced fear and privation and where she knew first love before the Gestapo raid which led to her death.

HALPER, Albert, *The Golden Watch* (New York, Henry Holt & Company, Inc., 1953).

His sister's first date, his older brother's disappointing first job and his own encounters with reality, idealism, and the peculiarities of adults make up this warm story of a Jewish boy who grew up on Chicago's West Side before World War I.

LEWITON, Mina, *The Divided Heart* (New York, David McKay Company, 1948).

Family life as Julie had known it for fifteen years is suddenly changed when her parents were divorced, and it was only gradually, through pain and struggle, that she established her life on a secure foundation again.

MOODY, Ralph, *Man of the Family* (New York, W. W. Norton & Company, Inc., 1951).

When his father died, Ralph Moody, though still in his teens, took over the responsibility for the family, working and scheming for their welfare and only occasionally slipping back into the role of the youngster he was.

MOODY, Ralph, *The Fields of Home* (New York, W. W. Norton & Company, Inc., 1953).

After a brush with the law, Ralph was sent to live with his cantankerous grandfather on his Maine farm, where with the help of Millie, the maid, and his Uncle Levi, he reclaimed the run-down farm despite his grandfather's opposition to new ideas and "upstart" youth.

O'HARA, Mary, *My Friend Flicka* (Philadelphia, J. B. Lippincott Company, 1941, 1944).

Ken's practical Wyoming father did not realize the depths of his son's longing for a horse, nor how love of a filly might teach the boy to face stern reality at last.

ROSE, Anna P., *Room for One More* (Boston, Houghton Mifflin Company, 1950).

The fun and security of wholesome family life so appealed to three foster problem children that they refused to leave the Roses' home when the welfare organization responsible for them pointed out that their "visit" was over.

RUNBECK, Margaret L., *Pink Magic* (Boston, Houghton Mifflin Company, 1949).

When Lambie Prowder, tall, bespectacled, and too intelligent for her own good, goes to Mexico with two seventeen-year-olds who know how to use pink magic on the men, she stumbles onto the secret herself and lands the prize catch of the season without even trying.

SALINGER, Jerome D., *The Catcher in the Rye* (Boston, Little, Brown and Company, 1951).

Just before Christmas, young Holden Caulfield, the iconoclast, knowing that he was to be dropped by his school, decided to leave early and not report home until he had to. In his own frank, adolescent way he tells what he did and saw and suffered in these three days in New York City.

SKINNER, Cornelia O., *Family Circle* (Boston, Houghton Mifflin Company, 1948).

Because her father was distinguished and urbane, and her mother was pretty and charmingly feminine, Cornelia's account of her eager, awkward adolescence is especially appealing.

SMITH, Betty, *A Tree Grows in Brooklyn* (New York, Harper and Brothers, 1947).

Francie Nolan grew up in a Brooklyn tenement like the indestructible tree of Heaven; for her mother's strength and her father's love were greater than the squalor of the city and her own imagination saw only beauty in the sordid slums around her.

STOLZ, Mary, *To Tell Your Love* (New York, Harper and Brothers, 1950).

Ann learned much about love one summer just by observing her older sister's happy romance and her best friend's hasty marriage, and by facing the fact that the boy she adored did not return her love.

STOLZ, Mary, *The Sea Gulls Woke Me* (New York, Harper and Brothers, 1951).

A summer away from home with other young people taught Jean to shake off the domination of her mother, to make her own decisions, to cultivate her own charms, and to get along happily with both girls and boys.

STOLZ, Mary, *Ready or Not* (New York, Harper and Brothers, 1952).

At sixteen, Morgan Conner, who had run the household since her mother's death, found she was ready for a deeper understanding of family and friends and also for romance.

WEST, Jessamyn, *Cress Delahanty* (New York, Harcourt, Brace & Company, Inc., 1954).

Cress had more emotions than she knew what to do with. She fell in and out of love, bought the wrong hat, changed her personality at intervals, and finally grew up with the unobtrusive help and understanding of her parents.

BIBLIOGRAPHY

Books

American Association for Gifted Children, *The Gifted Child*, ed. by Paul Witty (Boston, D. C. Heath & Company, 1951).

Association for Supervision and Curriculum Development, *Growing Up in an Anxious Age*, 1952 Yearbook (Washington, D. C., National Education Association, 1952).

CRUZE, Wendell W., *Adolescent Psychology and Development* (New York, The Ronald Press Company, 1953).

CUNNINGHAM, Ruth, *Understanding Group Behavior of Boys and Girls* (New York, Bureau of Publications, Teachers College, Columbia University, 1951).

FARNHAM, Marynia L., *The Adolescent* (New York, Harper and Brothers, 1951).

FRANK, Lawrence, and FRANK, Mary H., *Your Adolescent at Home and in School* (New York, Viking Press, 1956).

FRANK, Lawrence, and others, *Personal Development in Adolescent Girls*, Society for Research in Child Development Monographs (New Orleans, Child Development Publications, Louisiana State University School of Medicine, 1953).

GESELL, Arnold, *Youth, The Years from 10 to 16* (New York, Harper and Brothers, 1956).

GLUECK, Sheldon, and GLUECK, Eleanor, *Delinquents in the Making: Paths to Prevention* (New York, Harper and Brothers, 1952).

HAVIGHURST, Robert James, and TABA, Hilda, and others, *Adolescent Character and Personality* (New York, John Wiley & Sons, Inc., 1949).

HAVIGHURST, Robert James, STRIVERS, Eugene, and DeHAAN, Robert F., *A Survey of the Education of Gifted Children* (Chicago, The University of Chicago Press, 1955).

HORROCKS, John E., *The Psychology of Adolescence: Behavior and Development* (Boston, Houghton Mifflin Company, 1951).

National Society for the Study of Education, *Adolescence*, Forty-third Yearbook, Part I (Chicago, University of Chicago Press, 1944).

————, *Juvenile Delinquency and the Schools*, Forty-seventh Yearbook, Part I (Chicago, University of Chicago Press, 1948).

————, *Mental Health in Modern Education*, Fifty-fourth Yearbook, Part II (Chicago, University of Chicago Press, 1955), pp. 216–235.

WARTERS, Jane, *Achieving Maturity* (New York, McGraw-Hill Book Company, Inc., 1949).

Pamphlets and Periodicals

American Council on Education Studies, *Exploring Individual Differences*, Report of the 1947 Invitational Conference on Testing Problems sponsored by The Committee on Measurement and Guidance (Washington, D. C., American Council on Education Studies, 1948).

American Educational Research Association, "The Educational Program: Later Adolescence," *Review of Educational Research*, Vol. XXIV, No. 4 (1954).

Cleveland Welfare Federation, *Toward Better Adjusted Children*, Report of the Subcommittee on Early Detection of Maladjusted Children of the Committee on Juvenile Delinquency Prevention (Cleveland, Welfare Federation, 1955).

GUDRIDGE, Beatrice M., *It's High Time*, Guide for Parents of High School Students (Washington, D. C., National School Public Relations Association, National Education Association, 1955).

HAMRIN, Shirley A., and PAULSON, Blanche B., *Counseling Adolescents* (Chicago, Science Research Associates, Inc., 1950).

KUDER, G. Fredrick, and PAULSON, Blanche B., *Exploring Children's Interests*, Better Living Booklets (Chicago, Science Research Associates, Inc., 1951).

LEWIS, Gertrude M., *Educating Children in Grades Seven and Eight*, Bulletin 1954, No. 10 (Washington, D. C., Office of Education, 1954).

MENNINGER, William C., M.D., *Self-Understanding: A First Step to Understanding Children*, Better Living Booklets (Chicago, Science Research Associates, Inc., 1951).

MONTAGU, Ashley, *Helping Children Develop Moral Values*, Better Living Booklets (Chicago, Science Research Associates, Inc., 1953).

National Association of Manufacturers, *Your Future Is What You Make It*, 4th You and Industry Series (Washington, D. C., National Association of Manufacturers, 1949).

National Association of Secondary-School Principals, "High School Discipline in American Society," *The Bulletin*, Vol. 40, No. 216 (January, 1956), pp. 1–103.

OJEMANN, Ralph H., *Personality Adjustment of Individual Children*, What Research Says to the Teacher, No. 5 (Washington, D. C., Department of Classroom Teachers and the American Educational Research Association of the National Education Association, 1954).

School District of Philadelphia, *What Are Adolescents Like?* (Philadelphia, The Board of Public Education Printing Department, 1954).

REMMERS, H. H., and HACKETT, C. G., *Let's Listen to Youth*, Better Living Booklets (Chicago, Science Research Associates, Inc., 1950).

——, *What Are Your Problems?*, Life Adjustment Booklets (Chicago, Science Research Associates, Inc., 1951).

RIVLIN, Harry N., *Improving Children's Learning Ability*, Better Living Booklets (Chicago, Science Research Associates, Inc., 1953).

SEGEL, David, *Frustration in Adolescent Youth: Its Development and Implications for the School Program*, Bulletin 1951, No. 1 (Washington, D. C., Office of Education, 1951).

——, *Intellectual Abilities in the Adolescent Period: Their Growth and Development*, Bulletin 1948, No. 6 (Washington, D. C., Office of Education, 1948).

SHACTER, Helen, *Getting Along with Others*, Life Adjustment Booklets (Chicago, Science Research Associates, Inc., 1950).

THURSTONE, Thelma Gwinn, and BYRNE, Katherine Mann, *Mental Abilities of Children*, Better Living Booklets (Chicago, Science Research Associates, Inc., 1951).

U. S. Department of Health, Education, and Welfare, *The Adolescent in Your Family*, Children's Bureau Publication 347 (Washington, D. C., Social Security Administration, 1954).

WEITZMAN, Ellis, *Growing Up Socially*, Life Adjustment Booklets (Chicago, Science Research Associates, Inc., 1949).

WITTY, Paul, *Helping the Gifted Child*, Better Living Booklets (Chicago, Science Research Associates, Inc., 1952).

WRIGHTSTONE, J. Wayne, *What Tests Can Tell Us about Children*, Better Living Booklets (Chicago, Science Research Associates, Inc., 1954).

PART II

PART II
The Language Arts Program

PREVIEW OF CHAPTER 3

Taking Preliminary Steps

Sensing the Need for Change

Recognizing the Worth of the Individual Teacher

Involving All Concerned

Organizing for Curriculum Work

Planning the Village Curriculum Program

Improving the Curriculum in a City System

Working on the Curriculum through Study Councils and Regional Associations

Participating in Workshops under Sponsorship of Teachers Associations

Organizing Curriculum Study through a State-Wide Approach

Defining Goals

Setting Up Initial Agreements

Determining Scope and Sequence

Studying Relevant Factors

Student population

The community

Faculty resources

School facilities

Consultant services

Time and funds

Providing for Sequential Learning

Chart of sequential skills

Study of problems of articulation

Selection of instructional materials to fit the curriculum

Adjustment of grouping and promotion policies to curriculum needs

Use of cumulative records

Offerings in required and elective courses

Relating the Language Arts to the Total School Program

Evaluating the Program

Recognizing the Need for Continuous Curriculum Study

Bibliography

CHAPTER 3

Designing the Program

AFTER A GLIMPSE of the world the adolescent faces and a close-up of the adolescents the teacher faces, the reader of this volume is ready to consider problems in designing the language arts program.

These problems include (1) involving in the development of the program all persons concerned in putting it into action, (2) defining goals in terms of the needs of the adolescent and his world,* (3) planning co-operatively to create a design of adequate scope and sequence, and (4) developing methods to evaluate the effectiveness of the program so as to keep it ever responsive to the needs of the individual and of society.

TAKING PRELIMINARY STEPS

Out of the experiences of many schools have emerged certain principles of procedure and fruitful practices that can helpfully serve others inaugurating such a program.

Sensing the Need for Change

A first essential almost universally discovered is that a *need* for curriculum improvement must be genuinely felt by those who participate. Action undertaken by assignment from outside the group, or by administrative or supervisory direction alone, is almost certain to fail.

* See Chapters 1 and 2.

29

This sense of need may be so general and so acute among a faculty that no particular stimulus is required. Opportunity to work is enough. Often, however, it is desirable to plan ways by which to arouse a consciousness of the need for change. Some schools form small faculty groups for exchange of thinking about needs; reports from each group are made to the faculty as a whole. Where feasible, the entire faculty may approach the matter of need together—raising questions, exploring philosophies, discovering problems. Skilled and genuinely "permissive" leadership is essential at this point. There must be no sense of pressure for conformity or censure for honest differences. Respect for the sincerity of teachers as they consider their work must be the attitude that prevails.[1]

Stimulus toward such faculty thinking may come from workshops, locally organized; by participation in area study councils or regional undertakings; by bringing in consultants, lecturers, or teachers from other systems where curriculum work has gone well.

In many schools the impetus toward improvement comes from a serious study of the effectiveness of the existing English program. Questionnaires are used, addressed to graduates, employers, parents, members of the community. Students as well as other teachers in the system are queried. Such study is helpfully supplemented by evaluating the existing program against criteria shown in other studies to have considerable validity. Such criteria may be found in the Cooperative Study of Secondary School Standards, *Evaluative Criteria* (Washington, D. C., 1950); in *The English Language Arts;* and in this present volume, representing the work of the Commission on the English Curriculum of the National Council of Teachers of English. Self-evaluation may be facilitated by using experienced consultants from outside

---

[1] For further discussion of this point, see Association for Supervision and Curriculum Development, *Action for Curriculum Improvement*, 1951 Yearbook (Washington, D. C., National Education Association, 1951).

the system or skilled curriculum leadership within the school.

Of the many outcomes that will result from such preliminary steps, two are essential if later work is to succeed: (1) A genuine feeling of need for change must be aroused and some enthusiasm for undertaking the work must be felt, if possible, by a majority of the teachers concerned; (2) an understanding must be reached that curriculum development is something more than agreed-upon shifts of content. A decision as to whether *Silas Marner* or *A Tale of Two Cities* should be taught in the tenth grade, or how much emphasis should be given "verbals" in the ninth, are not the major outcomes sought through curriculum study. Until readiness and understanding are established to at least a reasonable degree, organizing for work will be premature and results discouraging. It is important to judge soundly the point at which actual work should be launched, for to continue preliminary discussion beyond the point where consensus emerges may be frustrating and lead to a lessening of interest. Sensitive leadership is essential here.

Recognizing the Worth of the Individual Teacher

It sometimes happens that the activities of individual teachers may bring about a recognition of the need for change. No classroom teacher need await a formal organization of his school or department in order to undertake curriculum work. Whatever may be the nature and extent of existing requirements, any teacher will find room and need for his own creative effort in developing his course of study. To aid such classroom teachers in their individual work, as well as to assist larger organizational undertakings, has been a guiding purpose of the Curriculum Commission of the National Council of Teachers of English in producing this present volume and its earlier reports.

Indeed, many a system-wide curriculum study has resulted from one teacher's work in his own classroom, becoming, as it inevitably does, a leaven working to raise the whole. A teacher not fully content with results he is achieving begins to study the problem afresh. He reads recent literature on instruction and curriculum planning in English. He attends conferences, enrolls in workshops, consults other teachers, examines new courses of study, or by himself thinks realistically and creatively about the objectives and goals that must guide his work with boys and girls. He investigates the kinds of experiences and activities he may use to these ends; he studies materials, instructional procedures, the nature of unit organization, and other means for improving the program he follows. A vitalized teaching of English in his classroom emerges. His colleagues hear about it and begin to study their own problems. Perhaps no method of curriculum change is more important than this grass-roots kind of study and experiment, in the laboratory of the classroom, under sincere and able individual teachers.

INVOLVING ALL CONCERNED

An effective method for setting up a curriculum development study is illustrated by the procedures used in appointing the Curriculum Commission of the National Council of Teachers of English.[2] The members of the Commission

represented all areas of the language arts and all shades of opinion concerning how they should be taught. Classroom teachers from the preschool through the graduate school, experts in child psychology, elementary school and high school principals, a librarian, and a college president all sat down together to consider the kind of program needed in school and college today. A general director headed the study with three associate directors, one for the elementary school, one for the secondary school, and one for the college and the university. Problems of articulation were both presented and met head on as discussion proceeded and manuscripts were read chapter by chapter by all members of the Commission.

[2] National Council of Teachers of English Commission on the English Curriculum, *The English Language Arts*, NCTE Curriculum Series, Vol. I (New York, Appleton-Century-Crofts, Inc., 1952), p. vii; and also Ch. 4, pp. 55–78.

Similarly on the local level, within a school or within a school system, individuals [3] might be chosen to represent the range of age-grade levels in the school, to include specialized competence in the various aspects of the language arts, and to bring in the point of view of librarians, guidance officers, administrators, and teachers of other subjects in which success is determined in large part by competence in writing and speaking or in reading and listening.

Representatives of the cultural agencies in the community (libraries, museums, experimental theater groups, literary and historical societies, youth recreation groups, radio and television stations, and motion picture exhibitors) are valuable as resource persons when the curriculum group is studying the out-of-school use of the language arts. Laymen representative of parents, business, industry, organized labor, and the professions in the community can also contribute to cooperative planning and evaluation.

ORGANIZING FOR CURRICULUM WORK

A teacher was examining some recently published courses of study in English. As she laid them aside she said, "These are excellent, certainly"; and then she added reflectively, "But I wonder by how many of the teachers they are actually used."

The answer would in all probability be directly related to the procedure under which these courses were developed. If the concept of a course of study as authoritatively mandated content-to-be-covered has been left behind, as it very generally has been, and if one's point of view is in harmony with

[3] This plan is being used in Atlanta, Georgia; Baltimore, Maryland; The Latin School of Chicago and the Chicago Public Schools; Cincinnati, Ohio; Concord, Massachusetts; Denver, Colorado; Florida State Department of Education; Gloucester High School, Gloucester, Massachusetts; Indianapolis, Indiana; Minneapolis, Minnesota; New England School Study Council; New York, New York; Seattle, Washington; St. Louis, Missouri; Syracuse, New York; Tulsa, Oklahoma; Tucson, Arizona; Wisconsin State Department of Education.

that set forth in this volume and others of the Commission on the English Curriculum, then it is apparent that courses of study must emerge from the thinking and effort of the teachers who are to use them, though guided by the experience and study of others. Indeed, if such courses are to be more than print-on-paper, the co-operative effort underlying them must represent a great many people—not merely the teachers, but pupils, parents, citizens of the community, administrators, supervisors, and experienced curriculum workers as well.

For example, the recent course of study in English for the secondary schools of Newport, Rhode Island (mimeographed, 1954), exemplifies this co-operative approach. The foreword states:

. . . teachers from grades 7–12 met together to study the needs of junior and senior high school students of Newport in the field of the language arts. In the spring and fall, committees sent questionnaires to teachers, students, graduates, and employers of Newport to discover the strengths and weaknesses of our English program. . . . The English teachers feel that this program of study is a tribute to the co-operation of teachers, pupils, parents, employers, and administrators in their desire to help the boys and girls of Newport achieve the power of effective communication.

The introduction to the course of study indicates the relation between the work of the local committees and such larger studies as that of the National Council of Teachers of English. The desirable outcomes of English as defined by the Council's Curriculum Commission in *The English Language Arts* (Chapters 1–4) were adopted as the basic platform for the new course. These outcomes were made specific to suit local conditions and needs. A section of the introduction entitled "Special Needs of Newport" lists among other items a changing relation between junior and senior high schools because of a new building arrangement, the strong influence of the Army and Navy in Newport, occupational demands, and facilities available.

The thinking of these teachers and their method of work illustrate throughout the co-operative approach now being used in developing an English curriculum for a particular community.

Examples from both small and large schools and school systems will illustrate ways of organizing that have been found effective for curriculum study.

Planning the Village Curriculum Program

A village system having one senior and two junior high schools decided to undertake curriculum work leading to a new program in English. The chairman of the senior high school, the supervisor of elementary schools, and the school superintendent served as an informal initiating committee. In the spring term they arranged for a workshop type of course on basic principles of instruction in the English language arts and the nature of a sound course of study. Teachers from kindergarten through Grade 12 participated in weekly meetings throughout the term. This workshop brought together the thinking of all teachers in the system. The sense of need for a new course of study became evident.

In the following fall, the superintendent arranged for meetings of all junior and senior high school teachers of English for curriculum work for one hour of one school day each week. The teachers decided to add a second hour of their own after-school time to make a two-hour session possible.

The workshop of the preceding spring had laid the foundation in a sense of need, desire to work, and understanding of the nature of the problem. The informal steering committee had secured facilities, including funds for books, for courses of study, for other needs that might arise, for the services of a consultant. The whole group started together, therefore, on their first question: "What do we want six years of work in English in our junior and senior high schools to contribute to boys and girls?"

In formulating objectives, they looked first at the over-all outcomes desired rather than at objectives at various stages or grades. In their thinking they were guided by the work of the National Council of Teachers of English as presented in *The English Language Arts*. Objectives were made concrete to meet the specific needs of their own high school population. Preparation for early marriage was one such need, and since the majority of the pupils grew up in that village and entered employment locally immediately after graduation, the group stressed the importance of using English to broaden horizons on the world.

When over-all objectives had been thought through together, experiences in reading, writing, speaking, and listening that would contribute to these outcomes were itemized. Charts were then prepared, allocating major responsibility for these experiences to successive grades. It was clearly stated that such allocation did not preclude earlier work if occasion demanded, nor did it insure mastery at one point; but the committee planned to assign responsibility for major emphasis on each experience at the point where they believed need and readiness would be greatest. For example, the experience of planning a program for a banquet and for receiving and introducing guests was allocated to the tenth grade because that class each year had responsibility for an interschool meeting and banquet. Although students had needed and had had this experience before, special emphasis on it at the secondary school level was considered a contribution to the continuing strand of "social competence."

When such responsibilities had been distributed, horizontal committees were formed by grade levels. Each committee planned an over-all course for its grade, including a general theme or problem that would tend to unify the year's work and would call for the experiences in speaking, reading, writing, and listening allocated to it. Various possible units of work were suggested. Materials, activities, books, and other resources were investigated. Each committee then brought its work back to the committee-of-the-whole for review and criticism. The department chairman drew together and edited the plans for mimeographing.

The next step was to plan resource units. This, they agreed, must be a continuing process over the years, but samples were prepared as guides. (Chapter 4 of this volume presents a similar example of a unit.)

Under this working plan, possible when all teachers of a system can work together, remarkable harmony of purpose was achieved and a clearly sequential, well-articulated program in English developed.

Improving the Curriculum in a City System

In a city system in the South, too large for all teachers to work together, an over-all curriculum committee was formed of thirty-two people representing all the secondary schools. These served as a steering committee and as a central co-ordinating committee as well.

The members of this central curriculum committee were divided into subcommittees by grade levels and into vertical committees for each of the strands of the language arts program—speaking, writing, reading, and listening. Each member was responsible in his own school for keeping the teachers informed of what was going on, and for securing from his colleagues suggestions and materials which the central committee co-ordinated. In this way, even though in so large a system a central committee was necessary, all teachers of English participated in the work.

A Western city followed a similar plan leading to a new course of study for the entire system from kindergarten through Grade 12. A central steering and co-ordinating committee was formed at the beginning under leadership of a supervising teacher from the school system. This committee represented all grade levels. Three curriculum committees, one for each of the three levels—elementary, junior, and senior high school—and additional committees on special problems, such as the use of the library, were formed to work with the central committee. The steering committee surveyed needs and present practices and drew up a tentative statement of philosophy for the new curriculum. This platform was circulated among all teachers and revised several times in the light of suggestions received. The central steering committee also planned the general allocation of goals and experiences appropriate to the various levels and assisted the curriculum committee at each level to develop materials and resources for the program of study.

Working on the Curriculum through Study Councils and Regional Associations

In some areas a number of schools (as many as seventy or eighty) unite in a school-study council for improvement of instruction in their geographical regions. Representative teachers are released, with expenses paid, for full-day meetings. Many aspects of the English curriculum have been studied and strengthened through such councils. In one, the center of attention was on the meaning, nature, and advantage of unit organization of the English course. Panels, consultants, and discussion groups attacked the matter in the general meetings. Volunteer groups, drawn from neighboring schools to insure opportunity for work between general sessions, undertook to prepare resource units around problems agreed upon as important. These units were mimeographed and distributed among all members of the council, revised in light of criticisms received, and then were published, along with summaries on the unit approach in general, as a guide for further curriculum work in the several schools.

Such school-study councils can greatly facilitate the curriculum work of the individual schools of which they are composed. In general they do not replace the work of local schools, but feed into it through study of special problems such as here described.

Similar curriculum work has been carried on through larger regional associations, often made up of several states.

Participating in Workshops under Sponsorship of Teachers Associations

Several state English councils have begun to sponsor workshops on the curriculum for their members, usually in cooperation with institutions of higher learning so that academic credit may be earned if desired. The council aids in planning and setting up the workshop and in some instances assumes a share of the financial responsibility. Such workshops have been held under the sponsorship of the National Council of Teachers of English since 1954.

Organizing Curriculum Study through a State-Wide Approach

As in local undertakings, so at the state level every effort is being made to use the co-operative approach in curriculum work. *The Course of Study in English for Secondary Schools in Pennsylvania*, published as a progress report in 1952, resulted from the work of district curriculum committees throughout the state under guidance of a State Production Committee. A statement from the "Introduction" defines the current attitude of state departments and their relation to local groups: [4]

No course of study will succeed unless the teachers on each faculty—through their own group and individual planning—adapt it to local needs. An effective curriculum grows in its own native soil. Pupils and schools are too varied for a committee in a distant conference to provide more than permissive ideas. . . . English teachers can readily adapt themselves to this new type of planning, for today they are coming to classrooms with more initiative and ingenuity, and with better preparation than ever before.

Another excellent example of co-operative planning is the Florida State Department of Education Curriculum Development Program. At teachers' requests, voluntary curriculum workshops were set up in eleven counties during 1945–48.

[4] Commonwealth of Pennsylvania, Department of Public Instruction, Bulletin 280, *The Course of Study in English for the Secondary Schools,* Harrisburg, 1952, "Introduction," pp. xi–xii.

This grass-roots approach to curriculum study involved an analysis of the pupil population, of research in child growth and language development, of instructional materials, and of staff resources. The participating teachers were also stimulated to prepare units and to share during the school year their teaching experiences in trying out the units.

In 1948, the state department invited master teachers, competent librarians, and creative supervisors from these eleven counties to come together on the campus of the Florida State University. The purpose of this five-week workshop was to prepare a bulletin * for the State Department of Education. The production group enjoyed the leadership of a curriculum co-ordinator from the State Department of Education and an out-of-state curriculum consultant who had had extensive experience in seven other states. Both the co-ordinator and the consultant had worked with the curriculum groups at the county level.

Because curriculum production workshops for the language arts, music, art, home economics, mathematics, science, social studies, and the school lunch program were meeting simultaneously on the Florida State University campus during the summer of 1948, it was easy for the language arts group to discover relationships among all subject areas. By having joint sessions with representatives from other areas, the language arts group was able to reach decisions as to how the language arts might reinforce the other areas and how they, in turn, might be reflected in the language arts program.

Likewise the preparation of the Minnesota State *Handbook in the Language Arts for Secondary Schools* shows how a state department of education works through teachers in the classroom to revise the curriculum. The Minnesota State Commissioner of Education, with the aid of a curriculum expert in the state department, appointed a committee of nine-

---

* Florida State Department of Education, *Experiencing the Language Arts,* A Guide to Teachers in Kindergarten to Grade Twelve, Bulletin No. 34 (Tallahassee, Florida State Department of Education, 1948).

teen to revise the old bulletin on English. Members included two junior high school teachers, two senior high school teachers, four who taught throughout the secondary school, one small-town superintendent, one city supervisor of the language arts, two junior-senior high school librarians, and five consultants from the state university and teachers colleges. These consultants represented speech, journalism, library, English, and education. The head of the high school English department in an average-sized town in the state was made chairman.

During the years when the work was in progress, all members were released from classes for two days each semester to attend committee meetings, with expenses paid, at the Center for Continuation Study at the University of Minnesota. Other work they did in writing the course was done on their own time.

The committee early accepted as its platform the one set forth in *The English Language Arts*, Volume I of the NCTE curriculum series. It agreed upon a unit plan of instruction, each unit involving all four of the language arts, although certain ones gave special stress to reading, writing, speaking, or listening. Skills were to be related to the purposes or topics under consideration. Variety in units was to be expected, some of them emphasizing problems of adolescents; some, topics of concern to the modern world; some, literary types or experiences directly related to the development of discrimination in choices of literature, moving pictures, television, and other mass modes of communication. Subcommittees concerned with the junior and senior high school prepared introductory sections of the handbook on points of view, organization, skills to be taught, and the like.

It was decided, in view of the fact that this kind of teaching was new to many teachers of the state, that units for each year of the secondary school would actually be constructed by individual members of the committee, worked out in their own classrooms or in those of other teachers in the state, submitted for criticism to the entire committee, checked by the librarians for books used, and revised by the writer in terms of suggestions made. Final editorial work was done by the chairman and by one of the consultants. It was clearly indicated in the handbook that the units were illustrative and that substitution of others similar in plan, but more suited to the localities concerned, was to be desired.

The National Council of Teachers of English proposed four areas of growth which should be stimulated by the secondary school program: growth of boys and girls as individual persons, as members of social groups, as citizens, and as workers. The committee tried to take all of these into account in the choice of language arts units for each grade. In the eighth grade, for example, the personal enrichment units included *Adventuring in Books, Exploring Leisure,* and *Entertaining Ourselves and Others,* the last including dramatics and puppetry. A unit concerned with social living was *Getting Along with Others.* Two which led to understanding our national heritage were *Our Country in the Making* and *Who Are Americans? What Is Success?* consisted of interviewing and also the reading of biography for the purpose of developing a personal sense of values and exploring backgrounds for choice of a life work. Mass modes of communication were related throughout to the work in progress. At some point in the senior high school each was studied in a separate unit as an important institution in American life. The eleventh grade was left as the American year, with these units giving special emphasis to literature and expression: *The Search for Freedom and Democracy, The Search for the Good Life in America, People Who Make Up America, Frontiers to the West, Enjoyment of American Humor,* and *The Role of the Press in American Life.* The history of literature as such was abandoned, since the colleges of the state indicated on a questionnaire sent out by the committee early in its work that chief concern should be with the development of skill in reading material, much of it prose, of a high level of maturity. Personal expression of ideas about the material read and critical evaluation of it were stressed. Units for the twelfth grade included those on *Drama, The Motion Picture, Understanding the World at Work, Modern World Problems and the Influence of Environment on Thought and Personality Revealed in Fiction of All Nations, The Development of a Personal Philosophy through Readings in Poetry and Essay,* and *What Shall I Read?*, a final unit on planning one's future reading and on learning to know sources of review and reference. Special emphasis upon skills in reading and expression and upon appreciation of the value of literature as literature characterized the program.

Throughout the years of the preparation of the handbook, the Spring Conference of Librarians and Teachers of the Language Arts, which is held each year on the university campus, devoted its sessions to discussion and demonstration of unit procedures. Sample units were mimeographed for distribution, so that many schools will have had some years of experimentation with the method before the course comes out. After the appearance of the handbook, meetings will be held at teachers colleges in different sections of the state explaining the program and having teachers already familiar with the course and the method describe their procedures and their difficulties for those unfamiliar with the plan.

DEFINING GOALS

Any such local group will find it useful to start its exploration by preparing a list of desirable outcomes for the language arts program. In doing this, they will need to have at hand whatever information is available on the nature of the student population and of the school community.[5] Some of these matters are discussed later in the section on the scope of the program.

[5] See Chapter 2 for specific leads in getting to know students and their community.

Language arts teachers throughout the nation accept personal, social, and occupational competence as the goal of education. Attainment of this outcome may be achieved within the limits of the capacity of the individual if his experiences with and through language are directed toward:

1. CULTIVATION OF WHOLESOME PERSONAL LIVING

   a. Sense of values.
   b. Perspective on one's self and one's time.
   c. Extension of experience so as to be good company *for one's self* as well as good company *for others* through such habits as continued personal reading of high quality and skill in social letter writing and conversation.
   d. Ability to use the cultural resources in one's community including the library, radio, television, motion picture, theater, and public platform.
   e. High degree of competence in the basic skills of reading, writing, listening, and speaking.
   f. Intellectual curiosity and creativeness (so far as possible) in all four of the language arts.
   g. Capacity for logical and critical thinking in expression of ideas and in acceptance or rejection of ideas of others.
   h. Personal integrity in thought and expression.
   i. Intelligent consumption of goods and services because of sensitivity to the denotation and connotation of words; that is, sales resistance without becoming a nuisance as a purchaser, emotional discount for unsubstantiated superlatives in advertisements and sales talks, alert attention to "small print" in contracts, guarantees, and cautions on how to use a product.

2. DEVELOPMENT OF SOCIAL SENSITIVITY AND EFFECTIVE PARTICIPATION IN GROUP LIFE

   a. Sensing values in the current scene and their relation to the contributions of past and future.
   b. Recognition of the dignity and worth of every individual.
   c. Control of one's prejudices so as to avoid giving offense or blocking important group action.
   d. Skill in the language arts of persuasion, co-operative planning, discussion, and decision.
   e. Recognition of the social and psychological factors involved in communication with people of different backgrounds.
   f. A sense of responsibility for critical (as well as imaginative) reading and listening in order to understand and appreciate elements in American culture and in that of other nations.

3. Linguistic Competence Necessary for Vocational
Efficiency

   a. Following and giving directions.
   b. Keeping up with technical knowledge in one's occupation.
   c. Maintaining effective interpersonal relationships: employer-
   employee, employee-employee, employer-public, employee-
   public.
   d. Developing needed skills in business letter writing, in persuasion and exposition, and in techniques of interviewing.

SETTING UP INITIAL AGREEMENTS

The importance of agreeing in advance upon a set of principles on which the program will be based cannot be over-
emphasized. Such agreements constitute a platform to guide
the makers of the curriculum, some of whom may not have
been present at the discussions. A list of agreements is useful
in handling differences of opinion which inevitably arise in
the course of working out the details of the program.

After defining goals, the Production Committee for this
volume agreed on these basic points:

1. The program in the language arts must be broad enough to
give students freedom and opportunity to develop their potentialities, to pursue their own ends, and to learn the processes of
effective participation in group life.
2. Growth in language power is gradual; it can be continuous; it
should be cumulative.
3. A study of child growth has established that no child can be
pushed into maturity by prearranged steps or at a predeter-
mined rate. What he *is*—his rate and pattern of growth—must
be known and considered in planning and in conducting his
educational experiences.
4. The rate of progress on the part of individual students and the
ultimate level of their accomplishments differ according to their
innate potentialities and to the stimulation of their surroundings.
5. What an individual takes to and gets from instruction will depend upon his *readiness* for the learning, his *identification* both
mentally and emotionally with the experience, and the *satisfaction* he can derive from the knowledge, skills, or appreciations
which are outcomes of the learning.
6. Language is part of all activity; language is involved in the
student's adjustment to the group.

7. Experience on the part of the student is the ground out of which language expression springs. The curriculum should provide activities which require and stimulate effective use of language.

8. Students' realistic and imaginative writing about their innermost concerns should be encouraged in order to help them develop an objective approach to their own experiences, leading to mental and emotional stability.

9. Language must be developed in relation to normal purposes and contacts of school, home, and community.

10. Language use is motivated by purpose. Whether the purpose is creative or utilitarian, young people are vitally interested in expressing themselves when to do so satisfies needs and purposes that are real to them.

11. Language power can be developed effectively only in the kinds of social situations in which it will be used.

12. Effective communication involves social and psychological adjustments as well as linguistic skill.

13. The meaning of words depends upon the way they are put together in sentences; a meaningful vocabulary grows from the association of words with non-verbal experiences.

14. Students need to become aware of language as an instrument of thought and of the language arts (speaking, listening, reading, and writing) as study procedures and as sources of recreation.

15. Effective habits of work should grow out of a well-balanced language arts program.

16. The language arts program should give practice in the skills needed by the learner as speaker, listener, writer, and reader and should develop the attitudes essential to proper use of freedom of speech, press, and assembly.

17. Attention to speech is important from the beginning of a child's schooling throughout his life.

18. Convention has established flexible but nonetheless important standards of language usage.

19. Students need to learn methods of observing current speech and writing and also how to find and to use authoritative sources of information on current usage acceptable in various situations.

20. Back of successful communication, whether in sentences, paragraphs, or longer discourse, is the power of sustained thinking.

21. The language arts program should stimulate intellectual curiosity and a capacity for critical thinking.

22. Balance is needed between the time spent on learning language skills and the time devoted to free and animated expression making use of these skills.

23. Students should be trained in the intelligent use of the cultural

resources in their community (libraries, museums, theater, and literary figures).

24. Refreshment of mind and spirit through imaginative release in literature, books, films, TV and radio plays, and recordings can further mental and emotional stability.
25. Students should be trained in the intelligent use of the mass modes of communication.
26. Reading is a means of emotional, aesthetic, and intellectual growth.
27. Sensing the values of silent reading for finding answers to questions and of oral reading as a source of enjoyment is an outcome of *dynamic* reading.
28. Through literature, students should have access to the spiritual experience of mankind—home, friends, church, nation, world.
29. The language arts program should be integrated with the work of the library and with the use of language and reading in all other subjects and activities of the school.
30. The student should leave high school with as great a mastery of specific skills in reading, writing, speaking, and listening as his ability will permit.

DETERMINING SCOPE AND SEQUENCE

In determining the scope and sequence of the language arts program for any secondary school, those engaged in curriculum planning need to give attention to these factors: the student population, the community, faculty resources, school facilities, and consultant services.

Studying Relevant Factors

Student population. Of primary concern are the interests, capacities, scholastic achievements, instructional needs, and occupational outlook of the adolescents for whom the program is planned. Cumulative records,[6] work-study experiences, scholastic and other aptitude tests, interest inventories, interviews, and exploratory situations in which linguistic competence is observable—these are some of the means by which the significant potentialities and present achievements of students are ascertained. Such data assembled for the student population in an individual secondary school, as well as

[6] See Chapter 2, pp. 13 ff.

in all the secondary schools within a school system, are basic to curriculum planning. In addition, follow-up studies of previous graduates who are currently employed or who are attending college reveal strengths and weaknesses in the language arts offerings of the school.

The community. The "life space" of the individual influences the development of his linguistic competence, discriminating taste, and satisfying relationships with boys and girls of his own age. In this connection, it is useful for the teacher to know where the student lives and the things, people, and animals he sees on his way to and from school. Of equal importance is the teacher's knowledge of the cultural and recreational opportunities in the community. These include libraries, museums, theaters, and sports arenas, as well as radio and television programs. Information concerning the open and closed meetings of youth organizations may also give the teacher clues as to how boys and girls are spending their leisure hours.

Many schools report the use of informal school-community surveys to locate informed and talented adults willing to share information either at school assemblies and in classrooms or by having groups of students visit these adults in their hobby rooms at home or at their places of work. Surveys of the employment opportunities for high school graduates also reveal job requirements related to competence in listening, speaking, reading, and writing. Studies of the entrance requirements of the colleges usually attended by the graduates of a high school furnish relevant information to those engaged in curriculum development.

Faculty resources. Another major factor in curriculum planning is the range of training and experience among the faculty. It is of first importance to discover the aptitudes, interests, and formal and informal education of the language arts teachers. Where gaps are found, these may be filled by utilizing special talents of teachers in other subject fields. It sometimes happens that a teacher of mathematics, of business education, of science, or of the fine arts has a special aptitude, interest, or experience through which that teacher may become a resource person in school journalism or in the speech arts.

Several school systems report the use of inservice workshops to develop new insights and skills among members of the staff.

In Baltimore, for example, an inservice workshop, "Reading in All Content Fields," has been used as one method of alerting every teacher to students' reading problems and of increasing his skill in dealing with them in a school-wide developmental reading program. Similarly, workshops for all subject teachers have been conducted in "Better Speech Health." The purpose has been to assist teachers in identifying cases which require clinical services and in guiding all other students in better speech habits.

There is a national trend toward participation of language arts, physical education, music, and fine arts teachers in workshops in the speech arts planned for a school faculty. This cooperation has resulted in a contribution from every teacher to the development in all students of linguistic competence, personal adjustment, and human relationships.

School facilities. The potentialities and limitations of the school plant also relate to curriculum planning. Ingenious teachers, with parent and student help, in some instances have created a learning environment favorable to language growth out of what seemed an impossible situation.

In schools built before the present-day audio-visual equipment was available, imaginative and inventive teachers, with the aid of pupils, parents, and the school custodian, have remodeled classrooms to gain some flexibility in the use of limited space.

In these days of extensive building programs, however, it is essential that classrooms be made large enough to permit several small groups of students to work independently of each other during a class period. Book shelves, poster cabinets, bulletin boards, and electric outlets are essential for effective use of classroom libraries and of loan collections of books, films, filmstrips, colored slides, tape recordings and records. Filing cabinets are needed for folders of students' writing and for recordings of their oral communication. If results of curriculum study are to be measured through the years, these papers and recordings need to be kept for use as diagnostic instruments, as well as evidence of students' growth in language power.

Consultant services. As has been mentioned earlier, resource persons may be found among the faculty, students, and parents of a school.

Specialists in aspects of the language arts and in curriculum research and evaluation are often available in nearby schools, colleges, and universities, as well as through the National Council of Teachers of English, the College Entrance Examination Board, the Educational Testing Service, the Educational Records Bureau, The College Conference on Communication and Composition, and the Association for Supervision and Curriculum Development.

Publications of the National Council of Teachers of English are an invaluable consultation service through print—inexpensive and easily available. Attendance at regional workshops and at the annual meetings of the National Council of Teachers of English is an additional way of securing consultant help in local curriculum planning.

Time and funds. Closely related to the problem of school plant facilities for carrying out the recommendations of a new curriculum is the foresight needed in providing funds and facilities for the work of the curriculum committee itself. A chairman or steering committee working with the administration should explore available resources and possibilities, for within the limitations of such conditions planning must take place. Among these important facilities is time for committees to work other than in the weary after-school hours of a teaching day. Gradually curriculum study is coming to be recognized as an important part of the work for which a teacher is employed. Some boards of education provide for closing school early once a month, bi-monthly, or even one day a week for such work. In some schools, committees rotate their meetings, so that teachers are available to take over the duties of those in session at any given time. Supply teachers may be provided to relieve the regular teachers for periods of curriculum work. Many schools also use pre-term or post-term curriculum workshops, for which teachers are remunerated. Certainly recognition must be given by the administration to the importance of curriculum work by teachers if wholehearted, continuing co-operation is to be expected.

Budgetary provisions should also be made for questionnaires or other survey and evaluative materials, and for curriculum guides, books, and courses of study. Fees for lecturers or consultants must be foreseen. Some schools send representatives to participate in workshops, conferences, study councils, and in the annual meetings of the National Council of Teachers of English. These are a few examples of the kind of advance planning that is needed to determine what can wisely be undertaken.

Providing for Sequential Learning

Reports to the Commission from all parts of the country indicate that everywhere an earnest effort is being made to provide a sequential language arts program from kindergarten through Grade 12.

Chart of sequential skills. Sequence is being provided not only through the method of setting up curriculum committees,[7] but also through systematic analysis of reading, writing, listening, and speaking skills. Curriculum workers in several school systems have charted the sequence of these skills.[8] Whenever such charts have been published in local

[7] See pp. 32–33.
[8] Chicago Public Schools, Indianapolis Public Schools, Minneapolis Public Schools, New York City Public Schools.

curriculum guides, teachers have been reminded of the wide range of abilities and of achievement likely to exist among the members of a single class.

Good practice over the country indicates that teachers attempt to find where each student is at the beginning of a unit of instruction and to provide learning situations and instructional materials appropriate to the rate and pattern of the individual's growth in language power. The teacher also relates to such charts what he knows about the stage of maturity of each child and the kinds of situations which will motivate the student either to feel a need for a new skill or to recognize an opportunity to apply an old one.

The publishers of many series of textbooks furnish charts indicating where skills are first developed and how they are maintained in later units. Again this device of charting a sequence is useful to those teachers who utilize scientific and creative methods of finding where each individual within a class is in relation to the sequence of skills.

Study of problems of articulation. In an effort [9] to provide for the continuous development of children from one school level to the next, articulation problems have been studied by groups representing each level.

For orientation purposes, elementary pupils are given an opportunity to visit the secondary school; and, when feasible, senior high school students visit the college which they are planning to enter. The junior or senior high school teacher confers with the former teachers of his students. Visits to classes are arranged. Teachers from "feeding" schools confer with teachers in the junior or the senior high school, as the case may be, and observe classes to which their students go. Teachers from the higher level visit classes in the lower school. At times, too, a teacher follows up a particular child as he moves on to the next school because of some special problem he has. Through these conferences and

[9] Baltimore Public Schools, reported by Helen Chambers, Josie Smith, and Katherine Templeton (Baltimore, Md.).

observations, a study is made of curriculum materials, techniques, and procedures at all levels.

Problems of articulation brought to light by these school groups are taken up by city-wide committees organized by the secondary supervisors. The various phases of the language arts program are studied in order to insure continuity in growth. Representatives from colleges receiving high school graduates meet with secondary school teachers and supervisors to discuss the objectives and programs of both schools and colleges and to plan ways of solving articulation problems.[10] In order to see the total picture, committees at times review the whole program of language arts from the kindergarten through Grade 12.

Selection of instructional materials to fit the curriculum. At the heart of a sequential program in the language arts is the selection of instructional materials to meet the wide range of differences among the students at any grade level. The wealth of recently published trade books and textbooks in literature, reading, speaking, listening, and writing offers a challenge to individual teachers and to curriculum workers to find the right books for the right student. In many communities [11] there are staff committees representing teachers of all subject areas and of all grade levels engaged in a continual study of instructional materials, including books, periodicals, films, filmstrips, records, slides, and flat pictures.

Through workshops, committees, and conferences, teachers are encouraged to extend their reading of books that might appeal to their students. School and public librarians have been of great assistance, calling attention of both pupils and teachers to books that might be of interest. In a workshop, "Literature for Adolescents," [12] each participant selected an area of interest, found many books relating to the area, examined them, and for each made an annotation in-

[10] For further examples see Chapter 12.
[11] Baltimore City Public Schools, *Criteria and Procedures for Selecting Books, A Committee Report* (Baltimore, Md., Bureau of Publications, 1955).
[12] Baltimore Public Schools.

cluding these items: *unit title, title of book, brief description of content, grade for which suitable, readability level,* and *other relevant hints for using the book.* The bibliographies that grew out of this professional activity were edited, mimeographed, and distributed to all secondary teachers. Through another workshop, "Utilizing Radio and Television in the Language Arts Program," a similar listing of radio and television programs was made available to Baltimore teachers. This latter list, of necessity, will need frequent revisions, but it served a valuable purpose in helping teachers to see radio and television as potential instructional material.

Adjustment of grouping and promotion policies to curriculum goals. Provision for sequential learning usually results from the co-operative study of grouping and promotion policies. Where secondary curriculum committees include representatives from elementary schools and from colleges, it has been possible to agree that the rate and progress of individual students and the ultimate level of their accomplishments differ according to their innate potentialities and to the stimulation of their surroundings.[13] Such committees also come to appreciate the fact that growth in language power is gradual; it can be continuous; and it should be cumulative. Faculty agreement is also achieved as to the kinds of growth (related always to the student's capacity and initial status in specific skills) which are essential for promotion to the next level. Equally important are decisions as to methods of determining when a student's best interest is served by his staying longer at the same grade level.

Some schools [14] report that in grouping students into class sections, consideration is given to the student's physical maturity, scholastic achievements, special interests and aptitudes, peer-relationships, and expected teacher-pupil adjustment. Some large schools reduce the range of abilities and achievement within a class but allow enough spread to chal-

---

[13] See pp. 13–14.
[14] Baltimore, Cleveland, Chicago, Indianapolis, Los Angeles, New York.

lenge the teacher and to guarantee that students will learn from each other. These same schools have developed accelerated and enrichment programs for superior students and "opportunity," "resource," or "special" classes for slow-learning pupils as ways of providing for extreme differences among secondary-school students.

Grouping within the class is an effective means by which a teacher leads his students, each according to his own growth pattern and rate of learning, into continuous development toward language competence. Groups [15] are set up for different purposes and their membership, size, and length of life vary with the purpose for which each one is formed. If, for example, the teacher's goal is to give a talented oral reader an opportunity to interpret effectively a literary selection, a whole class might form the listening group. If, however, the purpose is to give each student in the group a chance to react orally to what is read, the listening group will need to be small enough to permit every member to participate during the available time. If the purpose of grouping is to help the students gain a specific skill, only those who need directed practice on that skill should be included in the group.

Grouping is a means toward sequential learning when both student and teacher are aware of the student's need and of his progress toward his goal.

Use of cumulative records. As illustrated in Chapters 2 and 5–10, the perceptive study by the teacher of the cumulative records of an individual can lead to improved sequence in the student's learning experiences. To the extent that the teacher adds to the records significant data concerning the rate and pattern of the student's learning, the next teacher will be able to maintain an unbroken sequence of the student's development.

Offerings in required and elective courses. In designing

[15] Florida State Department of Education, *Experiencing the Language Arts,* Bulletin 34 (Tallahassee, Florida State Department of Education, 1948), pp. 70–71.

their language arts program, small and large schools provide some experiences for every student (required courses) and other experiences (electives) for those students with special interests, aptitudes, or instructional needs. The required courses and the electives in literature, language skills, reading improvement, and public speaking offered by the Los Angeles City Schools illustrate the principle that the design of the program should permit each student to attain his maximum personal development and to contribute his best to the group.[16] So, too, do the junior and senior high school courses of study for the New York City Public Schools.[17]

RELATING THE LANGUAGE ARTS PROGRAM TO THE TOTAL SCHOOL PROGRAM

In addition to developing a sequentially articulated program, it is important for curriculum committees in the language arts field to remember its relation to other aspects of the school program. Because language is social in content, social in significance, and social in the manner in which it is learned, a student may improve his linguistic competence through every occasion in and out of school which calls for speaking, listening, reading, and writing.

One school [18] launched a school-wide approach through a study by the English teachers of the habits and skills essential in their field. The list was mimeographed and submitted to the entire faculty, with the request that each teacher check the list using these symbols: √√ needed frequently, √ needed to some extent, x needed only to a very limited extent, m missing but needed, n not desirable or not applicable.

[16] Los Angeles City School Districts, *Graduation Requirements and Curricula,* School Publication No. 489 (Los Angeles, Calif., Los Angeles City Schools, 1950).

[17] New York City Board of Education, *English Language Arts Course of Study for New York City—Junior High Schools* (New York, September, 1956); *English Language Arts Course of Study for New York City—Senior High Schools* (New York, September, 1956). See also Chapters 5–10.

[18] Forest Park High School, Baltimore, Maryland.

A compilation of the replies from every teacher disclosed those habits and skills which were of general concern and those which were needed by students only in their English activities.

Through a series of group meetings, teachers of the same pupils evolved ways of encouraging students to make use of the basic training given in the language arts class. The teacher in each subject area assumed responsibility for the development of the special terms (meaning, pronunciation, and spelling) in that field. In addition, each subject teacher assumed responsibility for helping students to check their oral and written reports in that subject. Accuracy of facts, soundness of interpretation, and clarity and effectiveness of organization were the elements evaluated. From time to time, the teachers of the same students conferred to check what progress they were making in applying language skills developed in the English classroom and applicable in other fields. Wherever remedial work was needed in any aspect of the language arts, provision for it was made through the co-operation of the English and other subject teachers or in special classes organized by the English language arts department.

The Latin School of Chicago has developed an outstanding program in all-school English. Not only are the skills in reading, writing, speaking, and listening the concern of all teachers, but every teacher is co-operating in a recreational reading program which has increased both the quality and quantity of the reading done by every student in the school. The speech arts, likewise, have gained greater significance in the lives of the students because of the total involvement of the faculty in planning the program and the leadership of the headmaster.

The teachers in the Minneapolis, Minnesota, Public Schools have been working for several years with an all-school approach to communication. Representatives from all grade levels and from all subject areas have co-operated in the study of the communication needs of boys and girls at different age-grade levels.

As a result of this comprehensive program of curriculum development, several guides have been issued. *English and Social Studies, Grades 7, 8, 9* (1951), reports what is being taught in a two-hour course. This guide lists the learnings to be acquired cumulatively through experience in all three grades. Skills and competencies, as well as major concepts, in speaking and writing, and in reading, listening, and observing are identified. Attitudes and appreciations conducive to personal development are also listed. Learnings to be acquired in social behavior include skills and competencies and information important to good citizenship. *Achieving Objectives of Education* (1953), another guide for curriculum development, gives for each objective the basic concepts to be understood, desirable attitudes to be developed, major skills and competencies to be acquired, and types of experience which contribute to the realization of this objective. Language arts run throughout this guide. *Communication, A Guide to the Teaching of Speaking and Writing* (1953) lists the common goals to be sought at all levels and in all subjects; describes learning experiences in the elementary grades, junior high school, and senior high school; discusses the teaching of spelling and handwriting; and gives assistance in identifying growth in language use.

Unit Plans for the Language Arts developed by the Seattle, Washington, Public Schools (1952) presents a planned sequence from Grades 7 through 12.

EVALUATING THE PROGRAM

Certain broad criteria are applicable to the language arts program as a whole; others, to its facets—speaking, listening, reading, writing, and observing.

Concerning the program as a whole, teachers and administrators, as well as parents and other citizens, may well ask:

1. Are speaking, listening, reading, writing, and observing organized into a developmental program from grade to grade, from year to year in the student's life?
2. Has the curriculum stimulated teachers to individualize instruction within a class organization through flexible grouping, differentiated assignments, utilization of student leadership, and a variety of instructional materials?
3. Is provision made to meet the needs of students for enrichment and for remedial instruction in speaking, reading, writing, and listening?
4. Are movies, radio, television, recordings, and periodicals, as well as field trips, used to enrich experiences gained from reading books?
5. Is the literature presented for students' independent reading within their silent reading comprehension? Are superior students helped to read up to the level of their abilities?
6. Is literature beyond the students' *silent* reading comprehension, but within their emotional understanding, presented to them through oral methods?
7. Are experiences provided for developing in students discrimination in selecting books, periodicals, movies, radio and television programs, and recordings?
8. Is specific training provided for the various reading purposes of the students at each stage of their development? Speaking purposes? Writing purposes? Listening purposes?
9. Are the reading and library skills needed for study and recreational reading being developed and used?
10. Are grammatical concepts developed at the age-grade level where the students can use them to facilitate correct and effective oral and written expression?
11. Are listening skills developed through specialized radio and speech activities, as well as in the daily contacts of students in small and large groups?
12. Are language activities (in reading, writing, speaking, and listening) integrated with other subject-matter areas and with the total school and out-of-school life of the students?
13. Is there direct and well-motivated attack on difficult and specialized language skills?
14. Is there provision for individual students to proceed at their own rate?
15. Are students developing a sense of responsibility for proofreading and evaluating their own work and that of others?
16. Do students have the habit of proofreading and editing for correctness and effectiveness, as well as for accurate interpretation of facts, student-written resource material which is to be preserved in the classroom or school library?

If evaluation is to make its best contribution to the improvement of learning, evaluative criteria and plans for self-appraisal must be developed co-operatively by the teacher with his students. These criteria should identify growth in observing, listening, speaking, reading, and writing.

If samples of students' writing are collected for purposes of evaluation, it is desirable and necessary to record the source of motivation and the circumstances under which the writing was produced. It is also helpful on such a sample to record whether the writing was independent or co-operative composition, whether teacher consultation was available during its production, and whether time and training had been provided so that the student felt a desire to revise, knew how to revise, and had time to revise.

Similarly, when discs or tapes are used to record students' oral reading, special occasion talks, or oral responses to listening experiences, it is desirable to attach a notation stating briefly the nature of the speaking or listening situation and the speaker's or listener's purpose. If at least three recordings of a student's speaking (including oral response to listening experiences) are made during a semester, a comparison will indicate (1) the extent to which the curriculum is challenging students to speak and to listen and (2) the rate and pattern of their improvement. This kind of information is invaluable in a study of the curriculum.

Cumulative records of students' independent reading and listening not only furnish information immediately useful to their teacher, but also provide evidence of the effectiveness of the curriculum.

Results of standardized tests of reading and listening skills give the teacher additional information concerning his students' growth in linguistic competence and may indicate whether the curriculum needs further change.

Detailed suggestions for evaluating the various aspects of the language arts program are included in Chapters 4–10.

RECOGNIZING THE NEED FOR CONTINUOUS CURRICULUM STUDY

No classroom teacher or organized curriculum group can afford to call its work finished when a new course of study is produced. The fact that many courses recently appearing as printed documents have the subtitle "A Progress Report" is indicative of the realization that curriculum work must be continuous. The most important result that could emerge from a curriculum study—local, area, state, regional, or national—would be an awakened interest among all teachers in study of the needs of boys and girls, the impact of the changing times, the richness of materials available to improve teaching, and the almost limitless and tremendously important possibilities that challenge a teacher of the language arts continually to study and improve the curriculum.

BIBLIOGRAPHY

LANGUAGE ARTS

Books

Florida State Department of Education, *Experiencing the Language Arts*, Bulletin 34 (Tallahassee, Florida State Department of Education, 1948).

National Council of Teachers of English, Commission on the English Curriculum, *The English Language Arts*, NCTE Curriculum Series, Vol. I (New York, Appleton-Century-Crofts, Inc., 1952).

National Society for the Study of Education, *Adult Reading*, Fifty-fifth Yearbook, Part II (Chicago, University of Chicago Press, 1956).

———, *Mass Media and Education*, Fifty-third Yearbook, Part II (Chicago, University of Chicago Press, 1954).

———, *Reading in the High School and College*, Forty-seventh Yearbook, Part II (Chicago, University of Chicago Press, 1948).

SMITH, Dora V., *Communication, The Miracle of Shared Living* (New York, The Macmillan Company, 1955).

Pamphlets and Periodicals

American Educational Research Association, "Language Arts and Fine Arts," *Review of Educational Research*, Vol. XXV, No. 2 (April, 1955).

The English Journal (Champaign, Ill.).

FREEMAN, Frank N., *Teaching Handwriting, What Research Says to the Teacher*, No. 4 (Washington, D. C., Department of Classroom Teachers and the American Educational Research Association of the National Education Association, 1954).

GATES, Arthur I., *Teaching Reading, What Research Says to the Teacher*, No. 1 (Washington, D. C., Department of Classroom Teachers and the American Educational Research Association of the National Education Association, 1953).

HORN, Ernest, *Teaching Spelling, What Research Says to the Teacher*, No. 3 (Washington, D. C., Department of Classroom Teachers and the American Educational Research Association of the National Education Association, 1953).

ARTICULATION

Fund for the Advancement of Education, *Bridging the Gap between School and College*, a Progress Report on Four Related Projects Supported by the Fund for the Advancement of Education, Evaluation Report No. 1 (New York, Fund for the Advancement of Education, Established by the Ford Foundation, June, 1953).

General Education in School and College, a Committee Report by Members of the Faculties of Andover, Exeter, Lawrenceville, Harvard, Princeton, and Yale (Cambridge, Mass., Harvard University Press, 1953).

CHILD DEVELOPMENT AND HUMAN RELATIONS

American Educational Research Association, "The Educational Program: Later Adolescence," *Review of Educational Research,* Vol. XXIV, No. 4 (October, 1954).

BENNE, Kenneth D., and MUNTYAN, Bozidar, *Human Relations in Curriculum Change* (New York, The Dryden Press, 1951).

Educational Policies Commission, *Education of the Gifted,* Report of the Educational Policies Commission of the National Education Association of the United States and the American Association of School Administrators (Washington, D. C., National Education Association, 1950).

MILLARD, Cecil V., *Child Growth and Development in the Elementary School Years* (Boston, D. C. Heath & Company, 1951).

National Association of Secondary-School Principals, "Human Relations in Secondary Education," *The Bulletin,* Vol. 39, No. 209 (March, 1955).

MENTAL HEALTH

Department of Supervisors and Directors of Instruction, *Mental Health in the Classroom,* Thirteenth Yearbook (Washington, D. C., National Education Association, 1941).

National Society for the Study of Education, *Mental Health in Modern Education,* Fifty-fourth Yearbook, Part II (Chicago, University of Chicago Press, 1955).

REDL, Fritz, and WATTENBERG, William W., under the editorship of Willard B. Spalding and Ernest R. Hilgard, *Mental Hygiene in Teaching* (New York, Harcourt, Brace & Company, Inc., 1951).

EVALUATION

Books

The Commission on English, *Examining the Examination in English: A Report to the College Entrance Examination Board,* Harvard Studies in Education, No. 17, Charles Swain Thomas, Chairman (Cambridge, Mass., Harvard University Press, 1931).

Educational Testing Services, *Essential Characteristics of a Testing Program,* Education and Advisory Service Series, No. 2 (Princeton, N. J., Educational Testing Service, n. d.).

FUESS, Claude M., *The College Board: Its First Fifty Years* (New York, Columbia University Press, 1950).

GREENE, H. A., JORGENSEN, A. N., and GERBERICH, J. R., *Measurement and Evaluation in the Secondary School* (New York, Longmans, Green & Company, 1954).

LINDQUIST, E. F., *Educational Measurement* (Washington, D. C., American Council on Education, 1951).

Maryland State Department of Education, *Evaluating Maryland's Public School Program,* Third Annual Educational Conference of the State of Maryland Department of Education (Baltimore, Maryland State Department of Education, 1950).

ODELL, C. W., *How to Improve Classroom Testing* (Dubuque, Iowa, William C. Brown Company, 1953).

THOMAS, R. Murray, *Judging Student Progress* (New York, Longmans, Green & Company, 1954).

Pamphlets and Periodicals

American Educational Research Association, "Educational and Psychological Testing," *Review of Educational Research,* Vol. XXVI, No. 1 (February, 1956).

REMMERS, H. H., and GAGE, N. L., *Educational Measurement and Evaluation,* rev. ed. (New York, Harper and Brothers, 1955).

ROTHNEY, John W. M., *Evaluating and Reporting Pupil Progress,* What Research Says to the Teacher, No. 7 (Washington, D. C., Department of Classroom Teachers and the American Educational Research Association of the National Education Association, 1955).

WRIGHTSTONE, J. Wayne, *What Tests Can Tell Us about Children,* Better Living Booklets (Chicago, Science Research Associates, Inc., 1954).

GENERAL CURRICULUM PROBLEMS

Association for Supervision and Curriculum Development, *Action for Curriculum Improvement*, 1951 Yearbook (Washington, D. C., National Education Association, 1951).

————, *Creating a Good Environment for Learning*, 1954 Yearbook (Washington, D. C., National Education Association, 1954).

BLAIR, Glenn Myers, *Diagnostic and Remedial Teaching* (New York, The Macmillan Company, 1956).

CASWELL, Hollis L., and associates, *Curriculum Improvement in Public School Systems* (New York, Bureau of Publications, Teachers College, Columbia University, 1950).

Department of Supervision and Curriculum Development, *Group Planning in Education*, 1945 Yearbook (Washington, D. C., National Education Association, 1945).

HAVIGHURST, Robert J., STIVERS, Eugene, and DeHAAN, Robert F., *A Survey of Gifted Children*, Supplementary Educational Monographs, No. 83 (Chicago, University of Chicago Press, November, 1955).

KRUG, Edward A., *Curriculum Planning*, Education for Living Series (New York, Harper and Brothers, 1950).

LEONARD, J. Paul, *Developing the Secondary School Curriculum* (New York, Rinehart & Company, Inc., 1953).

McNERNEY, Chester T., *The Curriculum* (New York, McGraw-Hill Book Company, Inc., 1953).

National Association of Secondary-School Principals, "What Should We Expect of Education?" *The Bulletin*, Vol. 40, No. 217 (February, 1956).

National Manpower Council, *Improving the Work Skills of the Nation* (New York, Columbia University Press, 1955).

National Society for the Study of Education, *Adapting the Secondary-School Program to the Needs of Youth*, Fifty-second Yearbook, Part I (Chicago, University of Chicago Press, 1953).

————, *Audio-visual Materials of Instruction*, Forty-eighth Yearbook, Part I (Chicago, University of Chicago Press, 1949).

————, *General Education*, Fifty-first Yearbook, Part I (Chicago, University of Chicago Press, 1952).

————, *Learning and Instruction*, Forty-ninth Yearbook, Part I (Chicago, University of Chicago Press, 1950).

ROMINE, Stephen A., *Building the High School Curriculum* (New York, The Ronald Press Company, 1954).

SAYLOR, J. Galen, and ALEXANDER, William M., *Curriculum Planning for Better Teaching and Learning* (New York, Rinehart & Company, Inc., 1954).

SMITH, B. Othanel, STANLEY, William O. and SHORES, J. Harlan,

Fundamentals of Curriculum Development (New York, World
Book Company, 1950).

SPEARS, Harold. *The Teacher and Curriculum Planning* (Englewood
Cliffs, N. J., Prentice-Hall, Inc., 1951).

STRATEMEYER, Florence B., FORKNER, Hamden L., McKIM, Margaret
G., and members of the Childhood-Youth Education Committee,
Developing a Curriculum for Modern Living (New York, Bureau
of Publications, Teachers College, Columbia University, 1947).

TROW, William Clark, *The Learning Process*, What Research Says to
the Teacher, No. 6 (Washington, D. C., Department of Classroom
Teachers and the American Educational Research Association of
the National Education Association, 1954).

PREVIEW OF CHAPTER 4

Enrichment and Motivation of Teaching through the Unit Method of Instruction

Reading Skills for a Purpose
Literature for Insight and Enjoyment
Interrelated Development in the Language Arts
The Unit Method Defined

Back-Country America—An Illustrative Unit

The Teacher's Problem in Selecting the Unit
The Teacher's Part in Introducing the Unit
Getting Under Way with Reading
Enriching the Program with Special Reports
Sharing Reading through Informal Discussion
Varying the Program with Individual Contributions
Seeking Additional Materials and Ideas
Sharing Experiences through Speech and Listening
Preserving and Interpreting Findings through Writing
Examining the Literary Value of What Was Read
Evaluating the Results of the Unit

The Values in Unit Teaching

Problems Involved in Unit Teaching

Selecting Units of Instruction
Securing and Handling Materials
Consulting with and among Departments
Insuring Sequence in Unit Teaching

Bibliography

CHAPTER 4

Building Instructional Units

MUCH HAS BEEN DISCOVERED in recent years about how language grows and how literature, well taught, can enrich the lives of boys and girls.

ENRICHMENT AND MOTIVATION OF TEACHING THROUGH THE UNIT METHOD OF INSTRUCTION

Language power increases and words take on deeper and more precise meaning as young people extend and reflect upon their experience. As they grapple with more and more complex ideas, their sentences grow in maturity and therefore present problems of clarity and effectiveness in expression not encountered earlier. When students have genuine motives for communication, they see value in gaining skill in speaking, writing, reading, and listening. Because communication involves sharing or exchanging ideas in settings in which there are differences of opinion, emotional overtones, and variations in the meanings of words, the use of language is complicated by the social situation in which it is used.

Reading Skills for a Purpose

Skill in reading flourishes best when young people read for a purpose, looking for something. In the search for meaning, power in word recognition develops into something more fundamental than mere word-calling. Use of contextual clues becomes a normal procedure. Synonyms and antonyms serve as aids in pinning down ideas. Reading for details and distinguishing main points from subordinate ones become tools in the search for ideas. More complex processes, such as searching for clues in fiction, following a sequence of ideas by proper attention to transitions, and reading to visualize the setting, to interpret character, or to explore motive, take on a new significance when there is a purpose for which the reading is done. Once found, ideas must be fitted into the train of thought being followed in the classroom or must be used in the pursuit of problems that have meaning for the pupils.

Literature for Insight and Enjoyment

Literature provides insight into human experience. Its power lies primarily in its aesthetic values, which delight the reader as they enrich his spirit. English teachers are concerned both with *what* literature says to young people and with *how* it says it. Varied types of literature, each with its distinctive approach to human experience, offer rich rewards in a lifetime of reading to those who master the techniques of interpretation required by each of them.

Students differ greatly in the background of experience they bring to literature and in the reading skills they have at their command. In any class in the junior or senior high school, the range in reading ability is likely to be at least six or seven years. Some method of meeting these varied needs must be devised.

Interrelated Development in the Language Arts

Moreover, the language arts are closely interrelated. The day is past when English programs were organized with one term of writing, one term of literature, and one term of speech. The sequential program for all students utilizes all the language arts in every term. Where offerings related to special interests are scheduled for a semester, they are planned either as remedial programs for retarded students or as enrichment for superior students.

Enjoyment of reading leads to discussion (speaking and listening); discussion, to reading or writing. Writing and speaking pose similar problems in the selection and organization of material. Each involves a reader or listener to whom something is to be made clear or by whom something is to be imaginatively realized. Both depend upon reading, observation, and listening for motive and for content. They differ, however, in the final step of concern for the conventions of writing or speaking and the use and control of the voice or bodily movement.

What is a speaking situation for one student is a listening situation for another. In the oral interpretation of literature, discussion constantly follows reading. Reading frequently eventuates in written reaction to the ideas expressed or in the attempt to reproduce in imaginative form a similar experience of one's own.

The Unit Method Defined

Teachers seek some means of organizing instruction that implements the principle of learning through use in purposeful activities and at the same time recognizes the relatedness of all the language skills and literature. One effective organizational pattern is the unit method of teaching. There will be no effort in this chapter to argue the merits of different kinds of units. To some people a unit is an organized study of a topic such as *Romance Is More Than "Boy Meets Girl"* or *Getting Acquainted with Great Literary Personalities of America*. To others it involves pursuit of a problem such as *What Values Are of Most Worth?* or *How Does Effective Communication Influence Life in Our Town?* To still others, it means consideration of questions of moment to young people such as *Problems of Growing Up during Adolescence*. For yet others, unit teaching may center in experiences like *Adventuring in Books, Enjoying Poetry,* or *Understanding Drama*. All that is meant by the term here is that varied activities in the language arts are developed around a central theme or purpose, clear and significant to the student. It must be sufficiently broad to involve in some measure all four of the language arts and to permit each individual (1) to work in co-operation with his class and (2) to pursue certain special interests in a wide range of materials and experiences suited to his ability. In working through a unit, students need to think clearly and logically, to plan under the guidance of the teacher, to assign tasks and to accept responsibility either as individuals or in groups, and to learn such research techniques as use of library reference sources, directed observation, and the interview. At the same time, they have opportunity for practicing many forms of speech and writing with direct attention to these skills as the need arises. In a social setting, the students test their powers and have opportunity to note the results, both as regards the quality of their own performance and its effect upon the listener or reader.

BACK-COUNTRY AMERICA—AN ILLUSTRATIVE UNIT

Perhaps the best way to illustrate the possibilities in this kind of teaching is to present in some detail a unit, called *Back-Country America,* which has proved useful in a town of 35,000 and later in a university laboratory school.[1] It is suitable for the tenth and eleventh grades, according to the relative maturity of the class, and takes from five to eight weeks to complete, depending upon the interest of the students, the amount of material available, and the number of activities the teacher wishes to undertake.

The Teacher's Problem in Selecting the Unit

The teacher of this unit, at the suggestion of the school librarian, read Paul Annixter's *Swiftwater* when it first appeared in the library. Impressed by both its interest and its sensitivity in presenting the life of a boy and his father, who

[1] Virginia Alwin, teacher, Rochester, Minnesota, High School, 1951–52; University High School, Minneapolis, Minnesota, 1952–54; Arizona State Teachers College, Flagstaff, Arizona, 1955–.

are brought close to one another in their common interest in protecting the wild game of Maine, she began to relate it to other stories of back-country folk and their surroundings. It reminded her of *The Yearling* by Marjorie Kinnan Rawlings, and of *Hie to the Hunters!* by Jesse Stuart. Each had elements of appeal for individual boys and girls in her classes. Each dealt with one phase of *Back-Country America.* She culled from her memory of similar reading some fifteen or twenty titles that could be combined into a rich unit.

Possibilities for furthering the aims of the language arts. The teacher recognized the many possibilities in this unit for sensing the distinctiveness of life and personality in the back hill country and at the same time the universality of human behavior beneath outward manifestations and appearances. The study she had just finished with her class had emphasized informative reading, expository writing, and persuasive speaking. She saw in this one opportunity for a more varied program in reading—the novel, poetry, biography, and drama—with a wide range of difficulty in each.

Magazine articles and travel books with emphasis upon description and anecdote would furnish new examples of language used effectively. In *Holiday* for March, 1951, there appeared an interesting article by A. B. Guthrie, Jr., called "Kentucky," showing with accuracy and picturesqueness, accompanied by delightful illustrations, the many-sided life of the people of Kentucky, among them the Southern Highlanders. This would make a colorful bulletin-board display. Out of the reading of this unit could come the chance to contrast poor and good books, for the subject of back-country life attracts both the writer of cheap and ephemeral stories with an eye to the sales value of the different, the stereotyped, and the spectacular, and the serious writer whose own life and emotions have been deeply intertwined with those of the people about whom he writes.

Many skills in reading as well as in the use of library sources could be developed in the unit. There would be opportunities for clear thinking, for establishing purposes, for grappling with the selection and organization of materials to fulfill those purposes. The distinctive traits of speech of the back-country people would open up the whole field of dialect and its relationship to the development of the English language. There would be ample occasion for pursuit of individual and group interests in such subjects as mountain music, mountain ballads, mountain feuds, and the effect of environment on personality. There could be special stress upon informal writing which utilizes anecdotes for interest and illustration, upon excursions into imaginative writing, choral speaking, and the study of the ballad. For the class as a whole, there would be reading for characterization, for insight into the effect of environment on character, and for details to illustrate a point. There could be conversational discussion in which drawing generalizations from specific instances would play a large part. Practice in the skills of speech and writing would be continual. Many of these possibilities would occur to the beginner in unit teaching only as the unit got under way.

Richness of materials available. There was no doubt that the subject was rich in human interest, in furthering development of insight, and in possibilities for increasing powers in the language arts. The next question was whether enough material was available to make the unit a profitable one.

Jesse Stuart, Marjorie Kinnan Rawlings, MacKinlay Kantor, and Richard Chase were well represented in the school library. A search through anthologies available either in sets or in single copies brought to light several short stories related to the topic: "The Storm," "Eustacia," "The Champion," "The Thanksgiving Hunter," and "The Split Cherry Tree" by Jesse Stuart; "Journey to the Forks," by James Still; and "Georgia Mountain Men," an excerpt from *Deep River* by Henrietta Henkle. Poems were also included: Stephen Vincent Benét's "Mountain Whippoorwill," DuBose Heyward's "Mountain Woman," and others similar in theme and quality. Paper-bound books also helped with such titles as *The Voice of Bugle Ann* and Marjorie Kinnan Rawlings' *South Moon Under*. Today such additional titles are available as *The Burl Ives Song Book* and *Gal Young-Un and Other Stories of Cross Creek Country*.

Scholastic for December 3, 1945, offered an article on "The Changing Mountain Folk"; *Newsweek* for June 13, 1949, furnished "Coin of Plenty: Hillbilly Songs"; *Holiday* for September, 1948, provided "Carolina Mountain Folk"; the *National Geographic* for September, 1946, "Arkansas"; *Life* for December 28, 1949, "Fruitful Mountaineers"; and the *Ford Times* for April, 1948, "Ozark Vittles" and "Tall Tales of Arkansas." Many magazines proved invaluable: *Coronet; Reader's Digest; Holiday* for November, 1950, on "Tennessee" (Storied Land of the Bible and Fiddle, the Rifle and the Demijohn); and *The Saturday Review* for August 12, 1950, containing an article on the Southern mountains. The teacher discovered some of these articles through the *Reader's Guide to Periodical Literature* and stocked them from libraries and second-hand bookstores. As soon as she sensed the possibilities of the unit, she began watching for articles, which appeared with a frequency she had never been conscious of before. She kept a special file of them. Later the students helped by bringing materials from home, continuing in their search and in their contributions to the file long after the unit was finished.

The teacher and librarian together collected on special shelves all the books and magazines in the library which dealt with the theme. These were loaned to the classroom for the period of the study. Apparently the school was, or could be, provided with the material needed. The first year the unit was pursued successfully with a few books, some short stories, half a dozen magazines, and two or three poems. Others were added each time the unit was taught.

The teacher familiarized herself with the available materials. Her knowledge of others grew with the progress of the unit and increased notably each time she taught the material. She read as widely as possible in order to sort out those books which revealed different aspects of life in the backwoods country and to determine, within each topic, which books would stimulate the more intelligent readers and which would be of use for the retarded pupils; which would appeal more to boys and which to girls; and which, perhaps, would appeal to one boy because of his interest in music, to another because of his love of stories of feuds and fighting, or to a girl because of her interest in language or religion. She prepared a reading list, tentatively organized. Members of the class then found additional titles as they worked, and sometimes thought they saw in those already available, values which the teacher herself had not discerned.

The Teacher's Part in Introducing the Unit

Filled with enthusiasm for the unit and equipped with some background for it, the teacher was ready to capture the interest of the pupils and to help them think through for themselves the purposes and plans she had already tentatively formulated.

The first time she attempted the unit, she introduced it by means of a bulletin board showing colorful pictures of the life of the mountaineers of the Great Smokies, the Cumberlands, and the Ozarks. These came from the magazine articles already mentioned. Some of the class were interested at once and began to name the backwoods sections of the United States which they had heard of and would like to investigate further. In the course of the discussion, the teacher led the students to think constructively about what they could learn from such a study, what were the purposes toward which they might work. Some of these could be foreseen, but others had to evolve with the unit. The class could plan some activities, too, from the beginning. Others presented themselves as the work progressed.

Agreeing upon purposes of the unit. In the list of purposes which follows, those marked with an asterisk were agreed upon early in the unit. The others were added as need for them arose.

PURPOSES OF THE UNIT ON BACK-COUNTRY AMERICA

ATTITUDES AND INSIGHTS

*1. To gain insight into the lives of other Americans living under conditions very different from our own.
*2. To discover how the distinctiveness of these people has come about through their environment and conditions of living.
3. To find out how these people are like us; that is, have universal loyalties, loves, hates, and other attitudes as well as regional ones.

READING AND LITERATURE

*1. To discover reasons for the peculiar power of literature as literature to reveal the thoughts, feelings, and the conditions of living of these or any people.
*2. To become acquainted with noted works and authors that have revealed these people to us.
3. To develop standards of judging between cheap and melodramatic stories and those of real value as literature.
4. To learn to read and take notes so as to bring to bear the insights and events of each book on the topics being considered.
5. To learn to read literature of various types, adjusting our method of reading to our purposes.
6. To learn to use valuable reference sources in the library.
7. To appreciate the importance of dialect in revealing regional character.
8. To develop our vocabularies through wide reading and use of context clues, through intelligent listening, and through use of the dictionary.

SPEAKING AND LISTENING

1. To think clearly about problems discussed in the unit and to participate in class discussion so as to help to come to intelligent conclusions.
2. To organize carefully and present clearly and interestingly different kinds of reports on our individual findings.
3. To learn to tell an incident well to prove a point in discussion.
4. To listen intelligently to discussion so as to relate what is said to the topic.
5. To learn to listen for the main generalizations and relate incidents and subpoints to them.
6. To improve our ability to work in groups, sticking to the point, encouraging and using contributions of each member in preparing interesting and original presentations for the class.

7. To learn to carry on informal, conversational discussion.
8. To read aloud stories and poems with real interpretation; to share selections read or to prove a point.
9. To improve our choral reading of favorite poems.
10. To use new words frequently and to choose concrete and suggestive words to make our talks more interesting.
11. To improve our ability to use our voices well.
12. To learn to judge whether we have actually achieved our speaking purpose by interesting, informing, or persuading the class.
13. To eliminate from our speech those things which lessen the value of our presentation, such as unacceptable usage or poor articulation, pronunciation, or enunciation.

WRITING

1. To be sure that we know our purpose in writing and choose and organize ideas with our purpose in mind.
2. To learn to summarize in clear and logical form the ideas or the central idea we have gained from our reading and from the class.
3. To take initiative in carrying on various kinds of personal and imaginative writing suggested by the unit.
4. To learn to write reflectively about these regional people with use of interesting incidents to prove our points.
5. To improve the concrete and suggestive power of the words we use in writing as we see how the writers we read use them.
6. To think clearly, outlining topics carefully and showing the relationship between the outline and the paragraphs and larger divisions of what we write or present orally.
7. To learn to spell important new words to be used in this unit.
8. To assume responsibility for correct punctuation, spelling, capitalization, and manuscript form in all written work.
9. To learn to examine our sentences for completeness, clarity, acceptable usage, and effectiveness before asking anyone else to read what we have written.

Arousing individual interests and planning procedures. With another class, at a later date, the teacher introduced the same study by displaying in front of the room some thirty or forty books set in back-country districts of America. As she handled each book in turn, telling something of interest about it, she indicated which would be especially enjoyed by boys and which were better suited to girls, suggesting certain books to individuals whose interests she knew. She explained the relative difficulty of some of the books, showing the kinds of insights and reading ability each of them would require. For example:

We Took to the Woods is an objective story of outdoor life that is easy to follow and breezy in incident.

Swiftwater by Paul Annixter requires more sensitivity and insight to get beneath the mere story of setting up a game refuge and to appreciate the lasting effect of that common interest upon father and son.

Mountain Laurel is a simple story of the sacrifices of a girl whose mother died and left her with a mountain brood to take care of.

The Dollmaker by Harriette Arnow is a difficult book which goes deeply into the values and codes in social behavior brought into open conflict when a Kentucky family moved into wartime Detroit. I believe you could handle that, Helen, because you are interested in social problem novels. [Helen is a mature and gifted eleventh-grade reader.]

Hie to the Hunters! is full of mystery and excitement and of the outdoor life and hunting of the Kentucky mountains. It is rather easy to read. You would like it, Bill, because you are a Kjelgaard fan.

Jesse Stuart's The Thread That Runs So True captures the interest of a mature reader. Much social insight is woven into the thrilling fights of this mountain school teacher both with his pupils and with members of the community. It is an autobiography.

Schoolhouse in the Foothills is the same kind of autobiography of a woman school teacher.

The Yearling is a quiet, deeply sensitive story of a poor boy of the Florida swamps and his yearling. The father and mother play a big part in the story, which seems easy to read. Perhaps you read it in the eighth grade. If so, you will find yourself thinking more deeply about the story now that you are older. Marjorie Rawlings is a writer you will want to know. She won a literary prize for this book. Perhaps you can discover why.

Led by the teacher, the pupils made a list of some of the things they might look for in books they chose, for example: (1) the sense of place which permeated each book; (2) special insight into the character of the people; (3) problems peculiar to the life of the region; and (4) evidence of the language of the people, their literature, and their arts and crafts.

Before leaving class that day, students were asked to hand in a 3 x 5 card listing the books they would most like to read. They gave first, second, and third choices in case several people wanted the same book. After that, they listed the general kind of book they preferred or the title of a familiar one on the list which they had liked very much. With these choices in mind, the teacher sorted her materials and displayed them around the room, so that each individual could begin his reading immediately upon entering class next day. Waiting lists were set up so that all could ultimately read the book they had selected as first choice.

Some days later the class spent a full hour talking about what sections of the country could be included under the topic *Back-Country America,* what aspects of life there would be most significant for study, what writers they thought would prove most useful for the unit, what sources of additional books and magazines were at hand, and what plans the class could make for dividing up the task. That night the students were to list in their notebooks what they thought they might gain from such a unit, what activities they might engage in as individuals and as a group, and what helpful materials they had at home or could borrow from their local library.

Using a common selection to demonstrate approaches to reading. On yet another occasion, the teacher introduced the unit by having the boys and girls read together in class James Still's short story, "Journey to the Forks," from *On Troublesome Creek.* (Some teachers prefer this method of approach because it furnishes "a community" start—something which the entire class can approach together and from which they can learn techniques of reading and interpretations useful later in individual reading.) They found the following passage provocative.

"It's a far piece," Lark said. "I'm afraid we won't make it before dusky dark." We squatted down in the road and rested on the edge of a clay rut. Lark set his poke on the crust of a nag's track, and I took the saddlebag off my shoulder. The leather was damp underneath.
"I'm afraid we ought never thought to be scholars," Lark said.[2]

[2] James Still, "Journey to the Forks," in *On Troublesome Creek* (New York, Viking Press, Inc., 1941), p. 129.

Discussion of the story clarified the incidents and conversation, directed them toward the purposes of the unit, and then revealed methods of study needed to achieve purposes:

How much of an undertaking was it for Lark and his brother to go to the mountain school?

What excuses does Lark think up for not going? Why?

How common do you imagine Cain's attitude toward "larnin'" was in the hill country? What effect did his talk have on Lark? On the brother?

[Cain thought "larnin'" was not only superfluous, but evil. It taught that the earth is round, and the Bible says "hits got four corners."]

What evidence is there that Lark had a kind of "larnin'" all his own?

[He had extensive knowledge of nature and animals.]

From rumors the boys had heard about the school, what do you gather about the kind of farming and housekeeping done by the mountaineers of a generation ago?

[The boys were amazed at the amount of washing and sweeping done at the school and at the scrubbing of the cows: "Dee reckons they'll soon be breshin them cows' teeth."]

Do you think the author's main purpose is to give us information about the hill country or to make us *feel* with the boys? What passages make you think so?

How does he tell you the road was rough?

[The boys rested "on the edge of a clay rut." They set their "poke" on "the crust of a nag's track."]

How does he tell you the boys were hot? "I lifted the saddlebags off my shoulder. The leather was damp underneath." How important is it that the big brother tells the story in the first person?

Ballad writers often say that the mountaineers have a poetic language all their own. What examples of it are there in this story?

[*dusky dark* for *twilight*. "They ring a bell *before and betwixt* books." "The sun ball reddened, mellowing the sky." Brother says he wants to be the first member of the family to graduate: "Never a one went all the way through the books and come out yon side."]

Which words in the dialect recur often enough so that you can tell what they mean? Do you think the dialect hinders or helps the purpose of the author? Are there any especially quotable passages?

This story is only five pages long. How do you think the author managed to pack so much into five pages?

In the reading you are going to do by yourselves, you will be gaining impressions of the mountain people and their environment. If this story is a sample, what kinds of things should you watch for? What different hints make you *feel* for these people as well as *know* them? How much do the characters help? The conversation? The author's description? In what ways do you think the characters will be the product of their environment? In what ways are they like you and all other people? As you pick up each new piece of reading material, ask yourself this question: What contribution can this story or essay or poem make to my understanding and appreciation of these back-country people and their environment? Make notes with page references to especially good examples so that you may share them later with the rest of the class.

Presenting a reading list. The list that follows is a composite of those developed in various experiences with the unit in two schools. No teacher would have all these materials. One school would perhaps have a third of them, and another school a different third. In either event, the unit could be successfully carried out. The titles are presented here as organized by the teacher and pupils by region, by topic, and by literary type. Another useful way of presenting them might be in alphabetical order by authors, giving the students the responsibility of organizing them topically for the next class that tried the unit.

READING LIST FOR BACK-COUNTRY AMERICA

IN THE DEEP WOODS (of Maine)

SOCIAL LIFE AND CUSTOMS

> *We Took to the Woods.* Louise Dickinson Rich. Grosset
> *Happy the Land* ..... Louise Dickinson Rich. Grosset
> *My Neck of the Woods.* Louise Dickinson Rich. Lippincott

NOVELS

> *Swiftwater* .... Paul Annixter........ Wyn
> *Star of the Trail.* ...... Louise Dickinson Rich. Lippincott
> *The Trail to the North:*
> *A Bill Gordon Story.* Louise Dickinson Rich. Lippincott

UP IN THE HILLS AND MOUNTAINS (of Kentucky, Tennessee, North Carolina, and the Virginias, the Cumberlands, the Smokies and the Blue Ridge)

SOCIAL LIFE AND CUSTOMS

> *Children of Noah* ..... Ben Lucien Burman... Julian Messner
> *Smoky Mountain Coun-*
> *try* .... North Callahan....... Little

Handicrafts in the		
Southern Highlands	Allen Eaton.........	Russell Sage
Our Southern High-		
landers	Horace Kephart......	Macmillan
Miracle in the Hills....	Mary T. Sloop and	
	Blythe Liggett.....	McGraw
The Great Smokies and		
the Blue Ridge	Roderick Peattie (ed.)..	Vanguard
Nurses on Horseback...	Ernest Poole.........	Macmillan
Stay on, Stranger.....	William S. Dutton....	Farrar
Blue Ridge Country...	Jean Thomas.........	Little
The Singin' Fiddler of		
Lost Hope Hollow...	Jean Thomas.........	Dutton
Traipsin' Woman......	Jean Thomas.........	Dutton

POETRY

Kentucky Is My Land. Jesse Stuart.......... Dutton

Selected poems of Benét and others from anthologies

SHORT STORIES (COLLECTIONS)

Up Creek and Down		
Creek	Esther G. Hall......	Random
On Troublesome Creek.	James Still..........	Viking
Clearing in the Sky...	Jesse Stuart..........	McGraw
Head o' W-Hollow.....	Jesse Stuart..........	Dutton
Men of the Mountains.	Jesse Stuart..........	Dutton
Tales from the Plum		
Grove Hills	Jesse Stuart..........	Dutton

NOVELS

The Dollmaker........	Harriette Arnow......	Macmillan
Everywhere I Roam...	Ben L. Burman.......	Doubleday
Happy Mountain......	Maristan Chapman....	Viking
Home Place..........	Maristan Chapman....	Viking
The Singing Hills.....	Lillian Craig.........	Crowell
Mountain Laurel......	Anne Emery.........	Putnam
Mountain Girl........	Genevieve Fox.......	Little
Miss Willie	Janet H. Giles........	Westminster
Tara's Healing........	Janet H. Giles........	Westminster
The Enduring Hills...	Janet H. Giles........	Westminster
Roseanna McCoy......	Alberta Hannum......	Holt
Thursday April........	Alberta Hannum......	Harper
A Nose for Trouble...	Jim Kjelgaard........	Holiday
Trailing Trouble	Jim Kjelgaard........	Holiday
Rider on the Mountains.	Elizabeth Lansing.....	Crowell
Hill Doctor..........	Hubert Skidmore.....	Doubleday

Hill Lawyer	Hubert Skidmore	Doubleday
River Rising	Hubert Skidmore	Doubleday
River of Earth	James Still	Viking
The Good Spirit of Laurel Ridge	Jesse Stuart	McGraw
Hie to the Hunters!	Jesse Stuart	Harcourt
Mongrel Mettle	Jesse Stuart	Dutton
Taps for Private Tussie	Jesse Stuart	Dutton
Son of the Valley	John R. Tunis	Morrow
The Nine Brides and Granny Hite	Neill C. Wilson	Morrow

AUTOBIOGRAPHY

Forty Acres and No Mules	Janet H. Giles	Westminster
The Thread That Runs So True	Jesse Stuart	Scribner

IN THE BACKWOODS AND SWAMPS OF FLORIDA

NOVELS

Davey	Rubylee Hall	Little
The Wahoo Bobcat	Joseph Lippincott	Lippincott
South Moon Under	Marjorie K. Rawlings	Grosset
The Yearling	Marjorie K. Rawlings	Modern Library

SHORT STORIES

Gal Young-Un and Other Stories of Cross Creek Country	Marjorie K. Rawlings	Bantam
When the Whippoorwill	Marjorie K. Rawlings	Scribner

AUTOBIOGRAPHY

Cross Creek	Marjorie K. Rawlings	Scribner

IN THE SWAMPS OF GEORGIA

NOVELS

Swamp Boy	{Maribelle B. Cormack {Pavel L. Bytovetzski	McKay
Jareb	Miriam Powell	Crowell

IN THE OZARKS OF ARKANSAS AND MISSOURI

SOCIAL LIFE AND CUSTOMS

Schoolhouse in the Foothills	{Ella Enslow (pseud.) {Alvin F. Harlow	Simon

And Green Grass Grows.

All Around	Marguerite Lyon	Bobbs
Fresh from the Hills	Marguerite Lyon	Grosset
Take to the Hills	Marguerite Lyon	Bobbs
Ozark Mountain Folks	Vance Randolph	Columbia Univ. Press
Ozark Superstitions	Vance Randolph	Columbia Univ. Press
Down in the Holler	Vance Randolph	Oklahoma Univ. Press
We Always Lie to Strangers	Vance Randolph	Columbia Univ. Press
Ozark Country	Otto Rayburn	Little
Straw in the Sun	Charlie Mae Simon	Dutton
Backwoods America	Charles M. Wilson	University of North Carolina Press

SHORT STORIES

Ozark Anthology	Vance Randolph (ed.)	Caxton

NOVELS

The Daughter of Bugle Ann	Mackinlay Kantor	Random
The Voice of Bugle Ann	Mackinlay Kantor	Coward
Big Doc's Girl	Mary Medearis	Lippincott
Hirum, the Hillbilly	Phil Stong	Dodd

TRAVEL

Backwoods Teacher	Joseph Nelson	Lippincott

BALLADS AND FOLKLORE

BARNES, Ruth A.	*I Hear America Singing: An Anthology of Folk Poetry*	Winston
BONI, Margaret B.	*Fireside Book of Folk Songs*	Simons
BOTKIN, Benjamin A.	*Treasury of American Folklore*	Crown
BOTKIN, Benjamin A.	*Treasury of Southern Folklore*	Crown
CARMER, Carl L.	*America Sings: Stories and Songs of Our Country's Growing*	Knopf
CHASE, Richard	*Grandfather Tales*	Houghton
CHASE, Richard	*Jack Tales*	Houghton
FELTON, Harold W.	*John Henry and His Hammer*	Knopf
HOWARD, John T.	*Our American Music: Three Hundred Years of It*	Crowell
IVES, Burl	*The Burl Ives Song Book*	Ballantine

LOMAX, John A. and   *American Ballads and Folk Songs*   Macmillan
LOMAX, Alan, comps.
NILES, John J.   "Folk Ballad and Carol," pp. 217–
33 in Peattie, Roderick (ed.)
*The Great Smokies and the
Blue Ridge*   Vanguard
RITCHIE, Jean   *The Swapping Song Book*   Oxford
SANDBURG, Carl   *American Songbag*   Harcourt
SANDBURG, Carl   *Carl Sandburg's New American
Songbag*   Broadcast
SHARPE, Cecil   *English Folk Ballads from the
Southern Appalachians* (2 v.)   Oxford
WELLS, Evelyn K.   *The Ballad Tree*   Ronald

MAGAZINE ARTICLES ON BACK-COUNTRY AMERICA

BELL, Corydon, "The Fair at Gatlinburg," *Ford Times*, Vol. XLII (July, 1950), pp. 32–38.

BORAH, Leo A., "Home Folk Around Historic Cumberland Gap," *National Geographic Magazine*, Vol. LXXXIV (December, 1943), pp. 741–768.

BURMAN, Ben L., "At Home in the Hills" (excerpt from *Child of Noah*), *Reader's Digest*, Vol. LVIII (May, 1951), pp. 135–138.

———, "Everywhere I Roam; Travelogue," *Saturday Review*, Vol. XXXIII (August 12, 1950), pp. 18–20.

BURNS, Bob, "Tall Tales of Arkansas," *Ford Times*, Vol. XL (April, 1948), pp. 14–19.

CARTER, Hodding, "Tennessee" (Storied Land of the Bible and Fiddle, the Rifle and the Demijohn), *Holiday*, Vol. VIII (November, 1950), pp. 34–51 ff.

CULLIMORE, Don, "The Parable of Hemmed-In Hollow," *Ford Times*, Vol. XLIII (July, 1951), pp. 40–43.

DAWKINS, O. C., "Books in the Kentucky Hills," *Christian Science Monitor* (November 4, 1953), p. 9.

EDDY, Don, "Parson of Middle Laurel Fork, Ky.," *Reader's Digest*, Vol. LVI (January, 1950), pp. 85–90.

"Folk Singers: Mountain People Remember the Old American Music," *Life*, Vol. XXIII (October 20, 1947), pp. 63–66.

GIPSON, Fred, "A Hound-Dog Man," *Reader's Digest*, Vol. XLVIII (February, 1946), pp. 93–97.

GUTHRIE, A. B., Jr., "Kentucky," *Holiday*, Vol. IX (March, 1951), pp. 34–39.

HAM, Tom, "Close-Up of a Hillbilly Family," *American Mercury*, Vol. LII (June, 1941), pp. 659–665.

HENDON, Booton, "The Pathfinder of the Moonshine Mountains," *Saturday Evening Post*, Vol. CCXXIV (March 29, 1952), pp. 30–31.

HICKMAN, Herman, "Up in the Hills," *Coronet,* Vol. XXXV (January, 1954), pp. 34–35.

HUGHES, Carol, "Ozark School That Runs on Faith," *Coronet,* Vol. XXX (July, 1951), pp. 92–95.

HYLAND, T. S., "Fruitful Mountaineers," *Life,* Vol. XXVII (December 26, 1949), pp. 60–67.

JUSTUS, M., "In the Heart of the Great Smokies," *Junior Scholastic,* Vol. XXXIII (September 16, 1953), pp. 20–21, 24.

"Life Goes to a Kentucky Mountain Wedding," *Life,* Vol. XI (July 28, 1941), pp. 82–85.

"Light in the Mountains," *Time,* Vol. LVI (October 16, 1950), pp. 74–75.

LYON, Marguerite, "Ozark Vittles," *Ford Times* (April, 1948), p. 10.

MARKEY, Morris, "Carolina Mountain Folk," *Holiday,* Vol. IV (September, 1948), pp. 80 seq. to 134.

MARTIN, Harold H., "Bears Are No Darn Good," *Saturday Evening Post,* Vol. CCXXV (September 20, 1952), pp. 19–21.

MULLER, Edwin, "Wilderness Trail," *Reader's Digest,* Vol. LV (July, 1949), pp. 101–104.

RANDOLPH, Vance, "How Kate Got a Husband and Other True Lies from the Ozarks," *Minneapolis Sunday Tribune,* Vol. LXXXVI, No. 295 (March 15, 1953), pp. 2, 6 (Feature-News section).

———, "Tall Tales from the Ozarks," *Reader's Digest,* Vol. LX (April, 1952), pp. 19–20.

———, "We Always Lie to Strangers" (excerpt), *Reader's Digest,* Vol. LIX (November, 1951), pp. 82–83; Vol. LX (April, 1952), pp. 19–20.

RICH, Louise D., "A Backwoods Baby Is Born," *Reader's Digest,* Vol. XLI (October, 1942), pp. 21–23.

ROBINSON, Alice, "Angel Healer of the Backwoods," *Coronet,* Vol. XXV (March, 1949), pp. 142–144.

ROSS, Irwin, "Moonshining Is on the Rampage," *American Mercury,* Vol. LXXI (November, 1950), pp. 552–558.

SIMPICH, Frederick, "Arkansas Rolls Up Its Sleeves," *National Geographic,* Vol. XC (September, 1946), pp. 273–312.

SMITH, H. H., "Bright Promise in the Ozarks," *Collier's,* Vol. CXXVIII (September 15, 1951), pp. 32–33.

STAPLETON, Bill, and KALISCHER, Peter, "Now Everybody Likes Mountain Music," *Collier's,* Vol. CXXX (September 13, 1952), pp. 70–71.

STONG, Phil, "The Friendly Ozarks," *Holiday,* Vol. X (August, 1951), pp. 90–97.

STUART, Jesse, "What America Means to Me," *American Magazine,* Vol. CLI (May, 1951), p. 10.

THOMAS, Jean, "The Changing Mountain Folk," *Scholastic,* Vol. XLVII (December 3, 1945), pp. 17–18.

"Tragic Troubadour," *Coronet*, Vol. XXX (July, 1951), pp. 118–124.
WILLIAMS, Lawrence S., "Nag's Head Fox Hunt," *Ford Times*, Vol.
　　XLIV (February, 1951), pp. 23–24.

The particular method of introducing the unit will vary
from school to school and from unit to unit. The important
thing is that it should (1) arouse interest in the unit, (2)
give an overview of its possibilities, (3) probe the background knowledge of the students in the region to be studied, (4) help them to develop and define their purposes in
pursuing the unit, (5) introduce and stimulate the search
for appropriate activities and materials, and (6) give some
initial guidance in methods of study and co-operative procedures.

Getting Under Way with Reading

Students read for a period of about two weeks, browsing
among many magazine articles and books in the room. All
members of the class read at least one book and several articles. Some read four or five books and a dozen articles. The
work was done in the classroom under the teacher's direction,
and interest was sufficiently high that those capable of much
reading did it voluntarily at home.

Each student entered in his notebook his reactions to his
reading and the main points he wanted to remember under
such topics as the four suggested on the opening day (see
pages 77–78). As activities developed, other kinds of reading were required, such as looking up the history of ballads
or locating critical comments on the work of writers who
proved useful in the unit.

Reading with purpose in mind. During these days of reading, the teacher moved about the room throughout the hour,
helping individuals with vocabulary and reading problems
and discussing with them the value of their notes. Students
conferred with each other and in small groups as topics of
special interest came up or as they found new materials to
recommend to each other.

At the beginning of a period or at some appropriate time during a period, the teacher might interrupt the reading to help the whole class with taking and organizing notes or to ask whether anyone had found evidence in support of these statements she had heard on the radio program, Invitation to Learning: "The backwoods are wonderful for men and dogs, but hard on women and mules" and "Jesse Stuart's Greenup County is the sort of place where a good hound dog is worth more than an automobile and barn dances draw bigger crowds than movies." By such suggestions the teacher directed reading.

Sometimes opportunity was given to raise questions about the meaning of words or passages in the reading, or even to meet with the teacher in small groups for further explanation. At other times, the class stopped to report incidents illustrative of the topics or questions set up in advance of reading (pages 93–95), or to mention authors they were discovering who were especially gifted in characterizing the people or the region.

Developing skills in reading. From time to time, also, certain passages which illustrated important reading skills were studied by the class as a whole, so that each student might observe the techniques he would need in doing his own individual reading. In the quoted paragraphs which follow the meanings of some words had to be looked up in the dictionary—*dulcimer,* for example, and *sobriquet.* Others could be guessed from context clues: *economically self-sufficient, payment in kind, traditionally, endowment, archaic, illiterate, dialect, polite speech,* and *pithy philosophy.* Checking their guesses by dictionary definitions of words whose meaning had been inferred from context followed. Once established, this skill could then be used by the students in their own individual reading. The same passage was used to show how deftly pictures or examples may be employed to develop generalizations and to illustrate what to look for in the mountaineer's speech.

In the old-fashioned mountain home of thirty years ago, one finds the ideal conditions for the preserving of folk song. It provided complete *isolation* from the outside world and was almost cut off from the nearby haunts of men. It was *economically self-sufficient,* the family laboring for what they needed and resting when that was secured. When necessities come hard, people are satisfied to stop work when they have enough . . . As for money, there was practically no use for it. Even the country store accepted *payment in kind.* There was leisure then, and a man is not afraid of leisure when he possesses inner resources for using it well. . . .

The resources for leisure time were at hand—tales and songs, airs played on a homemade fiddle or banjo or *dulcimer,* passed on *traditionally* to each generation. The wealth of inheritance was a part of everyone's *endowment,* though naturally some people were better performers than others. Mrs. Jane Gentry sang for Cecil Sharp sixty-four songs. . . . "Singing Willie" Nolan, so called to distinguish him from other Willie Nolans in the neighborhood, came rightly by his *sobriquet,* having learned his songs from a mother who could sing all night and not repeat herself. . . . In this way, many a child grew up familiar with tales of the most approved classic fiction, though he did not get them from books. . . .

It was moreover natural for him to sing, for the lines of the ballads slipped from his tongue like his own spoken language. What is poetry to us was his natural expression, and words which seem to us *archaic* or *illiterate,* or poetic, were his daily speech. As his tunes belonged to the usage of a bygone day, rejected by the *literate,* so did his daily speech. It is of course not a new discovery that *dialect* was once *polite speech.* . . .

So we find that a doll is a "poppet," that maidenhair fern is "never-still." A young girl is "in the rise of her bloom," the white heads of old people are "a-bloomin' for the grave." . . . There is much condensed and *pithy philosophy:* "I'd druther not go, but a body don't allus git his druthers in this world." . . . The expression of pleasure in natural beauty is characteristic. The mountain is "October-colored"; a little boy dreams away a summer day "a-laying on my back in the field, a-studyin' how blue them clouds is a-gittin'." Lindy, who arrived at school with her entire wardrobe of four dresses sewed one on top of the other, talks in homesick vein of home, where she could run outdoors "atter dark," and see "the moon-ball a-glistenin' and a-gleamin' on Isaac's Run." . . . Thus the ballad's diction, imagery, force, and economy of words, and the ability to meet expressive demands are all reflected in the mountain singer's daily speech.[3]

By the use of such passages, reading skills may be effectively developed even though different individuals are read-

[3] Evelyn K. Wells, *The Ballad Tree* (New York, The Ronald Press Company, 1950), pp. 294–296.

ing different materials. Informative reading played an important part in the unit, especially in drawing generalizations from incident and example, selecting details significant for a particular topic, following a thought sequence, and distinguishing main from subordinate ideas.

Adjusting one's speed of reading to the tempo and mood of a selection proved necessary in many parts of the unit: following the slow pace of the boys to school in Still's story, already quoted, and speeding up for the moments of suspense in the exciting adventures in *Hie to the Hunters!* Suiting one's technique of reading to the nature, purpose, and significance of the material likewise proved important. Reading to interpret character demanded attention to the individual's manner of speech, his sense of values, his reactions in time of crisis. It required also recognition of the hints dropped by the author and by other figures in the story. Reading to determine the effect of environment was similarly important— ability to sense the inroads of isolation upon character and thinking, the strain of imminent danger upon one's attitude toward one's self, one's family, and especially toward strangers. It is obvious that skill in reading can be effectively taught even though the material read is different for different students.

Homely phrases, hostile innuendo, local dialect, and unfamiliar nature and surroundings demanded careful and thoughtful reading, often with recourse to the dictionary or to other sources of reference. Picturesque speech and highly imaginative and suggestive description called for creative reading, for ability to enter imaginatively into what was presented, enjoying the savor of words, recognizing their emotional tone, and re-creating in one's own mind the scenes and characters presented. All of these abilities were developed with the class in the course of the reading.

Fortunately, in unit teaching, the instructor is not carrying on daily "recitations," in the sense of asking questions of the entire class to be responded to by individual members. Often pupils are working alone or in groups on days when no class planning or sharing is going on. On these occasions the teacher, therefore, has much more time to move about the room, helping individuals and groups with reading problems not common to the class as a whole.

Since the students in this class were already familiar with the location of books on the library shelves, with the use of the catalog and the encyclopedia, special emphasis could be placed in this unit on use of biographical and poetry indexes and the *Reader's Guide*.

Emphasizing vocabulary. Throughout the unit, vocabulary was stressed in relation to context in speech and writing as well as in reading. *Realistic* and *romantic* presentations were contrasted and the meaning of the two words was progressively clarified. *Homogeneous* and *regional* were used to characterize the *communal* life of the people. *Theme* and *satirize* were often heard in discussion. So also were *local color, impression,* and *integrity* in writing. Such words as *demagogue* and *revenue, linguistic* and *dialogue, imagery* and *picturesqueness, secluded, inaccessible,* and *isolated* were learned in connection with the ideas read and expressed. Use of the dictionary revealed interesting word origins; and for individual students, study of the relation of dialect to locale and to the historical development of the English language proved fascinating.

The list of interesting words from the dialect of the hill folk was headed by a generalization which grew out of the study:

It would be a mistake to think of the language of our hill people as being marked by corruptions; it is, rather, marked by linguistic survivals.

bide	(stay)	gallivantin'	(roaming for
biggity	(overproud)		pleasure)
ding-donged	(annoyed)	hankerin'	(wanting badly)
I'd druther	(I'd rather)	kin-folks	(relatives)
drug	(dragged)	passel	(parcel)
fit	(fought)	mosey	(stroll)
a fur piece	(a long way)	plumb welcome	(very welcome)

poke	(sack)	traipsin'	(walking)
quare	(queer)	whole endurin'	(all day)
rabbity	(timid)	day	
sartin	(certain)	workin'est	(most industrious)
shucks of corn	(husks of corn)	you-uns	(you ones)
sight of	(great deal of)	spindlin'	(thin)

Enriching the Program with Special Reports

Seeking interesting topics. Very early the class began to discuss local dialects, where they come from, how they enrich the language, and how they aid the author in characterizing back-country folk. One person was appointed to be the class lexicographer. At the end of each day, the students handed to him on separate slips of paper interesting words like "poke" for "sack," "We're proud to have you" for "We're glad to see you," "youngun" or "least un" for "children," and "halped" or "hep" for "helped." Many of these were traced to the English of earlier periods. One of the more intelligent readers in the class found interesting material in a book by Vance Randolph and George P. Wilson called *Down in the Holler: A Gallery of Ozark Folk Speech,* published in 1953 by the University of Oklahoma Press. Such chapters as "Sayings and Wisecracks" and "Survivals of Early English" stimulated so much interest in the English language that a whole unit of study on that subject was undertaken by the same class later in the year.

On one occasion the reading was interrupted by a film like the one entitled *The Call of the Redbird,*[4] portraying the life and aspirations of certain people of the hill country.

Enjoying poetry together. Sometimes the class stopped to enjoy together a poem such as Stephen Vincent Benét's "The Mountain Whippoorwill" or "The Ballad of William Sycamore"—both revealing with sympathy and keen observation the mountain folk whom he knew so well. "William Sycamore" has characteristics of the old ballad, the spirit of the

[4] *The Call of the Redbird,* United Brethren Board of Home Missions, St. Paul, Minnesota.

mountaineer, a startlingly graphic use of words, and vivid local color in its comparisons.

"The Mountain Whippoorwill" or "How Hillbilly Jim Won the Great Fiddler's Prize" catches the spirit and the language of the hillbilly fiddler and the wild music of the annual competition. The poem is particularly good for oral interpretation, either by individuals or by the class as a whole in choral reading. A recording of it is also available from the National Council of Teachers of English.[5] The silence following the tense climax furnishes a superb contrast, showing the power of poetry to capture a mood. The picturesque use of words appeals to boys and girls instantly: "Old Dan Wheeling with his whiskers in his ears," "Old Dan Wheeling's got bee-honey in his strings" or "Little Jimmy Wheezer that can make a fiddle cry." [6]

The fact that the competition was won by a boy who "never had a mammy to teach him pretty-please," who "never had a brother nor a whole pair of pants," delights the hearts of adolescents. It is at moments such as this that broad units of instruction furnish excellent opportunity to teach literary appreciation. The "background" is ready-made, interest and emotions run high, and poetry triumphs. One of the girls who was particularly interested in creative expression brought in also a children's story of a similar competition in *One String Fiddle* by Allena Best.[7] The old fiddler instructed Irby in how to make an *original* hill-country tune.

"I can play *Turkey in the Straw*," said the boy, but that did not please Fiddler. "No, that's somebody else's tune, and this one's got to be 'riginal," he insisted. "Meanin' one all yer own, one ye've made up fer yerself."

"*All* out of my own head?" said Irby. That didn't seem possible.

"Well, mebbe not quite," admitted Fiddler. "Mebbe ye hear a bit

[5] National Council of Teachers of English. *Recordings of the Poets*— Stephen Vincent Benét, (Champaign, Ill., The Council, 704 S. Sixth).

[6] *Selected Works of Stephen Vincent Benét* (New York, Rinehart & Company, Inc., 1942), 2 vols.

[7] Allena Best, *One String Fiddle* (Eau Claire, Wis., E. M. Hale Company).

of a tune that a blackbird sings, and that'll give ye an idee. And mebbe ye'll heed the way a wagon wheel squeaks along the road on a hot sunny afternoon, and ye'll git a few more notes from that. And then mebbe ye'll git an idee from the rattle of the water over the stones as it runs down the mountains. And ye'll tie 'em all together and do a few more twists and taddiddles, and in time ye git a tune. What ye want is *mountain* music."

Sharing Reading through Informal Discussion

Selecting and organizing material for informal discussion. After everyone had finished at least one book, plans were made for discussing the reading together in class.

One whole period was spent listing on the chalkboard possible topics for discussion which had grown out of the reading. This kind of activity calls forth a contribution from every member of the class. The result is a conglomeration of topics without recognizable relationship one to the other. The teacher then demonstrated the necessity of putting these into some kind of usable order. Hard thinking had to be done to pull out the major points and to suggest the subtopics needed to elaborate each one. At the end of the hour the job was still unfinished. A committee was chosen to complete the outline and present it to the class for criticism and expansion next day. Discussion then centered on the logic of the outline and the fullness of treatment suggested by the subtopics. After the ordering of the ideas was completed, outline form and the necessity of parallel form for parallel topics were checked against textbooks and reference sources in the classroom and library. The following outline of topics, completed under the direction of the teacher, was finally agreed upon.

BACK-COUNTRY PEOPLE AND THEIR WAY OF LIFE

I. HOMES OF THE BACK-COUNTRY PEOPLE

A. Cabins in the Mountains
B. Huts in the Woods
C. Homes in the Swamplands

II. THEIR HISTORY

   A. Their Backgrounds
      1. Their Origin
      2. Their Ancestry
   B. Their Language
      1. Origin of Dialects
      2. Reasons for Their Persistence
   C. Names of Persons and Places
      1. Origin of Names
      2. Stories Back of Names
   D. Famous Backwoods People
   E. TVA
      1. Reforestation under TVA
      2. Rise of New Industries

III. THEIR WAY OF LIFE

   A. Housing and Housewarmings
   B. Occupations
      1. Farming
      2. Conserving the Soil
      3. Hunting
      4. Moonshining
   C. Crafts and Skills
      1. Weaving
      2. "Whittling"
   D. Religion
      1. Superstitions
      2. Morals
   E. Education
      1. Kinds of Schools
      2. Teachers
      3. Effect on Thought and Way of Life
   F. Health
      1. Medical Facilities
      2. Sanitation

IV. THEIR MEANS OF COMMUNICATION

   A. United States Mail
      1. The Mailman
      2. The Mail-Order Catalog
   B. Trading and Swapping
   C. The Community Store
   D. "The Grapevine"

V. THEIR CUSTOMS

A. Family Relations
B. Courtship and Marriage
C. Funerals
D. Superstitions
E. Community Life

VI. THEIR ENTERTAINMENT

A. The Place of Music and the Dance
 1. Mountain Ballads
 2. Folk Dancing
B. The Telling of Tall Tales
C. Sports
 1. The Fox Hunt
 2. Trapping
 3. Fishing
D. Holidays and Other Celebrations

VII. THEIR CODES

A. Morals and Taboos
B. Moonshining
C. Politics and Government
 1. The Law and the Courts
 2. Jails and Jail Breaks
D. The Family
E. Feuds and Land Disputes

VIII. THEIR PERSONAL CHARACTERISTICS

A. Their Attitudes
 1. Toward Nature
 2. Toward Work
 3. Toward Themselves and Outsiders and Vice Versa
 4. Toward City Slickers and People Who Leave the Community
B. Their Interests
C. Their Sense of Humor
D. Their Pride in Possessions
E. Their Ambitions
F. Their Philosophy

IX. THEIR FUTURE

Carrying on informal discussion. The teacher then suggested that conversational discussions would be better than formal reports because of the intimate character of the material to be shared. She presented the scheme to the class, illustrating the procedure by re-enacting a conversational discussion about Robert Lawson's dramatic readings—which all had recently enjoyed together at a convocation program —playing interchangeably the parts of chairman and members of the group.

Each class member was then asked to write on a slip of paper the topic which his book fitted best. Groups were then formed of those who had chosen the same topic, and a period was given over to planning the reports to the class. Each group elected a chairman (1) to get the discussion going (that is, introduce and define the topic); (2) to keep it going (by enlarging upon what was said, by pointing up or clarifying statements made, or by making comments on the subject); and (3) to end the discussion (by summarizing).

When it came time for presentation of its topic, each group sat around three sides of a table facing the class. After the topic was clearly stated for the audience by the chairman, each member of the group talked to it, presenting his anecdotes and evidence from the books he had read. The members were to interpolate remarks in conversational fashion so that each could contribute at the right moment something which might be out of place later.

There were about eight groups with three to five people in each. Usually three such groups could carry on their discussions in one period. For example, in the group which was to discuss the *Way of Life of the Mountaineers,* one girl led off with a description of the mountaineer's cabin in *Mountain Laurel* by Anne Emery. This reminded another of the old and new cabins displayed on the grounds of Berea College and still another of the cabin in James Still's "The Proud Walkers," which she had read. This in turn led to examples from Jesse Stuart of the mountaineer's attitude toward education, and so on until each member of the group (five in all) had contributed all he knew about the topic from reading which he himself had done. After the group had finished, the discussion was thrown open to the audience, who contributed additional incidents and information from their own reading. The remarkably lively discussion and response from the audience were attributed by the teacher to the keen interest of the students in the topic of the unit and to the broad reading on the part of the entire class before the group discussion began.

The success of group work depends largely upon the guidance given by the teacher before the groups are formed. Time spent in discussing how to get quietly into groups, how to insure each person's participating, and how to work without disturbing others pays dividends later on. Students need to know (1) where in the room or elsewhere each group is to meet, (2) how they are to proceed from the election of a chairman on, (3) what is to be expected from each group and when, and (4) what to do if they finish before the other groups. In this case, the members of each group were to define their topic clearly and discuss together the examples they had found illustrating it, so as to be sure that each member understood the procedure and had something ready to contribute to the class.

Varying the Program with Individual Contributions

From time to time during this part of the unit, variety was introduced by having individual talks on subjects of special interest or programs of a related character interspersed between the group discussions. One was on the *Origin and Nature of the Folk Ballads of the Mountaineers*. A committee composed of one girl in each of three classes, all singers interested in music, presented a ballad program to each class in turn. One of the girls gave an informative talk on the origin of the ballads of the hill country, their place in the life of the people, and the work of modern musicians and scholars in preserving them. In the ballad of "Barb'ry Allen," one read the part of the narrator, one was Barb'ry Allen, and the other was Sweet William. After that, they sang this and other ballads to the accompaniment of the zither. Next, they played two recordings of a ballad, one a commercial recording by Susan Reed and one by a mountain woman, a recording secured for the Library of Congress by Alan Lomax. Finally, a boy gave an interpretive reading of "The Mountain Whippoorwill" by Benét to contrast the early ballads with the modern literary form. Choral reading by the class as a whole would have served the purpose equally well.

The program closed with general class discussion of ballads which other members had come across in their reading. The work of Cecil Sharp, Francis J. Childs, Alan Lomax, Carl Sandburg, Carl Carmer, Burl Ives, and John Jacob Niles was specially mentioned and also the recent recordings of Jean Ritchie, the mountain singer from the southern Appalachians.[8] Favorites among the ballads were "Lord Randall," "Little Mattie Groves," and "I Wonder as I Wander Out under the Sky." Jesse Stuart's modern ballads in *Kentucky Is My Land* were also popular. The rise of the religious carols and the growth of secular ballads were topics of great interest.

The folklore of the highlands and the work of the Carolina Players were likewise presented as special reports. These were followed by group dramatizations of favorite scenes from books read or original presentations of incidents in the novels used. The class lexicographer gave a report on Mountain Language, and three boys presented an "Invitation to Learning" type of discussion on *Swiftwater* and how Annixter portrays his region and its people. Another three did the

[8] "Kentucky Mountain Songs," Electra Record, EKL25, EKL2, *Jean Ritchie Singing the Traditional Songs of Her Kentucky Mountain Family*, and EKL12, *Folk Songs from the Southern Appalachian Mountains* (New York, Electra Record Corporation, 361 Bleeker Street).

same kind of presentation of Jesse Stuart and his Kentucky stories.

Seeking Additional Materials and Ideas

During the entire period of the unit, magazine articles, pictures, phonograph records, and books were available in the classroom. For example, students brought in for the bulletin board pictures and clippings from magazines and newspapers which their families no longer wanted to preserve. They found books containing pictures like James H. Hopkins' *Kentucky Mountaineer* from the Art Institute in Chicago. They wrote to the Library of Congress for available recordings of mountain songs. They secured material from Berea College. They wrote for information about the Gatlinburg Fair, which revealed much about the arts and crafts of the mountaineers. One student studied in greater detail the work of the Carolina Players at the University of North Carolina, under Frederick H. Koch whose ambition was to help young people to make fresh dramatic forms out of the materials of their native localities.

"We have found," he wrote, "that if the young writer observes the locality with which he is most familiar and interprets it faithfully, it may show him the way to the universal. . . . Each of the American Folk Plays . . . is the work of a single author dealing consciously with his materials, the folkways of our less sophisticated people living simple lives not seriously affected by the present day complex social order. The plays are concerned with folk subject-matter: with the legends, superstitions, customs, environmental differences, and the vernacular of the common people." [9]

One of these plays was performed in assembly by a group of students.

Sharing Experiences through Speech and Listening

As the boys and girls were preparing to share their findings with the class, the teacher led them in setting up goals for

[9] Frederick H. Koch, *American Folk Plays* (New York, D. Appleton-Century Company, Inc., 1939).

effective informal discussion and for individual reports and in considering techniques for carrying on each of them successfully. The same procedure was followed for interpretive reading. Each student recorded in his notebook his own specific goals concerning contact with and influence on the audience, flexibility in the use of his voice, care in articulation and enunciation, and expressiveness in speaking. Each was impressed also with the importance of a clear understanding of any passage he chose to interpret orally, with insight into the characters portrayed and with effective interaction with the audience.

Interrelationships of speech and listening, as means to learning from others. The large part played by learning from the contributions of others in this unit gave special importance to listening. Careful attention and intelligent focusing of listening were imperative. Students were guided in what to listen for, just as they were guided in effective presentation of their own findings. Those who gave special reports were helped by the teacher in carefully organizing material, selecting illustrative incidents, and substantiating generalizations with evidence. The outline which ordered their own ideas in speaking became a guide for their listeners. Clear indication of main and subordinate elements and the adequate use of transitions were equally important for speaker and listener. These interrelationships were brought out constantly in the course of the unit, sometimes by the teacher, at other times by the class. Such topics as those listed on pages 93–95 became guides for both speakers and listeners. Listening for enjoyment and for interpretation of characters was also emphasized as oral interpretation and storytelling played their parts in the activities. Critical listening for noting improvement in speaking helped each student gauge his own success and that of others.

Using evaluation and remedial drill for purposes of improvement. At the close of this varied program of sharing findings with the class, students evaluated their performance in informal discussion, in interpretive reading, and in other oral skills. Some oral drill on verbs which had caused trouble was given in small groups to those students who had revealed a need for it. The usage test which appears in the final evaluation of the unit shows what some of these needs were. After a teacher has worked through the unit once, he may wish to use such a test as both pretest for diagnostic purposes and final test at the end of the unit to measure progress.

Preserving and Interpreting Findings through Writing

The unit proved particularly valuable also for the amount of composition work which it stimulated both from individuals and from the entire class—writing primarily of a creative rather than of an expository kind.

Individual creative writing. One month the *American Magazine* carried an article called "Newspaper Woman of the Ozarks," the story of Mrs. Maud Duncan, who in Winslow, Arkansas, writes and prints on a hand press a four-page weekly called *The Winslow American.* One student volunteered to write for a copy so that the class could read it. Out of this interest came one boy's decision to write a hill-country paper of his own, taking his ideas for the society column, the headline news, the advertisements, and similar sections from the stories and articles he had read. Another boy brought out a hill-country edition of *Life.*

Curiously interesting also was a current news item in the local daily paper about a prisoner of war returned from Korea to marry his bride in Big Stone Gap, Virginia. Neither his parents nor hers would attend the wedding because their families were not on speaking terms. The students immediately suspected a mountain feud of long standing between them. An interesting discussion arose over the difference in treatment of this incident in a newspaper and in a novel. This particular story of a Romeo and Juliet of the hill country (not to mention a Hatfield or a McCoy) became the basis of a short story written by one of the girls in the class.

Preserving a file of material. A permanent file of such stimulating material was developed in the classroom for use in
future years, and members of these classes continued to contribute to it as long as they were in high school. The long-
term interests developed by students through this kind of
teaching are among its greatest values. The opportunity for
individuals to pursue over a period of time topics of interest
to them makes for a kind of power not generated in day-by-
day assignments.

General class writing. The class finished their informal discussions with a keen sense of the human-interest value of the
material they had collected. It was worth writing down, the
teacher thought. She pointed out that here was a kind of
writing very interesting to readers. It was a cross between the
long expository paper and the short story. It demanded a
lighter touch than the so-called "long paper," with more of
the writer in it. It had a thread of logic, a topical outline running through it; yet its interest centered in just the right
anecdotes to prove the points. As a concrete example of the
informal essay she introduced to the class Caddy and Burman's article called "Everywhere I Roam," which appeared
in the *Saturday Review of Literature* for August 12, 1950. It
begins this way:

> The mountains are changing. The "good old days" when no moun-
> taineer ever locked his cabin door, are more and more becoming only
> a memory. Yet as the traveler walks through the streets of a little moun-
> tain town, or wanders up a pine shaded hollow, he constantly comes
> upon some remnant of an older frontier era that is in delightful con-
> trast with mechanized America.
> Nowhere, perhaps, are these contrasts more evident than in a moun-
> tain courtroom.

Then follow interesting anecdotes of mountain trials with
old Judge Honey and the young mountain lawyers furnishing
a striking contrast. "Honey, I hate to do this to you," declares
the old judge, "but I've got to sentence you to sixty days,
Honey." The mountain jail, the politician, the mailman, the

fiddler, and the fox race all follow as examples of the "good old days," each introduced by an arresting modern counterpart, as in the case of the fiddler: "The Juke Box, as elsewhere, has blasted its thunderous way into the hill towns."

The article demonstrated clearly the effectiveness of the mountaineer incidents for illustrating a point.[10] Students also drew examples from it of how to paragraph and punctuate conversation and how to capitalize and underline book titles. Among the most popular topics for the papers were these:

Backwoods Superstitions
Mountain Larnin'
Backwoods Dialects and Their Origins
Women in the Backwoods
Famous Feuds
Hillbilly Music and Square Dancing—Why Their Current Popularity?
Marjorie Kinnan Rawlings' Florida Folk
Jesse Stuart as a Painter of Life in the Backwoods
A Comparison of Realistic and Romanticized Versions of Backwoods Life
The Effect of Developments like TVA on the Hill People
"Li'l Abner" Compared with True Pictures of Backwoods People
The Carolina Players and Frederick Koch
Hill-Country Ballads, Their Sources, and Their Place in the Lives of the Mountaineers
The Mountain Mule
The Art of Swapping in the Hills
What Makes a Hill-Country Man a Success?
Mountain Men and Their Hound Dogs
The Mail-Order Catalog or "The Wish Book"
A Comparison of the Treatment of a Region by Four Different Authors

Each class member was held responsible for checking his own paper for sentence clarity and completeness, for correct punctuation and paragraphing of conversation, for correct capitalization and underlining of titles, and for those uses of the comma important in this unit, particularly in series and to set off interrupting modifiers. The spelling of *its, their,*

[10] Some teachers may prefer to develop these composition principles in relation to illustrations in a composition text available to their students.

and *theirs* and correct use of the apostrophe to show possession were in need of special stress. Those matters in which
the entire class proved weak were given attention both before
the papers were handed in and when they were returned.

After the papers were completed, the students met in committees of three to select those which they thought the class
would most enjoy hearing read aloud and those which should
be passed around for silent reading. The standards for judging were those drawn originally from the Caddy and Burman
article.

The need for attention to spelling. As the class took notes
and summarized their findings and as they wrote, both individually and as a group, stories and essays growing out of the
unit, problems of spelling came to the fore. Words already
mentioned under vocabulary had to be spelled. They included such literary terms as *dialect, satirize, regional, linguistic, imagery, realistic, romantic,* and others descriptive of
the locale: *isolated, homogeneous,* and *picturesque.* Among
other words included were the following:

grievance	affect	illustrative
violence	effect	environment
violent	character	suspicious
corrupt	loyalty	neighbors
corruption	integrity	literary
mountain	sincerity	dignity
mountaineer	exaggerate	description
mountainous	ballad	rugged
communal	musical	violin
community	secluded	quaint
geography	feud	competition
geographical	biography	anecdote

To these were added from such lists as Ayer's words in general use that are most frequently misspelled in high school,
and some from the intermediate grades, such as *its, they're,
across, already,* or *exercise,* frequently misspelled by upper-
grade pupils and falling naturally into the unit.[11] If a class

[11] Fred C. Ayer, *A Study of High School Spelling Vocabulary* (Austin,
Texas, The Steck Company, 1945); James A. Fitzgerald, *A Basic Life
Spelling Vocabulary* (Milwaukee, The Bruce Publishing Company, 1951).

has a spelling book or a graded list to "cover," since such lists invariably include the words most used and most frequently misspelled, they fit easily into any unit in progress.

Learning how to attack new words independently is as important as mastering any list of words. Adding of suffixes occurred frequently as in the words in the first column of the list above. The meaning of prefixes arose in the much misspelled *affect* and *effect*.

Capitalization and punctuation involved in the writing. Matters of capitalization and punctuation were discussed as the need for them arose. The question of how to punctuate and capitalize titles of books and magazines, and articles or stories within them, proved important throughout the unit. Geographical names such as *Ozarks, Tennessee Valley, Great Smoky Mountains,* and *Kentucky* occurred again and again. Writing *mountain, frontier,* and *government* and *fiddle* with small letters when occasion demanded proved equally difficult. Even *Indian, English,* and *British* troubled some students.

Typical sentences involving use of the apostrophe were these:

1. *Big Doc's Girl* has *its* setting in the Ozarks.
2. Writing *The Yearling* must have been several *years'* work.
3. City *people's* lack of knowledge about the backwoodsmen is unfortunate.
4. *The Thread That Runs So True* is Jesse *Stuart's* autobiography.
5. Is this your (or you're) copy of *Swiftwater?*

Exercises and tests contained sentences taken directly from the students' own writing. These are examples:

1. Marjorie Kinnan Rawlings, who portrays the Florida scene, won the Pulitzer Prize for her novel, *The Yearling.*
2. Our group discussed the following of Jesse Stuart's books: *Hie to the Hunters!,* a novel; *The Thread That Runs So True,* an autobiography; and *The Clearing in the Sky,* a collection of short stories.
3. In *The Singing Hills* a little boy says indignantly, "I wouldn't do such a dastardly deed as to report a still. You are just joking him, for you know I wouldn't."

Usage related to the unit. Of all the problems of verb usage, the most frequent and disturbing were concerned with distinctions between *lie* and *lay:*

1. A braided rug was (lying, laying) on the floor of the hill doctor's office.
2. Bugle Ann, the hound dog with the unusual voice, was (lying, laying) in front of the hearth.
3. Last night I (lay, laid) awake thinking about the experiences of the teacher in *The Thread That Runs So True.*
4. *We Took to the Woods* tells how the snow (lay, laid) ten feet deep.
5. Both *The Enduring Hills* and *Miss Willie* were (lying, laying) right here last night.

Other matters of usage which needed attention either in small groups or in the class as a whole were illustrated in the usage test given at the end of the unit.

The tremendous interest in dialect and in getting at changes in form and meaning opened the way for interesting discussions of how language changes through the centuries, of the effect of local usages upon it, and of how new words enter the language. The contrast between descriptive and prescriptive grammar interested these students, but careful consideration of the problem had to be left to a later unit.

Examining the Literary Value of What Was Read

Many opportunities had arisen during the unit for the teacher to emphasize the power of literature to reveal human experience, to give insight into human personality, and to show the interaction of people and place. Under her guidance, the class had begun to separate out those writers who succeeded best in bringing their characters to life. The teacher felt time should be given at this point to pull together these scattered examples into some kind of specific recognition of certain writers whose literary craftsmanship has given them a recognized place in American literature, to sense the unique power of different literary types, and to establish standards of appreciation which would serve in evaluating both the materials used in this unit and new materials which students might turn to later for personal reading.

Poe's theory of unity of tone and effect in a composition, of choice of characters, of incidents, and of setting in terms of a central idea or purpose could be well illustrated by the materials of this unit. The sincerity of the author could be demonstrated by the care with which he probed the motives and outlook of his characters, showing the inevitable conflict or interaction among them and between them and their environment. The use of concrete details, of the right figure of speech or twist of language, of emotional suggestion or pictorial imagery, could be clearly illustrated. A false emphasis, especially in regional fiction, betrays an insincere purpose— the effort merely to raise a laugh, to stimulate the catching of a breath, or to stereotype for effect. In order to stress these standards for judging material read, the teacher prepared the following set of questions for class discussion:

Topics for the Discussion of the Literary Value of Materials Read

Think back over the books, short stories, and magazine articles you have read for this unit:

1. Which gave you most insight into how the people of the backwoods lived and felt and thought? Explain what you think made the writer successful in doing this.

2. Choose a piece of literature you think showed the author's deep sincerity of purpose. Show how you think that purpose affected the unity of the story, what he told about the characters, the choice of incidents used, the description of place, the use of dialect.

3. What material you have come across do you feel satirized or exploited the people and life of the region? What elements received an emphasis out of proportion to their real place in the lives of the characters? What did such stories fail to reveal?

4. What effect did the use of dialect have upon the stories you read?

5. Were the best authors you read "outsiders" or "natives"? In what way were they qualified to write books about the region?

6. Do you think the authors you read gave a "realistic" or a "romantic" view of the backwoods people? Give illustrations.

7. Which authors in this unit have an established place in American literature? Why do you think they have achieved that place?

8. What is the difference between a regional story and one that re-

veals "universal" traits common to people everywhere? Can a novel be both "regional" and universally true? Give examples from your reading to back up your answer.

9. Think of the types of literature you have read or heard about in this unit—short stories, novels, biographies, dramas, poetry, and essays. Can you think of any incident or any character presented in books of two or more literary types? What can a poem do that a novel is not capable of doing? What can a novel do that a poem cannot do? What advantage has biography over the novel and vice versa? How would a play handle the same material? Give examples from your reading.

10. Why is it a good idea to read both fiction and nonfiction about a region? What is the function of each?

11. What standards of judging a book have you learned from this unit that would be useful for any kind of reading you do in the future? [Some questions like 3 and 9 brought forth reports by small groups of gifted students.]

Evaluating the Results of the Unit

Every worth-while unit eventuates in certain insights, attitudes, and appreciations, certain knowledge acquired, certain skills achieved, and certain behavior resulting from the combination of all of them. There are many ways of evaluating these results. Students and teachers together, in one instance, considered what growth they had made as a result of the study. After the discussion the class members wrote a paper, with illustrations from the work of the unit, concerning what they had gained from it. They also grappled with a concise statement of what they considered to be the theme of the unit.

Chief among their gains, they felt, was their increased knowledge of the life and people of the hill countries. They wanted to visit the Ozarks some day and the Southern Highlands. They had gained considerable knowledge of the work of notable writers and had read many more books than they usually did in the same period of time. They had become acquainted with some new magazines which they hoped to follow from month to month. They had come to know a people different from themselves. At the same time, they commented frequently on how universal were many of the traits revealed in any region. They had learned a good deal about the English language, about balladry and folklore, and about the inevitable relationship between today and yesterday, between people and place. They commented often on the "freedom" to learn which they had enjoyed in this unit, the "freedom" to read "what they wanted to read," to pursue together in planning and discussion topics of joint interest to members of the class. Over and over again they referred to learning together and from each other. Above all, they thought they had had "fun." "I don't like to say we were *studying* this unit," wrote one girl. "We were just *having fun reading and talking together.*"

This is the supreme test of good teaching, *provided that real learning accompanies the fun*—for the teacher to be able to hold the reins and yet appear unnecessary to the project. Care must be taken always to explain to the members of the community the elements of growth and hard work involved in such a unit, for occasionally a student is heard to remark, "We haven't done a stroke of work for two days. We're just having fun," when in reality he has been doing twice as much work as usual. He had not thought of it as work because he had enjoyed it.

Using standards for group work which had been set up during the unit, the class discussed together what progress they felt they had made in working in groups and in what ways they needed to improve.

The teacher examined the record of each individual's reading. In another class she prepared an essay-type test on the first four purposes of the unit, asking students to write on the "distinctiveness of these people and how it had come about through their environment and conditions of living." She asked for a discussion of what qualities in the back-country folk were regional and what were universal.

In most classes each member was asked to name two authors of distinction who had contributed to our knowledge of these people and to characterize the work of each.

Finally, in a class of very intelligent students, the teacher presented a copy of an unfamiliar short story, "A Piece of News," by a contemporary author, Eudora Welty, and asked each one to tell what he had learned from the unit about the back-country people that helped him to interpret this rather subtle story. He was then to tell what literary qualities he thought gave the story distinction.

Each piece of student writing was evaluated for selection and organization of ideas as well as for the effectiveness and appropriateness of expression.

Evidences of progress in speech and writing were available in the records of the students during the unit. A test of vocabulary (in context) and a test of spelling based on the words of the unit revealed the extent to which each individual had grown.

The final usage test was composed of sentences which were actually heard or written in the classroom and had been discussed as they arose:

USAGE TEST

1. (Us, We) boys all want to read *Hie to the Hunters!*
2-3. In fact, (almost, most) everybody in our class (has, have) already read it.
4-5. Jesse Stuart is one author (who's, whose) books are (very, real) popular with young people.
6. Many of his stories, like "Split Cherry Tree" for instance, are about teen-agers, probably because he was once the (principal, principle) of a high school.
7. (It's, Its) a wise idea to check what we find in books of fiction, like *The Voice of Bugle Ann,* by reading a book which is fact, like *Backwoods America.*
8. We noted that there (is, are) many people in the Kentucky
9. hills who weave, sing, and talk just as (there, their) great
10. grandfathers (did, done).
11. We talked about hill customs, superstitions, (and etc., etc.).
12. Someone mentioned that the mountaineers are (used, use) to "getting along without."
13-14. We (hadn't ought, ought not) to overlook the fact that there is such a thing as backwoods wisdom (to, too).
15. Mary, Ruth, and (I, me, myself) read *The Singing Hills.*
16-17. (Was, Were) you surprised to learn how many of (these, these here) people operated illicit stills?

18. The feuds of the Kentucky hills are (suppose, supposed) to be, for the most part, a thing of the past.
19. If we (wouldn't have, hadn't) checked our facts, we would have thought there were only thousands of backwoodsmen instead of millions.
20. This copy of *Hound Dog Man* has been read by so many people that it is (wore, worn) out.
21. The man from the Ozarks was telling a tall tale, but nobody (could have, could of) guessed by looking at his face that the story wasn't gospel truth.
22. To (who, whom) was the old fellow telling his lies, some unsuspecting tourists?
23-24. (Let's, Lets, Let us) see (your, you're) annotation of *Men of the Mountain.*
25. In many of the books about the hill people we can see (that, where) these people have prejudices against modern medicine.
26-27. Springfield Davis (sure, surely) seemed to love Bugle Ann, his hound dog, better (than, then) anything else in the world.
28-29. Fred says that he (doesn't, don't) want to miss (none, any)
30. of (them, those) books about hunting and trapping in the backwoods.
31. *Start of the Trail* appeals to those of (us, we) boys who like to camp out in the woods.
32. Will you (leave, let) me read *Big Doc's Girl* next?
33. (Since, Being that) our unit and our book list were titled "Back-Country America," our notations had to be written with that fact in mind.
34. The "Singing Fiddler" could sing the old Elizabethan ballads very (well, good).
35. Of the two books, *The Voice of Bugle Ann* is the (shorter, shortest), I'm sure.
36. The corn field (lay, laid), or maybe we should say it stood, at a 45-degree angle.
37. The men were (laying, lying) in wait for the stranger.
38. They had (laid, lain) there all night.

Tests given at the end of a unit may become the basis for an accompanying period of remedial work aimed at individual needs or they may be looked upon as serving a diagnostic purpose for what should be emphasized in the next unit. When a period of remedial work follows, it is most interesting if it is kept closely related to the material of the unit. Care should be taken to avoid the kind of alternation of activities described by a student who wrote: "First we have a unit, and then we have grammar."

THE VALUES IN UNIT TEACHING

Unit teaching, therefore, provides a natural situation for well-motivated learning. It places the skills of communication where they belong—in purposeful activity in a social setting. It demands orderly planning and assumption of responsibility for carrying out the plans. It furnishes opportunity for extensive group work and for individualized procedures to meet the needs, the interests, and the capacities of all members of the class. It stimulates curiosity and creativeness, giving those with unusual powers of self-direction a chance to forge ahead on their own. Yet it keeps the entire class working together on a common problem. It permits the use of all types of literature—new and old, prose and poetry, easy and mature— and the development of skill in reading each of them. It recognizes the place of the library in the learning activities of the classroom and teaches economical use of the facilities available. It takes advantage of the natural relationships between speaking and listening and writing and reading in the normal pursuit of well-integrated problems. It gives opportunity for enjoyment of literary selections by the class as a whole and at the same time develops personal standards of literary appreciation and personal habits of reading to suit individual interests. It gives opportunity for careful evaluation of progress by the students themselves and for the planning of next steps in learning.

PROBLEMS INVOLVED IN UNIT TEACHING

There are those who believe that units of teaching should come out of the inspiration of the moment, should spring from the students' undirected desires expressed in response to the teacher's question, "What would you like to study next?"

That is not the point of view of this chapter. It is true beyond a doubt that some of the most successful units of instruction arise from the inspiration of the moment, and good teachers are always alert for times of intense interest and drive on the part of pupils; but the program envisioned in this chapter involves a thoughtfully planned series of units which, though they may be constantly changing, are set within the framework of a careful study of the needs of the individuals and the demands of the society in which they live.

Selecting Units of Instruction

Volume I of this curriculum series suggests as a framework for English teaching the four aspects of the growth of young people with which secondary education is most concerned: (1) their growth as individual persons, (2) their development as members of social groups, (3) their preparation for citizenship, and (4) their training as workers. Each of these areas should be recognized at some time in any well-balanced program of instruction, although the first two find special emphasis in the language arts program. It is important that students should, through literature, come to know people and times different from their own. A unit on *What Values Are of Most Worth?*, introduced through biography, essay, and fiction, starts young people thinking about what makes life worth while. Poetry, too, has answers to that question. On the other hand, a love of poetry helps to enrich life; so also does a habit of reading good fiction. Hence in one unit, students may seek to discover what poetry holds for them and to learn how to read and enjoy it. In the tenth grade, young people are eager for exciting adventure and mystery whether on this planet or in the outer reaches of space. It is important that they should know how to choose wisely; hence some units at this level on *Adventuring through Fiction*.

Young people need to learn something of the struggle for freedom in this country and in the world at large. Understanding of the spiritual meaning of that struggle (not an outline of events) can come through literature. On the other hand, a commencement pageant may make an excellent base for a unit. The mass modes of communication have become important institutions in American life. Any one of them or all of them in combination will furnish a rich source for integrated teaching. A study of the place of imagination in American life opens up a fascinating area in American literary, intellectual, and artistic development as well as in invention and physical well-being. American humor offers another opportunity for varied study.

Growing Up During Adolescence has been an ever increasing favorite among units for senior high school boys and girls. It is often used as a basis for guidance. Getting acquainted with a new school—its purposes, its offerings, its life (not chiefly its physical plant)—offers opportunity for a wide range of writing, speaking, and listening. Reading in this unit centers on getting acquainted with the library, examining one's personal habits of reading, and starting off one's high school career by emphasis on personal reading and a reading plan for years ahead. At the end, opportunity is given for sharing that reading with other members of the class. At the same time, the testing of reading skills in this unit may give students incentive and goals to work toward during their high school years.

The range of units [12] should be carefully planned with all aspects of the students' development and interests in mind. Each in turn should deal with a problem or topic of importance to adolescents. It should permit emphasis in greater or lesser degree on all four of the language arts and should pro-

---

[12] In the secondary curriculum guides prepared by the Baltimore, Maryland, public schools, by Atlanta, Georgia, and by the Florida State Department of Education there are examples of units which arise in the speaking and writing needs and interests of teen-agers. These units (e.g., Writing Letters Which Will Be Answered, Winning an Audience, Making the Expression of Ideas Clear, Producing a Newspaper), though they begin with speaking, writing, or the functional study of grammar, require all four language arts and from two to three weeks of sustained work for the students to achieve their goals.

vide well-motivated practice in each. It should make possible much planning by the students and the carrying on of activities which have meaning for young people, emphasizing constantly the importance of clear and sustained thinking. It should foster individual interests, allow for individual differences, and provide opportunity for self-direction and long-term planning. It should also permit careful evaluation, at the end, of skills, habits, and knowledge in the various language arts, social attitudes and skills, and personal development— goals which have been carefully thought through from the beginning.

Securing and Handling Materials

No unit should be begun until the teacher is certain that adequate reading materials and other facilities are available in school and community. Otherwise, complete frustration may result for both teacher and pupils.

In large city systems where it has been customary to order textbooks in sets from an approved list, unit teaching sometimes necessitates changes in the general regulations governing the ordering of books. Oakland, California, for example, has developed a trial list of books of which from one to five copies may be ordered for try-out purposes in individual units. It is easier to add titles temporarily to this list than it is to go through the long process of "adoption."

Again, in large high schools with many sections at the same grade level, specific timing of units must be arranged from class to class so that not all of the sections will want the same materials at the same time. Avoidance of a small fixed number of units can be achieved by constant try-out of new and different units for the sake of variety both within and among schools whose students may have very different needs and interests. Flexibility in the program depends upon the constant trial of new units and the dropping of others which prove unsuited to particular schools or groups of students.

Consulting with and among Departments

Consultation with other departments and within the language arts department itself is imperative in the setting up of such units (1) to avoid overlapping; (2) to promote co-operation with other departments, such as home economics in family-life units, with the guidance department in units with a vocational emphasis or getting acquainted with the school, with social studies in units on the peoples who make up America, and with art and music in units involving aesthetic values; and (3) to made adequate use of all available facilities in the school.

It sometimes happens that individual members of the language arts department tend to go off on their own tangents and carry on units which may or may not fit into the school program as a whole. Furthermore, it occasionally happens that an individual class may repeat the same unit at too close intervals. It is desirable, of course, to keep all possible flexibility in the program and, within the framework of major objectives, to allow every possible freedom to individual classes and teachers in the choice of units for study. One school, for example, kept a bulletin board in the Staff Room with dates down the side and the departments of the school across the top. Every two weeks each member of the staff recorded in the appropriate space the units he was teaching. Overlapping was thus avoided, and many co-operative and integrating activities arose between classes and departments as a result of the information made available to them.

Overlapping or neglect of important areas of study is in no way inherent in the scheme of unit teaching and can easily be avoided by a little co-operative planning.

Insuring Sequence in Unit Teaching

Sequence in units is as important as a broad range. One type of sequence inheres in the growth of young people themselves. Characteristics of adolescents at different stages of their development from childhood to maturity are well known. For example, the hero worship stage in the junior high school makes useful a study of *Changing Styles in Heroes and Heroines* from the gods and goddesses of Olympus through the knights of the Middle Ages to the aviator of our own day and other less spectacular heroes of modern civilization. The tenth grade is a time when use of adventure thrillers parallels a stage of increasing vigor and admiration for physical courage. The twelfth makes possible consideration of other equally important aspects of courage. At the same time, fiction revealing mature phases of human personality comes into its own with older readers.

Units selected for different grade levels should take account of the characteristic interests and patterns of growth of the boys and girls concerned. This does not mean that the same theme may not recur at intervals during the high school period. A unit on family life, for example, is one thing in the seventh grade, when children are the center of attraction; another in the tenth, when conflict between the older and younger generation over "going steady" often looms large; and still another in the twelfth when relations of husband and wife may be of special interest. Radio, television, and motion pictures, which in the eighth grade may be part of a unit in *Communicating Together in Our Home Town,* may in the eleventh grade be units in themselves in which they are studied as powerful agencies in American life.

There is also a sequence of learning in the language arts. Use of complete sentences, avoidance of run-on sentences, and the search for variety in sentence structure are special problems at the junior high school level. Later, as thinking grows more mature, sentences become complex, causing new problems of clarity; and sustained thinking demands such elements of sentence structure as parallel construction or the long appositive modifier. Punctuation needs increase correspondingly.

Early in the junior high school students are still grappling with problems of the acceptable use of *see, do, come,* and *go,* of *ring, begin,* or *freeze.* Later such distinctions as those differentiating *sit* from *set* and *lie* from *lay* call for attention.

First, one learns to write single paragraphs, unified in theme and with a wealth of detail to build up or support the idea expressed. Later the adequate weaving together of paragraphs by appropriate transitions becomes part of a larger problem of the long composition.

After an initial try-out of units, it is possible and desirable for teachers to assign the teaching of specific skills to each unit. Doing this insures coverage of those aspects of punctuation, capitalization, usage, spelling, and choice and organization of material which research has shown of functional value in speech and writing. In allocating skills, teachers need to consider also the results of diagnostic tests, taken by the students, and other relevant information on the students' cumulative records. Similarly, letter writing, making reports, telling personal experiences, and panel discussions may occur in specific units found best suited to the development of these aspects of the language arts program. Examples of such planning may be found in the language arts bulletins of Denver, Seattle, and Minnesota and in the Communication Guides of Minneapolis.

Unit teaching, then, must not be hit-and-miss teaching. By examining the needs of their own students, members of a department may agree upon what is to be emphasized at different levels. Such elements of language then may be readily woven into whatever units are in progress. All individuals, however, will not achieve the same level of performance. Each must be helped at his own particular stage of development. The direction of progress may readily be mapped. How far each student may go in a given length of time cannot be prescribed. The teacher may rest assured, however, that with the stimulation of the richer background in unit teaching and the opportunity it offers for the exercise of personal initiative and of caring for the needs of individuals, each will go further than he would under a lock-step system.

BIBLIOGRAPHY
Books

ALBERTY, Harold, *Reorganizing the High School Curriculum* (New York, The Macmillan Company, 1953), pp. 421–517.

ANDERSON, Harold A., LEMON, Babette K., SCHULER, Marguerite E., and SHEPHERD, Edith, *Instruction in English in the University High School*, Publications of the Laboratory Schools of the University of Chicago, No. 9, August, 1941 (Chicago, University of Chicago Press, 1941).

APPY, Nellie, ed., *Pupils Are People*, Report of the Committee on Individual Differences, Monograph No. 13, National Council of Teachers of English (New York, D. Appleton–Century Company, Inc., 1941), pp. 131–140, 193–206.

BROENING, Angela M., ed., *Conducting Experiences in English*, Monograph No. 8, National Council of Teachers of English (New York, Appleton-Century-Crofts, Inc., 1939).

Chicago Public Schools, *Resource Units for English 1* (Chicago, The Public Schools), 104 pp. (mimeographed).

CROSS, E. A., and CARNEY, Elizabeth, *Teaching English in High Schools* (New York, The Macmillan Company, 1950).

DE BOER, John J., KAULFERS, Walter V., and MILLER, Helen R., *Teaching English in Secondary Schools* (New York, McGraw-Hill Book Company, Inc., 1951).

Florida State Department of Education, *Experiencing the Language Arts*, Bulletin No. 34 (Tallahassee, Florida State Department of Education, 1948), pp. 208–296.

GAY, Robert, ed., *Essays on the Teaching of English in Honor of Charles Swain Thomas* (Cambridge, Mass., Harvard University Press, 1940).

HOOK, Julius N., *The Teaching of High School English* (New York, The Ronald Press Company, 1950).

POOLEY, Robert C., and WILLIAMS, Robert D., *The Teaching of English in Wisconsin: A Survey of the Methods and Materials of Instruction and of Teaching Personnel in the Elementary and Secondary Schools, 1944–45* (Madison, University of Wisconsin Press, 1948).

POWDERMAKER, Hortense, *Probing Our Prejudices: A Unit for High School Students*, Bureau of Intercultural Education (New York, Harper and Brothers, 1944).

ROBERTS, Holland D., KAULFERS, Walter V., and KEFAUVER, Grayson N., *English for Social Living* (New York, McGraw-Hill Book Company, Inc., 1943).

St. Paul City Schools, *Revised Course of Study in English* (St. Paul, Minn., Department of Public Instruction).

SMITH, Dora V., *Communication, the Miracle of Shared Living* (New York, The Macmillan Company, 1955), pp. 62–78.

STEARNS, Gertrude B., *English in the Small High School* (Lincoln, University of Nebraska Press, 1950).

STEPHENS, Stephen DeWitt, *Individual Instruction in English Composition* (Cambridge, Mass., Harvard University Press, 1928).

TABA, Hilda, and ELKINS, Deborah, *With Focus on Human Relations* (Washington, D. C., American Council on Education, 1950).

VAN TIL, William, *Democracy Demands It: A Resource Unit for Intercultural Education*, Bureau for Intercultural Education, Public Service, Vol. 6 (New York, Harper and Brothers, 1950).

WEEKS, Ruth Mary, *Using Periodicals*, A Report of the National Council of Teachers of English Committee on the Use of Magazines and Newspapers in the English Class (Champaign, Ill., The Council, 1950).

Periodicals

ANTHONY, Mary, Sister, "Detroit Girls Study the Newspaper," *English Journal*, Vol. XXXVI (May, 1947), pp. 254–256.

BELL, J. W., "Chicago's English Curriculum for the High Schools," bibliog., *Bulletin of the National Association of Secondary-School Principals*, Vol. 30 (February, 1946), pp. 132–141.

BROENING, Angela M., "Trends in Secondary-School English," *Journal of the National Education Association*, Vol. XXXVIII (December, 1949), pp. 666–667.

CALLAHAN, G. M., "Plan for a Year's Work in Ninth-Grade English," *Journal of Education*, Vol. 136 (April, 1954), pp. 206–209.

CHAMBERS, H. L., "Organizing English Units," *Baltimore Bulletin of Education*, Vol. XXVII (March, 1950), pp. 7–9.

COX, M. S., "Meet the Myths: Our Tenth-Grade English Unit Gives Students a Literary Background and a Creative Opportunity," *Clearing House*, Vol. XXVIII (October, 1953), pp. 89–94.

DRAPER, E. M., and GARDNER, G., "How to Construct a Resource Unit," bibliog., *Clearing House*, Vol. XXVI (January, 1952), pp. 267–270.

DUFFY, M. E., "Unit in Reading and Thinking," *English Journal*, Vol. XXXV (January, 1946), pp. 43–45.

"English Unit on Housing Used by a Tenth-Grade Group," bibliog., *Bulletin of the National Association of Secondary-School Principals*, Vol. XXXII (May, 1948), pp. 53–59.

FINDER, M., "Units Aplenty," *English Journal*, Vol. XLII (September, 1953), pp. 324–329.

HENRY, G. H., "Our Best English Unit," *English Journal*, Vol. XXXVI (September, 1947), pp. 356–362.

LEESE, J., "Developing Units in the Modern Secondary School," *High School Journal*, Vol. XXVIII (November, 1945), pp. 259–262.

LOBAN, W., "Teaching Literature: A Multiple Approach," *English Journal*, Vol. XLV (February, 1956), pp. 75–78+.

LOVRIEN, M., "Studying the Cultural Diversity of a Great City," *English Journal*, Vol. XXXIX (May, 1950), pp. 262–267.

McCUTCHAN, Mary, "The American Dream: A Unit in Junior English," *English Journal*, Vol. XXXI (March, 1942), pp. 200–219.

McHARRY, Licsette J., "The Teaching of American Ideals: I," *Illinois English Bulletin*, Vol. XXXVII (November, 1949), pp. 1–18.

McKEAN, R. C., "Students Like Thematic Units," *English Journal*, Vol. XLV (February, 1956), pp. 82–83.

MOSING, H., "Appreciation through Units," *English Journal*, Vol. XLIV (February, 1955), pp. 80–86.

PEEL, L. S., "Teen-ager Takes a Look at Himself," *English Journal*, Vol. XLII (November, 1953), pp. 459–460.

SPINKS, Pearl, "Life Brought to Literature through Group Work," *English Journal*, Vol. XXXIX (April, 1950), pp. 201–205.

ZIEGLER, Caroline L., "Releasing Individual Expression," *Baltimore Bulletin of Education*, Vol. XXVII (March–May, 1950), pp. 34–35.

ZOLLINGER, Marian, "Five Units and How They Grow," *English Journal*, Vol. XXXIX (October, 1950), pp. 423–429.

PREVIEW OF CHAPTER 5

Literature for Discovery and Imaginative Insight

Recognition of the Needs of Youth

General and Individual Needs
The Wide Range of Individual Differences

Use of Literature to Meet These Needs

Broadened Thinking and Experience through Literature
Literature as a Source of Pleasure
Other Personal Values in Literature
The Place of the Emotions in Literature

The Importance of Choice in Reading

Unhappy Results of Prescribed Lists
Setting the Stage for Personal Reading
Progressive Experiences in Choosing
Variety to Be Expected in the Reading of the Same Individual
The Importance of Student-Teacher Relations in Reading Guidance
Relation to "Outside" or Independent Personal Reading

Methods of Organizing Literature for Classroom Study

Common Experience in Reading as an Aid to Growing Maturity
Centers of Interest for Units in Literature
Use of Literary Types
American, English, and World Literature

The Use of Periodicals

The Use of Related School Services

Audio-Visual Aids
Relation of Literature Teaching to the Library

Evaluating Outcomes in Literature

Use of Informal Student Reaction
Measures of the Amount and Nature of Voluntary Reading Done

Conclusion

Bibliography

CHAPTER 5

Meeting Youth's Needs through Literature

And these things I see suddenly, what mean they?
As if some miracle, some hand divine unseal'd my eyes,
Shadowy, vast shapes smile through the air and sky,
And on the distant waves sail countless ships,
And anthems in new tongues I hear saluting me.
WALT WHITMAN, "Prayer of Columbus"

LITERATURE FOR DISCOVERY AND
IMAGINATIVE INSIGHT

THE STUDY of literature in secondary schools should provide the experience of discovery. Many discoveries have been less heralded at the time of their happening than at a later date. No one of Columbus' contemporaries could have envisioned the results of his discovery. Nor can teachers or the public grasp the full significance of the intellectual and emotional experience that may come from the penetration of the ideas and feelings of human beings, recorded—whether in prose or poetry—with what may be called poetic truth. Poetic truth is the truth that is not factual, but that is true to the actions and aspirations of mankind.

Histories of wars, based supposedly on facts, become antiquated. Homer's *Iliad*, Shakespeare's *Henry the Fifth*, and Byron's "Battle of Waterloo," with imaginative, even fabulous accounts, because of their "higher truth," have persisted for generations. Mrs. Benary-Isbert's *The Ark*, Whitman's "Come Up from the Fields, Father," and McCrae's "In Flan-

123

ders Fields" tell younger students more about the real meaning of war than all the accounts of campaigns which fill the pages of textbooks.

In an age of science and mechanical development, it is almost inevitable that the importance of intangibles should be minimized or obscured. It is all the more imperative that the values of the study of literature should be clear not only to teachers of English in high schools, where masses of young people find terminal education, but also to the gadget-minded of the populace, short-sighted in their enjoyment of the immediate, the noisy and crowded, the active and unreflective.

Lives are being lengthened by science. A new motive has been introduced for the study of literature. Education today must consider not only the present, the job at the end of a high school course or admission to college; it must prepare for a long span of life.

Literature should be so studied that it will meet the needs of youth and promote growth. The approach to literature in the classroom should lift an Iron Curtain of indifference or antagonism toward books. It should provide a unique experience of entrance into a real world which students are likely to visit in other subjects, and into a world of imagination which they are unlikely to travel without the study of literature. Even with such an approach, students may not be able to travel without a teacher of perception and sensitivity who has himself happily explored the realm.

RECOGNITION OF THE NEEDS OF YOUTH

Sometimes the phrase "the needs of youth" seems vague, modish, or sanctimonious. It must be interpreted literally. It is incontrovertible that infants have unique needs; so have young people of fifteen or twenty; so, likewise, men and women of forty or of eighty years of age. Each group has certain general characteristics as well as marked individual variations. The accomplishments of Churchill at 77, Herriot at 79, Croce at 85, Santayana at 97, Orlando at 91, and Berenson at 96 [1] differed from the usual accomplishments of octogenarians; so, also, the achievements of a Mozart at five, a Shirley Temple at seven, a Macaulay at fifteen, a Gertrude Ederle at nineteen differed from those of most of their contemporaries.

General and Individual Needs

In planning the study of literature to meet the needs of youth, general traits as well as individual characteristics must be taken into consideration. Most students in high school are on their way to adulthood and to long lives, extended beyond the years of industrial usefulness. Their maturing is revealed not only in their physical status but in their intellectual and emotional development. The students must grow as individuals in self-realization, poise, judgment, and self-control. They must grow in their relations with people, their contemporaries and those of all ages, races, nationalities, and creeds. They must grow in their ability to work effectively in order to become self-sustaining, courageous workers and citizens.

Some students are individualists and cannot see their place in relation to that of others. Some are insecure and "troublesome" until the troubles are detected and, if possible, remedied.

Many high school students are interested in what they deem fair play; the conception of it at first may be narrow, but it can be broadened. Some have already achieved an objective and broad social view. Romantic students are numerous. So are students curious about the future and the world. They have an exploring turn of mind about places, experiences, and increasingly about people and human relations. Sometimes through life, reading, or work, they have an unusual insight.

[1] Harvey Breit, "Talk with Martin Gumpert," *New York Times Book Review*, Vol. XXVIII (September 2, 1951), p. 13.

No group is really homogeneous. Young teachers are some-times misled by the term and seek the transfer of students as soon as individual differences appear. The term is relative: a group can be only approximately homogeneous. It is the glory of a democratic and thinking people that there are individual differences; it is of the utmost importance that some individual differences—and individuality—be stimulated and cherished.

The Wide Range of Individual Differences

The range of differences is wide. In a given grade, students are at varying points of development. The place where each one is may be suggested by statistical records kept over a period of years in school. These records must be supplemented by the teacher's penetrating study of each student as he is revealed through his actions and reactions in class, in activities in school and out of school, and in his writing and conversation. Attention should be focused on the point at which he is, his present stage of development. The study of literature must be directed toward promoting growth. The specific means of doing so are likely to vary with each individual. In one class of tenth-grade students taking ninth-grade English, boys were strangely moved by Eugene O'Neill's *Ile*. After presenting it in class, they went home and read the play with or to their families. For one student it had special significance because his mother was perfect for the part of Mrs. Keeney, the Captain's wife.

Differences in ability to read. Individuals within each class likewise differ in their ability to read. In one study made in independent schools,[2] 9 per cent of the twelfth-grade students were found to be reading at or below the ninth-grade median. About 7 per cent of the ninth-grade students reached or exceeded the median for the twelfth grade.[3] The

[2] "1946 Fall Testing Program in Independent Schools and Supplementary Studies," *Educational Records Bulletin*, No. 47 (February, 1947), p. 19.
[3] Paul A. Witty, "Current Role and Effectiveness of Reading among Youth," in *Reading in the High School and College.* Forty-seventh Yearbook,

differences are also clear when Benjamin, dissatisfied with translations, reads *War and Peace* in Russian with understanding and appreciation; while Dan, also a senior, completes a simplified version of *Great Expectations*, the first book, he hesitatingly admits, that he has ever read on his own; and while Helen, who reads with eighth-grade ability, finds satisfaction in Rebecca Caudill's *Tree of Freedom*. Such evidence points to the necessity of furnishing, in classroom and library, reading materials paralleling in difficulty the range of ability among the members of the class.

Increasing differences with age. Economic factors, family patterns, and environment retard or accelerate physical, intellectual, and emotional development. Students differ when they enter their first class in school. Differences increase rapidly with years of schooling. They exist also because of other factors; possibly in junior high school they are accentuated by the more rapid physical and social development of girls as compared with boys. Rapid students in the senior high school have been gaining over slower students for ten, eleven, or twelve years. Those trailing behind rarely catch up. Sometimes they spurt and surpass those who have seemed more advanced. Like other human beings, students are not one thing or another; they are many different things at the same time and at different times.

USE OF LITERATURE TO MEET THESE NEEDS

The teaching of literature should be directed toward meeting the individual needs and stimulating the growth of young people, who are eager or apathetic, pulsating or unresponsive human beings. Many may be quickened to perceptiveness and insight. It is also well to remember that the apathy, unresponsiveness, and indifference may be turned into strong antipathy unless a teacher is understanding and skillful.

National Society for the Study of Education, Part II (Chicago, University of Chicago Press, 1948), p. 18.

Broadened Thinking and Experience through Literature

If the teaching of literature is successful, students will independently turn to books for information, ideas, and enjoyment. A seventh-grade boy of low reading ability may revel in Holling C. Holling's *Paddle-to-the-sea,* in the Haders' *Spunky,* or in Mildred Merriman's poem, "The Pirate Don Durk of Dowdee"; whereas a girl of average reading power may turn to Helen Adams' *Wonderful Year,* to Cornelia Meigs's *The Invincible Louisa,* or to Emily Dickinson's "A Day." In the tenth grade, superior students may be challenged by Thor Heyerdahl's *Kon-Tiki,* by Charles Dickens' *A Tale of Two Cities,* or by Carl Sandburg's "The People, Yes." Scenes from books, lines of poetry and prose, will remain in the memories of individual students and will take on new meaning as they flash into mind to illuminate reading and actual situations. Happy experiences—not necessarily easy experiences—with literature in junior and senior high school should give students broad and deep insight into themselves, into others, and into a world which is broadening astonishingly for them. The increasing scope results not only from the time in which they live, a period of rapid communication between places once remote, but from the stage of growth of the students themselves.

The study of literature may give information about parts of our country and of the world. By means of literature, students may travel into places that were not touched upon in traditional courses in English literature. They may visit unfamiliar homes and villages—back-country America, as suggested in the unit developed in Chapter 4. They may go to India with Kim. Defoe, Dana, Melville, Conrad, Maugham, Paton, Hemingway, Buck, and other writers too numerous to mention may give them insight into far-off places and strange experiences. For similar breadth of adventure, junior high school students are indebted to Louise Rankin, to Howard

Pease, and to Kate Seredy. Through books, young people may travel in the past, the present, and even in the future. They may come to realize how other human beings—in prehistoric, medieval, and more recent times—have reacted to situations and to people.

Ideas should result from the study of literature, whether prose or poetry, biography or fiction. Frequently they result from the study of essays and expository prose. When ideas are presented through emotional experiences they may have added power.

Literature as a Source of Pleasure

Strangely enough, the fact that literature is a source of pleasure is a point that needs stressing. The pleasure is not of one kind; there are infinite possibilities, depending upon interests and maturity. If the study of literature does not provide enjoyment, the teaching has been a failure. Time was when some English teachers saw only facts or moral values in literature and penalized students for finding pleasure in reading. The teacher of today knows that such an attitude drives young people from books and encourages hypocrisy. Theodore Spencer noted that Somerset Maugham was criticized for stressing novels as a source of entertainment.[4] What a dreary world this would be if books were to be read for direct moral instruction only!

Other Personal Values in Literature

Moral values, however, must not be overlooked.[5] They are implicit in the finest of books, leaving unforgettable impressions and also judgments of right and wrong. The way of art is often effective because of its indirect approach. The

[4] Theodore Spencer, "Somerset Maugham," *English Journal,* Vol. XXIX (September, 1940), p. 529.

[5] Educational Policies Commission, *Moral and Spiritual Values in the Public Schools* (Washington, D. C., National Education Association, 1951), p. 61.

biblical parables are but one example. Rudyard Kipling's *Jungle Book* is another, and so, too, are *Macbeth* and *How Green Was My Valley.*

Literature gives enjoyment by illuminating beauty, whether that of a Grecian urn, of the search for the Holy Grail, of stopping by the woods on a snowy evening, of a father and son by the Oxus River, of wild swans at Coole, or of the death of a hired man.

The Place of the Emotions in Literature

Whether students read for information, ideas, or enjoyment, the study of literature must involve their minds and their hearts. It is a special advantage for the teacher of literature that the emotions are involved, for they play a significant part in communication and in maturity. But emotions will be involved only if the material read is well within the ability and the experience of the reader, if the author is capable of carrying young people from the familiar to the unfamiliar, and if the teacher sets the stage for an emotional reaction. Dissection of lines and phrases and a plethora of facts and details about the life of the author, the circumstances under which he wrote the works, and the literary influences which caused him to write as he did, can easily sever the personal contact between writer and reader.

THE IMPORTANCE OF CHOICE IN READING

Unhappy Results of Prescribed Lists

The teaching of literature must emphasize choices. Conventional methods are prone to offer young people a prescribed book, the same for all students and too frequently the same for all teachers, regardless of whether either can see any reason for the selection. At one time books were imposed by outside agencies, perhaps outside a secondary school teaching situation, sometimes outside any teaching situation or any actual observation of groups of young men and young women. The requirements might come from a school head, a city, a state, or a college. Books were handed out to students in a perfunctory fashion and were received without enthusiasm or curiosity. Even teachers were not stimulated to read widely and to make choices. Theirs not to question why! Often their obligation was to prepare students for an intensive examination on facts about authors and titles and specific works, lines, and words in American and English literature. The idea of choice, philosophically basic, was entirely overlooked.

Setting the Stage for Personal Reading

Today programs of reading are more elastic. Classroom and school libraries make browsing possible. Class periods vary from occasional "recitation" to planning what to read next, conversing about books, sometimes reading silently throughout the entire period, conferring in small groups, and sharing reading in a wide variety of ways, from giving personal reactions to panel discussion and dramatization. Sometimes all students read together a single selection as a means of developing skills needed for a certain type of literature or for mutual enjoyment or understanding. This selection may then act as a springboard for individual reading on the same or related topics. Sometimes class members keep individual plan books in which they consciously map out a program of reading for themselves, considering carefully the breadth and depth of the reading they are doing.

Through personal guidance the teacher is in a position to help students develop methods of selection which will stand them in good stead when school days are over. What differentiates a good novel from a poor one? A Zane Grey from a Herman Melville? In one's program of reading, what purpose is served by biography? By the essay? What means has the reader of knowing whether a novel about India is true or untrue? Where can one find out what current authors are receiving favorable recognition and why? When one wishes to pursue reading about a special idea or experience, where can he find material? If one enjoys poetry and wants to delve more deeply into it, how can he go about doing so? Weak students need encouragement and guidance. Gifted students need suggestion, a vision of their own potentialities, and freedom to pursue reading in the direction of their own interests and at the level of their highest capacities. They need a teacher who has read so widely and who is so understanding that he will challenge them to broaden their interests, to deepen their insight, and to develop a personal attitude and philosophy commensurate with their powers. *Language Arts for Today's Children,* Volume II of this curriculum series, presents in Chapter 10 (pp. 307ff.) a most interesting junior high school Book Week Celebration in which young people were stimulated to both individual and group achievement.

Progressive Experiences in Choosing

Today, throughout the elementary school, children should be having happy experiences with choosing books from attractive displays and browsing corners in their classrooms. With this background, junior high school students will be ready to range and explore widely, feeling at home with books and with choosing among them. At this age, if ever, the habit of reading is for the majority of people established; and wide individual reading with opportunity to choose, reject, or accept from among a wealth of possibilities is the essential base for the habit of turning to books as sources of information, relaxation, and inspiration. That such experience with choosing has not been given some boys and girls is revealed in their attitudes toward literature when they reach senior high school or leave school for work. The helplessness of many a high school student when first called upon to make choices is significant. So, too, is the helplessness of many adults when visiting a library. They are unaware of their responsibility for choice, expecting—thoughtlessly, but not unreasonably, in view of their training—that books will always be placed in their hands by a book club or librarian, if not by a teacher. In school they accepted books passively or resentfully, seldom with curiosity or spontaneous warmth.

Variety to Be Expected in the Reading of the Same Individual

Students may surprise their teachers by their choices. Some senior boys, supposedly with serious reading difficulties, for whom mild and childish books have sometimes been deemed suitable, have discovered and read harsh books, especially those about war, including Norman Mailer's *The Naked and the Dead*. A senior college preparatory student, whose choices would be expected to be mature, discovered with pleasure Howard Pyle's simple *Men of Iron* along with Ernie Pyle's biography. Others were excited by Robert Frost's *Masque of Reason* and Robinson Jeffers' *Medea*. A tenth-grade general student read Mika Waltari's *The Adventurer* and asked questions about the continuity of this picaresque novel.

No one reads always at the same level of maturity. Sometimes he surprises himself and his teacher by the high level of his choices. At other times he relaxes with a simple, entertaining book or picks up something he has missed at an earlier period of his reading. One student's enthusiasm may incite many in a group to read, as it did in the case of a student who brought in Edith Wharton's *The Spark* in connection with Walt Whitman.

The Importance of Student-Teacher Relations in Reading Guidance

Students often astonish their teacher by the intimacy of their confidences concerning what they are reading. When they do, it is because the relations between teacher and student are frank, personal, and understanding. Under these circumstances, teachers can help students to achieve a kind of proportion in their reading, balancing distorted views of life and stretching horizons. As a result of such honest, informed, inspired teaching, students should be open-minded about literature of all types, aware of what each has to offer, and responsive to it. Many examples appear in print of how teachers have achieved this end.[6]

With a friendly relationship to books should come a realization of the fact that the content is more important than the cover. Students have grown when they cease to apologize for having read a paper-covered book, when they learn that a book in inexpensive format may be far more significant than an elegantly bound copy of Sabatini, for example. Students are growing when they become aware that the publication of a book in an inexpensive edition may indicate that it has had something vital to say to many people over a long time and that it is still speaking. Often they mistake such books for recent ones. Then a major antagonism is removed: that against old books. So are other antagonisms, such as those against poor type, worn covers, and marked or soiled pages. Paper-bound editions, by reviving old books, are reaching new readers. Many of them make young people aware of values in literature by authors who perennially speak to mankind.

Relation to Independent, Personal Reading

Emphasis on the choice of books and on unit teaching has tended to modify ideas of what used to be called "outside" reading, a formal, and too frequently a futile, activity. Often

[6] Lou LaBrant, "Guided Free Reading as a Means of Promoting Reading Interests and Tastes in High Schools and Colleges," in W. S. Gray, ed., *Adjusting Reading Programs to Individuals*, Supplementary Educational Monographs, No. 52 (Chicago, University of Chicago Press, 1941), pp. 242–248.

Esther Raushenbush, *Literature for Individual Education*, Sarah Lawrence College Publications, No. 1 (New York, Columbia University Press, 1942).

Louise Rosenblatt, "Development of Reading Interests and Critical Appreciation in Secondary Schools and Colleges," in W. S. Gray, ed., *Reading and Pupil Development*, Supplementary Educational Monographs, No. 51 (Chicago, University of Chicago Press, 1940), pp. 223–229.

one book read and retold by a class was followed by one book, possibly of similar type, read independently by individual students; in some cases the second book was identical for all. Sometimes a certain number of books was required for a year's reading, perhaps ten books from an outmoded list that the teacher may have borrowed. Usually a written report was required. Seldom was there communication between the book and the reader or a spontaneous sharing with classmates because of the joy of the experience or the possible contribution of the ideas to the solution of a human problem. Too often the requirement resulted in copying or paraphrasing another's report. Under the circumstances, a common greeting between English teachers was, "How many books do you require for outside reading?" Stress on the *requirement* and on the *number* ignored communication or growth in understanding, appreciation, and enjoyment.

METHODS OF ORGANIZING LITERATURE FOR CLASSROOM STUDY

When the dogmatic procedure of handing out a book for class study or for independent reading fell into disrepute, the reaction was too frequently the other extreme of never having all students or any two students read the same book. As a consequence, they read a wide diversity of titles or seemed to have read them. There was a minimum of challenge to choose books of increasing depth; too often there were no recognizable results from a kind of heterogeneous, undisciplined reading. In spite of the fact that students are at different stages of development, making it hazardous to grade books for them as groups, and although one book which could meet the needs of all would be more rare than a phoenix, there may still be some worth-while reading of the same book by interested groups of students and sometimes by the class as a whole.

Common Experience in Reading as an Aid to Growing Maturity

Reading may be a social undertaking, as music and painting often are. The common experience may be a point of departure for a wide variety of individual reading taking on meaning from the sharing of insights. Sometimes the book to be read by the class may be chosen by majority vote. Class discussion, focusing on one book, is likely to illuminate what the book has to offer. One student can find much more than another. A student's explanation of what he has found in given lines or scenes or chapters may help other students not only to see that they failed to reach the author but to discover what they must do or see or feel to be reached by him.

The danger of simplified editions. When an effort is made to center attention on a single book, teachers sometimes resort to the use of shortened and simplified versions of books which have been prepared to meet the needs of slow students, many of whom have resisted formal and traditional methods. Such books are not to be used thoughtlessly. Frequently when copies are available in schools, they are picked up carelessly and substituted for books that would be more challenging.

The question at issue is whether a different book, simpler in its original form, would not meet the need of the poorer reader more adequately. If *Treasure Island* is too difficult, there are other and easier pirate stories. If *Silas Marner* is beyond the reading ability of many tenth-grade pupils, there are other and simpler novels revealing human personality similarly changed by force of circumstances and by the influence of one human being upon another. Simplified editions are not to be used with any students who could read the original version, but unfortunately they have been so used. The versions are uneven in quality. Some have not caught the dignity and the spirit of the original; they give students no clue to the author's intent or achievement. A number of the simplified or shortened books have been cheapened by misleading or ludicrous illustrations. Such distorted versions are to be avoided, for there are many excellent simple books. Most teachers will use the substitutes only as a last resource and after a careful study of the new form in relation to the original.

Extensive and intensive study of literature. The study of literature should be both extensive and intensive. Jack O'Brien's *Silver Chief, Dog of the North,* John Tunis' many popular stories, Gregor Felsen's *Hot Rod,* or Cornelia Otis Skinner and Emily Kimbrough's *Our Hearts Were Young and Gay* are unquestionably suited for rapid reading. So are many other books not so easy as those named. But there must be some intensive reading, some attempt to stretch students to find treasures that are not to be discovered by those who race along in reading, throwing aside anything presenting an obstacle in detail, closely-reasoned thought, abstraction, or figurative expression.

Intensive study may be made of the depths and heights of human happiness and misery. Conrad's *The Rover* presents unforgettably an unschooled man with an impressive knowledge of the world, "the Brother of the Coast, the man of dark deeds, but of large heart."

Students cannot appreciate literature unless they understand irony, metaphor, and important allusions, not as decorations but as a means of expressing ideas. Without penetrating them, the study of literature is superficial.

Through extensive and intensive reading, students should gain power. They should learn to delight in a challenge and to ask without hesitation for assistance in arriving at the meaning. The skill or artistry of the teacher is called upon in judging when there should be extensive reading—where the less said the better; and where there should be intensive study. And a spirit of tolerance and humility should be devel-

oped in students that will make for a good-natured acceptance of Thoreau's statement on "Reading" in *Walden:* "It is
not all books that are as dull as their readers." [7]

Centers of Interest for Units in Literature

A most successful way of motivating reading and of providing for individual differences is through the idea-centered
unit. Penetration into the back country of America was the
purpose of the unit in Chapter 4, which served as a center
for class consideration of a unified theme and which introduced the use of related language skills. The ideas in which
to center units are myriad; finding an idea presents no problem for a resourceful, imaginative teacher with a wide and
deep range of interests. Choosing may be more of a problem.

The interest may be in sections of our country. Robert
Frost's pictures of bending birches, of snowstorms, of fences,
and of nature in New England—but with a universal significance—and Edith Wharton's granite outcroppings as revealed in *Ethan Frome* give a clue to what might be done
with New England. Other sections are rich in literature
which can bring to life the varied strains in our country.
Mark Twain, Hamlin Garland, Ole Rolvaag, Ruth Suckow,
and Willa Cather reveal something of the diversity of life in
the Middle West. For younger pupils also there is an abun-
dance of material in Doris Gates, in Florence Means, in Carol
Ryrie Brink, in the more mature books of the Wilder "Little
House" series, and in Borghild Dahl's recent *Homecoming.*
The same is true of other countries all over the globe. One
senior class gained much from a study of novels of many
countries, centering in the theme, *No Man Is an Island.* Sophomores enjoy pursuing the universal problem of "parent trouble" in such novels as Alice T. Hobart's *The Peacock Sheds
His Tail* (South America), Alice M. Huggins' *The Red Chair*

[7] Henry D. Thoreau, *Walden or Life in the Woods* (Mt. Vernon, N. Y.,
Peter Pauper Press), p. 97.

Waits (China), and John Drinkwater's *Bird in Hand* (Great Britain). A unit may be centered in fun—books of humor, tales of pirates, or sport stories. Standards of selection in these areas are very·important for recreational reading.[8] Another unit may be centered in frustration, a common theme in literature, as in *The Return of the Native, Giants in the Earth,* and *Cry, the Beloved Country.* Younger students may enjoy units centered in animals, introducing such books as *Smoky* and *The Yearling.* The latter, together with O'Hara's *Green Grass of Wyoming,* may lead into problems of growing up, in which Maureen Daly's *Seventeenth Summer,* Betty Cavanna's *A Girl Can Dream,* Mary Stolz's *In a Mirror* are especially interesting to younger teen-age readers.

Or pupils may like adventure in the air or on the sea. August Derleth, in an article in the *English Journal* for January, 1952, gives special help in choosing science fiction wisely. Materials vary from simple space-ship stories for junior high school boys, like Otto Gail's *By Rocket to the Moon,* to the sociological treatises of Ray Bradbury, solving man's problems in the expanding world of the planets, and the deeply philosophical literary work of Saint Exupéry in *Wind, Sand, and Stars.*

Older boys have seen the answer to their fears in *The Red Badge of Courage* and *Journey's End.* Both boys and girls are interested in family relationships in *Alice Adams, Of Human Bondage, Sorrell and Son, Hamlet,* and *Antigone.* Individual girls, and boys too, have asked for *Adam Bede* and *The Scarlet Letter.* Other seniors do well if they read Douglas Gorsline's *Farm Boy* or Betty Cavanna's *Going on Sixteen.* The problem is to help each pupil to find the books best suited to his needs and to his level of ability. Listings of themes are to be found in many anthologies and in accounts in *The English Journal,* which appear in the bibliography for this chapter.

[8] Margaret A. Edwards, "How Do I Love Thee?" *English Journal,* Vol. XLI (September, 1952), pp. 335–340.

Colleen Scury, "A Scorecard for Reviewers," *Horn Book,* Vol. XXVIII (October, 1952), pp. 348–351.

The basis of choice of the idea for the unit is significant. So is the carrying out of the idea to a definite conclusion. The study, though concerned with a wide range of resources, must have a center of gravity. The unit as a whole must achieve a sense of form.

Use of Literary Types

Students must be guided to make choices in all types of literature. Different reading skills are required to interpret different literary types. Young people must not follow the line of least resistance, concentrating on detective or adventure stories, or exciting fiction.[9] They should become familiar with all types, not with facts about a type as the issue but with types as varied forms of communication. Different things may be communicated most effectively in different ways. Some things need to be said in every possible way. For example, our heritage of freedom is effectively revealed in Paul Green's play, *The Common Glory*, in Clara Ingram Judson's biography of *Thomas Jefferson*, in Esther Forbes' novel, *Johnny Tremain*, in the Benéts' collection of poems called *Book of Americans*, in Walt Whitman's *Poems of Democracy*, and in Dorothy Thompson's powerful essay, *America*. These selections represent a wide range of difficulty, permitting students of varying ability to read materials suited to their individual needs and at the same time making it possible for each of them to contribute something worth while to the discussion. Consideration of these selections cannot fail to bring out the different way in which each literary type approaches the same theme.

Literary types as a mature approach to literature. The study of literary types as such is a mature approach to literature. It is inappropriate as a basis for organization of literary study in the junior high school, although pupils in Grades 7 through 9 may learn, in connection with units and other ac-

[9] May L. Becker, *First Adventures in Reading* (Philadelphia, J. B. Lippincott Company, 1947), pp. 271–286.

tivities in reading, a love of poetry, a consciousness of the dramatic power of plays, and an interest in the short story form. In the senior high school the study of types as such may be presented as a special-interest unit or an elective course for students of particular aptitude and maturity in reading.

Literary types and individual differences. It should be noted also that organization of literature by type, like that by theme, facilitates adjusting the level of difficulty in reading to the abilities of individual students, for there are easy plays and difficult plays, simple poems and mature ones, short, swiftly moving novels and long, complicated ones. Each student may be directed to material suited to his own needs; yet he is in a position to make a valuable contribution to the work of the group.

Literary types as distinct forms of communication. Certainly, however, consciousness of types should be a significant part of units. Students must realize how many different ways there are to communicate. They must learn to be flexible and respond to various types even by name, for the names give hints of the author's meaning and aid in interpretation. The terms *fiction, story, play,* and *poetry* indicate an imaginative approach: "Do not take this too literally, for this is drama." "This is biography; it is meant to be the truth."

In considering literary types as forms of communication, students are interested in discovering that the same writers at different times have taken different approaches. Saroyan wrote *The Human Comedy* as a motion picture; students may read it as a novel. *My Friend Flicka,* by Mary O'Hara, was first a short story; the same incidents were later woven into a long piece of fiction. Comparison of the two makes an interesting study. Nicholas Monsarrat's novel *The Cruel Sea* raised questions about classifications. What was the relation of the novel to *H. M. Corvette, East Coast Corvette, Corvette Command,* and *H. M. Frigate?* When questioned, Mr. Monsarrat called the books which had previously appeared notebooks. He said, "The facts had to be true, had to be based on reality, the framework exact. In the novel, however, I had the opportunity of selection and emphasis to a degree that I did not in the nonfiction accounts." [10]

Students read a novel with increased appreciation when they consider the breadth and depth of its scope in relation to life. Some students have felt they penetrated life with Sinclair Lewis or Sholem Asch, for example. Carl Sandburg tried to help people to an understanding of Lincoln, writing of him in poems, in a novel, and in a Pulitzer prize-winning biography. Young people can gain insight into Lincoln through Sandburg's writing or in many ways; for example, through Churchill's *The Crisis*, a novel; Walt Whitman's poetry; Drinkwater's *Abraham Lincoln*, Sherwood's *Abe Lincoln in Illinois*, plays; Ruth Painter Randall's *Mary Lincoln*, biography; or, of course, through Lincoln's own words. Students who have one form of communication only—possibly science fiction, a sentimental love story, or a predigested article—must be helped to realize the diversity of reading matter, the effectiveness of various types, and the satisfaction and enjoyment that may come through this diversity.

As students follow an idea in a unit through a wide variety of types of literature, each of them important in illuminating all sides of a central theme, they may be helped to grow in power to understand and to respond to each type in its unique way of communicating.

The drama, for example, may be read, but reading is secondary to seeing a performance with living actors, in a theater in which there is an audience of living people, more or less responsive to what they see and to what they hear. Attendance at plays is important in the appreciation of drama, and schools in or near large cities can co-operate in making attendance possible. TV drama presents possibilities for

10 Nash K. Burger, "Talk with Mr. Monsarrat," *New York Times Book Review* (August 19, 1951).

Marion C. Sheridan, "Teaching a Novel," *English Journal*, Vol. XLI, No. 1 (January, 1952), pp. 8–14.

realization of what acting contributes, though a large audience is lacking.

The necessity for action and movement in plays or scenes students themselves present for their group makes for enthusiasm.[11] It was true of a group who took into their own hands a class presentation of "The Doctor in Spite of Himself." Bubbling over with pleasure, they arranged for an account in the school paper. Young people enjoy taking part in acts and scenes from Shakespeare's plays—not only brilliant students but those sometimes deprived of acquaintance with Shakespeare by elders who forget—or never knew— that by some miracle Shakespeare spoke to groundlings as well as to philosophers. Since the language of Shakespeare is a foreign tongue to many boys and girls, use of recordings, of films, and of television is an invaluable aid to those incapable of discerning without assistance the meaning of the lines. Many students, also, who live far from the legitimate stage will be brought by these same devices to an appreciation of the dramatic power of plays.

Poetry, too, involves the use of the ears and sometimes of movement. So does some prose—rhythmical prose found, for example, in *A Tale of Two Cities* and *Cry, the Beloved Country*. Classes enjoy coming in with a refrain, as in "Sally in Our Alley," Browning's "Cavalier Tunes," and W. R. Benét's "Jesse James." Informal verse choirs add to appreciation. Dialogue enhances old ballads, as do refrains like those in the traditional English ballad, "The Coasts of High Barbary," and the American ballads like John Jacob Niles's version of "The Weep Willow Tree" and Richard Chase's repetitive refrains in his *Hullabaloo and Other Singing Folk Games* and in his *Grandfather Tales and Jack Tales*. Ichabod Paddock's "Blow, Boys, Blow" in Carl Carmer's *America Sings* is also a favorite with younger students. The martial rhythm of Chesterton's "Lepanto" is in marked contrast to the music of

[11] For a discussion of effective oral interpretation of literature, see Chapter 7, pp. 234–236 and Chapter 8, pp. 282 ff.

Wordsworth's "I Wandered Lonely as a Cloud." The changing rhythm of *John Brown's Body* gains in beauty through an understanding of the poet's purpose in varying it. Masefield's skill in "Sea-Fever" illustrates the beauty of variation in meter in an effort to communicate movement and experience: [12]

I must go down to the seas again, to the lonely sea and the sky,
And all I ask is a tall ship and a star to steer her by,
And the wheel's kick and the wind's song and the white sail's shaking,
And a grey mist on the sea's face and a grey dawn breaking.

Tone is exceedingly important in interpretation, particularly in plays and poetry. It may give clues to what puzzles in ellipses, as in the poetry of Browning or in Miller's "Columbus." It helps junior high school students to enter into the spirit of Charles Carryl's "Robinson Crusoe's Story," with its rollicking rhythms, its forced rhymes, its humorous use of surprise meanings for old words, its amazing concoctions in the way of food, and its new and startling accomplishments on the part of cat and goat.

The importance of hearing in interpreting the printed word emphasizes the need for the use of recordings of plays, of music such as the lyrics in Shakespeare's plays, of poetry, often read by poets themselves. Among readers appealing strongly are Maurice Evans, Robert Frost, and Dylan Thomas.[13]

A knowledge of types of literature helps with pace or timing. Students must learn to vary their pace, and one way to determine pace is recognizing a type and knowing what that type demands. They must not be impatient with a deliberate study of a poem, such, for example, as Alfred Noyes's "The

[12] John Masefield, *Salt Water Poems and Ballads* (New York, The Macmillan Company, 1953).

[13] National Council of Teachers of English, *List of Recordings for English Classes* (Champaign, Ill., Annual).

Edgar Dale, *Audio-Visual Methods in Teaching*, rev. ed. (New York, The Dryden Press, 1954).

Arno Jewett, *Recordings for Teaching Literature and Language in High School* (including a bibliography of 500 titles), Bulletin 1952, No. 19 (Washington, D. C., Office of Education).

Highwayman" for junior high school classes or Peter Viereck's "Kilroy" for senior high school students. And the study may be profitable not only in the interpretation of the particular poem but as a reserve, referred to in the report issued by the association of assistant masters in secondary schools in England: "When we take in class a play or an essay or an outstanding chapter of a novel we rely on and draw from a reserve that was mainly built up in the poetry lesson with its concentrated study of concentrated expressions." [14]

American, English, and World Literature

For many years, especially in the Middle West, courses in the history of literature—American, English, or World—have been common in high school programs. The gradual trend away from them has been accelerated in recent years by renewed emphasis upon reading literature itself rather than learning facts about it. Stress upon the point of contact between writer and reader has tended to discredit courses which begin in the early centuries and come only in the last months of the year to the period which young people know best and to which they must adjust. This does not mean that old literature is to be set aside for new or that the importance of perspective is to be forgotten. It means, rather, that literature is to be related directly to human experience, to aesthetic enjoyment, and to the needs of young people. The colleges, too, have urged emphasis upon acquaintance with good books and upon skill in reading and reflecting upon materials of a high level of maturity.[15] They are often opposed to anthologies that publish misleading excerpts from longer works and that tend to deceive readers of isolated contributions presented without their context.

Understanding life and thought in the United States and in foreign countries through literature is the goal toward

[14] Incorporated Association of Assistant Masters in Secondary English, *The Teaching of English* (Cambridge, England, Cambridge University Press, 1952), p. 27.
[15] See Chapter 12.

which courses in American, English, and World Literature are directed. Translations, however, must be recognized as such. Differences in translations should be made clear. Few today approve a course consisting solely of translations.

Americans should understand their country as it is revealed through literature. Units aimed at giving students a feeling for their heritage are fundamental. Many courses today center in such topics as *Our Heritage of Freedom, America's Concept of "The Good Life," The Diversity of Cultures in America* (people and regions), *Frontiers to the West, American Humor, American Folklore,* and *The Place of the Press in American Life.*[16] The unit in Chapter 4 showed one of many ways to have students reach out to penetrate their country. Other still broader units will make known to American young people the backgrounds of their country and its people—actual or fictional—among them such noted people as Benjamin Franklin, John Brown, Thomas Jefferson, Hamlin Garland, Otto Eisenschiml, Charles Lindbergh, and E. E. Cummings; or such characters as Ramona, "my Antonia," Per Hansa and Beret, "the lost Phoebe," and the Autocrat of the Breakfast Table, Johnny Tremain, and Henry Fleming.

Insight into Great Britain need not be achieved solely through literary surveys or through reliance upon Irving's *Sketch Book.* There is vicarious adventure in reading on such themes as England and the sea, which Masefield, Riggs's *Beowulf,* and Marryat have opened up to boys and girls; on her heroes and our heroes—King Arthur, Robin Hood, William Wallace, and St. Patrick. American young people cannot trace in literature their own country's faith in individual human worth without going back, the more gifted among them, to Chaucer's ploughman, his country schoolmaster, and

16 For a similar program, see:
Mary McCutchan, "The American Dream: A Unit in Junior English," *English Journal,* Vol. XXXI (March, 1942), pp. 194–200.
Liesette J. McHarry, "The Teaching of American Ideals: I," *Illinois English Bulletin,* Vol. XXXVII (November, 1949), pp. 1–18.
Marguerite R. Tupper, "The Teaching of American Ideals: II," *Illinois English Bulletin,* Vol. XXXVII (December, 1949), pp. 1–37.

his country parson—extolled in England when the rest of Europe devoted itself to romantic tales of lords and ladies. Later centuries picked up the theme in Gray, in Burns, in Goldsmith, in Housman, in Hardy, and in other poets of our day. Limits cannot be set to the possibilities of illumination of our common faith in freedom, integrity, and beauty revealed in such novelists as Scott, Dickens, and Thomas Hardy, or in poets like Keats, Shelley, Tennyson, Browning, and Auden.

An appreciation of literature of all countries is of deep importance. Often the best way to gain that appreciation is through a unit centered in an aspect of life in a particular country or designed to reveal universal human experience by focusing upon literature of many kinds and nations, bearing on such topics as war, social injustice, the devotion of men and women to each other or to a cause, love of nature, or the romantic view of life.

The study of world literature develops balance and induces humility. Americans were not the first to act or to write. How long ago Sophocles in *Antigone* told of the wonders of man beyond fancy's dream! The literature of the world emphasizes the oneness of mankind and its diversity. Such feeling may come through the folklore of Mexico, Ireland, South America, and Scandinavian countries, as well as of Greece and Rome. Units may be centered in humor, heroes, attitudes toward life, restraints, nobility, human nature. Older students might be interested in ways of governing, gleaning ideas from Plato's *The Republic,* Ibsen's *An Enemy of the People,* Drinkwater's *Oliver Cromwell* and *Abraham Lincoln,* Maxwell Anderson's *Elizabeth the Queen* and *Valley Forge.*

Younger pupils and those less mature among the older ones frequently find their best introduction to other countries in fiction written about young people like themselves who live in foreign lands: Fritz Muhlenwig's *Big Tiger and Christian,* for example, for China; Elizabeth Goudge's *Gentian Hill* for England; Dola DeJong's *Return to the Level Land* for Holland; Kate Seredy's *The Good Master* for Hungary; and for somewhat older readers, Margaret Bell's *Watch for a Tall White Sail,* for Alaska; Madeleine L'Engle's *And Both Were Young* for France and Switzerland; Alan Paton's *Cry, the Beloved Country* for South Africa; *People of the Deer* for the Eskimos of northern Canada; and Giovanni Guareschi's *Don Camillo and His Flock* for Italy.[17]

Mature students will read *War and Peace, Crime and Punishment, Kristin Lavransdatter,* and Conrad's *The Rover.*

THE USE OF PERIODICALS

Periodicals containing literary material or furnishing background for literary themes are valuable in the teaching of literature. A wide range of magazines, current and bound, may be used in the development of an idea-centered unit. *Holiday, Life, Coronet, The National Geographic Magazine, Reader's Digest,* and *The Saturday Review* proved especially useful in the unit described in Chapter 4. Much of the best of current fiction, which ultimately appears in book form, comes out in the issues of *The Saturday Evening Post, Good Housekeeping,* and similar journals. Some magazines specialize in literary themes—*Scholastic, Literary Cavalcade, The New Yorker, Harper's, The Theatre Arts Monthly,* and the various book review weeklies.[18] A few, like *The Horn Book, Young Wings,* and *Junior Reviewers,* are useful with

[17] George R. Carlsen, "Creating a World Outlook through Literature," *English Journal,* Vol. XXXIII (December, 1944), pp. 525–532.

Charlton Laird, ed., *The World through Literature,* Monograph No. 18, National Council of Teachers of English (New York, Appleton-Century-Crofts, Inc., 1952).

Louise M. Rosenblatt, "Toward a Cultural Approach to Literature," *College English,* Vol. VII (May, 1946), pp. 459–465.

Minnie M. Rugg, "In the Four Seas All Men Are Brothers," *English Journal,* Vol. XXXI (December, 1942), pp. 719–725.

[18] Laura K. Martin, *Magazines for High Schools: An Evaluation of a Hundred Titles* (New York, H. W. Wilson Company, 1950).

Ruth M. Weeks, *Using Periodicals, A Report of the Committee on the Use of Magazines and Newspapers in the English Class* (Champaign, Ill., National Council of Teachers of English, 1950).

younger students. For mature seniors, the *Atlantic Monthly* and similar magazines give perspective and excellent variety in the writing of today. There is writing on things of today in the language of today; there is writing of permanent interest bringing the past into the present. Such subjects in the *Atlantic* are Robert Hillyer's "In My Library, Late Afternoon," poetry; Lucien Price's *Dialogues of Whitehead;* the biography of Hemingway; and T. S. Eliot's "The Three Voices of Poetry." Insight into India, Holland, and Belgium is given not alone by facts but by imaginative writing. Stories and "Accent on Living," a section given over to humorous incidents and personal reflections, help to broaden the range of the student's reading.

THE USE OF RELATED SCHOOL SERVICES

Wise teachers of literature make constant use of such related services as the department of audio-visual instruction and the library.

Audio-Visual Aids

Films are an important ally in the study of literature. A traditional use of them has been showing, after the reading of a book, a film based on it; and many teachers have been disappointed unless they could have the entire film. Such a plan does not make for the maximum usefulness of films, nor does a reversal of the order—seeing a complete film first and then reading the story or play afterward. The latter may even prevent the reading of the book.

Instead of emphasizing the possible identity between the film and the book, teachers should use films to promote the reading of books or to stimulate thinking. A brief film based upon a longer book, whether or not it is part of an English unit, may be valuable in the study of literature. Discussion is essential if the presentation is to be significant. Since that is so, the trend in the films prepared by the Committee of the

National Council of Teachers of English to co-operate with Teaching Film Custodians, Inc., has been to choose comparatively brief excerpts—fifteen or twenty minutes in length. The excerpt, which must be challenging, should be more or less complete in itself. Such brief films can be shown and discussed in a class period.[19] Study guides make it possible to anticipate the showing and indicate a wide variety of ways in which the films may be used.

An excerpt was devised from Dana's *Two Years Before the Mast*. It was not prepared because schools were teaching the book or because they should be encouraged to do so. The film was to be provocative. It should be significant for students faced with entering the Army or Navy, where questions of discipline or restraint might arise. What are one's rights? Questions of discipline arise in school; what has the film to say? The film may easily lead into a unit or contribute to one; possibly one on books that have influenced practice as Dana's log did and as Galsworthy's *Justice* did. Students may not read Henry James's *Washington Square*, but the film excerpt, ending with a question, raises interesting problems of family relationships and the development of personality. *Meet the Forsytes*, an excerpt from the film based on *The Forsyte Saga*, should help in introducing the characters of the novel. It also may precipitate consideration of an era in England or, again, of family relationships. "The Telltale Heart" is a short story, well told through symbolism and useful in that connection alone. It could also be a part of a unit on guilt or conscience. An excerpt in color from *Kim* may lead not only into Kipling's novel of that name and into his other books, but into India and Pakistan, into the responsibilities of young boys, into questions of holiness and philosophies, and into an unlimited range of reading that might include E. M. Forster's *A Passage to India*.

Understanding Movies, a 17-minute film, provides a valu-

[19] Study guides may be secured by sending a postcard to Teaching Film Custodians, Inc., 25 West 43rd Street, New York 36.

able introduction to the showing of films in connection with the study of literature. Brief scenes memorably illustrate directing, acting, photography, editing, and art and music.

Likewise, radio and television may be tools. Transcriptions of *Invitation to Learning* and of other programs have contributed to the discussion of literature. A television version of *Coriolanus* prompted mature students to read the play. Television's *Hamlet* and *Macbeth* had a similar effect.

Filmstrips, which may be stopped at will for comment, offer a rich background for the study of literature.

Students enjoy making tape recordings of their reading, of passages they have memorized, of their programs, and perhaps of the culmination of a unit.

Though pictures and other audio-visual aids have a place in the enrichment of the teaching of literature, they are but tools to help students to translate, as it were, printed words into the scenes and thoughts for which those symbols stand. They make, even in high school, for "reading readiness."

Relation of Literature Teaching to the Library

The study of literature requires close co-operation with librarians,[20] who may provide stimulating exhibits, aid in the securing of books and pictures, and help to encourage students to read by gently and wisely guiding them. In such co-operation, the librarian is assisted by knowing what the teacher is aiming to do and by being informed far enough in advance to gather together all the resources of the library that will be useful in a unit. The teacher also is helped by knowing the resources of the library. How otherwise can he make adequate preparation for teaching a unit, or for guiding the reading of individual students?

It is important also that if personal choice is to enter into the experience of reading, boys and girls should learn how

[20] Frances Clarke Sayers, "The Hills Beyond," *Baltimore Bulletin of Education*, Vol. XXXI (June, 1954), pp. 23–31.

Amelia H. Munson, *An Ample Field* (Chicago, American Library Association, 1950).

to use book lists, catalogs, and other sources of reference in the library. They should know where books are on the shelves and how they are catalogued. In years to come the public library will be their chief source of reading materials. One function of the high school English program, therefore, is to facilitate the carry-over from school to public library.

EVALUATING OUTCOMES IN LITERATURE

It is obvious, as has already been said, that many of the most significant and personal outcomes of the teaching of literature are imponderables and cannot be measured by any known statistical procedures. Perhaps consideration of certain questions teachers inevitably ask about the results of their teaching may help to focus attention on what is important and on what efforts have been made to measure pupil attainment:

1. To what extent have students in my classes learned to relate literature to their own personal living?

2. To what extent have they used reading voluntarily for pleasure, for understanding their own problems, for insight into their world?

3. How much voluntary reading do they do?

4. How much have they grown in power to read literature, to use those reading skills adapted to comprehension of it, to enter imaginatively into its manner of expression, its depth of insight, and its creative power?

5. How able are they to distinguish between the ephemeral and the lasting, the dull and the imaginative, the aesthetic and the pedestrian, the false and the true?

6. What acquaintance have they gained with well-written books of today and yesterday, of our country, of Great Britain, of lands beyond the English tradition?

7. What resources are they familiar with for wise guidance of their own reading after school days are over?

Use of Informal Student Reactions

The answers to some of these questions can be given only after intimate observation of, and conversation with, individual students. Teachers and librarians working with the same individuals can learn much from each other.

Students may be asked to keep a plan for reading, to write answers to questions directed toward an evaluation of the effect of their reading upon their thinking, their attitudes toward others, and their understanding of their world. No topic is more stimulating to some students than "The Autobiography of My Life of Reading." The American Library Association has published such a story.[21]

A part of the evaluation of every unit in literature might well be a subjective question or a brief essay on how the student's reading has affected his pleasure in books, his standards of selection, or his understanding of life. The guidance of such thinking about reading reveals to students some of the major aims of the literature course.

Measures of the Amount and Nature of Voluntary Reading Done

Studies of the amount and nature of voluntary reading done by students are available in many places. Too often the results lack adequate interpretation as to the kinds of reading done, the sources of books read, the motivation for reading, and the breadth and quality of the selections. Much valuable data which would help answer these questions for individuals and for groups lie concealed in file folders kept by certain schools for a period of six years in the life of the same persons. Often the information is kept by columns headed:

Date	Author	Title	Where I Got It	Why I Read It	How I Liked It

---

[21] Margaret A. Edwards, "A Little Learnin'," *ALA Bulletin*, Vol. 50, No. 5 (June, 1956), pp. 379–386.

The replies in the last three columns may be coded with a list of possible responses suggested in advance by the students and mimeographed for filing in the folder. What is *done* with the data is all-important. Stock-takers' reports and evaluations, written once or twice a year by the students themselves following class discussion, are invaluable. So, too, are personal conferences with the teacher to discuss what individuals should do next in their reading. Vertical studies of the reading of the same students over a period of years are much needed as clues to what it is that really influences reading choices.

Personal reaction to each book read, at the time of the reading, is also important—not merely a retelling of the story. Growth can be stimulated as well as measured by the types of techniques used for evaluation.[22]

CONCLUSION

If the study of literature is truly discovery, young people should be stirred and awakened by the thoughts and emotions that come only through reading. They must discover that literature offers experience and insight and enjoyment for meeting their needs.

The time to penetrate the rich offerings of literature is in youth. No one can wait until old age, as Trollope pointed out in *The Claverings:*

[22] Harold B. Dunkel, *General Education in the Humanities* (Washington, D. C., American Council on Education, 1947).

Lou LaBrant, *An Evaluation of Free Reading in Grades 10, 11, and 12 for the Class of 1935,* Ohio State University Studies: Contributions in Education No. 2, rev. ed. (Columbus, Ohio State University Press, 1936).

Dora V. Smith, *Evaluating Instruction in Secondary School English. A Report of the New York Regents Inquiry,* Monograph No. 11, National Council of Teachers of English (Champaign, Ill., National Council of Teachers of English, 1939), o.p.

Eugene R. Smith, Ralph Tyler, and Evaluation Staff, "Record of Reading," in *Appraising and Recording Student Progress* (New York, Harper and Brothers, 1942), pp. 319–328.

If a man have not acquired the habit of reading till he be old, he shall sooner in his old age learn to make shoes than learn the adequate use of a book. And worse again;—under such circumstances the making of shoes shall be more pleasant to him than the reading of a book. Let those who are not old—who are still young, ponder this well.

Implicit in all that has been said is that a teacher of literature must be imaginative, sensitive to literature, aware of the values inherent in it. He must be well read so that he will have wide resources for comparison and allusion. If he has not himself *experienced* literature, it is unethical for him to attempt to teach literature. Every one of his resources is needed urgently to make the little black marks against a white background become symbols of hopes and fears and pleasures, of thoughts and emotions.

The present world invites people to dodge the reading of words. Devices for hearing and seeing, including picture newspapers and magazines, discourage effort to read unadorned pages of print, cold in comparison to brilliantly colored flamboyant illustrations, with hit-and-run headlines. At the same time, the present world makes greater demands on maturity than previous ages.

Growth in the understanding of literature and in its appreciation is growth in maturity as a human being. The result of the study is not a matter of standardized testing, though certain phases, more often intellectual ones, may be tested to a certain extent. But there is no adequate test for emotional growth or aesthetic response.

Literature, the written record of the defeats, victories, dreams of mankind, the record of human reflections and emotions in every conceivable situation, the record of individuals —when individuals are losing their identity—can in a significant and unique way meet the varied needs of youth. Through it man may learn to feel with man. He may gain objective judgments of the course of human life. He may gain a sense of values, of what things are of worth.

BIBLIOGRAPHY
Books

ADAMS, J. Donald, *Literary Frontiers* (New York, Duell, Sloan and Pearce, Inc., 1951).

American Council on Education, *Literature for Human Understanding* (Washington, D. C., The Council, 1948).

————, *Reading Ladders for Human Relations* (Washington, D. C., The Council, 1947).

AMES, Van Meter, *Aesthetics of the Novel* (Chicago, University of Chicago Press, 1928).

BARZUN, Jacques, *God's Country and Mine* (Boston, Little, Brown & Company, 1950).

BIRKETT, Sir Norman, and others, *Books Are Essential* (Toronto, Ambassador Books, Ltd.; London, André Deutsch, Ltd., 1951).

BROENING, Angela M., ed., *Conducting Experiences in English*, Monograph No. 8, National Council of Teachers of English (New York, Appleton-Century-Crofts, Inc., 1939), pp. 13–107.

BROWN, John Mason, *Broadway in Review* (New York, W. W. Norton & Company, Inc., 1940).

COOK, Elizabeth Christine, *Reading the Novel* (Boston, Little, Brown & Company, 1933).

DEBOER, John J., KAULFERS, Walter V., and MILLER, Helen R., "Literature for Human Needs," in *Teaching Secondary English* (New York, McGraw-Hill Book Company, Inc., 1951), pp. 204–230.

Denver Public Schools, *Literature Guide for Use in Junior High Schools* (Denver, Colo., Public Schools, 1951).

EASTMAN, Max, *Enjoyment of Poetry* (New York, Charles Scribner's Sons, 1921).

HIGHET, Gilbert, *People, Places, and Books* (New York, Oxford University Press, 1953).

HOOK, J. N., "Using the Approaches: Fiction and Drama," *The Teaching of High School English* (New York, The Ronald Press Company, 1950), pp. 135–175.

JELINEK, James J., *Experience through Literature* (New York, Exposition Press, Inc., 1948).

LABRANT, Lou, *We Teach English* (New York, Harcourt, Brace & Company, Inc., 1951), pp. 264–311.

LAIRD, Charlton, ed., and others, *World through Literature*, Monograph No. 18, National Council of Teachers of English (New York, Appleton-Century-Crofts, Inc., 1952).

MARK, Milton, *Enjoyment of Drama* (New London, Conn., Arthur C. Crofts Publications, 1940).

MIRRIELEES, Lucia B., *Teaching Composition and Literature in Junior and Senior High School* (New York, Harcourt, Brace & Company, Inc., 1952).

MUIR, Edwin, *Essays on Literature and Society* (London, Hogarth Press, 1949).

National Council of Teachers of English, Commission on the English Curriculum, *The English Language Arts*, NCTE Curriculum Series, Vol. I (New York, Appleton-Century-Crofts, Inc., 1952), pp. 374–396.

RICKERT, Edith, *New Methods for the Study of Literature* (Chicago, University of Chicago Press, 1927).

ROSENBLATT, Louise M., *Literature As Exploration* (New York, Appleton-Century-Crofts, Inc., 1938).

SMITH, Dora V., *Communication, the Miracle of Shared Living* (New York, The Macmillan Company, 1955), pp. 62–78.

SMITH, James Harvey, *The Reading of Poetry* (Boston, Houghton Mifflin Company, 1939).

SMITH, Reed, *The Teaching of Literature in the High School* (New York, American Book Company, 1935).

SPRAU, George, *The Meaning of Literature* (New York, Charles Scribner's Sons, 1925).

STEFFERUD, Alfred, ed., *The Wonderful World of Books* (New York, The New American Library of World Literature, Inc., 1952).

THOMAS, Cleveland A., Chairman, Secondary Section Committee, NCTE, *They Will Read Literature*, A Portfolio of Tested Secondary School Procedures (Champaign, Ill., National Council of Teachers of English, 1955).

WILKINSON, Bonaro, *The Poetic Way of Release* (New York, Alfred A. Knopf, Inc., 1931).

Periodicals

ABBOTT, Allan, "Imaginative Element in Poetry," *Teachers College Record*, Vol. XXVIII (October, 1926), pp. 105–117.

BROWN, John Mason, "American Tragedy," *Saturday Review*, Vol. XXXII (August 6, 1949), pp. 124–129.

———, "Art of Keeping the Mind Refueled," *Vogue*, Vol. 121 (May 1, 1953), pp. 102–103+.

———, "Operation Caesar," *Saturday Review*, Vol. XXXVI (August 15, 1953), pp. 24–26.

BURTON, Dwight L., "Teaching Literature to Our Youth Today," *English Journal*, Vol. XLIV (May, 1955), pp. 274–279.

———, "There's Always a Book for You," *English Journal*, Vol. XXXVIII (September, 1949), pp. 371–375.

———, "Solving Problems of Adolescence through Literature," *English Journal*, Vol. XXXVI (November, 1947), pp. 469–473.

CADY, EDWIN H., "The Role of Literature for Young People Today," *English Journal*, Vol. XLIV (May, 1955), pp. 268–273.

CARLSEN, George R., "Contributions of English to Home and Family Living," *Junior College Journal,* Vol. XX (December, 1949), pp. 209–217.

———, "Creating a World Outlook through Literature," *English Journal,* Vol. XXXIII (December, 1944), pp. 526–532.

———, "Literature and Emotional Maturity," *English Journal,* Vol. XXXVIII (March, 1949), pp. 130–138.

DEVERE, Eona, "Novels Revealing the Development of Character," *English Journal,* Vol. XXXI (January, 1943), pp. 44–45.

EDMAN, I., "Spoken Word: Recordings of Their Own Works by T. S. Eliot and R. Frost," *Saturday Review,* Vol. XXXVI (April 25, 1953), pp. 71+.

EDWARDS, Margaret A., "How Do I Love Thee?" *English Journal,* Vol. XLI (September, 1952), pp. 335–340.

ENO, Isabel V., "Books for Children from Broken Homes," *English Journal,* Vol. XXXVIII (October, 1949), pp. 457–458.

FREEMAN, Bernice, "Teaching Short Stories," *English Journal,* Vol. XLIV (May, 1955), pp. 284–287.

FRY, Christopher, "Poetry in the Theatre," *Saturday Review,* Vol. XXXVI (March 21, 1953), pp. 18–19+.

HARTLEY, Helene W., "Developing Personality through Books," *English Journal,* Vol. XL (April, 1951), pp. 198–204.

KIRCHER, Clara J., "Character Formation through Books: A Bibliography; An Application of Bibliotherapy to the Behavior Problems of Childhood" (Washington, D. C., The Catholic University of America Press, 1945).

McHARRY, Liesette J., "The Teaching of American Ideals: II. An Annotated Bibliography of Books Related to American Life," *Illinois English Bulletin,* Vol. XXXVII (November, 1949), pp. 1–18.

MACLEISH, Archibald, "Why Do We Teach Poetry?" *Atlantic,* Vol. 197 (March, 1956), pp. 48–53.

MEADE, Richard A., "Organization of Literature for Juniors and Seniors," *English Journal,* Vol. XXXVI (September, 1947), pp. 366–370.

MORTON, Charles W., "Accent on Living," *Atlantic,* Vol. 197 (March, 1956), pp. 90–91 (comics).

RAUSHENBUSH, Esther, "Literature for Individual Education," Sarah Lawrence College Publications, No. 1 (New York, Columbia University Press, 1942).

ROODY, Sarah I., "Personality through Literature," *English Journal,* Vol. XXXVI (June, 1947), pp. 299–304.

SAYERS, Frances C., "The Hills Beyond," *Baltimore Bulletin of Education,* Vol. XXXI (June, 1954), pp. 23–31; revised, *NEA Journal,* Vol. 43 (December, 1954), pp. 548–550.

SHAFFER, Virginia, "Broad Reading Program," *Baltimore Bulletin of Education,* Vol. XXVII (March, 1950), pp. 22–25.

SHAFFER, Virginia, "They Can Take It," *English Journal,* Vol. XLI (December, 1952), pp. 526–530.

SHERIDAN, Marion C., "Beyond Fancy's Dream," *English Journal,* Vol. XXXIX (February, 1950), pp. 57–64.

——, "Life Without Literature," *English Journal,* Vol. XXXVII (June, 1948), pp. 291–297.

——, "Teaching a Novel," *English Journal,* Vol. XLI (January, 1952), pp. 8–14.

SMITH, Dora V., "Teaching Poetry for Appreciation," *Educational Outlook,* Vol. IV (January, 1930), pp. 89–104.

SPINKS, Pearl, "Life Brought to Literature through Group Work," *English Journal,* Vol. XXXIX (April, 1950), pp. 201–205.

TUPPER, Marguerite R., compiler, "The Teaching of American Ideals: II. An Annotated Bibliography of Books Related to American Life," *Illinois English Bulletin,* Vol. XXXVII (December, 1949), pp. 1–37.

WAGNER, Martha, "College Students Evaluate High School Readings," *English Journal,* Vol. XLI (May, 1952), pp. 251–253.

WILSON, C. E., and FRAZIER, Alexander, "Learning through Listening to Each Other," *English Journal,* Vol. XXXIX (September, 1950), pp. 367–373.

PREVIEW OF CHAPTER 6

Reading—An All-School Responsibility

Developmental Reading
Remedial Reading
The Need for a Carefully Devised Testing Program

Major Strands of the Developmental Program in Reading

Developing Meaningful Reading Vocabulary
Expanding Recognition Vocabulary
Improving Skill in Attacking Words
Using Context Clues
Adjusting Speed in Reading
Developing Basic Silent Reading Skills
Developing Skill in Oral Reading
Promoting Habits of Reading for Personal Pleasure and Profit

*The Special Province of the English Teacher: Developing
the Essential Skills for Reading Literature*

Reading Fiction
Reading Poetry
Reading Drama
Reading Biography
Reading the Essay or Article

Remedial Reading in the Classroom

Identifying Retarded Readers
Grouping for Instruction within the Class
Assisting Readers with Specific Disabilities
Furnishing a Needed Range of Difficulty in Reading Materials

Identification of Individuals Needing Clinical Help

The Role of the Classroom Teacher
Resource Help

Bibliography

CHAPTER 6

Developing Competence in Reading

IMPROVEMENT of reading in the secondary school has in recent years become the common concern of all teachers. Conditions of life in the mid-twentieth century place increasing demands upon every individual to be able to read intelligently. More and more pupils in the lower ranges of ability are now in high school. Research has revealed the complex nature of reading and the necessity for adapting skills learned in the early grades to the more mature tasks of the high school. This challenge is being met by recognizing the need for both a developmental and a remedial program—the first to develop more mature powers needed to cope with more complex learning activities in secondary schools and the other to aid those pupils who need further assistance with the skills to which they have already been exposed in the elementary school.

READING—AN ALL-SCHOOL RESPONSIBILITY

Developmental Reading

The developmental reading program in the junior and senior high school begins with the first meeting of the classes in September. Up and down the corridors, from Mr. Wallace who teaches industrial arts in the seventh grade to Miss Foster who teaches senior English, the teaching of reading is vital in any class where reading is used as a tool of learning. Until he is graduated, no secondary school student is through with reading instruction though, unlike the elementary school pupil, he may never enroll in a class entitled "Reading." If Miss Foster, Mr. Wallace, and their colleagues are to fulfill their responsibilities in the developmental reading program, they must be aware of several facts concerning reading:

1. *There is a wide range of ability in reading in any secondary school class.* Though Mr. Wallace's students are all classified as seventh-graders, there may be boys and girls who read at the average level of the second and third grade and others who are the equal of tenth- and eleventh-grade students. Some of Miss Foster's seniors may be fifth- and sixth-graders in reading ability while others are at the level of college seniors. Classes above the sixth-grade level commonly present ranges of at least eight school years in ability to read. By the time they reach high school, pupils of high ability have had eight or nine years to outstrip their less favored classmates. The weak become increasingly handicapped through the years. The challenge to adjust methods and materials of instruction to these ranges of ability is among the most serious faced by modern secondary school teachers.

2. *Reading skills differ from subject to subject.* No teacher in the secondary school can afford to yield to the temptation to "let George do it" so far as the teaching of reading is concerned. Differing materials and purposes for reading from class to class impose different reading demands upon students. One of the major aims of the developmental reading program is to train students to "shift gears" from one reading situation to another. Mr. Wallace is destined for disillusionment, for example, if he relies upon the English teacher to teach his seventh-grade class to read the blueprints, diagrams, and directions necessary in industrial arts work. The chemistry teacher who complains that it is his job to teach chemistry, not reading, is hiding his head in the sand. Silent reading ability is related importantly to achievement in almost all subjects; thus, attention to reading and study skills

in each subject area is one of the most profitable avenues to improved learning. No one untrained in the vocabulary and concepts of science is capable of teaching reading in that subject. Fundamental to successful teaching in any subject are an analysis of the reading skills made essential by the purposes and materials of the course and a careful provision for developing these skills within the framework of the course of study.

3. *New and more complex reading demands are made upon students at each level of the school.* Complaints such as "I could teach these students something if they had learned to read in the elementary school" are less and less frequent in secondary schools as teachers become increasingly aware of the complexity of the reading process. Reading is not a simple skill like knitting, which can be mastered at a given point and then applied in any situation ever after. Rather, reading is a complex network of abilities which continues to develop through all the years of school. Although it is impossible to designate any one point at which reading instruction can stop, many secondary schools, assuming that the sixth grade is some kind of magic point of climax in reading development, have allowed reading ability to grow by chance. In the field of literature alone, the road to maturity in reading that lies ahead of the seventh-grade pupil bristles with new, sophisticated skills. Accustomed to following the sequence of events in the conventional story, the seventh-grader will soon read stories which end at the beginning and begin at the end. Shortly he will be required to keep track of many plots and hosts of characters in the novels he reads. If *Ivanhoe* is still in his course of study, for example, he will be required to follow four sets of two chapters each in which Scott brings all the characters up to date with the sound of a bugle. Later, he will be asked to interpret the story in which nothing happens except in the mind of a character, to follow narrative which is furthered by the "stream of consciousness" technique, to recognize the allegory in *Huckle-*

berry Finn or *Moby Dick*. If he reads certain character novels in the tenth grade, he may be asked to trace examples of "foreshadowing" in the narrative. Within two or three years, he may be reading Shakespearean drama, in which time has distorted both the denotation and connotation of words— "the hardest reading in the world," according to one authority.[1] These are but a few illustrations of new reading skills in literature which the student must develop through the high school years. At the heart of the concept of developmental reading is the aim of developing in students at all levels "the increased power in reading demanded by the more complex tasks imposed upon them." [2]

Remedial Reading

In any secondary school class there may be students whose reading ability lags behind their mental ability. These students are in need of remedial or corrective reading based upon careful diagnosis of their disabilities. Too often such students are ignored or labeled as "slow learners," and their problems become increasingly serious as time goes on. A few of these students presenting complex disabilities are in need of individual clinical assistance which goes beyond what can be given by the classroom teacher. Many, however, can be given the help they need within the individual classroom. Clinical phases of reading, together with the possibilities for remedial reading within the classroom, are explored later in this chapter.

The Need for a Carefully Devised Testing Program

It goes without saying that a carefully devised testing program under the direction of experts is necessary to determine where each student is in his progress in reading. Excellent

---

[1] Matthew W. Black, "Hardest Reading in the World," *Education*, Vol. LXIX (May, 1949), pp. 579–589.

[2] National Council of Teachers of English, Commission on the English Curriculum, *The English Language Arts*, NCTE Curriculum Series, Vol. I (New York, Appleton-Century-Crofts, Inc., 1952), p. 397.

survey tests are available to reveal the range of abilities in any given class. These tests are useful for screening out the mature readers from those who merely live up to expectations and for revealing those whose reading ability is far below their intellectual capacities together with those, extremely low in reading ability, who are, however, reading as well as can be expected of them. Such evidence should be available to each teacher for every class he meets. In addition, diagnostic tests of developmental reading skills in various subjects can add much to the teacher's understanding of the reading problems faced by his pupils. Tests in the primary skills of reading can then be given to those in special need of remedial help. The relationship of these results to social and emotional factors is dealt with in the later analysis of remedial reading.

MAJOR STRANDS OF THE DEVELOPMENTAL PROGRAM IN READING

The developmental program in reading includes many different strands, among them enrichment of vocabulary, adjusting speed to purpose and material, improving basic silent and oral reading skills, promoting habits of reading for personal pleasure and profit, and, in the language arts, promoting special skills for the reading of literature.

Developing Meaningful Reading Vocabulary

Basically, reading may be thought of as a process of attaching meaning to symbols. Each word on the printed page acts as a stimulus, directing the reader to certain referents in his experience. A totally strange word has no value as a stimulus unless the reader can analyze it in some way that will unlock meaning in terms of his experience. On the other hand, a reader may recognize a familiar word such as *liberal* or *conservative* and still be unable to bring to it any real meaning from his experience. A word remains meaningless for silent reading purposes unless it has some basis in the reader's experience. Growth in reading vocabulary, which is basic to the development of any skill in comprehension, depends upon: (1) a constantly expanding store of words which can be recognized at sight, and (2) development of skills by which the meaning of new words or familiar words used in new ways may be determined. Each teacher in the junior and senior high schools has a stake in promoting this two-pronged growth in vocabulary.

Each subject area in the secondary school imposes a "technical" vocabulary of new terms and familiar terms carrying new meanings. The social studies, for example, impose a particular burden of abstract and metaphorical terms: *culture, inflation, laissez faire, justice, parity, free enterprise, reactionary, radical, on the fence, pork barreling, tariff wall, pump priming.* These terms cannot be explained by synonyms or graphic portrayal; their meanings must be built inductively through specific illustrations which are related at the students' level of experience. Science materials are replete with long, formidable words often built with Latin and Greek roots, prefixes, and suffixes. The science teacher finds it necessary to teach certain prefixes such as *mono* (monoxide), *di* (dioxide), *tetra* (tetrachloride), *hydro* (hydroelectric), and *endo* (endothermic) and certain suffixes such as *ate* (chlorate), *ite* (chlorite), and *ide* (chloride). The teacher of the language arts, in addition to putting meaning into terms specific to the study of language and literature, has a key responsibility in developing general facility in dealing with words.

Expanding Recognition Vocabulary

Wide reading of material adjusted to the reader's level of ability is undoubtedly the best general means of expanding recognition vocabulary, since new words are encountered constantly and reinforced in context. However, more direct methods are needed, also, to enrich meaning and establish relationships between the verbal symbol and experience.

Ability to deal with new terms sometimes can be developed through direct experience. For example, a junior high school class about to undertake a unit on the sea in literature might visit a nearby shipyard or harbor. A half hour on a real ship would build valuable readiness for such terms as *binnacle, bridge, bulkhead, forecastle, hawser, starboard.* A senior high school class dealing with terms like *impressionistic, symbolistic, romantic,* or *realistic* in writing might visit an art museum to view examples of these approaches in painting.

Opportunities for direct experience of this kind are limited, but possibilities are virtually unlimited for developing meaning through indirect experiences in the form of audio-visual aids—films and filmstrips, recordings, pictures, models, and bulletin boards. For the class studying the various attitudes of authors toward their material, the Charles Laughton–Frederic March film of *Les Miserables* furnishes a common, specific basis for discussing the characteristics of romanticism. Models of stages help students to interpret stage directions in reading drama. Pictorial scenes of the Southeast will help those reading regional literature of that area to visualize *water prairie, bayou, canebrake,* or *Spanish moss.* Preceding a unit on the small town in American literature, the teacher may arrange a bulletin board of scenes from small towns in which certain items in the pictures are numbered and the words with corresponding numbers are listed below. For example, the theater marquee is numbered 4 in one picture, and the word *marquee* is listed as number 4 below it.

Word study aimed at expanding and enriching vocabulary can be individualized to a great extent, and students may share in the teaching. They may keep individual notebooks of alphabetically listed words encountered in their reading which they have trouble recognizing on sight. Or they may keep files of cards with words on one side and meanings on the other, which they can run through quickly from time to time. Using these individual notebooks or files, they may test each other in pairs or small groups. Occasionally, students may be asked to make the meanings of new words clear to the class through pictures, slides, drawings, models, skits, or pantomimes. For example, one senior high school class drew up a list of foreign expressions—*savoir faire, coup de grâce, tour de force, factotum,* and so forth, from their reading. Small groups within the class were given responsibility for presenting one of the terms in skit or pantomime.

For purposes of enlarging vocabulary, the study of word meaning should grow naturally out of the students' reading. Of little value are periodic lists of isolated words for which definitions are looked up in the dictionary and handed to the teacher. However, it may be useful for a class to study short lists of words in connection with a specific reading assignment. For example, in a class about to read Poe's "The Telltale Heart," the teacher may write the following list on the chalkboard:

courageously	suppositions
profound	uncontrollable
sagacity	precautions
causeless	dismembered
motionless	dissemble

Preliminary discussion of the words may help in the reading of the story which follows immediately. Some of the words may be approached through relation to more familiar words: *courageously—courage; sagacity—sage; suppositions—suppose.* The key to others is found in prefixes or suffixes: *causeless, motionless, precautions, dismembered.* A follow-up in which the words are considered in context should be included.

Improving Skill in Attacking Words

The reader at any level may encounter strange words or known words used in unfamiliar ways. If he is efficient, he is able to use one of several types of skills to unlock the meaning of such terms; and the cultivation of these skills of analysis is important in developing reading vocabulary.

Structural analysis, the breaking up of words into smaller parts, is important for successful word attack. Although elementary school programs include considerable training in this type of analysis, junior and senior high school students vary widely in their ability to apply it. They need further training in analysis of words met in their reading in the various subject areas. Reference was made earlier to the science teacher's need to teach certain prefixes and suffixes, and functional teaching of structural analysis of words in the English class was cited above with the example of words from "The Telltale Heart."

Syllabication of words remains a problem for many secondary school students. Knowledge of vowel and consonant sounds and blends is essential to success in syllabication. Most students in the secondary school will have such knowledge, but those who do not will need work in phonetics in special remedial groups. However, facility in the vowel and consonant sounds will not guarantee skill in syllabication; definite teaching of it in context may still be necessary. Some group training might be given in listening for syllables as the teacher reads words orally and the students tap lightly on their desks to indicate the number of beats or syllables they hear. This may be followed by having students write the number of syllables they hear in several words and then check the accuracy of their count in the dictionary. Through the work in reading, spelling, and dictionary study, the teacher should build the following principles of syllabication: (1) If two consonants occur at the end of the first syllable in a two-syllable word, the second consonant usually goes with the second syllable (let-ter, mas-ter) unless the consonants make a diphthong (fa-ther). (2) If a single consonant stands between two syllables, the consonant usually goes with the second syllable (la-bor). (3) If a word ends in *le* (lit-tle, peo-ple), the consonant preceding *le* usually goes with it. (4) When a verb ending in silent *e* drops the *e* and adds *ing*, the consonant is kept with the first syllable (hid-ing). (5) A compound word divides itself between the words (mail-man). (6) Prefixes and suffixes are separated from the root syllables (re-turn-ing).

Using Context Clues

Skill in the use of context clues to meaning helps the secondary school student in attacking unknown words independently. The context in which a word or term is used offers various kinds of clues from which the approximate meaning can be guessed. Some of these types of clues with examples are: [3]

1. The experience clue:
   A pair of crows called *raucously*. (What does "raucously" mean? It means the way crows sound. Everyone has heard the cawing of crows.)
2. The comparison or contrast clue:
   (1) John was *loquacious* while his friend Bill was the silent type.
   (2) The eagerness of the others was in marked contrast to Helen's *apathy*.
3. The synonym clue:
   He laughed. He danced. He had never been so gay.
   He was simply *buoyant*.
4. The summary clue:
   He was completely *disheveled*. His hair was mussed, his shirttail was out, and his trousers were wrinkled. (The summary might precede the word rather than follow it.)
5. The association clue:
   He was out of it in an instant with the *agility* of a pickpocket. (Associating agility with a pickpocket gives a clue to the meaning.)
6. The reflection of a mood or situation clue:
   During the whole of a dull, dark, and soundless day in the autumn of the year, where the clouds hung oppressively low in the heavens, I had been passing alone through a singularly dreary tract of country. At length I found myself, as the shades of evening drew on, within view of the *melancholy* House of Usher.

[3] A number of examples are taken from:
Helen D. Gibbons, "The Meaning Side of Reading," *California Journal of Elementary Education*, Vol. IX (May, 1941), pp. 224–228.
Carol Hovious, *Suggestions for Teachers of Reading, Grades 7–12* (Boston, D. C. Heath & Company, 1939).
Constance M. McCullough, "Learning to Use Context Clues," *Elementary English Review*, Vol. XX (April, 1943), pp. 140–143.

(*Melancholy* sums up the whole mood of the passage and the rest of the passage makes the meaning of *melancholy* clear.)
7. The previous contact clue:
   The cotton gin *emancipated* the southern farmers. (Previous contact with the word, probably in connection with the Emancipation Proclamation.)

These clues to meaning seem obvious to the mature reader, but many high school students are in the habit of skipping unfamiliar words rather than attempting to determine the meaning from context. They need to be made aware of these types of clues and given practice in using them. Teaching of context clues can be incorporated with dictionary study. Since more than one meaning will be given for most words a high school student looks up in the dictionary, he still must determine from context which meaning is appropriate. Students may guess meaning from context clues and then check their accuracy with the dictionary.

Adjusting Speed in Reading

Speed of reading, although it cannot be considered in isolation, is an important aspect of the reading process. Fast reading may not be beneficial nor slow reading harmful per se. Speed in reading is merely a product of the purpose in reading and the nature of the material read. It is virtually impossible to read swiftly through a recipe, a footnote in a biology book, or the fine print on an income tax form; and even if it were possible, it would not be wise in view of the purpose of the reading. Reading is a psychological, not a mechanical, process. Although the reader may be able to read an article in the *Reader's Digest* very rapidly, it is important that he pause on occasion to examine what he has read or to reflect upon an idea.

Plans to increase the rate of reading through use of material flashed on a screen or by means of light bulbs controlling speed frequently disregard the fundamentally psychological nature of reading. Naturally, the student who has a meager vocabulary or poorly developed skills for attacking new words will be a slow reader; consequently, as such skills are stressed in the reading program, speed is directly affected. And since speed is so much a product of purpose in reading, the student is constantly learning to adjust speed in terms of purpose as he is given practice with the basic silent reading skills discussed in the following sections. Thus a major responsibility of the developmental reading program is to help students adjust their speed of reading to various situations. Slow, painstaking reading may be at a premium in reading algebra problems or a Shakespearean play but not in reading an essay by James Thurber. Direct attention can be given to speed to serve specific purposes. For example, the English teacher may occasionally give timed drills in reading magazine articles or short stories. The students may keep records of their rate of reading over a period of weeks, in terms of words read per minute. These drills should be accompanied by appropriate checks on comprehension. Many students will be able to read considerably faster than they do with no adverse effect upon comprehension. They should be encouraged to do so. Others will need much more help with such aids to speed as proper phrase reading, increasing eye span, selecting key words, and recognizing different types of connectives—causal, for example, or additive, and the like.

Developing Basic Silent Reading Skills

A major responsibility of all secondary school teachers is to aid students in developing the skills needed to read successfully for a variety of purposes. The essence of the task is to train students to think with printed material according to their purpose in reading. Among the silent reading skills which junior and senior high school students need to develop are:

1. Reading to follow directions.
2. Reading for details.
3. Reading for main points or ideas.

4. Reading to select data bearing on a question or problem.
5. Reading to determine relationships. (For example, in literature, the student might be reading to understand how a character was influenced by his environment.)
6. Reading to organize. (Some reading situations require the student to organize the material as he reads so as to keep the whole pattern in mind. This he must do, for example, if he is to keep straight the various plots in *Ivanhoe*.)
7. Reading to evaluate or criticize.
8. Reading to compare or contrast.
9. Reading for implied meanings. (This skill, involving constant inference by the reader, becomes increasingly important in the high school. In literature, it involves, for example, determining the significance of an act, understanding symbolism, detecting satire and irony, recognizing allegory.)
10. Reading to form sensory impressions. (The ability to enter imaginatively into a selection through the senses by translating words into sounds, sights, tastes, smells, feelings.)
11. Reading maps, graphs, charts, tables, and so forth.
12. Skimming.

The need for a cumulative attack on skills. Because these basic skills involve thinking with printed material, they need to be refined and expanded at each school level as reading materials become more complex and challenging in line with the students' increased power of thought. Teachers from the seventh grade to the twelfth should teach all of these skills, although the level of material to which the skills are applied will vary according to the maturity of the young people. For example, most students in eighth grade would be able to give the moral of Laing's "The Date Catchers" whereas many seniors would have trouble stating the theme of Hemingway's "The Killers," although the basic skill involved in the two situations is identical.

Teachers may find it helpful to make a master chart of reading skills upon which a record can be kept of the status of each student. From this chart the teacher can tell at a glance which skills need to be especially fostered for individuals or small groups and which skills seem generally weak in the class. In addition, the teacher can check on the chart the frequency of his treatment of these skills, making sure that over a semester or year he will repeat several times and at frequent intervals work with each skill.

Two simple, fundamental principles, therefore, undergird an effective program for developing basic reading skills: (1) Each teacher should make systematic provision for teaching reading skills important to learning in his subject. The importance of the various basic skills varies from subject to subject. For example, reading to form sensory impressions is of little importance in science or mathematics, while reading of maps, graphs, or charts is unimportant in English. (2) Teaching of reading skills should be a functional part of the regular class work. The teacher does not teach English or social studies at one point and reading at another. Although some students may need special remedial work in comprehension skills, reading skills should be dealt with when they are needed in doing an assignment.

Relation of the assignment to the teaching of reading. Each reading assignment presents an opportunity to teach reading skills and should include discussion of the purposes of the reading and directions on how to read for these purposes. The teacher who merely assigns the next 15 pages or a certain short story for the next day and lets the matter drop is missing an important teaching opportunity. Guide questions which emphasize the purposes for reading help students to read more efficiently.

In the literature program, English teachers have an excellent opportunity to provide practice of the basic skills of comprehension.

Developing Skill in Oral Reading

Oral reading skill, like every other reading skill, is developed and maintained by practice. Students should ordinarily be called upon to read aloud only after they have read the material silently. This helps to assure an understanding of the meaning of the passage, so that the oral expression will convey the meaning. It also assures a better quality of performance and less chance of boredom and wasted time for the listeners.

Further assurance of improved performance results when the student reading aloud is the only one looking at the passage. This creates a real audience situation, and quality of performance assumes importance as the reader realizes that the ideas will be brought out only through his effective presentation.

A final assurance of better oral reading lies in the purposeful nature of the situation: the passage is being read for appreciation, better understanding, proof, or some other definite purpose. After a class has read a humorous short story, the teacher might ask, "What were the most attractive characteristics of this story? Who would like to read his favorite passage?" Each student selects a part to read, and as each reads, members of the audience listen to enjoy the humor and to see whether the passage is the same one chosen by them or by someone else. Perhaps the discussion shows that something is misunderstood in the story, and the teacher says, "Find the place that tells. . . . Who will read it for us?" If there is a difference of opinion, the teacher might ask the student to skim for proof and read the passage aloud. Occasionally unison reading of something well liked, such as a poem or a dramatic piece of prose, helps the poor oral reader learn to phrase expressively and to use pitch to heighten meaning.

A student who reads aloud can be no better than his audience.[4] Teaching of listening goes hand in hand with oral reading as the teacher leads the class in considering how to listen. Not only does this involve courtesy to the reader, but in each oral reading situation it demands of the audience clear responsibility for listening for definite purposes. The teacher may say, "Now let's listen to this to decide . . . ," and follow the listening with, "What did you find out about . . . ?" Oral reading should not be a tête-à-tête be-

[4] See Chapter 8, pp. 281 ff.

tween the teacher and an individual student. If the teacher alone understands or is interested, the presentation has little value.

Promoting Habits of Reading for Personal Pleasure and Profit

An all-school opportunity. A good developmental reading program is not limited merely to improving reading skills, for the skills grow in barren soil unless students develop an awareness of the personal rewards in reading. Teachers in all subject areas share the responsibility for promoting life-long reading interests. Different students seek different rewards in reading, and teachers in various subjects may be in a position to foster special interests and to create enduring reading patterns while at the same time enriching study in their fields. In a presentation of the Westward Movement, the social studies teacher might use with junior high school classes such books as Shannon Garst's biographies of Sitting Bull and Buffalo Bill or James Daugherty's *Of Courage Undaunted,* a fictionalized account of the Lewis and Clark Expedition, while at the senior high school level Conrad Richter's *The Sea of Grass* or Walter Van Tillburg Clark's *The Oxbow Incident* would be appropriate. Why not a special bookshelf of the better "Westerns" such as Ross Santee's *Hardrock and Silver Sage,* Lee Leighton's *Law Man,* and Jack Schaefer's *Shane* and *the Canyon?* Supplementary reading for a study of the American Revolution might include such novels as Esther Forbes' *Johnny Tremain* and Emma Patterson's *The World Turned Upside Down,* in which young people live through the thrilling and turbulent events of the Revolution. Contemporary events and problems, too, are personalized and humanized in current literature for young people. Junior high students enjoy Lucy H. Crockett's *Pong Choolie, You Rascal,* a young Korean's adventures in the war; Clara I. Judson's *City Neighbor,* the biography of Jane Addams of Hull House; and Jesse Jackson's *Call Me Charley,* the story of a lone Negro boy in a northern school. Senior high school students may read James A. Michener's gripping *The Bridges of Toko-Ri,* dealing with the Korean War; Jean Gould's *Sidney Hillman, Great American;* or Robert Sherwood's *Roosevelt and Hopkins.*

Some high school boys, and occasionally girls, are science enthusiasts. General reading in science has mushroomed since the dropping of the atomic bomb. The science teacher may recommend science fiction of the quality written by Robert Heinlein, A. A. Van Vogt, and Ray Bradbury, or related nonfiction such as Jonathan Leonard's *Flight into Space* or Charles Coombs' *Skyrocketing into the Unknown.* The immediate environment, too, provides a springboard for building reading interests through use of such books as Rachel Carson's *The Sea Around Us* or, at a less mature level, *The Inexhaustible Sea* by Hawthorne Daniel and Francis Minot. Books like Ruth Fox's *Milestones of Medicine* and *William Crawford Gorgas: Tropic Fever Fighter* by Beryl Williams and Samuel Epstein furnish other possibilities for broad reading in science.

Similar avenues to personal reading interests are open in other classes. The physical education teacher might direct students to a wealth of books and magazines in sports, hobbies, and recreation, while in home economics such topics as etiquette, grooming, home decoration, and family living are points of departure for individualized reading. To many boys, the field of automobiles, hot-rods, and airplanes is all-engrossing. Might not teachers of industrial arts capitalize on this interest in guiding reading?

The key role of the English teacher. Through literature, the English teacher makes an especially important contribution to the development of reading interests and tastes. A broad program of individual reading guidance is essential in any well-rounded curriculum in literature. Such guidance,[5] often carried on through broad topical units in which

[5] See Chapter 5, pp. 126–135; 138.

students read many different selections bearing on a central topic or theme, must be based upon a keen awareness of the general interests and preoccupations of adolescents at various levels, for these interests are important in motivating reading. Seventh- and eighth-grade pupils are universally interested in animals, for example. With reading guidance they may go from the dog stories of Jim Kjelgaard and the horse stories of Dorothy Lyons to *Lassie Come Home, My Friend Flicka,* and ultimately perhaps to *Moby Dick.*

Relations with parents and other adolescents, particularly those with the opposite sex, are especially acute concerns of ninth- and tenth-graders. A basis for enduring interest in reading has been built when students find their own emotional experiences in imaginative literature. The opportunity for building and broadening this base is excellent at this level as young people read imaginative treatments of their own culture. The key to the continuing popularity of Maureen Daly's *Seventeenth Summer,* for instance, lies in the essential truth with which it presents a first love affair. Other books which treat adolescent problems artistically are Mary S. Stolz's *To Tell Your Love,* Betty Cavanna's *Going on Sixteen,* Paul Annixter's *Swiftwater,* and James Summers' *Prom Trouble.*

Among students at the eleventh- and twelfth-grade levels there is an intangible but compelling curiosity about what people live for, which leads to interest in novels like F. Scott Fitzgerald's *The Great Gatsby,* Thomas Wolfe's *You Can't Go Home Again,* and biographies like Joseph Gollomb's *Albert Schweitzer, Genius in the Jungle,* Rachel Baker's *Sigmund Freud,* and Catherine Marshall's *A Man Called Peter.*

Love remains a predominant interest at the upper levels, and for the girls, especially, furnishes powerful motivation for reading, though sometimes at no higher level than *True Confessions.* From Daphne Du Maurier's fiction, girls may be guided to Benedict and Nancy Freedman's *Mrs. Mike* and Rose Wilder Lane's *Let the Hurricane Roar,* and then perhaps to the Brontë novels and Elizabeth Barrett Browning.

It is impossible to analyze the genesis of all reading interests. Each personality finds its own rewards in reading. Escape from the confines of the moment, a universal appeal of literature, may lie for some students in the humor and whimsy of Ogden Nash, James Barrie, or James Thurber; for others, in the sea adventure of Armstrong Sperry, Edward Ellsberg, Robert Louis Stevenson, or Joseph Conrad; for others, in the introspection of Emily Dickinson; for still others, in science fiction. Through variety and breadth of offerings, the literature program aims to involve each student in reading experiences that are rewarding to him.

THE SPECIAL PROVINCE OF THE ENGLISH TEACHER: DEVELOPING THE ESSENTIAL SKILLS FOR READING LITERATURE

Maturity in appreciation of literature presupposes the development of the skills essential to reading the various literary types—novel, short story, poetry, drama, biography, and essay or article. In general, these skills involve specific application to literature of the basic silent reading skills with the additional consideration of difficulties posed by the different literary types. Again, the teacher's essential task is to train students to think with various kinds of literary material according to the purpose in reading. Of course, these skills, like any reading skills, will develop gradually according to the reader's intelligence, interest, and general maturity.

Reading Fiction

Skills involved in the reading of fiction are many and complex. Students must learn to evaluate the truth or falsity of the author's presentation of human experience. They must discover the central theme of the work and relate the details to it. They must learn to follow different types of structure in the plot.

Evaluating truth to human experience. Young people frequently report that they liked a story or novel because "it was so true to life" without any real understanding of what they are saying. They need practice in evaluating fiction in terms of elements which make for real truth to human experience or lack of it. Among the skills essential to this purpose are:

1. *Reading to determine cause and effect in events.* The happenings in good fiction, like happenings in life, rest upon a basis of cause and effect, whereas inferior fiction is characterized by rootless accumulations of events. Students should be taught to ask themselves, "Was there any preparation for this happening, any reason for it in what has gone before, or did this happen purely by chance or coincidence?" Senior high school students may look for examples of foreshadowing in skillful writing. After reading an O. Henry short story, they may look back to see if the writer purposely led them astray in order to trick them at the end or whether the surprise ending could grow logically out of the story.

2. *Reading to discover whether there is development or metamorphosis of character.* Students need to be made aware of the difference between changes in characters which are based upon skillful development and changes based upon sudden, magical transformations. Junior novels frequently present "mousy" little heroines who blossom into vivaciousness overnight because a wise aunt comes to town and changes the hairdo and style of dress of the heroine. This can be contrasted to the logical development of the main character in something like Betty Cavanna's *Going on Sixteen.* "The Outcasts of Poker Flat" presents a good example of metamorphosis of character in the short story. A frequent guide question in reading fiction should be, "Were the person's acts predictable from his character?"

3. *Reading to judge precision and originality in character*

portrayal. Another helpful guide question in reading fiction is: "Are the characters real or merely representatives of types?" Immature fiction often resorts to stereotyped or stock characters. Students enjoy finding in their reading stereotyped little grandmothers, old-maid school teachers, visor-wearing, gum-chewing newspaper editors, stupid Irish policemen, or fabulously virtuous football coaches who are interested only in building character. Radio programs and movies might be a starting point for the study of character stereotypes with junior high school students. The stereotype of the adolescent in the Henry Aldrich–Corliss Archer tradition is one that interests and infuriates adolescents.

4. *Reading to judge authenticity of dialogue.* This skill is developed, of course, only as students acquire basis for judgment. For example, most high school readers are in no position to judge the authenticity of dialogue involving two tradesmen of Elizabethan London, but they may act as critics of the speech of American high school students or New York taxi drivers or Middle West politicians in fiction. Most junior high school students could detect in a recent novel the falsity in this bit of conversation by a seventeen-year-old baseball player who has just been offered an athletic scholarship: "I appreciate the offer more than I can tell you, sir. But it isn't a real business proposition. I mean you are offering to lend us considerably more money than we can offer security for, are you not?"

5. *Reading to judge validity of description.* Inferior fiction is larded with description which fills no essential purpose or which resorts to clichés like "black as pitch," "swarming like ants," and "shivers ran down his spine." Students should be given practice in noting description carefully to see if it is related to the central theme or purpose of the story and actually creates a sensory impression. Description of action, such as in sports fiction, might be a good starting point with seventh-grade pupils who could rule on quality of description in a recent basketball story which insists that

"Whiz! Boom! Swish!" represents the pass, the shot, and the resultant basket.

Discovering theme or central purpose. Fiction may have various purposes: simply to entertain through an unusual, gripping, or humorous story; to present a serious social or philosophical idea; to satirize; to create an effect or impression. Students need practice in reading fiction of all these types in order to discern the theme or purpose. Most students will have little difficulty in following the sequence of events in an adventure story, but they will need much training in reading stories which merely reveal a character or present an idea in a subtle fashion. Group reading and discussion of these kinds of stories will help young people learn to infer character from scanty clues, to seek allegorical significance beneath surface events, and to look for meaning in symbols. Well-selected guide questions will help students to center attention on important details. In group reading these guide questions may be differentiated according to the range in ability and maturity of the class. In a class reading Ernest Hemingway's *The Old Man and the Sea,* for example, one group may work with questions purely on the literal level of interpretation while the superior group may be assigned questions dealing with the allegorical significance of the story. Of course, as students develop an acquaintance with authors, they will know what to expect from Edgar Allan Poe and Nathaniel Hawthorne, from James Thurber and John O'Hara.

Relating detail to central theme or purpose of the selection. Mature discrimination in reading literature is dependent upon several types of skill in relating details to the central theme or purpose of a selection. The first of these is skill in determining the attitude of the author toward his material. Details in a piece of fiction take on different significance depending upon the writer's attitude, and senior high school students may be made aware of these different attitudes. At the one extreme is the naturalistic writer who is bent upon presenting a "slice of life," a stark cross section of reality. This type of story, frequently found in *The New Yorker* magazine, for example, tends to baffle and irritate adolescent readers until they realize the purpose of naturalistic writing. At the other extreme is the symbolist whose details, unimportant at the literal level, are merely symbolic representations of experience. Only a few of those in high school will be able to comprehend Joyce and Lawrence, but an acquaintance with symbolism and a habit of looking below the surface of details can begin early in the junior high school as students discuss the significance of the blue willow plate in Doris Gates's *Blue Willow* and the black coffee in James Street's *Goodbye, My Lady*. This can lead to a consideration of the symbolic value of the wolverine in Paul Annixter's *Swiftwater* and later of the green light in F. Scott Fitzgerald's *The Great Gatsby*.

Skill in recognizing "point of view" in fiction is also important in relating detail to the central theme or purpose of a selection. Most students are accustomed to the "omniscient" point of view in which the author projects himself into all characters, but they find it harder to interpret the story or novel written from the point of view of a specific character. Ninth- or tenth-grade readers may be asked to tell how Maureen Daly's "Sixteen" might have been different if written from the point of view of an adult rather than a teen-ager, and older students might be asked the same question about Sherwood Anderson's "I'm a Fool."

Skill in relating detail to the central purpose of a selection will enable superior senior high school students to make several additional distinctions which denote mature reading: (1) between journalism and literary art in fiction which deals with historical events; (2) between propaganda and literary art in fiction which deals with social problems; (3) between relevance and irrelevance of sordid material in fiction.

In order to make the first distinction, the reader must

have practice in answering the questions: "Does the book stress the universals of experience—the thoughts and feelings of people—or the external happenings? Does the choice of detail make us live through historical events or merely view them?"

All fiction which deals with social problems is special pleading of a sort, but some rises above the propaganda level. One of the main criteria is the author's handling of detail. A novel such as Laura Z. Hobson's *Gentleman's Agreement*, a protest against anti-Semitism, fails to rise above the propaganda level because the reader's emotions are strictly channeled. Through a series of scenes he is made angry about anti-Semitism and the people who practice it, but there is no real penetration into the motivations of these people. A novel like Richard Wright's *Native Son*, an angry protest against the Negro's status, rises to literary art because it studies the nature of race hatred through the motivations of people, giving the reader alternatives in emotion.

Fiction of the past three decades has frequently included sordid experience and language. Controversial books like John Steinbeck's *The Grapes of Wrath*, Thomas Higgins' *Mr. Roberts*, and James Jones's *From Here to Eternity* have been problems to high school librarians and teachers of literature.

These are some of the attitudes expressed:

1. Literature is one of the most potent sources in public schools for developing moral and spiritual values. What is read and what is talked about affect behavior.

2. Since the amount of free time which a teen-ager has for reading is limited, he should be encouraged to read literature which is most likely to facilitate his own personal and social adjustment at the same time that it increases his enjoyment of life.

3. Until young people have read creatively a wealth of literature which offers adequate personal and social adjustment, they will not see as unsatisfactory (both individually

and socially) the pathological or sordid behavior with which such books deal.

If teachers or librarians find that teen-agers are reading or are talking about such books—even the motion picture versions of them—discussion should center on whether the sordid details are essential for developing the theme of the book. Are these details necessary (a) to the reader's understanding of what motivates the character and (b) to his judging the adequacy of the character's adjustment to life?

Following different types of plot structure. High school readers will meet various types of plot construction in the stories and novels they read. Most will have little trouble with the plot which presents a straight chronological sequence of events, but they will need training in following the story which starts with a problem, regresses in time to tell how it arose, and moves forward in time to tell how it was solved; or the one which starts at the end, goes back to the beginning, and runs on to meet the starting point, the end of the person's life. In their early acquaintance with plots of this type, it may help students to draw jagged time lines to show the chronology of the story. In the novel, particularly the long nineteenth-century novels, students have the problem of following several plots involving various groups of characters through hundreds of pages. Simple charts showing the various plot strands and the characters involved may help, although the need for too many charts and diagrams may indicate that the novel is too difficult for the level of ability of the readers.

Reading Poetry

The unique characteristics of the other types of literature demand additional skills. Poems, like individual pieces of fiction, may have different purposes. The didactic poem like Holmes's "The Chambered Nautilus" must be read slowly and reflectively and paraphrased if the reader is to get the idea the poet is expressing. On the other hand, it is needless to try to paraphrase a poem like Sandburg's "Fog" which seeks only to create a word picture or impression. Narrative poetry may have a regular time pattern like fiction.

Perhaps the primary purpose of poetry is to produce an emotional impact. Students need to be made aware of the devices through which this is achieved. The first of these devices is rhythm. Most teachers have discussed with students the galloping rhythm in "How They Brought the Good News From Ghent to Aix," the rhythm of bird flight in Shelley's "To a Skylark," the rhythm of the sea wave in "Sea Fever." But fewer have made students aware of the rhythm, based upon the cadences of the human voice, in poetry like that of Carl Sandburg or Robert Frost. Oral reading and listening to recorded readings by professional artists will help to develop a feeling for this type of movement.

Rhyme is a second device by which emotional effects are produced. Two rhymes coming together produce a gayer effect than two far apart. Students often enjoy discussing the effects of various kinds of rhymes. Of course, rhyme patterns may also serve as the key to the organization of ideas in a poem. In the Italian sonnet, for example, the first eight lines (*abbaaba*) set forth a problem or situation while the last six (*cdcdcd* or *dcedce*) may present a solution.

Word color involving groupings of sounds is another device for creating effects. Students may look for the long sounds in "The Raven" (*oo, ee,* and *ie*) which produce an effect of dark melancholy and the quick sounds in "L'Allegro" which express gaiety. Imagery created by figures of speech—simile, metaphor, personification—is another means by which the poet reproduces emotional experience. In reading a line such as "The street light like a lonely sentinel," the reader, if he is to reproduce the effect, must reach into his experience to turn the simile into a mental picture. Of course, definitions and abstract discussion of imagery and figures of speech will not help students to enter imaginatively into the poem, or to re-create the sensory impression, which is the aim of teaching. Young people need much experience in turning words into mental pictures and sensory effects. It may be helpful occasionally for the teacher to read a selection aloud and have the students attempt to write what it made them see or feel.

The mechanics of poetry cause difficulties especially for junior high school students, many of whom attempt to read line by line even if there is no punctuation to indicate such stops. They need to be made aware that a line in poetry has nothing to do with a sentence or thought unit and that, as in prose, one must read according to the punctuation. Inversion in word order is another stumbling block to comprehension in poetry:

> Full many a gem of purest ray serene,
>   the dark unfathomed caves of
>   ocean bear . . .

Practice and group reading and discussion of poetry will make the inverted sentence pattern familiar.

Reading Drama

Drama places upon the reader a tremendous burden of conjuring up mental pictures and inferring ideas from scanty clues. Many students need much more help in establishing the scene in their minds than they get, for example, from the opening of Lady Gregory's *The Rising of the Moon:*

> SCENE: Side of the quay in a seaport town. Some posts and chains. A large barrel. Enter three policemen. Moonlight.
>
> Sargeant, who is older than the others, crosses the stage to right and looks down steps. The others put down a paste-pot and unroll a bundle of placards.

"Side of the quay in a seaport town" may mean little in terms of visual images to many students. Pictures or drawings, slides, filmstrips, and motion pictures are especially important to students reading "period" plays which demand the visualizing of types of dress, architecture, and the like.

In reading drama, as in some types of fiction, the reader

must form his estimates of character completely by indirect means—what the character says and does, what others say about him—just as one does in real life. "Characterize Lady Macbeth" (or any other character) assumes that a student has developed the ability to infer from clues. Many plays commonly read in high school were written in earlier centuries. Students need to be taught to think about these plays in terms of the time and place they represent. For example, many people of Shakespeare's day believed seriously in witches and ghosts; and the ghosts and witches in Shakespeare's plays are real, important characters, whereas contemporary plays usually introduce spirits for symbolic or humorous purposes. Allusions to contemporary events or people, now obscure, present a reading problem in older plays. The background of key allusions should be presented, by the teacher or individual students, before or during the reading of a play.

Stage directions create another specific reading problem in drama. Students should form the habit of noting stage directions carefully rather than skipping over them, which is the natural inclination. Careful reading of the first scene is especially important in many plays. In general, drama requires a slower reading rate than fiction.

Reading Biography

Mature reading of biography demands two major skills with which junior and senior high school teachers may be concerned: (1) skill in following various patterns of organization, and (2) skill in critical evaluation. In organization, biographies are either narrative, in which the events of the subject's life are presented in chronological order; or expository, in which various types of organization may be used. Junior high school teachers should be concerned primarily with narrative biographies, which furnish a natural bridge from fiction to the more difficult expository biography. But comprehension and enjoyment of biography in the senior high school will be enhanced if students learn to recognize some of the ways in which expository biographies are organized. For example, one biography of Mark Twain deals in turn with various influences upon him—his family, his boyhood experiences, his travels abroad. Lincoln's character and importance are estimated in one treatment through an analysis of a number of key episodes in his life, not necessarily in chronological order.

Critical reading of biography may be started early in the junior high school. For example, the student reading Shannon Garst's *Sitting Bull, Champion of His People* may be asked to find incidents which are obviously fictitious and those that could be based upon factual record. This can lead in the senior high school to checking the documentation of the biographer. For example, the reader might be suspicious of a recent biography of Carlos Romulo based almost entirely upon Romulo's own speeches and writings. Beginning in the junior high school, too, students should be taught to check the biographer's relationship to his subject. One would be more inclined to take seriously Mabel Robinson's *Runner of the Mountain Tops*, a biography of Agassiz, than one by a person with no scientific background. *A Man Called Peter*, a biography of Peter Marshall written by his wife, is meant as a monument and is therefore a very different type of biography from a study of Franklin Roosevelt by a lifelong Republican in which debunking may be the objective.

Reading the Essay or Article

Because of their diversity in form and content, essays and articles require the use of the whole gamut of reading skills. One ninth-grade anthology, for example, includes eight different essays and articles ranging from a humorous sketch by James Thurber to a deductively organized discussion of the habits and characteristics of Britons. Magazine articles are excellent for teaching basic reading skills. Essays and articles frequently change from one type of discourse to another. Within a single essay there may be shifts from enumeration to explanation, to chronology of events, to analysis, to exhortation or persuasion. This is often true, too, of textbook material. Occasionally, senior high school students may make rough outlines tracing the changes from one type of presentation to another. Practice in recognizing inductive and deductive patterns of organization also will help students increase their efficiency in reading general expository material. In the deductive pattern, the author presents general principles or conclusions first and then develops them with details, illustrations, or anecdotes; whereas in the inductive pattern, details are used to build up to a generalization.

REMEDIAL READING IN THE CLASSROOM

The dividing line between developmental reading and remedial reading in the classroom is a tenuous one. The general program stressing vocabulary development, basic comprehension skills, and interests in reading strikes at the heart of reading disability among high school students. The more effective the developmental program becomes, the less acute is the need for remedial work. Yet there are those who need specific, intensive reading instruction to correct deficiencies, and most of them can be assisted through remedial instruction within the regular classroom.

Identifying Retarded Readers

Initial diagnosis. Simply through observation, teachers can identify many of the students with reading problems. Common symptoms are inattentiveness, confusion concerning the class work, and poor achievement. However, as has already been said, more systematic diagnosis through standardized tests is needed as a basis for a plan of attack on reading problems. Measures of mental ability and of overall silent reading ability are needed in order to identify stu-

dents who are retarded in reading. Any class will present a
wide range in both mental age and reading age; but when
the teacher compares the two, he will find that the reading
ability of some individuals lags behind their mental ability.
These students are the retarded readers. When reading age
is two or more years behind mental age, reading disability
is becoming serious. Among the nonretarded readers may
be slow learners whose reading ability, though very low, is
consistent with their mental ability. The majority of the
genuinely retarded readers will come from the average and
above-average range in mental ability.

Categories of retarded readers. Even though the retarded
readers have been identified in a class, further diagnosis may
be necessary before the students are grouped for special instruction. Some of the general tests of silent reading ability
give little indication of specific weaknesses, and it may be
well to administer to the retarded readers useful measures
such as the diagnostic sections of the diagnostic reading
tests which cover vocabulary, auditory and silent comprehension, rates of reading, and word attack. After diagnosis,
teachers will usually find three types of retarded readers:

a. Generally retarded readers who are deficient because of absence
   from school, lack of interest, lack of maturity, or trouble with
   hearing and vision.
b. Readers with specific disabilities in word recognition, comprehension, or speed.
c. Readers with complex disabilities who need individual, clinical
   help.

Grouping for Instruction within the Class

After the different types of readers have been identified,
provision must be made for caring for the needs of each of
them. In most schools, this will be accomplished by the formation of small groups within the class or by flexible assignments involving special tasks for special groups.

The nonretarded readers. For the nonretarded readers, the
special small-group activities will be an extension of the de-

velopmental reading program and will provide opportunity for further enrichment and individualization. Superior readers may be given a chance to deal, individually or in a group, with very mature material and practice some of the more mature critical skills. Some of these students would profit from working with the special reading exercise material which accompanies some of the current magazines. Occasionally, superior readers might be used as "coaches" in the remedial groups. With the slow learners in the nonretarded group, that is, those whose reading level is low but in line with their intelligence, the main aim is horizontal enrichment—wide reading suited to their level of ability. The slow learner whose reading ability is correspondingly low needs material with a high interest value for his level of maturity but a feasible level of reading difficulty. In addition to appropriate trade books, anthologies prepared especially for retarded readers may prove useful.

The generally retarded readers. The group of generally retarded readers is in need of varied practice in reading skills. Creating interest in reading is usually a vital problem with these students who will show swift gains if a real interest is aroused. In the beginning, current newspapers and magazines are useful in motivating reading. Later, general workbooks or manuals available from many publishers prove helpful.

Assisting Readers with Specific Disabilities

1. *Lack of recognition vocabulary.* Meager recognition vocabularies can best be augmented through wide reading of easy material. Again, current newspapers, magazines, and trade books of appropriate difficulty will be important for this group. Along with wide reading, more direct techniques should be used. Teachers and students may make sets of flash cards with words which should be recognized instantly at the particular grade level of the members in the group. Practice sessions with these flash cards should be frequent

and brief. The students may also keep individual dictionaries of words which they have trouble recognizing on sight. Occasionally those in the group might test each other with sentences which contain words from material they are reading in the class or the small group.

2. *Insufficient or faulty methods of attack on words.* Since meager recognition vocabulary and deficiency in skills for attacking new words may go hand in hand, it is often unnecessary to deal with the two disabilities in separate groups. Some students may lack ability in phonetic analysis, structural analysis, use of context clues, or all three. Some readers, especially in the junior high school, may not have mastered the printed representation of initial consonant sounds, the consonant blends (*bl, br, ch, cr, dr, gl, gr, sch, scr, skr, squ, thr,* and the like), and the vowel sounds. Some possible techniques for helping them are these: writing from dictation words with troublesome combinations; oral reading and hearing the teacher and others in the group read orally; listing on the chalkboard words which contain the same sound; completing rhymes, for example, writing or choosing a word that rhymes with "tilt"; collecting from their reading words which contain various sounds and testing others in the group on them; using the pronunciation key in the dictionary; and using workbooks which contain material on phonics. In addition to the work in phonetic analysis which may be needed, students in this group will require much more experience in structural analysis and use of context clues of the type discussed under the developmental program.

3. *Poor comprehension.* Some students who have adequate command of skills for attacking new words but are deficient in comprehending what they read may form another group for remedial work. Their need is particularly acute for learning to read for a variety of purposes, to think with the words they are reading in relation to a definite purpose. For these students the teacher should devise exercises involving reading for various purposes in appropriate ma-

terial. Some of the reading workbooks available will help.
The remedial work should especially stress practice in getting the central thought of a sentence, paragraph, or longer
selection. Some useful exercises are: (1) underlining key
words in sentences; (2) reducing passages to 15-word tele-
grams; (3) building sentences by starting with subject and
verb and adding qualifiers; (4) selecting the most important
sentence in a paragraph; (5) giving appropriate titles to
paragraphs and longer selections; (6) matching clipped
newspaper articles with the appropriate headlines; (7) outlining; (8) writing précis.

4. *Lack of speed.* It was pointed out earlier in this chapter
that speed of reading cannot be considered in isolation but
that direct concern with speed in relation to material and
purpose for reading is important for all students. In general,
speed of reading and power of comprehension correlate
highly, and most high school students will learn to adjust
speed as they develop general reading proficiency and become aware of varying purposes in reading. However, some
students, ranking relatively high in comprehension, may be
habitually slow readers who carry on a painstaking, word-by-
word process in all situations. These individuals may form
another remedial group for specific attention to reading rate.
Within the group, further timed drills, such as those discussed earlier, should be given. When the student discovers that his comprehension does not suffer with increased
speed, he may break away from his overintensive habit in
reading. Reading for the main point or gist of a paragraph or
selection should be particularly emphasized in the group.
These students will need further help in reading by phrases
rather than by individual words. Drill material for this purpose is easily prepared. Mimeographed sheets of material in
pyramid form with lines of gradually increasing length are
useful. The student can practice reading each line at a glance
and mark his own progress in increasing eye span. Or material may be prepared in regular paragraph form with lines

separating logical reading phrases as in: A tall man/wearing high boots/sat across the room.

Furnishing a Needed Range of Difficulty in Reading Materials

It should be emphasized again at this point that grouping students within the classroom in order to furnish appropriate help or stimulation to those similarly gifted or handicapped is only part of the answer to the problem. Furnishing a wealth of reading material suited to the range of ability and interests represented in the class is all-important. When a seven-year spread separates the best from the poorest reader in the class, a similar spread of reading materials should be available in the classroom. This does not mean that a third-grade reading textbook with pictures of happy children at play should be furnished to a thirteen-year-old boy who reads at the third-grade level. It means that simple magazines and easy articles clipped from adult periodicals, and books prepared especially for overage readers, should be assembled. Helps for the selection of such materials appear in many sources.[6]

The Children's Catalog, a buying list for elementary school libraries, published by the H. W. Wilson Company, and Eloise Rue's *Subject Index to Books for the Intermediate Grades* are also useful. Nothing, however, can take the place

[6] Glenn M. Blair, *Diagnostic and Remedial Teaching in Secondary Schools* (New York, The Macmillan Company, 1946).

Anita Dunn and others, *Fare for the Reluctant Reader,* rev. ed. (Albany, N. Y., Capital Area School Development Association, Albany State Teachers College, 1952).

Donald D. Durrell and Helen B. Sullivan, *High Interest–Low Vocabulary Booklist* (Boston, Mass., Boston University, School of Education, 1950).

Margaret K. Hill, *Bibliography of Reading Lists for Retarded Readers,* Extension Bulletin, No. 681, rev. ed. (Iowa City, Iowa State University, 1953).

Cloy S. Hobson and Oscar M. Haugh, *Materials for the Retarded Reader* (Topeka, Kan., State Superintendent of Public Instruction, 1954).

George D. Spache, *Good Books for Poor Readers* (Gainesville, Reading Laboratory and Clinic, University of Florida, 1954).

Ruth M. Strang, Christine B. Gilbert, and Margaret C. Scoggin, *Gateways to Readable Books: An Annotated Graded List of Books in Many Fields for Adolescents Who Find Reading Difficult,* 2nd ed. (New York, H. W. Wilson Company, 1952).

of personal conference between student and teacher and constant try-out of books to suit the individual interests and needs of the reader.

The problem is not peculiar to English. No student reading with seventh-grade reading ability in the eleventh grade can possibly keep up with a class using an eleventh- or twelfth-grade textbook in science or social studies. He may even impair his reading ability and develop emotional blocks by attempting to do so. There are helps in these subjects also: for example, Helen M. Carpenter's *Gateways to American History; An Annotated Graded Bibliography for Slow Learners in Junior High School,* published by the H. W. Wilson Company in 1942. There is no field in which more good, simple books have been published in the last twenty years than in the field of natural science. They are listed in all elementary school indexes and in many courses of study.

It goes without saying that more intelligent readers also need the stimulation of materials which challenge their best efforts. Many such titles appear in the books mentioned in this chapter. The teacher should constantly check the range of reading materials in use in his classroom against the range of reading ability represented in his students. No one textbook can possibly meet the needs of all. How members of the class can work together on a single theme with widely differentiated reading materials furnished in classroom and library is illustrated in Chapter 4. The cost may seem prohibitive, but, in reality, schools that have tried it find it less expensive than furnishing a large anthology or a ponderous textbook in physics to everyone in the class.

IDENTIFICATION OF INDIVIDUALS
NEEDING CLINICAL HELP

In secondary schools, everywhere in the United States, there is awareness of a need for direct and continuous instruction in reading. In several large cities, the number of cases requiring attention is of sufficient size to warrant a full-time staff to assist the classroom teacher in the reading improvement program.

The Role of the Classroom Teacher

The classroom teacher, in such cases, plays an important role (1) in helping to identify individuals who should be referred to the central office division of reading analysis, and (2) in assisting the student to maintain a high level of skill after he returns to a regular English class from a clinical or remedial program.

In Baltimore, the classroom teacher is the key person in identifying a student as a reading problem.[7] Some indications of trouble are: limited growth in classroom situations, achievement on a standardized reading test below grade level; and a minimum Stanford-Binet IQ of 85. Students rating below 85 are considered if they do not present problems of general retardation.

Since it is recognized that in most instances reading disabilities are brought about by more than one cause, diagnostic reading tests alone are not considered sufficient for the study of a student's reading problem. Information on personality characteristics, on the incidence of irregular attendance and on physical defects is also secured. To aid in a better understanding of the student, an interview with the parent is arranged whenever possible.

Each Baltimore student referred to the clinic is given four basic tests: (1) a vocabulary sampling which provides an index to his sight vocabulary level; (2) an informal reading inventory which yields an index to his instructional or teaching level, his frustration, and his hearing comprehension level; (3) the vocabulary subtest of the Stanford-Binet Scale; (4) visual and hearing screening tests. Continuous study of the reading growth of the students under instruc-

---

[7] Mary Shapiro, Specialist, Reading Analysis Program, Baltimore, Maryland, Public Schools.

tion is maintained in order to further validate this pretesting program.

Philadelphia [8] has had a comprehensive secondary school reading program since 1948. Early emphasis stressed remedial work with small groups having low achievement in reading but average (or better than average) ability. Of comparable importance is the developmental work in which teachers and students of regular classes are involved in a directed program of reading improvement in all subject areas.

The remedial classes, also called "special English" or "reading improvement" classes, are held daily for at least a full term of five months. The maximum number of students in each group is set at fifteen. Classroom teachers and counselors recommend individuals whose needs warrant consideration for inclusion in the program, and the reading teacher makes the selections from these recommendations following a personal interview, an informal reading inventory, and a study of each student's cumulative records and his counseling and psychological records, as well as the results of reading achievement and nonlanguage tests.

Teachers from the fields of English, science, or common learnings are assigned to this program on a full-time basis after special training in remedial and developmental reading. The number of teachers allotted to each school depends both on the need and the school's readiness for the program.

Based on the principle of the interrelation of reading, writing, speaking, and listening, the program in the seventh and eighth grades includes all four, with materials ranging in difficulty from the level of the gifted to that of the slow learner. In one senior high school, students in the English department have specific time allotted each week for reading improvement.

Average demonstrated student growth, based on reading

[8] Rosemary Green Wilson, Special Assistant in Remedial Reading in Secondary Schools, Philadelphia, Pennsylvania.

test results, has been two terms in one, with considerably greater gains by some individuals and an over-all, notable improvement in study habits and attitude toward school. The success of the program, in the opinion of the Philadelphia School System, rests upon (1) the teachers' interest in extending their training through workshops and other in-service activities, (2) the skillful use of resource materials co-operatively developed by members of the staff, and (3) the acquaintance of teachers of other major subject fields with the service of the remedial classes and the techniques used to help students improve in reading.

Resource Help

Smaller school systems which do not require a full-time staff for clinical services report the use of services available at nearby colleges and universities. In every report received by the National Council of Teachers of English Curriculum Commission, it is clear that the teacher's role in identifying cases and in assisting the student after his return from a special program cannot be delegated to anyone else.

BIBLIOGRAPHY

BETTS, Emmett A., *Foundations of Reading Instruction* (New York, American Book Company, 1946).

BOND, Guy L., and BOND, Eva, *Developmental Reading in High School* (New York, The Macmillan Company, 1942).

CENTER, Stella S., and PERSONS, Gladys L., *Experiences in Reading and Thinking* (New York, The Macmillan Company, 1948).

Chicago University, *Clinical Studies in Reading*, I and II (Chicago, University of Chicago Press, I-1949, II-1953).

DOLCH, Edward William, *Problems in Reading* (Champaign, Ill., The Garrard Press, 1948).

DURRELL, Donald D., *Improvement of Basic Reading Abilities* (New York, World Book Company, 1940).

DURRELL, Donald D., and SULLIVAN, Helen B., *High Interest–Low Vocabulary Booklist* (Boston, Boston University, School of Education, 1950).

EPHRON, Beulah Kanter, *Emotional Difficulties in Reading* (New York, Julian Press, Inc., 1953).

GATES, Arthur I., *Improvement of Reading, A Program of Diagnostic and Remedial Methods* (New York, The Macmillan Company, 1947).

GRAY, William S., ed., *Classroom Techniques in Improving Reading*, Supplementary Educational Monographs, No. 69 (Chicago, University of Chicago Press, October, 1949).

————, *Improving Reading in All Curriculum Areas*, Supplementary Educational Monographs, No. 76 (Chicago, University of Chicago Press, 1952).

————, *Keeping Reading Programs Abreast of the Times*, Supplementary Educational Monographs, No. 72 (Chicago, University of Chicago Press, 1950).

————, *Promoting Growth toward Maturity in Interpreting What Is Read*, Supplementary Educational Monographs, No. 74 (Chicago, University of Chicago Press, 1951).

————, *Promoting Personal and Social Development through Reading*, Supplementary Educational Monographs, No. 64 (Chicago, University of Chicago Press, October, 1947).

————, *Reading in an Age of Mass Communication*, Report of the Committee on Reading at the Secondary School and College Levels of the National Council of Teachers of English (New York, Appleton-Century-Crofts, Inc., 1949).

————, *Reading in the Content Fields*, Supplementary Educational Monographs, No. 62 (Chicago, University of Chicago Press, 1947).

HARRIS, Albert J., *How To Increase Reading Ability* (New York, Longmans, Green & Company, 1948).

HAVIGHURST, Robert J., "Characteristics, Interests, and Needs of Pupils That Aid in Defining the Nature and Scope of the Reading Program," in W. S. Gray, ed., *Adjusting Reading Programs to Individuals*, Supplementary Educational Monographs, No. 52 (Chicago, University of Chicago Press, October, 1941), pp. 53–59.

JENNINGS, Frank G., "That Johnny May Read," *Saturday Review*, Vol. XXXIX, No. 5 (February 4, 1956), pp. 7–9, 39–41.

LABRANT, Lou, *An Evaluation of the Free Reading in Grades, 10, 11, and 12 for the Class of 1935*, Ohio State University Studies: Contributions in Education No. 2, rev. ed. (Columbus, Ohio State University Press, 1936).

————, *We Teach English* (New York, Harcourt, Brace & Company, Inc., 1951), pp. 52–60, 225–263.

LOBAN, Walter, *High Interest–Low Vocabulary Booklist*, B1158, Contra Costa County Schools (Martinez, Calif., 1951).

MCKILLOP, Anne Selley, *The Relationship between the Reader's Attitude and Certain Types of Reading Response* (New York, Bureau of Publications, Teachers College, Columbia University, 1952).

MORSE, William C., BALLANTINE, Francis A., and DIXON, Robert W.,

Studies in the Psychology of Reading (Ann Arbor, University of Michigan Press, 1951).

National Council of Teachers of English, Commission on the English Curriculum, *The English Language Arts*, NCTE Curriculum Series, Vol. I (New York, Appleton-Century-Crofts, Inc., 1952), pp. 397–413.

National Society for the Study of Education, *Reading in the High School and College*, Forty-seventh Yearbook, Part II (Chicago, University of Chicago Press, 1948).

Pittsburgh University, *Report of the Sixth Annual Conference on Reading* (Pittsburgh, University of Pittsburgh Press, 1950).

ROBINSON, Helen M., ed., *Promoting Maximal Reading Growth among Able Learners*, Supplementary Educational Monographs, No. 81 (Chicago, University of Chicago Press, December, 1954).

ROBINSON, Helen M., *Why Pupils Fail in Reading* (Chicago, University of Chicago Press, 1946).

STRANG, Ruth M., GILBERT, Christine B., and SCOGGIN, Margaret C., *Gateways to Readable Books; an Annotated Graded List of Books in Many Fields for Adolescents Who Find Reading Difficult*, 2nd ed. (New York, H. W. Wilson Company, 1952).

STRANG, Ruth, McCULLOUGH, Constance M., and TRAXLER, Arthur E., *Problems in the Improvement of Reading*, 2nd ed. (New York, McGraw-Hill Book Co., 1955).

WITTY, PAUL, *How to Become a Better Reader* (Chicago, Science Research Associates, Inc., 1953).

PREVIEW OF CHAPTER 7

The Importance of Competence in Speech

Evidences of Competence in Speech

Activities Recommended for Developing Competence in Speech

    Informal Social Activities

    Formal Group Activities

    Informal Business Procedures

    Processes of Sharing and Reporting

    Techniques of Evaluating Speech Activities

Methods of Working with Boys and Girls

    Group Planning of Activities Involving Speech

    Using Mistakes as Stepping-Stones to Improvement

    Weaving Speech into Broad Units of Instruction

    Directing Speech Work toward Improved Human Relations

    Helping Students Perceive Goals

    Making Evaluation Encourage and Instruct

    Varying the Activities to Meet Varying Needs

    Using Mechanical Devices

The Relation of Speech to Radio, Television, Stage, and Screen

    Discussion of Films

    Radio and Television

Speech and the Teaching of Literature

    Choral Speaking

    Sharing Reading

    Play-Making

    Interpretation and Appreciation of Drama

Criteria for a Sound Speech Program

    Provision for All of the Students

    Furnishing Teachers with Training in Speech

    Administrative Responsibility for the Speech Program

A Final Word

Bibliography

CHAPTER 7

Developing Competence in Speaking

No ASPECT OF the curriculum is more important to the schools of a democracy than the teaching of speech.

THE IMPORTANCE OF COMPETENCE IN SPEECH

In a land that maintains freedom of speech, the schools must prepare boys and girls to speak with a sense of responsibility and to understand the ways in which language is used to sway opinion and to determine action. Young citizens thus equipped are not only able to resist the fallacious persuasions of others but are competent to think about problems with clarity and precision and to express their views in ways that win support. Such persons are leaders with a social conscience; they are intelligent champions of worthy causes. Without them, a democratic society is doomed.

In today's world, the increase in the number of voices and the extension of their range by machines necessitate more than fluency of language and showmanship in performance. In addition to speech skills, a genuine integrity of purpose, accuracy of facts, reliability of opinions, and sincerity of feeling are required if speaking is to be a forthright and trustworthy medium of contact between mind and mind.

Speech is intimately tied up also with the development of personality. More than any other one thing it is an index to the self, and on it the expansion of the self depends to a significant degree. One's personal effectiveness is determined in large measure by what one says and how one says it. Witness the following comments on the part played by individuals in daily conversation: [1]

John is a good conversationalist; he never bores you with his troubles.

I always talk to Mary. She makes me feel that I am an interesting person.

He talked for an hour about his trip through the desert. All I remember is that the desert was dry and so was he.

He said about a dozen words the whole evening, and ten of them were either "yes" or "no."

It's nice to talk to Emory. You can disagree with him without hurting his feelings.

Mrs. Smith is a good hostess. She stimulates conversation. She doesn't monopolize it.

Because speech is the basic language activity by which people relate themselves to one another, the development of speech competence should come about through practice in using speech effectively in group relationships.

There is great need in these days for speech skills that go beyond the individual, that enable him to live as *a man among men,* not apart from them. As Bonaro Overstreet has said, "We live in a world where our lives so impinge upon one another that only a widespread spirit of trust and affection can save us from disaster." [2] Such trust and affection can hardly grow save by satisfying experiences with others. Teachers who utilize speech activities in combination with other language arts often find their work broadened and deepened in effectiveness through the extended contacts and the variety of speech situations which such a program affords.

EVIDENCES OF COMPETENCE IN SPEECH

Since speech exists for the interchange of ideas and experience and since it is the chief instrument of common under-

---

[1] Seth A. Fessenden, Roy Ivan Johnson, and P. Merville Johnson, *The Teacher Speaks* (Englewood Cliffs, N. J., Prentice-Hall, Inc., 1954), pp. 50–51.

[2] Bonaro Overstreet, *How to Think about Ourselves* (New York, Harper and Brothers, 1948), p. 167.

standing and co-operation, the teacher's purpose is to increase the competence of boys and girls in these phases of the process:

1. Having something worth while to communicate.

2. Presenting original thought with appropriate organization and development.

3. Interpreting with clarity the meanings expressed by others.

4. Being aware of others and gaining insight into their true responses. This implies understanding and accepting one's limitations, and thereby achieving a healthy personal adjustment to others rather than withdrawal from or aggression toward them. For example, teachers can aid shy children by helping them to *think toward the listeners* rather than *into themselves;* to be *idea conscious* rather than *self-conscious.*

5. Having sufficient range and flexibility in skills of language, voice, and action to meet the varying demands of specific speech situations.

6. Knowing sources and resources for speech materials.

7. Being aware of the symbolic nature of language and of the ways in which it influences human behavior.

8. Understanding and accepting the need for honesty in the use of one's abilities, such as they are, and facing realistically the consequences of using them; developing a social conscience.

9. Developing appreciation of the rich personal and social values in poetry and drama through effective use of oral interpretation.

10. Enjoying the imaginative experience of creative dramatics and play production.

11. Understanding the place of radio, television, stage, and film in American life and developing standards for effective use of them.

12. Evaluating one's participation in speech activities so that growth can continue.

ACTIVITIES RECOMMENDED FOR DEVELOPING COMPETENCE IN SPEECH

Reports from seventy teachers in twenty-five different communities widely scattered throughout the United States indicate the activities which they have found most useful for developing these competencies. The various procedures group themselves naturally into *Informal Social Activities, Formal Group Activities, Informal Business Procedures, Processes of Sharing and Reporting,* and *Techniques of Evaluating Speech Activities.*

Informal Social Activities

1. Participating in conversation; telephoning.
2. Introducing each other; inviting, receiving, and introducing family members, friends, and fellow students.
3. Storytelling and relating personal experiences.

Formal Group Activities

1. Making announcements of coming events.
2. Giving directions; explaining school or other regulations.
3. Planning with the group, solving group problems; serving as group leader, recorder, or observer.
4. Participating in informal class and group discussions, both impromptu and prepared. Sometimes these are carried on with simple parliamentary procedure. Sometimes they involve other group techniques and methods of directing cooperative thinking, such as the use of questions to carry thinking forward, the use of recorder and observer, the development of permissive rather than prescriptive or authoritarian situations, the effort to achieve consensus rather than majority vote, and improved group understanding and thinking rather than victory of one faction over another.
5. Participating in prepared panels, symposia, or forum

discussions in more formal situations, which may be as simple as an effort to increase understanding within a class or a school or as complex an undertaking as a radio, television, or other public presentation. The reports indicate that teachers believe the more formal, more complex enterprises should be carried on infrequently and as the culmination of efforts centered within the school as a whole or in school-community projects.

Informal Business Procedures

Interviewing and face-to-face conferences, involving personal discussion and the seeking or giving of information, permission, or co-operation. In the upper years these include vocational exploration and personal application for employment.

Processes of Sharing and Reporting

1. Oral reporting to groups, with and without follow-up discussion; announcing committee decisions; reporting with demonstration methods, such as chalk talks, showing of equipment, models, charts, graphs, maps, or other visual aids; summarizing information.

2. Presenting facts from individual research, from personal investigation through interviews, reading, travel, or other observation; use of demonstration methods wherever feasible.

3. Oral reading and declamation, with emphasis on conveying meanings and furnishing enjoyment. These activities afford motivation for developing variety in diction and command of voice, in pitch, rate, volume, and vocal quality for the sake of better communication. They give opportunity to enter personally into the mood or purpose of a selection and to grow in power to transmit the author's meaning and emotion to others. They promote fuller enjoyment of literature as well as reading skill and interest in reading.

4. Informal play-reading and classroom dramatization to

provide experience with dramatic material and to develop appreciation of the fun and the artistic qualities involved. At the same time, such dramatic reading gives opportunities for developing insight into human behavior as well as for improving individual poise and emotional control. Teachers occasionally utilize role-playing and sociodrama for improved insight and understanding, not only of situations in plays but of those in real life as well.

5. Choral speaking, so that participants share experience in interpretation and in creative group effort. Such activity should furnish keen insight into the effects of tone quality, of rhythm, of intelligent phrasing, and of variation in mood dependent upon sound and movement. In general, shared enjoyment and appreciation take precedence over public appearance.

6. Dramatic production, often so simply done as to require little or no staging, with an occasional more elaborate presentation. Every student, at some time in his school career, should have the opportunity to take part in a public performance.

7. Personal sharing of literature and reading in a wide variety of ways to stimulate interest, the desire to read, and standards of evaluation for further reading.

8. Radio and television programs, both simulated and real, as a part of, or perhaps the culmination of, other activities.

Techniques of Evaluating Speech Activities

1. Observing professional speakers, actors, commentators, and the like, in person and on the screen, radio, television, or recording, developing from such observation standards for critical examination of what is said and how it is said.

2. Being filmed or making speech recordings on tape, wire, or disc for purposes of record and evaluation.

3. Evolving co-operatively sets of standards for various speech activities and applying them to activities in progress.

4. Setting goals for future performance in the light of the results of the evaluation.

METHODS OF WORKING WITH BOYS AND GIRLS

The setting in which improvement in speech is stimulated is all-important if social and personal factors as well as speech skills are to be taken into account. How teachers work with boys and girls, how they motivate speech activities and relate them to the on-going life of the school day are vital factors in the development of a sound program.

Group planning, the division of tasks, caring for the varied needs of individuals and at the same time utilizing the peculiar talents and interests of each in the service of the class or school as a whole are techniques in which both students and teachers are becoming more and more proficient.

Group Planning of Activities Involving Speech

Teachers are becoming increasingly aware of the values inherent in planning with boys and girls. They are also cooperating with other teachers and with specialists. They are finding ways to open classroom doors so that boys and girls from one class can work with those in other parts of the school and also with parents and groups and agencies in the community. Above all, they are coming to grips with, and finding good solutions to, the problem of giving enough freedom for *student initiation, planning,* and *execution of* many projects. They even risk failure of a project for the sake of the growth which students gain in insight as to what responsibility really means in action. For example, Elizabeth R. Barlow, State Teachers College, Worcester, Massachusetts, tells how seventh-grade students worked together on an important school enterprise that took them into the community:

It was decided by vote that proceeds from an all-school Christmas sale should be spent to help less fortunate boys and girls. Enthusiasm for the project lent impetus to group discussions, interviews, informal talks, and finally to a pupil-planned assembly program. Pupil discussions covered (1) the responsibilities involved in the assignment, (2) ways of determining the wisest purchases, (3) ways of keeping cash records. Interviews included (1) consultation with authorities at two children's hospitals and one boys' home concerning needed recreational materials, and (2) conferences with local merchants concerning possible discounts. An assembly program rendered an "account of stewardship."

Pupils gained a sense of responsibility for making clear explanations and convincing statements of viewpoint. They recognized the value of concrete and acceptable expression both for its effectiveness in conveying ideas and for its attendant contribution to the speaker's own poise. Enthusiasm for the job at hand resulted in spontaneous, confident expression. Pupils grew in their ability to plan and carry through a courteous, efficient interview. "Arrange for time and place in advance," they said. "Be prompt and courteous. Have specific questions planned beforehand. Come quickly to the point to avoid wasting the other person's time. Listen attentively and take notes on important points. Thank the person and promise to quote him accurately."

They formulated similar standards for effective speaking before an audience. Some who previously had shrunk from talking before an audience volunteered to present periodic reports to the school on the progress of the activity. Certain shy pupils acted as gracious hosts and hostesses at the exhibit of purchases which had been arranged to permit the rest of the school to see how the money had been spent. A pupil-planned and conducted assembly made a competent report to the school.

Oral language activity permeated the entire undertaking. It also augmented and strengthened the activities in written expression for which the program provided opportunity.

Similarly an eighth-grade class in Worcester, Massachusetts, improved in speaking when it helped a new and inexperienced mothers' club to conduct a food sale, the proceeds of which were to be used in the purchase of baseball jerseys for the school team.[3]

They tabulated results of interviews with pupils as to their preferences in fruit juices, cakes, and sandwiches and negotiated purchases with wholesale merchants. They delivered speeches to pupils of the other grades, telling the purpose of the sale and emphasizing that loyalty to the school team could be shown by donating supplies and making purchases.

A better spirit developed throughout the school. The younger pupils were pleased with the attention from the older ones, who looked on them as potential customers. Speaking before the classes, the timid

[3] Woodland Street School, Helen Lombard, teacher.

gained some confidence. The overconfident realized the difficulties of speaking before new audiences. A third group discovered that they enjoyed public speaking. All members of the class had practice in building up a main thought that to them was very vital—"The Food Sale Is Our Sale." After assembling their thoughts, they had practice in delivering speeches that were not memorized.

In evaluating results, pupils listed the qualities which had made their speeches successful and later used these standards when arguing before the younger pupils in the school assembly the relative merits of two different proposals for use of land purchased by the local school committee. To note the improvement in these speeches over their earlier attempts was a real pleasure for all concerned.

Using Mistakes as Stepping-Stones to Improvement

Boys and girls working together on such a major project have the motivation that comes from genuine interest in achieving good results. Furthermore, in such a group situation, no student need fail for lack of opportunity to contribute what he can do or can learn to do. The range of abilities needed is as broad as the range of individual abilities in the group. Moreover, a student may sometimes spur others to learn even when his own achievement is slight. A teacher with ingenuity is quick to make use of unexpected opportunities to help young people learn from their own mistakes and those of others.

For example, in Memorial Junior High School in Passaic, New Jersey, when an incomplete announcement resulted in questions and confusion, the teacher led the class to list the kinds of information which must be furnished by an effective announcement.[4]

1. What is this about?
2. Why should anyone care?
3. Where will it happen?
4. When?
5. Who will take part?
6. Who should come?
7. What will it cost?

Trying out these standards in announcements of their own, students found themselves falling into dull, routine,

[4] Dorothy R. McConkey, teacher.

and monotonously similar performances. They discussed how a messenger might attract and hold interest. Next came the question of how to finish and to leave the room. So an understanding of form was built—introduction, body, and conclusion.

On another occasion, students developed spontaneous, informal, and highly imaginative endings for a story which a confused teller was unable to finish.[5] Later they read the original and discovered how it really ended.

Weaving Speech into Broad Units of Instruction

Though many speech activities evolve naturally out of individual and class projects under the guidance of the resourceful teacher, others must be definitely planned for in relation to major units in progress.

A TENTH-GRADE UNIT ON LIVING WITH OTHERS

A tenth-grade program, for example, in Brooklyn, centered about the theme of *Living with Others*.[6] During the early days of the term, while programs were unsettled, pupils were led to discuss problems of living today which young people face in home, school, and community. A check-list was evolved from the discussions, from which each pupil selected a topic for a short talk. Some pupils talked of unsupervised homes where both parents are at work all day. They raised problems of the narcotics racket and other unsavory community influences, of the need for recreation centers away from drinking and gambling. They were concerned that programs in theaters and on television and radio be improved. They felt the need of active rather than passive entertainment. The teacher led them from these negative reactions to a study of positive forces in the community, of resources available to offset these influences and to a recognition of the importance of personal choice in all matters of this kind.

Reading entered the program next with a study of successful men and women and how they met such problems in their lives. It was February, and Washington and Lincoln were in everyone's mind. Stories of Thomas Edison, of George Washington Carver, of Jane Addams and others were read and incidents chosen for reading aloud to the class to demonstrate the character of the choices made by these men and women. Lincoln's sense of humor saved the day for him on many occa-

[5] Oliver Hazard Perry Junior High School, Providence, Rhode Island, Margaret R. Deery, teacher.
[6] Erasmus Hall High School, Brooklyn, New York, Evelyn M. Hill, teacher.

sions. Examples of how a sense of humor influences human relations could also be found in the materials read as well as in fiction and poetry which could be used for this purpose later.

Many stories revealing problems of adolescents were available, some of them involving love affairs, winning independence of one's family, or choosing a career. Sometimes talks and discussions could lead out from a variety of solutions by the characters in different books—*Seventeenth Summer, Going Steady, Green Grass of Wyoming*, or *Huckleberry Finn* —and sometimes they led directly to similar situations in the pupils' own lives. Career stories are always popular—*The First Woman Doctor, Mary McLeod Bethune, A Man Called Peter*, and *Jim Bridger*.

Reading tastes, the pupils decided, were both a measure of one's success and an aid in developing an understanding of life and of human nature. The class discussed what functions books can serve in life and members of a panel presented specific books useful for different purposes. Breadth of reading, amount of reading, and quality and maturity of reading, they decided, were all measures of the extent to which an individual was making the most of books. Some books, they found, were mere stereotypes; they made both life and character development too simple and too easy, and success too sure. Similar standards could be applied to radio, television, motion picture, and stage.

An important part of the unit was concerned with the choice of a career. Inventories were made of personal abilities and the requirements of jobs and discussion ensued as to how the two could be matched. Illustrations abounded in the biographies read.

Many of the pupils actually worked out a personal program for purposeful living and for their own growth in personality.

A final discussion and report period was held at the end of the term. In preparation, students read books that would give an appreciation of life in other lands—the modes of life, the achievements, the activities of the world neighbor. Their reports showed that many of them had begun to develop attitudes of appreciation and acceptance of others whose backgrounds and whose race, language, religion and customs were different from their own. They noted that education and broader knowledge of the world tended to break down the barriers that lead to world problems.

Training and practice were given during the course of the unit in these speech activities: parliamentary procedure, group discussion, debate, social conversation, sharing books, research, documenting and organizing of oral presentations, oral reading and interpretation, dramatization of interviews and matters of social etiquette, and evaluation of personal progress, using a scheme such as that worked out by Benjamin Franklin for himself. After each activity pupils assessed their strengths and pointed out weaknesses to be improved in their next attempt.

The speech skills acquired in these various enterprises were studied in context as they were needed. Teachers are finding that developing skills in this way results in improved learning and in better retention.

A full description of how similar speech activities fitted into a unit on Back-Country America appears in Chapter 4 of this volume.

Use of records to maintain balance in activities. Teachers who fear speech skills may be lost sight of in such a unit may find useful the kind of record-keeping suggested by Weaver, Borchers, and Smith.[7] A chart may be prepared by the teacher with the names of the students in a column at the left and the types of speeches in which everyone should have practice across the top. In the resulting squares opposite each individual's name, the teacher may record 1, 2, 3, 4, or 5 for each occasion on which the student participated in that particular activity: 1 for inferior, 2 for below average, 3 for average, 4 for above average, and 5 for superior. One glance at the chart will indicate for the teacher both the number of times each student has engaged in the activity in the course of the unit, and the measure of success he attained on each occasion.

A similar chart may be kept by each learner in his notebook together with additional devices for evaluating each performance in greater detail. The students, perhaps, have agreed on certain standards for evaluating oral presentations to the class in which each may rate himself Excellent, Good, Fair, Poor:

1. Was my voice pleasant to hear, well modulated and varied in tone?
2. Did I choose a topic which held the attention of the class?
3. Was my material full enough and interesting?
4. Was my outline clear to everyone?
5. Did I adapt my material to my audience?
6. Did my manner and my eye contact set my audience at ease?
7. Did I suit my actions to my words?
8. Did my use of language add to or detract from the success of my speech?
9. What do I need to work on most before my next speech?

[7] Andrew T. Weaver, Gladys L. Borchers, and Donald Kliese Smith, *The Teaching of Speech* (Englewood Cliffs, N. J., Prentice-Hall, Inc., 1952), pp. 109–113.

Directing Speech Work toward Improved Human Relations

As the units cited have already demonstrated, the speech arts may be so taught as to develop attitudes of high social importance. Some of these are mere matters of saying "Please" and "Thank you" in a wide variety of ways and in numerous kinds of situations. Such amenities are the outward expression of an inner courtesy and consideration for others. The tone in which a request is made often determines the tone used in reply. Feelings are smoothed or ruffled by the manner in which one person addresses another. An atmosphere of gracious living, of mutual consideration and tact is particularly important in a classroom where speech is being taught. Nowhere does the example of the teacher do more to condition the behavior of the learner. Learning how to disagree with courtesy, learning to make the most of each person's contribution, however meager, learning to change the course of a discussion at just the right moment to avoid a deep hurt for another, learning to distinguish between fact and opinion, between honesty and dishonesty in thinking— these are fundamental matters of human relations intimately tied up with speech. Through dramatics, also, a boy or girl can develop social imagination and can learn to co-operate with others, to assume responsibility, to accept criticism, and to respond resourcefully in solving group problems.

Beyond this, the speech class may include frank and informed discussion of prejudices and how they arise, of platitudes and unthinking acceptance of them, and of clear differences of opinion among people brought up under widely different circumstances.

Combatting prejudice. Such an occasion arose when a tenth-grade class in Brookline, Massachusetts, was reciting the pledge of allegiance to the flag.[8]

" 'With liberty and justice for all' isn't true," said one boy. Out of the discussion came a study of the status of eight minority groups in the

[8] Brookline High School, Alice Howard Spaulding, teacher.

United States: the Chinese, Japanese, Scandinavian, Italian, Irish, Jewish, Negro, and Indian.

The following questions became the basis for reports:

1. How many _____ are there in the United States and where are they located?
2. On what basis do the prejudiced discriminate?
3. What handicaps do the _____ suffer under?
4. What can these _____ do themselves to improve their status?
5. What contribution have the _____ made to the betterment of the United States?
6. What can I, a high school student, do to bring about liberty and justice for all?

One week was given for research, organizing material, preparing outlines. These pupils, being retarded groups, worked slowly. Three days were devoted to the oral reports and discussion. There was an unusual amount of participation by the pupils, many of whom were often mute. A personal note was often sounded. Again, several times the remark was made: "Young people wouldn't discriminate if they didn't hear prejudice in their parents' talk."

Learning the need for facts. Another teacher describes a similar situation in a tenth-grade class in Passaic, New Jersey: [9]

Entering a classroom during World War II, the instructor heard a student say, "The only good Jap is a dead Jap." Since the members of the class were studying discussion, this seemed an opportune time for some practice. It took only a few minutes of talk before everyone became aware that knowledge of Japan and her people was sadly wanting. Right then and there, the class agreed that the next lesson would be one of research in preparation for a more enlightened discussion of Japan and the Japanese people.

With the help of the librarian, pupils used the encyclopedia and such books on Japan as the following: Frank Carpenter's *The Pacific: Its Lands and Peoples;* John Gunther's *Inside Asia;* Grace S. Yaukey's *Understanding the Japanese;* and Marion M. Dilts's *Pageant of Japanese History.*

After about three days of reading and research, the pupils were eager to tell what they had learned. They were alert, and they were all keen to contribute to the discussion. All points of view were exchanged in a quiet manner. This time the students were informed, so that they could speak more intelligently upon the subject.

Although there was difference of opinion, there was no shouting; no one tried to out-talk the others. The students listened to one another and so learned much about these Eastern neighbors, our enemies at the

[9] Ruth H. Thomas, formerly of the Passaic public schools.

time. At the end of the class hour, all realized that there were good and bad persons among all groups of people. The greatest lesson learned was expressed in the words of one girl: "I think maybe I have learned not to express my opinion until I know what I am talking about."

How well they illustrated Gordon Allport's definition of prejudice: "Being down on something one isn't up on"! [10] Superior readers would enjoy immensely his discussion of the subject in the Claremont College Reading Conference proceedings.

Helping Students Perceive Goals

None of the speech arts is studied exclusively as an end in itself, for each boy or girl usually achieves best in the context of a real speech situation. For this very reason, however, it is especially important for both teacher and student to have their speech goals set clearly before them.

One teacher in Roosevelt High School in New York City approached the development of the goals of public speaking by asking a group of pupils extremely hesitant to appear before an audience to carry on chatty conversations in groups of three or four. Analyzing their purposes later, they found them to be the same as those of public speaking: to amuse, to explain or to instruct, and to persuade or to convince. They then set out to achieve these same ends in more formal talks before the class as a whole.

As part of their preparation, the young people proposed listening to specific radio programs, to able preachers in various churches, to competent guest speakers in the school assembly, and to teachers who are effective speakers. They determined to observe specific aspects of these speeches, to become aware of the techniques employed by skillful speakers in attracting and holding the attention of an audience, and in effectively impressing their hearers. After close observation the pupils reported their discoveries, including the fact that good public speaking is conversational in effect.

The speeches which the students presented as a result of this unit indicated that they had come to recognize the conversational quality of public speaking. Through preliminary preparation they had acquired genuine interest in their topics and had developed a lively sense of communication. They had also learned to realize their own limitations and

[10] Gordon Allport, "Reading the Nature of Prejudice," *Seventeenth Yearbook, Claremont College Reading Conference* (Claremont, Calif., 1952), pp. 51–64.

the necessity of consulting reference works and other sources of information to enrich their own backgrounds. They had gained practice in selecting facts, in unifying notes, and in organizing data logically for lucid presentation to others. They had recognized the value of the right word and had tried to express themselves not only adequately but effectively. Moreover, they had become familiar with worth-while radio programs and had realized the advantages of intelligent listening. . . .[11]

Another group of high school students established their goals through a "get-acquainted activity" at the opening of school.[12] Seated two or three at a time before the class, they interviewed one another. Topics brought up in the interviews included personal experiences, places visited, hobbies, family customs, childhood fancies, and individual problems. Out of this activity grew a consideration of class goals in speech. They discussed the interviewing experience informally and, encouraged by the teacher, each student tried to pick out his two or three greatest language needs and those of the group. This procedure gives a good example of objectives arrived at co-operatively. A course so introduced and subsequently directed toward the achievement of these goals will have a maximum of meaning for the young people involved.

Making Evaluation Encourage and Instruct

Perhaps the hardest part of the teacher's responsibility in developing good habits of speech is to learn how to criticize wisely and to direct criticism by the class. Appraisal must be in terms of the goals set up jointly by teacher and class before the activity is begun. It must begin with consideration of merits, for *approval,* always a potent teaching device, is especially important in anything so personal as speech. It must push through to specific consideration of what the student needs to do better next time and must be accompanied by concrete suggestions as to *what to do* about weaknesses

---

[11] Theodore Roosevelt High School, the Bronx, New York, Mrs. Clara Bernhard, teacher.
[12] Modesto High School, Modesto, California, Margaret Painter, teacher.

revealed. The individual must feel certain of the good will and confidence of his critics and of their interest in helping him to improve.

Discussion of what the speaker said is both motivation and implicit criticism. "Did he inform, persuade, or entertain as he intended?" If needed, the teacher's criticism and/or that of a student partner can be set down in writing during the discussion, perhaps formulated in the light of the discussion. Principles, even of delivery, need to be taught, preferably in sessions evaluating a round of speeches. Rating does not need to be on all elements of speech, but on special merits and needs in relation to the purpose of the talk.

Balancing teacher-, class-, and self-criticism. Some teachers prefer, early in the term, to do all the criticizing themselves, centering first on the value of what was said and on its effect upon the audience. Detailed aspects of technique can then be considered as elements of the program for improvement. Sometimes the teacher's comment is made in front of the class; sometimes on a small sheet of paper of which the teacher keeps a copy; sometimes in private conference later; and sometimes by means of a combination of methods.

Techniques for reviewing goals and helping students progress toward them may then be made the subject of discussion in class before the boys and girls themselves earn the right to evaluate by discovering that evaluation is intended to *encourage* and *instruct*.

An important aspect of the evaluation is the speaker's own reaction both to the effectiveness of his speech and to the reasonableness of the criticism. He should be given the privilege of judging his own speech in terms of what *he* was trying to do. Sometimes he will be his own most severe critic and must be saved from himself. Sometimes he will be confused about his own goals and should be helped to write them down before he speaks again. An indication as to what he intends to do about the criticism the next time he talks is a necessary element in the procedure. He may record it in his notebook or on the note he returns to his teacher after copying it.

Using a rating device. Some schools have set forms for evaluation prepared co-operatively by teachers and students and used at the close of a speaking experience. Unless these are adapted from one speech situation to another, they are likely to become cut-and-dried.

Marvin Cohn of James Monroe High School in New York City describes the procedure used in his department where a rating form has been developed on which the teacher makes notations following specific items listed. After each talk, discussion is called for from the group, the teacher being the last one to react to the speech:

> The audience is thus encouraged to comment on the mechanics of the speech or some phase of the content. The last one to evaluate is the teacher, who takes a minute or two to indicate some especially outstanding aspect of the talk or to criticize constructively some weakness. As one might expect, the amount of discussion will vary from speech to speech, depending upon the quality, the interest for the audience, and the skill which the speaker has manifested in his presentation.
>
> The teacher has constantly to emphasize, however, that nothing succeeds like success, and to ask the pupils to be *helpful* in their comments. There are times when the peculiar problems a pupil has in speaking can be identified and attacked only by the pupil and the teacher working together. In such cases, the teacher so guides the class procedure as to save the pupil in question from discussion by his classmates.

Varying the Activities to Meet Varying Needs

The range of speech activities is wide; each one seems susceptible of almost infinite variation if developed by capable teachers in the interest of the student's growth in communicative skill and understanding.

Gadgets to help the shy. One teacher, for example, faced a group of shy, reticent, but conscientious students. Merely to get them on their feet to talk to their classmates with a modicum of ease and comfort was a major problem.[13]

[13] Jerome Dwelly School, Fall River, Massachusetts, Louise M. Murphy, teacher.

The scheme that broke the ice for them was asking each one to bring to class a gadget that might be new to the class and to explain the use of it. Six pupils volunteered for the first group of talks which showed the effects of home preparation and parental interest. The pupils were successful in arousing interest and curiosity. Many questions followed each talk. The old barrier, self-consciousness, diminished as they held in their hands such gadgets as a Wonder Wood-Burning Pen Set, special shears to crack nuts, others for cutting fish fins or for pinking, an onion chopper with a cover which was guaranteed to "Spare These Tears," or a jewelry box with a secret opening.

Pantomime and dramatization. Another teacher, working with a more mature class with considerable background in pantomime and dramatization, wanted to help them achieve their goal of forgetting themselves and "living" what they presented.[14]

Original monologues were used for the purpose, building on previous acting and pantomime techniques. They tried to develop stories with a struggle—man against nature, man against man, man against his conscience, and the mental struggle of man against man. An effort was made to incorporate a contrast of emotions, a strong climax, and a swift falling action.

Each student built a story from his own experience, often amazing himself with the success of his dramatization. He developed ease before his audience, sincerity of expression, and an awareness of the need for flexibility in his vocal expression and for meaningful bodily action. Student evaluation after each monologue developed constructive criticism and a good class relationship—these motivated another speaking experience. Students found they were observing people more closely; by using their imagination, they were able to lift themselves over the hurdle of stage fright.

This project, used many times with variations, is always the most enjoyed in the speech course. The class discovers unsuspected abilities in its members; originality and self-expression are encouraged; relaxation and expressive bodily movement are facilitated.

An attack on nasality. Still another class contained several students who spoke with unpleasant nasality.[15] Since the teacher herself had not had sufficient training to attempt to correct such a fault, she called upon the speech specialist for help.

14 Atlantic City High School, Atlantic City, New Jersey, Ruth E. French, teacher.
15 Passaic High School, Passaic, New Jersey, Hazel K. Weber, teacher.

In her visit to the class, the speech consultant discussed briefly several varieties of voice quality and read a short selection in a nasal voice, then with a throaty tone, and again with the pinched tones resulting from tense jaw and nearly closed mouth. Finally she read it in good voice. Students listened, then criticized each version. With the specialist's help, they worked out why one reading was better than the others, and they learned from her some ways of correcting each difficulty—with particular emphasis on nasality. Their regular teacher was learning with them and worked later with the speech consultant so that she could continue to help her students. Again, with new insight and opportunities for practice, the class evidenced real growth.

A search for voice color. A somewhat similar approach was used in a speech class which had been giving reports that were good in content but lacked voice color in delivery.[16]

The teacher suggested that students pair off and carry on conversation in which one speaker spoke only numerals and the other only letters. Their aim was to show their meaning simply by inflection. They gossiped, reported a fire, scolded a small child, fed a baby. After half a minute, they exchanged sides so that each party to a conversation had an opportunity to act out two parts purely with voice color. "With twenty students chattering at once," said the teacher, "the room was noisy, but the results were worth it!" As a follow-up assignment, each student was asked to prepare a nursery rhyme in three different ways: like a teacher scolding a student, like an umpire calling pitches, and like Tallulah Bankhead registering great emotion. The next day, the efforts were tape-recorded and played back.

In evaluation, the teacher wrote:

These simple methods facilitated work all the rest of the year. Both experiences were dramatic enough and had enough appeal for students to make a lasting impression. Perhaps they would fall flat with some classes and be only a source of tumult in others. But in these classes they are the most effective ways yet found for strengthening weak inflection.

Improvement of usage. A class of students with severe language difficulties felt the handicap of many lapses from acceptable English in speeches they hoped eventually to give in the school assembly.[17]

16 Lebanon, New Hampshire, High School, C. Paul Quimby, teacher.
17 B. M. C. Durfee High School, Fall River, Massachusetts, Edna U. Delehanty, teacher.

The teacher, eager to teach good usage through ear training, helped the pupils organize a direct attack on the problem. A tabulation was made of items misused in class recitations and in diagnostic tests; then a blackboard listing was made of ten examples of one type of usage. Oral drill with the whole group came next, until most of the pupils were aware of the *sound* of an appropriate expression to replace the unacceptable one. Then the class was divided into groups, each with a leader to conduct further oral drill and to assist anyone having difficulty. The teacher was free to help the pupils who most needed her. Review tests were used from time to time, given orally at conversational tempo, and competition was keen among the groups for the best composite scores. The whole procedure convinced the teacher that pupils are likely to modify their speech habits more readily from listening and speaking than from writing.

Using Mechanical Devices

The recording machine and playback are immeasurably valuable in the teaching of speech. A person who has never heard a recording of his own utterance has little notion of how it actually sounds. It makes small impression on him to be told that he speaks with nasality, and it may be hard to persuade him to do something about his poor enunciation, his foreign accent, or his monotonous tone. But let him hear a good record of his speech, and all this is changed. He now hears himself as others hear him and can consider his utterance objectively. He and his teacher can analyze his sounds together; then he can record again and compare results *himself*. Work in interpretation of literature, too, is greatly assisted by a tape or wire recorder. On such an instrument, without the expense of discs, the student can experiment with a reading to his heart's content until he has just the interpretation that suits him. Timing, emphasis, inflections— every detail of oral expression—can be tested and perfected. Speech training of a high order is the result.

Improvement through use of recordings. That the recording machine has other advantages is demonstrated by the reports that follow. A striking instance of growth occasioned by its use is described by Florence Hogan of the Burdick Junior High School in Stamford, Connecticut:

A group of ninth-grade boys with I.Q.'s ranging from 63 to 91 and with reading levels varying from high second through high sixth grade were the behavior problems of the school. They experienced obvious difficulty in conducting a discussion because of their lack of self-control and their lack of consideration for each other.

The teacher suggested that the class be divided into groups of five or six boys, each to conduct a discussion while the others observed. A series of guideposts for such discussion was then developed. After each group had "performed," the teacher allowed them to do a tape recording of their discussion.

The boys were very enthusiastic; they did a commendable job. On the playback they were able to evaluate their performances amazingly well. Next *they* requested an opportunity to perform individually. This was granted with alacrity. These pupils who usually made many grammatical errors were quick to recognize them and to note the most glaring types of weakness in sentence structure as well. Perhaps even more significant was their awareness of faulty enunciation. One boy with a very pronounced foreign accent was startled to find he could not understand his own recording.

Since then all have made a conscious effort to improve their speech and they have learned some social amenities regarding group discussions. They have talked so eagerly to their home-room companions that the English teacher of the other group (with superior ability) has received an avalanche of requests for an opportunity to use the tape recorder. Actually the superior pupils want to emulate those whom they have heretofore regarded with a certain amount of condescension. What this turn of events has done for morale is wonderful.

Self-criticism through use of recordings. A novel use of recording apparatus is reported by Dorothea Fry of John Muir High School in Pasadena, California, in her account of how she handled a group of boys who tried to make up in noise for what they lacked in self-confidence:

For that group, on the third day, I set up a machine which records sound on a magnetized steel tape for one minute at a time. I had it recording when these boys entered the room, very noisily indeed. Their noise continued after the bell—that, too, was typical. After I had a good noisy minute recorded, I turned the control to repeat, turned the volume control up full, and let the machine blast their own noise right back at them. Literally, they outshouted themselves. At first, they could hardly hear the machine. But a few of them were watching me out of the corner of an eye—and wondering with one brain cell what I was doing. Little by little all of them were attracted. A vigorous whistle came through from the machine, and then they really began to listen to themselves. The tape ran on, and on, until somebody asked the inevitable question—"Is that us?" I smiled and nodded, then turned the volume way down. Somebody else said, "Let's listen to it again!" One chap said, "It was pretty bad," and others agreed. *They* said it, not I. *They* had made the discovery for *themselves.* I didn't rub it in. I didn't say anything—we just went on with our class work. But for a fair proportion of the group there was a real improvement, and I was grateful.

Continuity for films. Homemade silent films often intrigue young people and lead them to furnish the needed conversation and commentary. One junior high school class, for example, having a film collection in its audio-visual department, made its own silent color movie of episodes in United States history. Since there was no sound track, conversation and commentary were written out and the lines spoken. A similar program based on Longfellow's *Courtship of Miles Standish* followed. Much practice in discussion grew out of group planning of costumes, properties, and action. Use of colorful conversation was also imperative. The films were excellent program material both for the school assembly and for the next Parent-Teacher Association meeting—all of which suggests how mechanical equipment, if used with imagination, can give impetus to learning. Schools without films can do the same thing with a camera and slides.

Radio broadcasts. Radio broadcasting, simulated or real, depending upon the equipment available in the school, is an effective source of motivation for speech. News commentary, speech-making, and radio drama all furnish excellent opportunity for communicating to a high school audience.

In Nashua, New Hampshire, two classes co-operated on a project in listening, radio broadcasting (simulated), and interviewing.[18]

The classes met together for planning, each member drawing by lot the name of a person in the other class who would work with him in the preparation of an interview. Later each interviewer submitted to his partner the general plan of the interview and the questions. A careful schedule was prepared with the visitors coming in groups of three for fifteen-minute radio interview programs, complete with name, announcer, producer, commercials, and stop-watch timing. Competi-

[18] Nashua Senior High School, Elizabeth F. Cornell, teacher, reporting.

tion among groups for excellence in performance was a factor, too. The entire series of programs was tape-recorded for later study and evaluation.

By way of results, there were greater appreciation of a good radio interview, much more understanding of differences in ability to answer questions satisfactorily and in poise, and a better background for evaluating the pupils' facility in speech.

Literary recordings and tapes. Use of literary recordings will be discussed in connection with the relation of speech to literature. Tape recordings of political and other speeches have been successfully used to demonstrate the elements of effective speaking and clarity of thought and organization. Some schools with considerable audio-visual equipment tune in on panels and forums, recording as students listen, shutting off the channel to the classroom just as the summary and conclusions are reached. The boys and girls are then asked to draw their own conclusions and make their own summaries, later comparing them with those recorded from the broadcast to which they were listening. Such an experience dramatizes for students the processes of logical thinking always involved in the communication of ideas.

Linguistic recordings. Observation of levels of language, so frequently advocated by linguists today, can also be stimulated by the use of recordings representing the speech of various sections of the country and of varying levels of society. Among the most popular displays in the Festival of Britain in London were the three-minute recordings of the speech of gentlemen before Parliament, of Welsh miners in their homes, of cockneys in the streets of London, of charwomen in office buildings and of ladies at social gatherings, each accompanied by a film revealing the setting of the speech.[19] Similar recordings are available for regional speech in the

[19] Address Linguaphone Institute, Rockefeller Plaza, New York City, for recordings by Cabell Greet. Disc records for research purposes are on file at three universities: for the *Linguistic Atlas of New England*, address Hans Kurath, University of Michigan, Ann Arbor; for the Upper Midwest, Harold B. Allen, University of Minnesota, Minneapolis; for the United States as a whole, C. K. Thomas, Cornell University, Ithaca, New York.

United States, by means of which consciousness of levels and characteristics of speech may be developed.

THE RELATION OF SPEECH TO RADIO, TELEVISION, AND SCREEN

No program in the language arts can fail to recognize the impact of the mass modes of communication upon American life. All of them bear direct relationship to the development of power in speech and of power to evaluate the effects of speech.

According to *The English Language Arts,* Volume I of this curriculum series, each of the modes of mass communication may be approached from three points of view: (1) as an institution in American life with clearly defined techniques for influencing the public; (2) as a source of entertainment and personal enrichment during leisure time; and (3) as an aesthetic medium with art forms peculiar to itself.[20] How each of these can be developed for students in school and college has been described in detail in that volume.

Discussion of Films

Group discussion of a specific motion picture is a common activity in the speech class. Students may be led to sense both the actual and potential power of the motion picture, to view it as an art form and as an educational force. They may develop standards of evaluation such as those prepared by Donald K. Smith of the Department of Speech at the University of Minnesota to illustrate their use with high school seniors of the state:

STANDARDS FOR JUDGING FILMS

A. STORY AND SCRIPT
  1. Does it distort life?
  2. Does it glorify unworthy goals or acts of living?

[20] National Council of Teachers of English, Commission on the English Curriculum, *The English Language Arts,* NCTE Curriculum Series, Vol. I (New York, Appleton-Century-Crofts, Inc., 1952), pp. 348–373.

3. Is it a stereotyped, predictable plot?
4. Does it give any insight into truth?
5. Is it worth telling? Worth seeing?
6. Are the lines clever, striking, or in any way distinctive?

B. CASTING AND ACTING

1. Do the actors develop interesting characters or simply exploit their own public personalities?
2. Do the actors heighten and sharpen all possible meanings in the story?

C. MUSIC AND SOUND

1. Do sound and music support and heighten the story or call attention to themselves?
2. Is there evidence of imaginative taste in the selection of sound and music?

D. PHOTOGRAPHY

1. Does it suggest story rather than call attention to itself?
2. Is there evidence of imagination and taste in the selection of camera angles, effects, and scenes?

The film, *Understanding Movies,* prepared by a committee of the National Council of Teachers of English in co-operation with Teaching Film Custodians, Inc., is especially useful for this kind of discussion.

Special reports can deal with the characteristics of types of films such as documentary, historical, animated, musical, and the like. Others may delve into the influence of propaganda on films, the relation of attendance to film production and selection, and sources of review of films.

Radio and Television

The wide range in radio and television offerings suggests as wide a range in the tastes and interests of the listeners and viewers. Students profit from a discussion of the reasons for their likes and dislikes and of the influence of different kinds of programs on American life.

Most closely allied to the problems of speaking, however, are analyses of speech and voice techniques of noted speakers on radio and television. Those programs which aim to influence thought or to inform are most useful. "Who is speaking?" students learn to ask. "Why? Under what sponsorship?" and "On what authority?" Ability to detect bias in point of view, unsubstantiated generalizations, or inferences inadequately drawn is particularly important in a land where freedom of speech gives equal rights to the informed and to the uninformed, to the straight and to the crooked thinker, to the sincere and to the insincere. Critical examination of what is heard is vital in today's world. Some understanding of the meaning of "the cold war" and its power over the minds of men should be given to older high school students in these times.

SPEECH AND THE TEACHING OF LITERATURE

Proficiency in speech adds zest, insight, and a heightened sense of appreciation to the study of literature. Poetry invites oral interpretation and takes on new color and life when read aloud. Witness the oral interpretation of Benét's "The Mountain Whippoorwill" in the unit on *Back-Country America* described in Chapter 4. As for the lyric poets, many a student for the first time grasps the full meaning of some passage from "Il Penseroso" or "Ode to the West Wind" as he practices in preparation for reading it to the class. The search for meanings before reading aloud develops ability to understand unusual word relationships and to recognize the pattern of many of the involved sentences common to poetry.

Choral Speaking

A teacher in Champaign, Illinois, describes how choral reading came to her aid when she approached the study of poetry with a lively group of sophomores in a required English class—a group who had not just a mild distaste but a pronounced dislike for poetry in any form: [21]

[21] Champaign High School, Marion Stuart, teacher.

Deep within the heart of the instructor was the feeling that the best of all rewards from the study of poetry is the personal enjoyment that comes from living a great poem and wanting to share the experience with others. . . . How was the instructor to break down this sense of determined opposition and lead her pupils to a realization of the richness of experience which a unit in poetry has to offer?

The backgrounds of individuals in the class showed great differences of preparation. One boy during his ten years of schooling had attended seventeen schools in ten different states. His intense dislike for poetry stemmed from the fact that he was poorly prepared in the fundamentals of reading, yet he expressed his distaste in his own way by saying he "just didn't get poetry." To ask such a boy to read verse aloud to the group would increase his aversion. . . .

Sharing a common indifference to school in general, a majority of the class had no desire for individual distinction and craved only the satisfaction of being one of the "gang." Any activity that was going to win approval would necessarily be one in which they participated as a group.

The teacher chose to introduce the study of poetry by means of choral speaking. Through reading aloud in unison, she hoped to offset personal limitations and dislike and to release the beginnings of appreciation and enjoyment of poetry.

Principles of interpretation were discussed. As the class read aloud, each individual found pleasure in an expression of himself that was submerged in the performance of the group. Opportunities for socialization, for developing a sense of belonging, for erasing the marks of previous unsatisfactory experiences were provided by this technique of group speaking.

Poems were studied by the class for personal enjoyment. The author's thoughts and meanings were discussed. The class searched for logical and emotional details that would reveal the spirit of the poem. Structure was considered, and its bearing on interpretation.

Rhythmical appreciation was developed. Prosody was learned as pupils clapped out the rhythms of ballads. Sensory appreciation was heightened as the group became aware of the onomatopoetic language in such a poem as "By the Turret Stair." Responding to the images of "A Winter Twilight" by Angelina W. Grimke, "Deserted" by Madison Cawein, and "A Wanderer's Song" by John Masefield, many pupils began to realize the possibilities of poetry. Metrical patterns of timing and phrasing were discovered in pieces like "The Skyscraper" by Carl Sandburg and "Kit Carson's Ride" by Joaquin Miller.

If results may be judged by a group request for a second unit of poetry, then the choral speaking techniques awakened intellectual curiosity and aesthetic appreciation among the sophomores. They found pleasure for themselves in "loving a good thing" and wanting to share the experience with others.

A similar shift in attitude accompanied the use of choral speaking in the Brookline, Massachusetts, High School where a dissatisfied group had announced its dislike of poetry: [22]

We discussed informally the rhythms of various objects—machines, airplanes, walking, dancing, heartbeats, the seasons,—all we could think of. Then we listened to music in various rhythms. The class listened to several poems, tapped out the rhythm as I read, noted variations in it, discussed why the rhythm was chosen and why it varied. We moved across to the music room and played and sang as many lyrics from Shakespeare through the nineteenth century as I could find.

A number of poems were memorized almost painlessly, the music of them was so thoroughly known. The boys and girls began to discuss narrative poems as possible subjects for musical settings. Finally, we had a panel on the theme, "We are the music makers. We are the dreamers of dreams."

A rewarding experience also came to a group of boys in the Boston Latin School: [23]

Much to my surprise the class was enthusiastic about choral reading. The timid, who feared facing a group, joined ir wholeheartedly, for they felt more anonymous. Often I would select the more timorous to do solo parts in a longer selection. We practiced on such selections as "O Captain! My Captain!", "The Highwayman," and especially the Psalms. The boys loved to chant the verses like the monks at choir. They became keenly aware of mispronunciations and other mechanical faults of oral reading, absorbed the cadences and phrasing of the selections, and developed a deeper insight into the beauties of the spoken word. The class not only derived enjoyment but also advanced rapidly in oral delivery.

Sharing Reading

Buzz sessions, panel discussions, and dramatized interviews helped an average group of students in a bi-racial section of Oakland, California, to share the insights gained through the reading of biography: [24]

The low ten's agreed that they wanted success. They had just made a study of occupations. Over and over again they wondered if they

[22] Brookline High School, Alice Howard Spaulding, teacher.
[23] Latin School, Boston, Cyril J. Neville, teacher.
[24] McClymonds High School, Dorothy Petitt, teacher.

would be successful secretaries, mechanics, teachers, nurses, electricians. But what was success? Did you get it by hard work? What better place to seek the ingredients of success than in the lives of men and women as recorded in biographies?

To find out what a successful person was like, each student chose with the teacher's help the biography of a person who interested him, a book, in each case on his own level of reading ability. A girl who found reading difficult became absorbed in a simply written biography of Queen Elizabeth II, which first attracted her because of its brevity. A boy who would read only animal stories had one standard for his choice: the man had to live out-of-doors. He chose to read about Cochise, the Indian chief. Whatever the reason for the choice, each student was searching for the qualities which made the person successful.

Groups of students who had read about successful athletes, scientists, statesmen, teachers, writers, and so on, met together in buzz sessions to talk over the lives of these people. One class had five people who had read the life of George Washington Carver, and so there was a special Carver committee. Each group planned a discussion to present to the class, which identified the ingredients of success in their particular occupation. Some used a panel. In general, each student presented a different person about whom he had read, illustrating his qualities by specific actions or accomplishments recounted in the book. The chairman was then responsible for summarizing the main points made by all members of the group.

Oral reports and oral presentation of projects comparing what people did in the days of Homeric Greece with what they do today followed the reading of the *Odyssey* in the high school in New Rochelle, New York:

The best of these were illustrated with maps, designs, fashion drawings, miniature stage sets and properties, even puppets. Plans and maps of cruises were offered, large collections of things parents had acquired on such travels, and reports of routes followed by relatives in World Wars I and II. Fashion reports showed styles of the earlier period which influence us even now. Frequently, tape- and wire-recorded reports were prepared by the group in the home of a member. One group spent long hours working out a puppet performance.

All in all, the early question of "How modern is the *Odyssey*?" led to rich rewards. Not only did the prejudice against the *Odyssey* evaporate; to some the book became a good blood-and-thunder tale, to others a delightful tale of adventure. And the study led to extensive individual reading of the wave of "odyssey" books coming from the press.

There was variety, and to spare, for several interesting class sessions. A number of extremely shy youngsters were able to lose their self-consciousness and develop the security they needed. In their evaluations of each other's reporting, the pupils laid real stress on historical accuracy —they had become research-conscious and research-proud. At the same time they developed standards of voice, action, presentation, and audience contact which led to more vigorous and effective speaking.

Play-Making

An experience which utilized several language arts skills in combination comes from a ninth-grade class at the University High School at the University of Iowa. It is reported by M. Agnella Gunn, now of Boston University:

While my class was discussing and reading aloud some short stories by Saki [H. H. Munro], they commented that in many ways short stories and plays were very much alike. They decided to try to convert some of the stories into plays and produce one.

The class members divided themselves into groups according to the story they chose to work on, and began to plan. We discussed together the necessary changes: What could be retained as it stood? What had to be changed? How? What could be dropped? What must be added? Narrative was re-evaluated and converted into dialogue or dropped. Such problems as inventing a new character or carrying information and description by the device of a narrator were handled before those of casting or direction were met.

The changing of one form into another resulted in a growing and healthy respect for the skills both of the short story writer and the playwright. Seeing how a clever phrase could lose its luster when it was tampered with resulted in an increasing respect for *form* of expression. Finally, the composite classwork on a one-act production of "Quail Seed" brought about an increased understanding of the techniques underlying both forms of expression, increased ability to share responsibility in committee work, and increased skill in oral interpretation.

The mysterious actions of the artist and his model gave ample opportunity for dramatic action. The guesses of the customers as to who the strange man was who daily sought the boy ordering pomegranates and quail seed furnished leads for the interpretation of character. And the unique descriptive power of Saki [H. H. Munro] gave hints for costumes and background which aroused the admiration of all concerned.

Other outgrowths which paid dividends in keener self-appraisal and in increased interest in further experience were the discovery that memorizing lines was almost effortless when it was based on real familiarity with the material and that naturalness of oral interpretation, conversational quality of voice, and ease of manner are best when they grow out of real understanding.

Interpretation and Appreciation of Drama

One of the major contributions of speech to the language arts program is the interpretation and appreciation of drama. In an elective course in Advanced Speech for the twelfth grade, a group of highly selected high school seniors did a unit on Shakespeare following the study of ancient and medieval drama.[25]

The purpose of the unit was to give these mature students an understanding of the elements which combined to make Shakespeare a major playwright, an appreciation of the place of his plays in the history of dramatic presentation, criteria by which to judge modern drama, and a recognition of the universal quality of great art. The class considered the ideas which Shakespeare explored, the human values he dramatized, the language forces he employed to create major poetic expressions, and the story outlines he used to communicate these ideas and values effectively. Having done a unit on classic drama and having been alerted by their teacher to the modern theater, the students were in a position to compare and contrast the "classic greatness" of plays like *Oedipus Rex* and the neo-classic formality of *The Cid* with Shakespeare's techniques, which led to easily recognized influences upon the modern stage—in both melodrama and such serious plays as *Winterset*. In developing standards for judging the theater of today, students were in a position to use measures derived from the past as well as present-day considerations.

During the course of the three- or four-week unit, each student read at least one play, most of them read two, and several read ten or twelve. The teacher tried to match the plays with the known interests of individuals. Those read are represented in general by the recordings listed below, which proved exceedingly useful:

Hamlet—Olivier	10″ Victor LCT 5298
—Gielgud	2–12″ Victor LM 6007
Henry VIII	12″ London LL578
Julius Caesar	2–12″ Columbia EL 52
Macbeth	2–12″ Victor LM 6010
Midsummer Night's Dream	3–12″ Victor LM 6115
Othello	3–12″ Columbia SL 153
Richard II	12″ Allegro 8001
Richard III (Barrymore)	12″ Audio Rarities 2203
Romeo and Juliet	3–12″ Victor LM 6110
The Tempest	12″ Royal 1440

[25] University High School, Minneapolis, Arthur Ballet, Assistant Professor of Speech, University of Minnesota, instructor.

Before letting the students settle down to reading in class for the better part of a week, the teacher read aloud three or four typical scenes, each from a different play. He did this to give a concrete example of how to interpret drama, how to read character from soliloquies, how to pursue hints for future action and how to relate each scene to what has gone before. Sometimes recordings were used to illustrate the voicing of lines by different actors, or such varied interpretations of character as exist between Sir Laurence Olivier's *Hamlet* and that of Arthur John Gielgud.

Often the unit is timed to coincide with a Shakespearean play which is on campus or is coming to a town theater. Sometimes a television performance is available like *Macbeth* or *Hamlet*. Frequently preview films are used, like Hollywood's (MGM) *Julius Caesar*, Sir Laurence Olivier's *Henry V* or *Hamlet*, Max Reinhardt's (MGM) *Midsummer Night's Dream*, the new Italian film with English dialogue for *Romeo and Juliet* or the older film from MGM, starring Norma Shearer and Leslie Howard. Often a very poor film like Orson Welles's *Macbeth*, which can be used along with condemnatory reviews by professional critics, makes a good jumping-off place for the development of critical judgment.

Activities carried on during the unit are many and varied. Small groups of students who have read the same play produce illustrative scenes from it. Panel discussions compare, for example, the Shakespearean tragic hero with the Sophoclean tragic hero, or Shakespeare's renascence view of man with the medieval view as personified in *Everyman*. Sometimes individual students give oral interpretations of famous soliloquies. For the intellectually alert, a stimulating project is to investigate those criticisms which have been completely adverse to Shakespeare, like Voltaire's, and those which have been enthusiastic like Lessing's. Inasmuch as the colorful Minnesotan, Ignatius Donnelly, wrote voluminously on the subject of the Bacon-Shakespeare conflict, the whole controversy that still surrounds the actual authorship of the plays is a research subject of great interest to Minnesota students. Again, individual pupils sometimes pursue research into the changes that have been wrought on Shakespeare's plays quite literally (as by Garrick and Colly Cibber) and by way of interpretation, a study of how the healthy Elizabethan action, for example, has been currently watered down into psychopathic mind-action after the influence of Freud.

Students who are more manual-minded and less interpretative engage in a wide variety of activities: the construction of models of Elizabethan stages *accompanied by demonstration speeches illustrating how they were operated in relation to some specific play*, the construction of Elizabethan costumes, a study of Elizabethan music, examination of Elizabethan foods, a search for present-day colloquialisms derived from Shakespeare ("Something is rotten in Denmark," for example), or a similar investigation of descriptive passages made necessary by the absence of scenery from Shakespeare's stage.

Interest runs high in this unit, and the level of performance is mature. The objectives stated in the beginning are largely realized. Above all, superior students work up to capacity and like it.

CRITERIA FOR A SOUND SPEECH PROGRAM

Increasing recognition is being given to the importance of speech in the high schools of today. The emphasis upon the arts of communication places speech and listening on an equal footing with reading and writing. Training in speaking and listening begins at least five years earlier than training in reading and writing and continues for numbers of students throughout college. Some high schools have set up separate departments of speech in the belief that work can function most efficiently if relatively autonomous. The Commission on the English Curriculum envisions a program in which speech takes its place among the offerings of the total program in the English language arts, hoping to bring about in this way a close interrelationship among the various aspects of the program in communicative arts. Because of the effort toward integration, it is especially important to guard the place of speech in the program and to see that its claims are not ignored in a traditional emphasis upon reading and writing; for in the schools of a democracy the ability to think clearly and honestly, to speak with vigor, and to examine critically what is said by others is of paramount importance.

It is well, therefore, to set up certain criteria of a sound program in speech which must be observed whether it is taught in relation to or in segregation from the other arts of language:

1. It should provide for *all* students—those with defective speech, poor speech, average speech, or superior speech.

2. It should be inclusive in scope and substantial and varied in offerings in the regular required courses in the language arts, in special elective courses, and in extracurricular activities.

3. It should be taught by teachers whose program of prep-

aration includes specific training in the arts and science of speech.

Provision for All of the Students

In too many instances the students already competent in speaking are the ones who receive the lion's share of available training. They are the window dressing with which the teacher impresses the school and the school impresses the public. This situation is natural; up to a point it is desirable. Youngsters capable of responding brilliantly to special instruction deserve the opportunity to develop their talents. Fellow students are stimulated by their example, and society has need of their accomplishments. But society has need also of the contributions of their less able schoolmates.

At the same time, the school should be teaching the inarticulate to speak, making the poor speakers average and the average speakers good. Remedial services for the handicapped are imperative, a speech clinic, for example, and wherever possible a specialist in general speech and speech correction, to assist classroom teachers throughout the school system. There should be instruction in the fundamentals of voice and diction and there should be application of these fundamentals to the speech activities of everyday life for all pupils in the regular language arts courses. In addition there should be special opportunities in the speech arts for advanced students in elective courses and in extracurricular activities.

The well-rounded speech program is commonly concerned with providing experience and rendering services in three areas: (1) applied speech, leading to proficiency in the kinds of daily speech activities enumerated earlier in the chapter; [26] (2) speech improvement, with emphasis upon speech fundamentals leading to refinement in the individual's mode of speaking; and (3) speech rehabilitation or

[26] Adapted from Ollie L. Backus, *Speech in Education* (New York, Longmans, Green & Company, 1943).

speech correction, leading to the removal of defects. These areas extend to the activities of oral interpretation and those of social and business communication, such as conversation, interviewing, discussion and conference, public speaking, and debate. In all of these, social etiquette and parliamentary procedure offer indispensable codes of conduct.

As already demonstrated, radio, television, telephone, recorder, and record player are media which stimulate interest and vitalize instruction. Some of the activities mentioned under applied speech are more important than others. Many teachers, for example, feel discussion to be a more valuable social medium than debate and less likely to develop contentious habits of thought and manner. Declamation offers less, according to the thinking of some teachers, than informal oral interpretation and dramatics.

Speech electives. Speech electives serve two groups of students. There are those who, recognizing their need for guided speech experiences beyond those available in the regular required courses, wish advanced work in public speaking or additional practice in oral interpretation. On the other hand, there are those gifted young people who seek the satisfaction of using and developing superior ability in such areas as dramatics and radio production. The latter tend to outnumber the former. Deterred by heavy curricular requirements or vague fears of not being able to "make the grade" in specialized speech activities, many boys and girls who would profit from these electives fail to avail themselves of their benefits. To the superior student, the school's obligation is heavy in proportion to his abilities. Especially through work with dramatics and public performance will this talented person gain experience in teamwork and group responsibility, factors tending to improve citizenship and social behavior. It should be noted here that it is a disservice to the student to permit him to look upon such studies as career training. The school makes no pretense of turning out actors, radio announcers, and other professional performers. Emphasis should be placed upon development of skills and deepening of understandings and appreciations. In most small schools, a single elective course combines practice in all the fields which engage the interest of advanced speech students.

Extracurricular activities in speech. Extracurricular activities supplement the credit-yielding courses, provide further special opportunities for able students, and facilitate the production of plays and radio programs and the development of verse-speaking choirs and discussion teams. In many schools these activities are handled largely through clubs. The device gives continuity and organization to the work. Care must be taken to keep membership accessible to all interested students. As with the electives, the purpose of these activities is to help produce an effective and well-rounded person rather than a professional performer.

Speech and drama teachers themselves are the first to say that some of the finest training in their field is enjoyed as a by-product of extra-class or extracurricular activity programs, the latter sometimes called co-curricular, or conceived of as part of the curriculum itself. Where these are developed for the sake of student growth and not for the personal glory of director or individual performer, excellent results obtain. Here again, a nice balance is not easy to achieve; but it is certainly worth the effort it requires.

Speech therapy. Speech therapy is a science rather than an art. Without it many boys and girls not only fail to succeed in the speech arts but, because they are socially frustrated, develop serious maladjustment in personality. The mission of the program of speech correction is to save the defective student from defeat. Here the boy barred from dramatics by a lisp receives help; the girl whose foreign accent cost her a good job has her fault corrected. Improvement of speech is accelerated by raised hopes and better mental health.

It is obvious that the correctionists in any school system

cannot shoulder the remedial program alone. If the school is large and therapists are few, many students in need of corrective help will be neglected unless the entire faculty participates in the program, especially the teachers of the language arts courses. They may assist in these ways:

1. By helping to make a screening survey of the speech of the student body as early in the school year as possible. Once the program is in operation, all but seniors may be surveyed in May or June for the following year, leaving only the incoming freshmen to be considered in the fall. A logical group to conduct this survey is the English or language arts faculty, who meet every student in the school and have responsibility for both oral and written expression. The director of speech therapy, at a meeting of the department of English or language arts, may suggest testing materials and procedures and ask that the teachers list all students who give evidence of needing speech help.

2. By helping with remedial measures when the therapist confers with the students listed. Using appropriate diagnostic procedures, the specialist finds cases where the teacher can, with guidance, render effective assistance. It is often desirable to request the presence of this teacher at a later conference between correctionist and student. On such an occasion, the teacher has opportunity to observe the procedures used to aid the pupil and can, after the departure of the boy or girl, discuss plans with the consultant for giving further help in the classroom. Certain cases of faulty speech may be satisfactorily handled in this manner with only occasional checking by the therapist. With other types of defects the classroom teacher will deal only indirectly. To correct stuttering, for example, classroom procedures can be recommended that will produce conditions in which the student can be expected to experience a maximum of success. Actual treatment of such cases will, however, be confined to the clinic.

Some students require the continuous attention of the therapist. Where possible, a schedule of speech correction classes should be set up whereby small, homogeneous groups can meet one or more times a week. Students may be grouped according to types of difficulties: problems of rate (stuttering), problems of voice (inaudibility, nasality—including cleft palate speech, hoarseness), problems of sound (foreign accent, sound substitution, lisping, lalling).

Difficulties in programming are inevitable. High school schedules tend to be tight and rigid. Here again the whole school faculty can co-operate. Nothing that the school offers the speech defective is so vital to his future as the removal of his handicap. When this fact is recognized by a staff, program troubles disappear. The sympathetic teacher relieves the student of worry caused by missing class work while in clinic, for apprehension of incurring the disgrace of low marks may seriously retard the work of correction.

To the speech correctionist falls the duty of enlisting the aid of all the agencies promoting the physical and mental well-being of the pupil. He should utilize the services of the health and guidance departments. In addition to a substantial background in speech pathology and therapy, he should have sufficient acquaintance with the work of other specialists—such as the physician, the psychologist, the psychiatrist, or the oculist—to know when to seek their help and how to interpret their findings.

Unfortunately, many teachers function in small school systems where the services of a speech correctionist are not available. In conjunction with a selected member of the staff, probably the school nurse or guidance officer, they should become familiar with the speech services available through the state university, the state teachers colleges, and the state department of education or welfare, so that they may help handicapped students to avail themselves of whatever clinical assistance is provided through these agencies.

Furnishing Teachers with Training in Speech

It is obvious that no teacher can hope to handle even the general aspects of a broad program in the language arts without specific training in speech. Preparation confined to college English, which too frequently excludes speech, can never be sufficient for teaching the program envisioned in this volume. On the other hand, preparation in college speech without strong supporting work in literature, reading skills, and composition would be equally ineffective.

In recognition of this twofold fact, there is a definite

trend in programs of teacher education to combine work in the two fields in the training of teachers. In 1953, according to figures in the United States Office of Education, the number of English teachers graduated was, roughly, equal to the demand for them. The colleges and universities of this country, however, trained three times as many teachers of speech as there were positions available in speech alone.[27] It is important that the two fields come together to meet the needs of the schools.

Major universities like those of Syracuse, Kansas, Utah, and Minnesota now have extensive majors in the language arts, which by uniting the old major and minor requirements maintain the same level of scholarship formerly required in each subject separately. The major may be in speech with a strong supporting minor in English, or in English with a strong supporting minor in speech. With this kind of background, teachers are in a position to do justice to the speech program outlined in this chapter. For speech correction and clinical services, they must add considerable work in the science of speech and in related sciences, into which they may move with increased confidence which comes from classroom experience.

High schools which have more than one teacher in the language arts commonly select their staff with the various aspects of the program in mind—someone with major interest and specialized training in speech, someone in reading, someone in writing, and someone in literature. In departments of even moderate size there should be at least one speech specialist. In situations where the department chairman is lacking in speech training, he should ask advice of the department member who knows most about speech. In-service training in the speech arts is recommended where teachers' preservice preparation has not included the funda-

[27] Ray Charles Maul, "The 1953 Teacher Supply and Demand Report," *Journal of Teacher Education,* Vol. IV (March, 1954), p. 3.

mentals of speech.[28] In addition, certain consultants will be required for remedial reading and speech correction. It should be possible for teachers to secure broad training in speech without undue specialization. Completely differentiated requirements for "general speech" and "theater arts" in some instances split college speech departments beyond the point of usefulness to the small school, in which, according to the figures, more than half the country's teachers are at work. A sensible program of co-operation could greatly enhance the possibilities for achieving, in the average American secondary school, the program for which criteria have just been given.

Administrative Responsibility for the Speech Program

The success of any educational program depends upon the understanding and support of the school administration. This seems particularly true of the program of speech, which makes its best contribution only if the vital nature of its offering is appreciated and protected.

The good administrator promotes intradepartmental and interdepartmental co-operation. Responsibility for the improvement of language competence should be accepted by all teachers in all departments. The success of an all-faculty effort to promote linguistic proficiency depends to some extent upon the staff's sharing a realistic philosophy of language founded on common understandings. Insofar as possible, the student should meet with consistent attitudes toward the importance of effective English expression on the part of all teachers as he moves from class to class. Only through the school administration can this favorable climate be produced. A useful approach would be for the administrator to request that the department dealing most directly with reading and expression undertake, in one or more

[28] In Baltimore, since 1952, the public schools have conducted workshops for teachers in these areas.

faculty meetings, to lead the staff in discussion of the problems most readily discernible in all classrooms of the school and make available to them current materials and thinking in the field. Another method would be for the administrator to appoint an interdepartmental committee on communication under the chairmanship of an interested and trained teacher.

The administrator should be sensitive to the teaching load of individual members of the staff. There is a tendency to treat certain speech activities as extras which may be added to a teaching load without recognition of their time-consuming nature. A dramatic production, for instance, requires uncounted hours of patient and creative effort. Yet a teacher may be asked to direct extracurricular plays with no thought of modifying the responsibilities he already carries. The same may be said of the oratorical contest, the speech choir, the student forum, and the radio club. An alert administrator recognizes the importance of these activities and adjusts the programs of teachers working with them.

Classroom speech activities are time-consuming. Only a limited number of students can participate in a public speaking activity within a single class period. Classes should be small and the number of hours allotted for the class should be as generous as possible. Teachers should see to it that each performance is full of meaning for each student and leads directly to clearly defined goals. Mere perfunctory "giving of talks" is inexcusable when time is at a premium. Small-group activities within the large class, as illustrated frequently in this chapter, will also help.

A FINAL WORD

Throughout the materials which have been supplied for this chapter from all parts of the country, there are certain trenchant and notably important implications for teachers of language arts:

1. Meeting the varied speech needs of individual students is vital. Essential for the purpose are flexibility and variety in methods, materials, and experiences.

2. Helping boys and girls relate themselves to the society, as well as to the neighborhood and school of which they are a part, is a process which may be substantially facilitated by guided speech experience.

3. More than has usually been realized, or even accepted in practice, communication is the goal of speech skills.

4. Integral to this concept of communication are the factors of individual and group appreciation and practice of accuracy, integrity, and responsibility for the end product, which may be—indeed, often should be—action in the interest of society itself.

5. Speaking is one half of the two-way process of oral communication; as listening improves, speaking becomes more effective. (See Chapter 8.)

Speech is not a natural gift; it is learned. A high degree of proficiency in speech is requisite to successful living. Few people meet with competence the infinitely varied speech situations involved in vocational, civic, and recreational activities. That the development of speech competence in boys and girls is a major aim of the secondary school is an inescapable conclusion.

Speech succeeds to the degree that it helps achieve the speaker's purpose. Mere fluency and showmanship without communication represent failure. Granting that the able speaker influences his fellows, it is important to society that his skills be directed toward socially desirable ends, that he respect truth and the rights of others, that he foresee and accept responsibility for the results of his words. Clearly, the school's program must not confine itself to developing mastery of skills; it must aim also to cultivate attitudes and ideals consistent with the highly co-operative society of America and with her significant role in the world community.

While there is no one golden road to sound speech training, the program should be systematic and should extend over a long portion of the student's schooling. Skill in speech is not developed quickly; it is the product of growth and requires time and guidance. This guidance should be provided by teachers whose preparation includes specific and adequate training in the field of speech. Instruction should be flexible and varied as to method and choice of materials and experiences.

The speech program can render its proper service only when the school's administrative and instructional personnel, sharing a common concern about the student's speech needs, are stimulated to purposeful and consistent collaboration toward a mutually accepted educational goal.

BIBLIOGRAPHY

Books

American Council on Education, *Sociometry in Group Relations* (Washington, D. C., The Council, 1948).

APP, Austin Joseph, *Making Good Talk* (Milwaukee, The Bruce Publishing Company, 1950).

BRETZ, Rudy, and STASHEFF, Edward, *The Television Program: Its Writing, Direction, and Production* (New York, A. A. Wyn, Inc., 1951).

BRIGANCE, William Norwood, *Speech: Its Techniques and Disciplines in a Free Society* (New York, Appleton-Century-Crofts, Inc., 1952).

BROENING, Angela M., ed., *Conducting Experiences in English*, Monograph No. 8, National Council of Teachers of English (New York, Appleton-Century-Crofts, Inc., 1939), pp. 121–258.

COBBY, M., *We Play and Grow* (New York, Pitman Publishing Corporation, 1954).

Educator's Washington Dispatch Staff, *Portfolio of Teaching Techniques: Group Dynamics and Role-Playing* (New London, Conn., Arthur C. Croft Publications, 1950).

ELSON, E. Floyd, and PECK, Alberta, *The Art of Speaking* (Boston, Ginn and Company, 1952).

FREEMAN, William, *An Informal Guide to Public Speaking*, illustrated by Gluyas Williams, ed. for America with additional chapters by Quincy Howe, a revised edition of *Hear, Hear!*, published in 1941 (New York, Simon & Schuster, Inc., 1953).

FRIEDERICH, Willard J., and WILCOX, Ruth A., *Teaching Speech in High Schools* (New York, The Macmillan Company, 1953).

GLASER, Edward M., *An Experiment in the Development of Critical Thinking*, Contributions to Education, No. 843 (New York, Bureau of Publications, Teachers College, Columbia University, 1942).

GLASGOW, George M., *Dynamic Public Speaking*, illustrated by Warren King (New York, Harper and Brothers, 1950).

GOUGH, Vera, *You're the Speaker: A Handbook on Effective Speaking for All Business and Social Occasions* (New York, Whiteside, Inc., 1954).

JOHNSON, Wendell, *Your Most Enchanted Listener* (New York, Harper and Brothers, 1956).

——, and others, *Speech Handicapped School Children*, rev. ed. (New York, Harper and Brothers, 1956).

LABRANT, Lou, *English and the Common Learnings* (Chicago, National Council of Teachers of English, 1951), pp. 105–142.

——, *We Teach English* (New York, Harcourt, Brace & Company, Inc., 1951), pp. 105–142.

LAIRD, Charlton G., *The Miracle of Language* (Cleveland, World Publishing Company, 1953).

LEE, Irving J., *How to Talk with People: A Program for Preventing Troubles That Come When People Talk Together* (New York, Harper and Brothers, 1952).

LEVENSON, William B., and STASHEFF, Edward, *Teaching through Radio and Television*, rev. ed. (New York, Rinehart & Company, Inc., 1952).

MACGOWAN, Kenneth, *The Living Stage* (Englewood Cliffs, N. J., Prentice-Hall, Inc., 1955).

MULGRAVE, D. I., *Speech for the Classroom Teacher*, 3rd ed. (Englewood Cliffs, N. J., Prentice-Hall, Inc., 1955).

National Council of Teachers of English, Commission on the English Curriculum, *The English Language Arts*, NCTE Curriculum Series, Vol. I (New York, Appleton-Century-Crofts, Inc., 1952), pp. 302–327.

OLIVER, Robert Tarbell, *Persuasive Speaking: Principles and Methods* (New York, Longmans, Green and Company, 1950).

RAUBICHECK, L. M., *Speech Improvement* (Englewood Cliffs, N. J., Prentice-Hall, Inc., 1952).

REAGER, Richard Cranston, *You Can Talk Well* (New Brunswick, N. J., Rutgers University Press, 1946).

ROBINSON, Karl F., *Teaching Speech in Secondary Schools*, 2nd ed. (New York, Longmans, Green and Company, 1954).

ROSS, Russell Conwell, *Speak with Ease* (Princeton, N. J., D. Van Nostrand Company, Inc., 1950).

SMITH, Dora V., *Communication, the Miracle of Shared Living* (New York, The Macmillan Company, 1955), pp. 78–94.

SONDEL, Bess Seltzer, *Are You Telling Them? How To Converse Well and Make Speeches* (Englewood Cliffs, N. J., Prentice-Hall, Inc., 1947).

United States Department of Agriculture, Ohio State University Agricultural Extension Service, *Playing Out Our Problems in Socio-Drama* (Columbus, Ohio State University Agricultural Extension Service, July, 1948).

UTTERBACK, William E., *Group Thinking and Conference Leadership* (New York, Rinehart & Company, Inc., 1950).

VAN RIPER, C., *Speech Correction,* 3rd ed. (Englewood Cliffs, N. J., Prentice-Hall, Inc., 1956).

WEAVER, Andrew T., BORCHERS, Gladys L., and SMITH, Donald Kliese, *The Teaching of Speech* (Englewood Cliffs, N. J., Prentice-Hall, Inc., 1956).

Wisconsin State Department of Public Instruction, *Guides to Curriculum Building: Junior High Level* (Madison, The Department, 1950).

Periodicals

ADLER, C. E., ed., "Developing Oral Communication Skills," *English Journal,* Vol. XLI (January, 1952), pp. 24–30.

AINSWORTH, Stanley H., chairman, "Speech and Hearing Problems in the Secondary School," prepared under the editorial supervision of the American Speech and Hearing Association with the co-operation of the Speech Association of America, *Bulletin of the National Association of Secondary-School Principals,* Vol. XXXIV (November, 1950), pp. 3–139.

BERNSTEIN, Julius C., "Recording and Playback Machines: Their Function in the English Classroom," *English Journal,* Vol. XXXVIII (June, 1949), pp. 330–341.

BRICKELL, Henry M., "What You Can Do with Sociograms," *English Journal,* Vol. XXXIX (May, 1950), pp. 256–262.

CONN, Milford, "How To Make Cultured Conversation: Satire," *Collier's,* Vol. 125 (May 6, 1950), p. 50.

COUFOS, Dorothy, "Telephoning Is Language," *Exceptional Child,* Vol. XXII (November, 1955), pp. 75+.

DAWSON, Mildred A., "Interrelationships between Speech and Other Language Arts Areas," *Elementary English,* Vol. XXXI (April, 1954), pp. 223–233.

DIETER, Otto A., "Classics and Speech," *Quarterly Journal of Speech,* Vol. XXXVII (December, 1951), pp. 479–482.

"Drama and Discussion in International Understanding," *Quarterly Journal of Speech,* Vol. XXXVI (October, 1950), pp. 345–350.

FURNESS, Edna L., "Remedial, and Developmental Speech Program," *Elementary English,* Vol. XXXII (May, 1955), pp. 289–295.

GREEN, Paul, and COCHRANE, Cliff, "Your Speaking Voice," *Journal of Business Education,* Vol. XXVII (January, 1952), p. 215.

HARRINGTON, Elbert W., "Role of Speech in Liberal Education," *Quarterly Journal of Speech*, Vol. XLI (October, 1955), pp. 219–222.

HAUGH, Oscar M., "English Teacher as Teacher of Speech," bibliog., *English Journal*, Vol. XLIV (April, 1955), pp. 205–210.

HOCHMUTH, Marie, "Speech and Society," *Bulletin of the National Association of Secondary-School Principals*, Vol. 32, No. 151 (January, 1948), pp. 17–33.

JAFFRAY, N. R., "Hi, Bud, What's Cookin'?", *Collier's*, Vol. 123 (June 11, 1949), p. 10.

JOHNSON, John L., "Minimum Speech Program for the Small High School," *Bulletin of the National Association of Secondary-School Principals*, Vol. XXXIX (May, 1955), pp. 121–125.

National Association of Secondary School Principals, "Speech Education for All American Youth," *Bulletin 32* (Washington, D.C., National Education Association, January, 1948), pp. 5–222.

OLSON, Helen F., "Speech for All," *English Journal*, Vol. XL (April, 1951), pp. 204–209.

PLETCHER, James D., "Persistent Problems in the Teaching of English," *Bulletin of the National Association of Secondary-School Principals*, Vol. XXXIX (September, 1955), pp. 82–84.

POOLEY, Robert C., "English Teacher's Preparation in Speech," *English Journal*, Vol. XLV (April, 1956), pp. 181–187.

"Symposium on Forensics in Secondary Education," *California Journal of Secondary Education*, Vol. XXVII (December, 1952), pp. 450–488.

"What Is Speech?", symposium, *Quarterly Journal of Speech*, Vol. XLI (April, 1955), pp. 145–153.

PREVIEW OF CHAPTER 8

The Impact of Radio and Television

Support from Research

The Values of a Listening Ear

The Individual Gains

The Group Gains

Listening as a Total School Problem

Students Bring Some Skills from the Elementary School

Elementary and Secondary Schools Differ as Listening Environments

Students' Listening Habits Influence the Staff's Satisfaction

Ineffective Listening Causes Inappropriate Behavior

Instruction Can Improve Classroom Listening

Assemblies Offer Opportunities to Improve Learning Skills

Teachers Identify Essentials in a Developmental Listening Program

Listening as a Study Procedure

Students Need Training in Listening to Directions

Planning Sessions Are Made Effective through Better Listening

Techniques for Listening to Lectures Can Be Taught

Students Need Training in Listening to Panels and Forums

Language Can Be Learned by Ear

Skill in Spotting and Remembering Oral Information Can Be Developed

Listening as an Aesthetic Experience

Training in Ways of Responding to Oral Language Increases Enjoyment

Listeners' Participation Can Improve Choral Reading

Evaluation of a Developmental Listening Program

Bibliography

CHAPTER 8

Developing Competence in Listening

THE LEVEL of living and learning attained by any individual is directly related to his competence in listening.

Listening can make the difference between knowledge and ignorance, information and misinformation, involvement and detachment, enjoyment and boredom. The way an individual listens is as important as what he listens to.

THE IMPACT OF RADIO AND TELEVISION

In today's world, individuals and institutions assume that information which is broadcast will be heard and heeded by all concerned. The air waves are used daily to communicate headline news; emergency decisions; weather warnings; campaign appeals; calls for help in locating escaped criminals, missing or kidnapped persons, relatives of individuals unable to establish their identity, and owners of unidentifiable animals and articles; information about salable products and services; and to provide instruction along many lines.

Within any week on radio and television there is also available a variety of entertainment. Music, art, science, literature, and sports may be heard through a single broadcaster, an interview, a panel, a symposium, a dramatization, a demonstration—to mention but a few types of presentation. Often the participation of listeners is secured through a studio audience or by telephone. Music is frequently used to establish a mood for an otherwise nonmusical program. The

251

responsibility placed upon the listener is the heavy one of selection, for what he hears will be no better than what he dials. And what he gains from the experience will be directly related to his competence as a listener.

The tremendous impact of radio and television may be gauged from the number of sets in American homes and from the amount of time spent in listening to programs. About 97 per cent of the homes in America are equipped with radio receiving sets, a majority having more than one. About two-thirds of the automobiles in this country are radio-equipped. In the four or more years in which television service has been provided, the percentage of homes with television receiving sets is already in the 80's.[1] Four hours and 57 minutes daily per television set and considerably more per radio set is the estimate of time spent in listening.[2]

The whole world is an "audible book" for today's youth. Training in how to listen will determine, in no small measure, how well young people differentiate truths from half-truths, facts from opinions, sensations from emotions, propaganda from education.

Though radio and television listening may seem to be a one-way process, it actually does not need to be. The listener can react critically, can take notes, and later through discussion with others, through reading relevant material, and through writing to the station can clarify misinterpretations and can register approval or disapproval.

What young people listen to on radio and television can change their knowledge, skills, attitudes, and behavior patterns. If the change is to be for the good of the individual and of society, instruction in how to listen is as urgently needed as is instruction in how to read.

Long before radio and television were invented, listening was a rich source of information, verification, entertainment,

[1] National Society for the Study of Education, *Mass Media and Education*, Fifty-third Yearbook, Part II (Chicago, The University of Chicago Press, 1954), pp. 80–81.

[2] A. C. Neilson in *Television Broadcasting Magazine* (April, 1955).

and inspiration. But these inventions, like sound films, added a range of speakers not available to any individual on a face-to-face basis. These new media also created a listening environment in which half-listening, not listening at all, or talking to a companion while listening are not looked upon as undesirable listening habits.

Teen-agers have on occasion transferred such habits of listening to the classroom and the school auditorium. Yet long before mechanical devices were invented for measuring listeners' boredom, teachers recognized signs and symptoms of inattentive, inaccurate, unimaginative, and unresponsive listening.

The new inventions and the new knowledge from child study and human relations training have served to convince teachers of the need for a developmental listening program in secondary schools.

SUPPORT FROM RESEARCH

Research studies reveal that listening is a factor in scholastic achievement,[3] that poor listeners can be helped to improve their skills,[4] that listening is subtly modified by attitudes toward the speaker, the situation, and the audience,[5] that mass listening is modified by the social nature of the situation (the same listener responds variously to the same speech in different audience contexts),[6] that poor listening with or without hearing impairment retards normal language development,[7] and that listening is so important in

[3] Thomas T. Blewett, "An Experiment in Measuring Listening at the College Level," *Journal of Communication*, Vol. 1 (May, 1951), pp. 50–57.

[4] Don Brown, "Teaching Oral English," *English Journal*, Vol. 39 (March, 1950), pp. 128–136.

[5] Carl I. Hovland, Irving L. Janis, and Harold H. Kelley, *Communication and Persuasion* (New Haven, Conn., Yale University Press, 1953).

[6] Eliot Freidson, "Communication Research and the Concept of the Mass," *American Sociological Review*, Vol. 18 (June, 1953), pp. 313–317.

[7] Don Brown, *Auding as a Primary Language Ability*, doctoral thesis (Stanford, Calif., Stanford University, 1954).

business and industry that many large enterprises have offered to their employees (at all levels) training courses in listening.[8]

With this evidence of research and a knowledge of individual development and of the importance of training in human relations, the teacher is aware of the need to help the student improve his attitudes, skills, and habits of listening and is ready to create a school environment conducive to effective listening.

THE VALUES OF A LISTENING EAR

The Individual Gains

To listen creatively adds flavor to life. The individuality of the speaker, his attitude of friendliness or antagonism, the interest of his experience, and the sense of belonging which the listener feels in the midst of conversation give him a glow of satisfaction at the same time that he can live vicariously in the lives of others.

The good listener finds pleasure in daily conversation, and in the informal programs of radio and television which offer him a comfortable way of learning what happens to his fellow men, why people act as they do, what they think, and how they feel. If one is capable of responding to the flavor as well as to the substance of words, he has a never-failing clue to the quality of feeling and thinking of the speaker, to his mood at the moment, and even to the region from which he comes. These experiences he will pass on to others, for ideas for conversation and letter writing often spring from talk remembered in colorful context.

[8] Thomas L. Dahle, *An Objective and Comparative Study of Five Methods of Transmitting Information to Business and Industrial Employees,* unpub. doctoral thesis (Lafayette, Ind., Purdue University, 1953).

Irving G. Lewis, *A Survey of Management's Attitudes Regarding Oral Communication Needs and Practices in Large Industries of Los Angeles County,* unpub. doctoral thesis (Los Angeles, University of Southern California, 1954).

Life for young people, as well as adults, is filled with many hours of waiting—for buses, cabs, trains, planes; for delivery of goods; for a turn to be served; for a show to begin; for an appointment with friends, dentists, doctors, and others. In such situations, a listening ear can relieve tension and reduce impatience, for the person who listens to the sounds and words around him is pleasantly diverted.

Listening is also a rich source of information and a valuable extension of familiar knowledge. Through radio and television today one comes into contact with life in every corner of the globe. One may learn, as well, what each candidate stands for in a local or national election, why the president has vetoed a bill, what experiences an explorer has had in Antarctica, and what happens in London when a queen is crowned.

At the same time he may enjoy the thrill of a Shakespearean play, hear a poet read from his own work, or listen to a modern actor present a first performance of a radio play.

Research has proved also that alert and accurate listening is an asset in the worker, and that attentive and responsive listening is necessary to successful supervision.[9] One firm has reliable evidence that the improvement of listening ability on the part of all members of the staff improved both morale and productivity.[10] In addition, the good listener improves as a speaker, for he learns from others a sense of organization and a consciousness of how words, used with precision and imagination, can capture attention and convey meaning.

The Group Gains

In the schoolroom, as well as in political, social, and service clubs, listening is a major element in influencing others and in getting work done on a co-operative group basis.

[9] Thomas L. Dahle, *op. cit.*, and Irving G. Lewis, *op. cit.*

[10] Reported by Leland Bradford at Assembly 6, *Human Relations Training*, Association for Supervision and Curriculum Development Conference, New York City, March 21, 1956.

Group discussion, planning, and decision depend for their effectiveness as much upon the listener as upon the speaker. Ability to follow a carefully prepared report and skill in selecting from ideas presented the one best suited to the needs of the moment are listening skills basic to carrying on business in groups.

In the schoolroom where modern methods aim to help young people learn from one another in co-operative group activities, failure to follow the ideas of another may mean loss of information vital to the problem in hand. The teaching of listening, therefore, has won an important place in the language arts program of the school.

The listener—whether in a conversational small group, or an auditorium situation—can contribute to the better listening of others. He can and should assume responsibility for correcting any physical interference with effective oral communication. If the public address system is not working and no one is taking care of it, the listener should rise to announce that the public address system is not operating. If the listener cannot hear and there are no closer seats available, he should rise to ask the speaker to speak louder. If the speaker is too close to the microphone or is using too much volume, again the listener has responsibility for bringing this fact to the speaker's attention.

If the temperature or lighting in the room interferes with the speaker's or the listener's comfort, he can and should take the necessary action to have corrections made.

If persons near the listener are conversing or otherwise distracting attention from the speaker, the good listener can courteously but firmly solicit their quiet attention.

If a question period is announced, the good listener will ask a pertinent, briefly worded question. If no questions are asked, after a short pause, the good listener may rise to offer a motion of appreciation for the inspiration (or whatever is the appropriate comment) of the talk.

LISTENING AS A TOTAL SCHOOL PROBLEM

Students Bring Some Skills
from Elementary School

Few students in the junior or senior high school are *naturally* good listeners. Some arrive in the secondary schools with an emerging skill in group discussion procedures, in listening to each other and interrupting courteously, in offering and seconding motions, in asking questions following a talk, and in participating as listener and as speaker in informal conversation situations both face to face and over the telephone. Many, by the time they leave the sixth grade, have been helped to achieve some discrimination in the choice of radio, television, and movies to which they listen.

Elementary and Secondary Schools
Differ as Listening Environments

Though the student's developing skill should not be ignored, continuous and cumulative training in listening will be required if the teen-ager is to adjust to the increasingly complex situations in secondary schools. The entering pupil will find listening problems in the larger building, the greater number of students from a wider geographic area, the diversified curricula and equipment, and a schedule which involves moving from one room to another as he works with several different teachers during the school day.

This difference between elementary and secondary schools is not something to be deplored but rather to be regarded by the teacher as a challenge. Seeking to create an environment conducive to effective oral communication, the junior or senior high teacher will see in before-school homeroom activities, for instance, situations in which the social amenities can be learned and practiced.

Purposeful grouping within a class during instruction periods can facilitate listening as a means of effective learning and gracious living. In classes continuously kept as a whole (25 or more in one group), many are likely to listen passively without profit to themselves or stimulus to the speaker. In groups of ten or fewer students, they are challenged to listen alertly and responsibly.

Students' Listening Habits Influence the Staff's Satisfaction

Studies [11] of "What makes the day hard for a teacher" reveal that the listening habits and attitudes of students play a large part. Typical irritants include interruptions of a whole class either by announcements over the public address system or by messages delivered orally by a messenger; interruptions of the teacher's work with one student or with a small group by others calling for his attention; delays in the progress of an activity either because of an individual's failure to complete an assignment given orally or because of a student's absence or lateness which caused him to miss an oral assignment or directions. Many instances of inappropriate behavior were found to have their origin in the offending student's failure to listen alertly and responsively when classroom procedures were co-operatively developed by teacher and students.

Evidence was found that whenever a teacher identified a listening problem and provided instruction, the attitudes and habits of his students improved and his personal satisfaction in teaching increased.

Announcements over the public address system. Stimulating immediate and alert listening to an announcement over the public address system was found to be one means of reducing the amount of listening needed by eliminating the occasion for repetition. A reduction in the number of such messages, as well as improvement of the wording of those sent, was achieved by training students to listen for the important items in the announcement and to appraise the mes-

[11] Conducted by Angela M. Broening.

sage for its clearness, conciseness, and appropriateness for delivery over the public address system. Through discussion, students discovered that some of these messages should have been written and sent to the individual classrooms concerned. Some of the announcements could have been timed for a cafeteria period, thereby interrupting fewer class sessions.

Students involved in the study developed the following questions for consideration before making announcements or explanations over the public address system:

1. Is this a message that everybody needs to hear simultaneously?
2. If so, what are the fewest words in which it can be clearly stated?
3. What incentive can the message give for good listening?
4. How can attention be alerted so that listeners hear the *first word* of the message itself?
5. What follow-up, if any, will be needed to check listening comprehension?

Oral delivery of messages. Interruptions caused by a student's bringing an oral message for some individual can be handled by a student host or hostess. Training can be given to all members of the class in how to listen and how to record the message. During the year, each student in the class may be given a turn as host or hostess. This experience has concomitant learnings for the listener and eliminates needless interruption of the entire group.

Interruption of teacher by groups. When a teacher is working with one group and a student from another group interrupts to ask help for his fellows, neither group profits. Such interruptions can be channeled so that good listening environments are maintained. Co-operatively the teacher and students may plan that any group wishing help may write the name of its chairman on the chalkboard and the teacher, as soon as convenient, will come to listen to its problem.

Annoyance caused by students' failure to listen immediately and alertly. The need for alert and prompt listening is recognized by teachers in all fields. The habit of alert listening *from the first word* can be developed when the teacher and students together explore the personal and social advantages of giving prompt attention. Together, they can decide upon cues for everybody to stop what he is doing to listen to the teacher, to a classmate, to a visitor, or to the presiding chairman in an assembly.

Having established the rationale for prompt and alert listening, the teacher may give specific training in a variety of purposeful situations. Using questions to focus attention during listening, checking what was heard and remembered against a written or mechanically recorded copy of what was said, and appraising, at regular intervals, student progress in listening comprehension and enjoyment are ways to sharpen skill and to help the class understand the importance of prompt and accurate listening.

Such training given in an English language arts class will be utilized wherever applicable if every member of the faculty is aware of what has been taught and not only expects but requires his students to use what they know.

Ineffective Listening Causes Inappropriate Behavior

Sometimes disciplinary problems turn out to be, in reality, problems of listening. For example, one day in a large city high school, announcement was made of a special assembly arranged that morning. Instead of locker-to-home-room-to-first-period class, the students were called to the auditorium. They were busily talking about the unexpected change in schedule. The principal explained from the stage that the city was celebrating the one hundredth anniversary of the establishment of a dental college and that two distinguished dentists were present to say a few words to the students.

When the first speaker began to talk, his regional accent provoked laughter. He was unable to turn the students' lack of familiarity with his Georgian speech to his advantage. He stumbled through his notes and after some fifteen minutes sat down. The students applauded loudly, no doubt to make amends for their earlier discourtesy. Their English teacher was sitting with her home-room group in the assembly and listening earnestly for what points were scattered through the talk. When she met the students in their first-period English class, they exclaimed, "Wasn't that speaker terrible? He rambled. . . ." The teacher interrupted, "You and all the other students were *terrible* for laughing at that beautiful Georgian accent. Now tell me what the speaker said."

It was quite an ordeal. From all of them, only four of the speaker's ten points were recovered. The teacher then asked for "the opening sentence" which, she said, was buried in his talk. No student could remember the sentence. The teacher wrote on the board, "You face the world with your teeth." The students then recalled it. The teacher listed the other six points she had noted and asked, as an assignment, that each student reconstruct the speech and be ready to give his version the next day.

Their talks were more than creditable. After hearing five, the teacher led the group to see that *good listeners,* when confronted by a disorganized talk, can by their own efforts find something to listen to. If they do this during the talk, the speaker usually improves, for an attentive audience brings out the best in any speaker. Learning how to accept and to profit from an inadequately organized talk is one way the listener can protect himself from boredom and can avoid discourtesy.

Utilizing such a dramatic opportunity to bring home to students why they should be good listeners is desirable; but continuous improvement in listening will result only if every teacher is aware of students' habits of listening and is alert to ways of helping them improve.

Instruction Can Improve Classroom Listening

Every teacher in the junior and senior high school, both in his home-room and classroom relationships with students, can bring about improvement in listening. One means is to discuss with his students the talks and the sound films they have listened to in the classroom, the club, and the auditorium.

Prompt attention to the speaker should be required, for it is an essential of learning and a requirement of courtesy.

Listening to relate new information to old is a skill which can be sharpened in every subject area. Previewing an announced discussion and listing pertinent questions can help the student to identify what he already knows, believes, or thinks about the subject to be discussed. Doing this will stimulate him to listen for what is new and for what confirms or refutes his ideas or beliefs. Remembering what is heard becomes easier when the alert listener selects and makes special mental note of what he desires to recall.

Students become better listeners if they listen for specific things. The class, for example, may be divided into small groups, each listening for a different point. *Group 1* may be asked to listen for new ideas; *Group 2*, for familiar ideas aptly expressed; *Group 3*, for the speaker's plan of organization; *Group 4*, for effective ways used by the speaker to hold or to reclaim attention; *Group 5*, for quotable phrases or sentences; *Group 6*, for unsupported generalizations; *Group 7*, for clues to questions to be raised in the discussion period.

After the talk, each listening group is allowed five minutes to share within the group what was heard. One member is chosen by the five as their spokesman in the general discussion. What each representative brings out will help the entire class to see what can be done in purposeful listening. Discussion under the guidance of the teacher will also reveal how listeners can focus their attention and how they can school themselves to remember whatever they decide they will want to recall.

When possible, it is desirable to play back a recording of the talk so that all listeners may re-listen to check their skill in (a) sensing the speaker's organization, (b) discovering new ideas, familiar ideas, quotable phrases and sentences, unsupported or questionable generalizations, or unwarranted inferences, and (c) being alert to a need for questions to clarify or to extend what the speaker said.

From time to time, when several students or the entire group are presenting ideas orally, it is useful to have two or three students serve as *listeners with specific purposes*. These listening observers may later assist their classmates in an appraisal of how well the students listened, how well they participated in the discussion, and what, at any point or points, seemed to block the flow of ideas.

Listening to a playback of such a discussion is a revealing experience to all participants, those who took part orally and those who served as "listeners with specific purposes."

Every student would profit from the experience, at least once during the year, of taking the role of listening-observer for the class as a whole to check on the flow of participation, the relevancy of questions and comments, and the quality of thinking evident in the discussion.

From such activities the substance of a discussion is learned. Equally important, the techniques of effective participation as listeners and as speakers are identified as guides to self-improvement.

It is also necessary to train students to listen to the presiding officer when he outlines the scope of a panel discussion and indicates the procedure to be followed; for example, "A brief statement is to be made by each member in succession," or, "The topic is to be tossed out for the entire panel, each panelist speaking as he feels moved." This second kind of panel discussion is more difficult for immature students to follow than is a symposium of short, but related presentations. High school students should learn to listen to both kinds.

Designating listening groups with specific assignments is also a useful technique in a discussion after viewing a film. If a documentary film is being viewed, groups may listen for new ideas, familiar ideas in a fresh context, well-supported generalizations, unsound inferences, emotional appeal, use of music, sound effects, quality of voice, or whatever aspects the teacher and students agree upon in advance.

For films presenting a story, these items prove useful guides: How does dialogue reveal character? How does action relate to words? How do environmental sounds create a sense of reality?

Students should note, however, that to be effective listeners they must eventually be able to listen for all these things at once.

Assemblies Offer Opportunities to Improve Listening Skills

The less than satisfactory attitudes and habits in some school assemblies, an example of which has already been given, may be a transfer by students of their habits of passive listening to radio, television, and sound films. Or, ineffective listening may be caused by lack of training in how to listen to the kind of presentation offered in the assembly. A less likely reason is that the program is inappropriate for the teen-age audience.

Improvement of listening through student-teacher planning committees. The involvement of students in planning, in preparing listeners for the kind of program to be presented, and in evaluating both the presentation and the audience's reactions increases the value of assemblies as listening opportunities. Student-teacher planning committees soon identify the kinds of speakers whose personal magnetism can hold the attention of the entire assembled group without previous preparation of the students for the event. There are some speakers and some topics, however, that require preliminary discussion with the teacher to create readiness on the part of students if they are to get the most out of the program.

Different listening skills required by different programs. Varied programs require varied listening skills. If the teacher takes the opportunity to discuss with his students the kind of listening skills required by the program to which they are going, the quality of listening and of behavior will both improve. For example, if the program is a play or a dramatic skit, listening to the flavor as well as the substance of dialogue, responding to facial expressions and gestures as accompaniments of spoken words, hearing environmental sounds which influence feelings and actions of characters—all of these aspects of listening need to be learned if one is to have maximum enjoyment and appreciation of the program. It is helpful, too, to provide time in the first period following the assembly to encourage students to share what they have heard and how they feel about it.

Aesthetic experiences are gained from appreciative listening at assemblies featuring talented men and women, travellers, and persons with creative hobbies which can be exhibited or demonstrated and talked about. When such programs include a variety of talents (those of actors and writers, physical and political scientists, artists, inventors, and business executives), they demand skill in following a sequence of ideas, recognizing transitions, and separating main points from subordinate ones and generalizations from examples.

Critical listening is required when students hear election promises of student candidates for office. Analysis of *what* they heard may reveal that their personal attitudes toward a candidate have led them to incorrect impressions rather than to accurate recall of what was said. Some of them will enjoy reviewing studies that have been made of the effect of one's previous mind-set upon listening.[12]

Listening to campaign talks on radio and television in a school assembly can contribute to critical thinking if students are trained to differentiate facts, opinions, and sugges-

---

[12] University of Chicago, Graduate Library School, Library Institute, *Youth, Communication, and Libraries,* papers edited by Frances Henne and others (Chicago, American Library Association, 1949).

tions for action. Knowing the background of a speaker and the authority by which he speaks is also important.

Training can be given prior to and following assemblies in which informed students or adults come before the school to discuss public affairs or controversial questions. On such occasions a listener needs to be able (1) to identify statements which conflict with his previous knowledge and (2) to seek further verification either from the speaker or from other sources. Awareness of devices for making an emotional appeal can be developed in a setting which puts responsibility upon the listener to recognize when he has responded emotionally rather than intellectually and to be alert to the consequences.

Orientation assemblies conducted by many junior and senior high schools for new students (freshmen) are exploratory listening opportunities through which a faculty can assess the level of listening skills and attitudes of the newcomers. Such an assembly stimulates alert and accurate listening on the part of the new students. The upperclassmen who are serving as hosts and hostesses must also hear and heed the directions given by the persons who speak to the students.

From an analysis of such experiences, both speakers and listeners come to realize their mutual responsibilities when directions are given orally and action is expected.

Many secondary schools present assemblies showing curricular offerings and club activities. The purpose is to acquaint *all* students with the range of available opportunities. The listener's responsibility is to hear the facts, to remember what is relevant to his interests and abilities, and to make appropriate choices.

Guidance conferences, at times scheduled for large groups in the auditorium and at other times for smaller groups in classrooms, are additional occasions for hearing what is said, for remembering what is important to the listener, and for asking questions necessary to the listener's understanding of the information communicated.

Other occasions, such as those on which athletic and non-athletic awards are presented, furnish opportunity for students to hear how their classmates have earned their awards and how skillfully they acknowledge the receipt of them.

Good practices reported by many secondary schools indicate that a negative approach—disciplining students who are inattentive and talkative in assemblies—has been replaced by positive instruction in how to listen for various purposes and by good example on the part of the faculty. As attitudes and habits improve, the behavior of students, as well as of teachers, reflects the belief that listening is more than courteous silence while another is speaking. To trained youth and adults, listening is a personal act of lending their ears so that a speaker may reach their minds and hearts.

It is significant, too, that reports from schools make it obvious that no additional "courses" or "subjects" are required to provide instruction in listening. What is needed, teachers of English claim, is fuller utilization, by all teachers and students, of the listening opportunities which present themselves in the course of every school day.

TEACHERS IDENTIFY ESSENTIALS IN A DEVELOPMENTAL LISTENING PROGRAM

Among the essentials of a good listening program, teachers have identified seven which should receive special attention. The first is that the entire English department or the entire faculty should provide listening experiences of graduated difficulty. Repeated practice of the same listening skill in fresh and well-motivated situations is necessary to the fixing of permanent habits. Reinforcement by the entire staff of the efforts of each teacher should be earnestly sought to increase the students' competence in listening.

Sharing of experience among the staff makes all members aware of the relative effectiveness of various techniques of questioning, of reporting, and of evaluating student participation in discussion. Skills developed in one teacher's class will then be applied by the student in another teacher's room because the student is himself aware of the relevancy of the skill and his teachers know that he has received training.

In the second place, listening should not be considered a thing apart. It should be taught in relation to all the listening situations of the classroom, auditorium, and club activities of the school program, a listing of which should be a first step in curriculum planning.

Third, a careful analysis should be made of the skills in listening needed in each of these situations. These skills can then be allocated according to difficulty and applicability to the work of each grade.

Fourth, students should be given special preparation for listening experiences beyond their immediate interests or present understanding. Preliminary discussion, background reading, vocabulary training and the use of visual aids can create readiness for listening and can ensure comprehension and enjoyment. Lack of such necessary preparation usually leads to ineffective listening and inappropriate behavior.

Fifth, the interrelationships of speech and listening should be explored so that the two may be taught in mutually helpful fashion. Reaction of the listener is an important measure of success in speaking. Poor results in listening may be due to poor speaking as well as to ineffective listening.

Sixth, what is taught should be related to the uses of listening in home and community as well as to the activities of school and classroom. Both teachers and pupils should explore the out-of-school listening habits of each class. Teachers speak favorably of periodic surveys planned and conducted by students to discover what radio and television programs are regularly heard, how much time is being spent in listening, and what, if any, use is being made of what is heard. Similar studies of the live and filmed plays which students choose for their recreation reveal the listening taste and comprehension of the individuals concerned. Teachers also report that informal diaries kept by students, as well as periodic surveys containing questions which yield comparable data, give useful information. Through both sources, standards of selection and of methods can be developed by teacher and students.

Seventh, a program of evaluation should be set up to discover as objectively as possible what progress students have made in the improvement of their listening.

LISTENING AS A STUDY PROCEDURE

Learning to listen is fundamental to listening to learn. In schools where *listening* has received as much attention as *reading*, improvement has been seen not only in the quality of learning but also in the pleasure of teaching.

Students Need Training in Listening to Directions

Alert listening to oral directions was ranked as most important in a list of seventeen desirable habits of work identified by teachers of all subject areas at the Forest Park High School in Baltimore.[13] Recognition by teachers of this need was a first step to involving students in learning how to listen promptly, alertly, accurately, and responsively. When students came to realize that they could save time and reduce boredom caused by needless repetition, they were motivated to try to listen more effectively.

An analysis of directions given by teachers and students not only provided the listeners with instruction in what to listen for and what to remember, but also assisted the person giving directions to consider their clearness, conciseness, and completeness. This experience in every subject field during a period of two weeks brought about improvement in listening and satisfaction in teaching.

[13] Co-operative Evaluation of the Forest Park High School, Baltimore.

Planning Sessions Are Made
Effective through Better Listening

How effectively a unit gets under way depends, in no small part, upon the quality of listening by students and teacher. As approaches to the study are explored, the significant ideas, keen interests, and relevant skills of different members of the group are revealed. Out of co-operative planning come reasonable goals and suggestions for individual and group study.

Here is an opportunity not only to launch a unit by involving the students intellectually and emotionally, but also to have them experience the personal and social values of alert listening. They learn to avoid repeating suggestions already given and to concentrate on adding new ideas and organizing all ideas into a workable plan of study. The focus of the teacher's questions during such co-operative planning sharpens listening by assisting the recall of relevant experiences and by giving promise of new experiences.

If this is to be a *learning to listen,* as well as a *listening to learn* situation, the teacher will need to select students or invite volunteers to listen for specific purposes, a procedure mentioned earlier in the chapter. A guide to listening can be handed to each listening-recorder so as to simplify his task and to guarantee full coverage of the discussion. *Recorder 1* might listen for approaches to the study; *Recorder 2,* for key words or questions in searching for material; *Recorder 3,* for resources among students and staff; *Recorder 4,* for books, periodicals, records, films, radio and television programs mentioned as sources. Being a listening-recorder does not, of course, eliminate a student from oral participation.

When possible, it is desirable also to make a recording of the discussion so that it may be played back to check what individuals remembered without taking notes and how well the recorders' notes captured the essentials of the discussion.

If any student has been unable to remember the significant points in the discussion, the teacher will help him analyze his listening experience to show him how to listen for whatever he needs to satisfy his purpose.

It is important to note and to recommend programs. When radio and television programs are used as sources of information, it is important that students quoting them in class give exact and specific reference to the program in question. Sometimes it is helpful to have several students listen to the same program so that they may share their reactions to it with the class. This experience sharpens "listening to remember" and puts a social value on sharing what has been heard.

This kind of sharing often spreads interest in an on-going program which is a good listening experience. Such programs as "Conversation," "Author Meets the Critic," "Playhouse," "Omnibus," "Invitation to Learning," and "University of Chicago Round Table" are opportunities for learning to listen and listening to learn.

When a teacher listens to the students' favorite comedy program, he will gain some insight into their sense of humor, the simplicity or complexity of the listening situation involved, and the level of language which the students are enjoying. Such knowledge furnishes a basis for the improvement of habits of choice. The teacher may also find a clue to developing standards which will be useful in selecting humorous literature to read aloud to the class.

Techniques for Listening to Lectures Can Be Taught

There are many common elements in listening to lectures, whether face to face, by radio, or on a recording. First, one must listen for the organizational pattern of the talk and adjust accordingly his method of note-taking. Yet, while the student is listening to the substance of the talk, he should not miss the flavor of it. If the topic is controversial, the listener should assess the speaker's fitness to talk on the subject. What the chairman says about the speaker will give him a clue. But as he listens, the student should be alert for any statement of bias, point of view, or documentation for generalizations. Notice should be taken of points which the speaker says are facts and those which he characterizes as opinions.

When some visual method (or material) effectively supplements oral words, the listener should make use of it. He must, however, keep his ears open while his eyes look.

Listening to detect false inferences and unsupported generalizations is a skill that can be developed as students listen to each other, to adult speakers at school assemblies, and to speakers in lectures and on the air. Reserving judgment in listening to different viewpoints and being alert to indefinite or emotionally charged words (when listening to campaign talks and to discussions of public affairs) are necessary and desirable habits.

It is important for the teacher to watch for distortions and confusions in students' reports of what they hear. Sometimes statements are attributed incorrectly to a speaker because of the convictions of the listener. To help correct this kind of listening, a teacher will need to analyze with the students a transcript or a recording of the talk. If neither is available, a comparison of reports of listeners of different convictions will reveal differences in recall and point up dangers of inaccurate listening. Occasionally it is necessary for the teacher to furnish background information which will enable his students to listen intelligently to the discussion of a controversial question. In this connection, also, it is as important to train listeners to record sources of oral information as it is to train readers in correct bibliographic form. Half listening, misquoting, and failing to credit the source of ideas and statements are pitfalls of untrained listeners.

Students Need Training in Listening to Panels and Forums

Many students find it more difficult to listen to a panel than to a single speaker. In a symposium, a sequence of short talks on a common topic, the listener is responsible for getting the main ideas of each speaker and for relating them to each other. If there is conflict between the panelists, the listener has to weigh the statements in the light of evidence presented and of his own knowledge of the subject.

If the panelists are talking in a conversational style in an unrehearsed session, the listener has to be alert for agreement and disagreement among them and has to be aware of the influence of his own point of view upon his reaction to the speaker's ideas. The logic of the argument must be carefully explored.

From time to time, it is a valuable learning experience to listen, teacher and students, to the same radio or television program. "Television games" like "What's My Line?" or "Hidden Biographies" are one kind of panel which proves entertaining and also enlightening in respect to techniques.

An article, "How to Be a Panelist" (*Time*, April 4, 1955, p. 64), was a springboard in one class for a pleasurable and profitable analysis of a series of telecasts regularly viewed by many of the students. They were impressed with this observation: "On the art of playing TV games, all panel members (What's My Line?) agree that the most important knack is to be able to listen. Explains Arlene Francis: 'Newcomers on a panel are always too tense to listen well, and sometimes will ask questions that have already been answered.' "

Panels such as "The American Forum of the Air," "University of Chicago Round Table," and "Invitation to Learning" require more sustained and alert listening than TV games, if the listener is to remember what is said and evaluate its validity and reliability.

"Conversation" and "Author Meets the Critic" offer listening opportunities similar to some informal situations in school and in life.

If students, through the teacher's assignments, feel strong purpose in turning on any of these programs, they not only increase their listening skills but also have something useful and enjoyable to share with classmates.

Language Can Be Learned by Ear

Absorption and imitation of the effective and correct speech of educated people are by-products of listening to good talk in conversation; to speeches on the public platform, over the air waves, or in the theater; and to recordings of forums and of readings of poetry and plays.

"Watch Your Language," a series on semantics, and "Shakespeare on TV" have provided enjoyable and profitable listening experiences for teen-agers and adults.

Students may also learn to listen for the level of language used in different broadcasts and may attempt to discover to what kind of listeners each is addressed. (See Chapter 10.) Many elements of usage can be learned better by ear than by eye. Listening to record players or to a partner's reading aloud sentences containing the language usage in question sometimes helps pupils to focus their own practice.

A listening partner can help a speaker or writer. Talking himself out or reading aloud his first draft of a paper will help a speaker or writer, although he should, of course, do some independent reading and thinking before he tries his ideas on a partner. Then he will jot down the ideas he thinks he wants to present. The next step is to talk himself out to his listening partner, who is responsible for testing the appeal of the speaker's opening, the consistency of his point of view, the adequacy of details, and the correctness and effectiveness of his words and sentences. Without interrupting the speaker, the listener notes what needs to be done to strengthen either the soundness of the ideas or the effectiveness of the presentation. With this help, the speaker is enabled to revise his plans and to rethink, if necessary, his opening and closing sentences. He will be helped to discover the need for deleting irrelevant ideas or for expanding points not fully developed.

When a student has prepared a first draft of a piece of writing, he will find help in reading it aloud to an alert and responsive listener who should react to the appropriateness and force of the ideas, the clarity, conciseness, and completeness of the sentences and to the concreteness and effectiveness of the words. After the writer has revised his copy, he should then test his revision by reading it aloud to his listening partner.

Skill in Spotting and Remembering Oral Information Can Be Developed

Having clearly in mind the specific question he wants answered is an aid to the listener in spotting information in oral sources. If the source is a recording of the weather or the time, the listener, after dialing the appropriate telephone number, needs to listen only long enough to get his question answered. Cutting off immediately without an acknowledgment is acceptable when the voice giving the information is recorded. But when a listener is seeking information by telephone or in a face-to-face interview, he must word his question clearly, ask it courteously, listen for an answer, and, if the answer is not complete, ask another question. Listening will be selective in that he will ignore whatever is irrelevant to his question.

If several questions are required in an interview, the listener needs to be alert for information relevant to his purpose even when not a direct answer to his question. It may be desirable to ask other questions in the light of the answer rather than to ask the questions he had planned in advance of the interview.

Hearing and recording essential information in a telephone call are important skills useful in social and business relationships. Classroom practice in a simulated situation can give teacher and students opportunities for training in how to listen and for appraising improvement.

It is a useful skill to listen alertly in order to remember the bibliographic or purchasing information which is given in a live or televised demonstration or exhibit. Having several students or a student and a teacher listen to the same program makes it possible to check the accuracy of what is recalled.

LISTENING AS AN AESTHETIC EXPERIENCE

Training in Ways of Responding to Oral Language Increases Enjoyment

Capacity for appreciative listening developed through talking things over. A functional approach to developing students' capacity for appreciative listening is found in the countless opportunities in any school day for talking things over. As students thus clarify, intensify, and interpret the experiences being shared, they discover that when they are not doing the talking they like to listen. Instinctively they realize that active listening is a creative part of talking things over.[14] The teacher's skillful questions and comments stimulate appreciation of the miracle of language. Thus, the student-listener grows in enjoyment of the verbal imagery and sentence patterns through which the speaker reveals sensory impressions and the emotional tone of his experience.

The student learns, too, how to utilize the resources within his community for extending his enjoyment of oral language. Among these resources are the book and film talks and the recordings made available through public libraries for use in group discussions.

Many public libraries throughout the country have instituted such groups, some meeting at regular intervals throughout the year. The Louisville (Kentucky) Public Library, to mention a good example, since 1948 has been using films on such subjects as art, history, and the dance, illuminated by comments of a guest authority in the field, followed by a general discussion by the audience.[15]

[14] Russell Potter, "Talking Things Over," *Saturday Review*, Vol. 37 (May 22, 1954), p. 11.
[15] "The Private Life of the Public Library," *Saturday Review*, Vol. 37 (June 26, 1954), p. 15.

The American Heritage Project initiated by the American Library Association in 1951 has been a source of "free and full investigation of ideas" and of aesthetic enjoyment of oral language.

The recordings in many public libraries include poems read by poets, plays and speeches read by gifted actors and speakers, vocal music of a wide range, choral speaking choirs, and transcriptions of public addresses faithfully recording vocal qualities which make listening an aesthetic experience.

Listening can be as creative an experience as any of the speech arts—conversation, special occasion talks, storytelling, interpretative oral reading, or dramatics. What is needed is that the listener receive the experience with his senses alert and his mind and heart ready for the flavor, as well as the substance, of what he hears.

Creative experience gained through listening to plays, concert reading of parts of a book, theater-at-the-lectern. A senior class in drama was helped to develop this view of listening as an aesthetic experience by hearing the teacher read aloud Christopher Fry's *An Experience of Critics.*[16] As he told of his five-year-old son's first visit to the theater, Fry identified the characteristics of a creative listener: readiness to receive, sensibility, awareness of when he is touched.

From Ivor Brown these students, who were listening to plays on the stage, TV, and radio, and to recordings, picked up another important idea. "No critic (listener) has any right to his place of privilege if he has become bored with the art in question. . . . Weariness is unforgivable." [17]

There are aesthetic elements in presentations on the stage, the screen, and the air, which make special demands on the listener or viewer. Some of the most beautiful descriptive lines in English poetry have been attributed to the absence of scenery from Shakespeare's

[16] Christopher Fry, *An Experience of Critics and The Approach to Dramatic Criticism* by Ivor Brown, W. A. Darlington, Alan Dent, Harold Hobson, Philip Hope-Wallace, Eric Keown, J. C. Trewin, T. C. Worsley, edited by Kaye Webb, with a prologue by Alec Guinness, drawings by Ronald Searle (New York, Oxford University Press, 1953), pp. 16, 17, 18.
[17] *Ibid.*, p. 35.

stage. In radio drama, not only the scene is hidden from view, but also the actors. Voice and language alone must differentiate one character from another until the unfolding of the plot permits actions to speak together with words. Specific techniques of listening must compensate for the lack of visual presentation.[18]

The students' checking their own listening reactions to a live play, a movie, or a radio or TV play with a dramatic critic's (in the daily or weekly newspaper to which they have access) promotes interesting conversation and keener listening.

Conversation improved through creative listening. How to make conversation in the presence of strangers is a serious problem with many teen-agers. This is especially acute for those whose language skills have not kept pace with the conversational opportunities of such social occasions as teas, receptions, picnics, dances, and banquets.

Some students find it easy to talk; few find it easy to listen to a talkative friend or stranger. What all need is greater awareness of the contribution which both eager listening and effective speaking make in promoting good talk in good company. They need to realize that conversation is a two-way process.

If listening in conversation is treated as a potentially aesthetic experience, speaking as well as listening improves.

One teacher approached this goal through two pieces which she had clipped for oral reading to her students: Emily Post's "On Making Conversation" [19] and Christopher Billopp's "Silent People." [20]

Emily Post advised:

> If you happen to be one of those who dread meeting strangers because you can't think of anything to say, you should console yourself with the fact that the faults of conversation are committed not by those who talk too little but by those who talk too much. To "listen eagerly"

[18] Dora V. Smith, *Communication, The Miracle of Shared Living* (New York, The Macmillan Company, 1955), pp. 100–101.

[19] "On Making Conversation," *Baltimore Sunday Sun,* May 22, 1955, Section A, p. 5, col. 1.

[20] *The Baltimore Evening Sun* (February 26, 1955), p. 4, col. 3.

is really the best possible advice to give on conversation, since the person whom most people like to sit next to is a sympathetic listener.

Christopher Billopp discussed humorously the silent people who listen alertly and sense when they need to talk.

The class discussion turned naturally to what makes a good conversationalist. This alert teacher, who had planned to involve her students in this exploration, had ready for oral reading to the group John Mason Brown's "The Uniform of Justice." [21] She read aloud passages which directed attention to qualities, including listening, that contribute to good talk.

Interestingly enough, students found some of these qualities, in varying degrees of perfection, among their classmates and teachers. The students cited conversations with club sponsors, year advisers, and home-room teachers who found time for informal conversations before the more structured part of the school day began.

It was useful, too, to take a backward look upon their own contributions to conversations in which they had had an aesthetic experience in listening: an unexpected and unusual snowstorm which had closed school early and which had tied up traffic for several hours; an intruder at 3 A.M. in the apartment home of one of the pupils; the acquisition of a new automobile, after demonstration rides in several different makes; a serious accident witnessed on the way to school.

In each of these situations, they discovered that the speaker had stimulated their creative listening because of the sensory impressions, emotional tone, imaginative thought, and universal significance of his performance.

Their listening, they concluded, had been creative because they had listened with all their senses and were emotionally stirred so that they identified themselves with the person who was telling his experience.

They realized, too, how their *silence* had been *articulate listening*, heightening the total pleasure of the group in-

[21] *Saturday Review*, Vol. 37 (October 30, 1954), pp. 9–11, 45–47.

volved in the conversation. They noted, also, that the range of their interests and the keenness of their observation increased as they listened more alertly to plays, recordings, sound films, radio and TV shows, and in face-to-face conversations.

Sharing experience in listening to the radio program "Conversation" proved mutually helpful to students and teacher. On four Saturday evenings, they had heard informed and engaging men and women converse about four different subjects: the qualities of the ideal spouse, modern music, a Broadway play "The Bad Seed," and impressions of Boston as a social and cultural center.

The student listeners were fascinated by their discovery of how natural it was for these men and women to bring into their conversation what they had seen, heard, read, and written. Facts and opinions were exchanged. Conversation was lively and informative. The students relished the flavor of this good talk. They recalled with enjoyment sense-appealing words and apt comparisons, pleasing voice qualities, and the give-and-take of stimulating ideas—all of which, they concluded, contribute to conversation as a two-way process.

They noted how humorous situations, a slip in use of words, misunderstanding of a person's intent or meaning were treated by the host and his guests.

From the more direct experience of their "show and tell" [22] conversations in the elementary schools, these students had matured to a point where they enjoyed listening with the inner ear to conversation in fiction, in plays on stage and screen, and in radio and television programs.

To their developing competence in listening, the other language arts—speaking, reading, and writing—continued to make a contribution.

[22] National Council of Teachers of English, Commission on the English Curriculum, *Language Arts for Today's Children*, NCTE Curriculum Series, Vol. II (New York, Appleton-Century-Crofts, Inc., 1954), pp. 116–117.

They concluded with Russell Potter [23] that television can never give the auditor the feeling of immediacy and of personal participation which he experiences in an auditorium with others listening to a speaker.

The experience of secondary school teachers corroborates Gorham Munson's advice: [24]

Exercises for quickening one's ear for the actual sound, mode, and idiosyncrasies of speech pay handsome dividends in reader-agreement when you come to write fiction or plays. . . . First the ear, then the mind selecting from actual talk the little characteristics that make it tangy, vital, natural, and finally discrimination in getting suggestion of naturalness rather than unedited recording. . . .

Fun derived from collecting spoken words. An interest in words, so natural in childhood, should be cultivated at secondary school level. Listening to the conversation of cultivated people, to talks of informed individuals, and to recordings of plays, poetry, and speeches is one means of collecting words. The listener hears how to pronounce the word and from the context gets a clue as to its meaning.

Every secondary school pupil should be introduced to the anthologies written by Ivor Brown, who has this to say for words: [25]

Words, like flowers, have colour and bloom and aroma. They are to the writer as paint to the artist and, while they have been scientifically examined and listed and defined without cease by learned men and lexicographers, they merit also the purely affectionate approach of the collector who assembles his favourites in order to gratify both his sense of meaning and his sense of beauty in verbal shape and sound. . . .

Words, like precious stones and cut flowers, depend upon their grouping and the choice of neighbours. They may be strange or beautiful or amusing in isolation, but they will be doubly so when an author of judgment has put them in the right company.

[23] Russell Potter, *op. cit.*, p. 39.
[24] Gorham Munson, *The Written Word, How To Write Readable Prose* (New York, Creative Age Press, 1949), pp. 139, 140.
[25] Ivor Brown, *A Word in Your Ear* (London, Jonathan Cape, 1944), pp. 5–6.

Listeners' Participation Can Improve Choral Reading

For full enjoyment of choral reading, students need experience in listening creatively to a variety of literary selections read by a single reader. When listening to one reader, they are able to catch the differences in voice qualities which reflect the author's meaning and mood.

Many teachers who have attended the conventions of the National Council of Teachers of English have vivid memories of aesthetic experiences through listening to poets recreate their poetry. These teachers instinctively realized in the midst of the performance that had their students heard the poet read aloud they would have been moved by the imaginative thought, verbal magic, and marked rhythm through which he illuminated experience.

Fortunately, these teachers can share their joy in poetry without taking their students to a convention, for the National Council of Teachers of English has made available poetic recordings of high fidelity.[26]

Students find John Masefield's "Aloft in a Gale" [27] an exciting experience when they hear it read aloud. Silent reading does not do justice to the magic of the words and the music of the sentences, as the following excerpts will prove:

> In the nights, in the winter nights, in the nights of storm when the wind howls, it is then that I feel the sweet of it. Aha, I say, you howling catamount, I say, you may blow, wind, and crack your cheeks for all I care. Then I listen to the noise of the elm trees and to the creak in the old floorings, and aha, I say, you whining rantipoles, you may crack and you may creak, but here I shall lie till daylight.
>
> There is a solid comfort in a roaring storm ashore here. But on a calm

[26] Recordings available from the National Council of Teachers of English (704 South Sixth Street, Champaign, Ill.): LP's—*Robert Frost Reading His Own Poetry, John Barrymore Reads Shakespeare, Poetry of Edna St. Vincent Millay Read by Judith Anderson, Ogden Nash Reading His Own Poetry;* and 78 rpm records by Vachel Lindsay, Archibald MacLeish, Stephen Vincent Benét, Wystan Hugh Auden, E. E. Cummings, and Robert P. Tristram Coffin.

[27] "Aloft in a Gale," quoted by Raymond McFarland in *Sea Adventure* (New York, Harper and Brothers, o.p.) from John Masefield, *A Tarpaulin Muster* (New York, Dodd, Mead & Company, Inc., 1919), pp. 179–182, 185.

day, when it is raining, when it is muddy underfoot, when the world
is the colour of a drowned rat, one calls to mind more boisterous days,
the days of effort and adventure; and wasn't I a fool, I say, to come
ashore to a life like this life. . . .

It is at such times that I remember the good days, the exciting days,
the days of vehement and spirited living. One day stands out, above
nearly all my days, as a day of joy.

We were at sea off the River Plate, running south like a stag. The
wind had been slowly freshening for twenty-four hours, and for one
whole day we had whitened the sea like a battleship. . . . For that one
wonderful day we staggered and swooped, and bounded in wild leaps,
and burrowed down and shivered, and anon rose up shaking. The wind
roared up aloft and boomed in the shrouds, and the sails bellied out
as stiff as iron. We tore through the sea in great jumps—there is no
other word for it. She seemed to leap clear from one green roaring
ridge to come smashing down upon the next. I have been in a fast
steamer—a very fast turbine steamer—doing more than twenty knots,
but she gave me no sense of great speed. In this old sailing ship the joy
of the hurry was such that we laughed and cried aloud. The noise of
the wind booming, and the clack, clack, clack of the sheet blocks, and
the ridged seas roaring past us, and the groaning and whining of every
block and plank, were like tunes for a dance. We seemed to be tearing
through it at ninety miles an hour. Our wake whitened and broadened,
and rushed away aft in a creamy fury. We were running here, and
hurrying there, taking a small pull of this, and getting another inch
of that, till we were weary. But as we hauled we sang and shouted.
We were possessed of the spirits of the wind. We could have danced
and killed each other. We were in ecstasy.

Teachers report that the emotional impact of some short
stories is doubled when they are read aloud. Wilbur Daniel
Steele's "The Body of the Crime" [28] was difficult to experience when a group of twelfth-graders read it silently. But
when their teacher read it aloud, they responded fully to its
haunting atmosphere, compelling characterization, and interesting plot.

Meaning and mood understood through listening. The
meaning and mood of the writer must be conveyed by the
manner of delivery of the oral reader. To interpret the author sympathetically, the reader must master the thought
and words of the selection and the use of his own voice.

[28] Wilbur Daniel Steele, *Best Stories* (New York, Doubleday & Company,
Inc., 1946).

Even when all three—meaning, mood, and manner—are in tune, listeners must co-operate with all their senses and sensibilities in order to achieve an aesthetic experience.

Students may respond emotionally to the pitch, intensity, and resonance of the reader's voice. They may, in addition, recognize the flexibility with which an effective reader uses his natural voice qualities to interpret an author's meaning and mood.

Voices chosen by listening. From appreciative listening to one voice reading aloud, students can be led to choose appropriately what needs to be read by a soloist; what by a group; what by high voices, middle voices, low voices; with what change in inflection and at what speed.

A group of seventh-graders had a rewarding listening experience when their teacher read aloud Psalm 46. They discovered that Verses 1, 2, and 3 were effective when read in unison. Verses 4 and 5 were given to one soloist; 6 to another; 7 to a third. Verses 8 and 9 were read, with volume and at increasing speed, by the entire group. Verse 10 was said by a soloist who could use the lowest range of his voice and who could speak with solemn firmness. The entire group shouted joyously Verse 11.

Psalm 46

1 God is our refuge and strength, a very present help in trouble.

2 Therefore will not we fear, though the earth be removed, and though the mountains be carried into the midst of the sea;

3 Though the waters thereof roar and be troubled, though the mountains shake with the swelling thereof.

4 There is a river, the streams whereof shall make glad the city of God, the holy place of the tabernacles of the Most High.

5 God is in the midst of her; she shall not be moved: God shall help her, and that right early.

6 The heathen raged, the kingdoms were moved: he uttered his voice, the earth melted.

7 The LORD of hosts is with us; the God of Jacob is our refuge.

8 Come, behold the works of the LORD, what desolations he hath made in the earth.

9 He maketh wars to cease unto the end of the earth; he breaketh the bow, and cutteth the spear in sunder; he burneth the chariot in the fire.

10 Be still, and know that I am God: I will be exalted among the heathen, I will be exalted in the earth.

11 The LORD of hosts is with us; the God of Jacob is our refuge.

Oral interpretation improved by listening to others. Edgar Allan Poe's poem "The Bells" is unique in the English language for the way in which the poet has translated sounds into words. The words themselves actually repeat the sounds of different kinds of bells. Then, too, the slow, solemn beat or the hurried, frenzied rhythm accents the bell sound and carries the reader through a strange poetic experience. This poem is particularly impressive when given as a choral reading.

One teacher reports using "The Bells" with unusual success with ninth-graders.[29] She had the class read the poem silently. Then she read it aloud attempting to reveal the sounds of the different kinds of bells. The class listened for what each stanza told about bells and what people feel when they hear that kind of bell. Individually, the students made notes of how they thought the poem should be read. They tried out, in small groups, reading in turn. In this way they discovered what parts required solo reading and what parts needed a group of voices to interpret the meaning. Each student then edited for choral reading a copy of the poem.

There were more than a dozen listening experiences, for they tried out every suggestion which gave promise of an improved effect. The results of this co-operative listening appear in the accompanying copy of "The Bells," edited for choral reading.

[29] Angela M. Broening at the Forest Park High School, Baltimore.

The Bells

EDGAR ALLAN POE

I

First girl soloist, gay　Hear the sledges with the bells,
　　　　　　　　　　　　　Silver bells!
All girls, light, clear,　What a world of merriment their melody
gay　　　　　　　　　　　foretells!
　　　　　　　　　　　　　How they tinkle,/tinkle,/tinkle,/
　　　　　　　　　　　　　In the icy air of night!
high-pitched　　　　　　While the stars, that oversprinkle
　　　　　　　　　　　　　All the heavens, seem to twinkle
　　　　　　　　　　　　　With a crystalline delight;
faster　　　　　　　　　Keeping time, time, time,
　　　　　　　　　　　　　In a sort of Runic rhyme,
say "t's" clearly　　　　To the tintinnabulation that so musically
　　　　　　　　　　　　　wells
　　　　　　　　From the bells, bells, bells, bells,
　　　　　　　　　　　　Bells, bells, bells—
　　　　　　From the jingling and the tinkling of the
　　　　　　　　bells.

II

Second girl soloist　　Hear the mellow wedding bells,
First boy soloist　　　　　Golden bells!
Boys and girls, happy　What a world of happiness their harmony
　　　　　　　　　　　　　foretells!
　　　　　　　　　　　Through the balmy air of night
raise voice　　　　　　How they ring out their delight!
　　　　　　　　　　　　From the molten-golden notes,
　　　　　　　　　　　　　And all in tune,
　　　　　　　　　　　　What a liquid ditty floats
slower　　　　　　　To the turtle-dove that listens, while she
　　　　　　　　　　　　　gloats
　　　　　　　　　　　　　On the moon!
　　　　　　　　　　　Oh, from out the sounding cells,
surprise　　　　　What a gush of euphony voluminously wells!
Second girl soloist　　　How it swells!
First boy soloist　　　　　How it dwells!
Boys and girls, swing-　On the Future! how it tells
ing motion　　　　　　Of the rapture that impels
　　　　　　　　To the swinging and the ringing
　　　　　　　　　Of the bells, bells, bells,
　　　　　　　　Of the bells, bells, bells, bells,
　　　　　　　　　　　Bells, bells, bells—
　　　　　　To the rhyming and the chiming of the bells!

III

Third girl soloist, ex-
  citedly
Girls

loud

louder

faster

slower

Boys

distress
loud and strong

die down

Girls

beat out rhythm

anger

marked rhythm

Hear the loud alarum bells,
Brazen bells!
What a tale of terror, now, their turbulency
tells!
In the startled ear of night
How they scream out their affright!
Too much horrified to speak,
They can only shriek, shriek,
Out of tune,
In a clamorous appealing to the mercy of
the fire,
In a mad expostulation with the deaf and
frantic fire,
Leaping higher, higher,
higher,
With a desperate desire,
And a resolute endeavor
Now—now to sit or never,
By the side of the pale-faced moon.
Oh, the bells, bells, bells!
What a tale their terror
tells
Of Despair!
How they clang, and clash
and roar!
What a horror they outpour
On the bosom of the palpitating
air!
Yet the ear it fully knows,
By the twanging
And the clanging,
How the danger ebbs and
flows;
Yet the ear distinctly tells,
In the jangling
And the wrangling,
How the danger sinks and
swells,—
By the sinking or the swelling in the anger
of the bells,
Of the bells,
Of the bells, bells, bells, bells,
Bells, bells, bells—
In the clamor and the clangor of the bells!

IV

Second boy soloist, solemn	Hear the tolling of the bells, Iron bells!
Boys, sorrowfully	What a world of solemn thought their monody compels! In the silence of the night How we shiver with affright At the melancholy menace of their tone! For every sound that floats From the rust within their throats Is a groan./
slower	And the people/—ah, the people,/ They that dwell up in the steeple, All alone,/
slow	And who tolling, tolling, tolling
bass tone, steady, solemn	In that muffled monotone, Feel a glory in so rolling On the human heart a stone—
Girls, raise voices	They are neither man nor woman, They are neither brute nor human, They are Ghouls:/
beat out rhythm	And their king it is who tolls; And he rolls, rolls, rolls, Rolls
begin to get faster	A paean from the bells; And his merry bosom swells With the paean of the bells,
faster	And he dances, and he yells: Keeping time, time, time,
marked rhythm *faster*	In a sort of Runic rhyme, To the paean of the bells, Of the bells:
Boys, steady	Keeping time, time, time, In a sort of Runic rhyme,
faster	To the throbbing of the bells, Of the bells, bells, bells—
Girls	To the sobbing of the bells; Keeping time, time, time,
faster	As he knells, knells, knells, In a happy Runic rhyme,
happy	To the rolling of the bells, Of the bells, bells, bells:
Boys	To the tolling of the bells,

Of the bells, bells, bells, bells,
faster   Bells, bells, bells—
Girls and boys, slower   To the moaning and the groaning of the bells.

EVALUATION OF A DEVELOPMENTAL LISTENING PROGRAM

The true measure of a developmental listening program is its impact upon the students' attitudes, knowledge, skills, and behavior patterns. To be effective in the fullest sense, the program must contribute toward the personal, social, civic, and occupational competence of the individual.

The immediate outcome observable to both student and teacher is improvement in the student's use of listening as a study procedure and as a source of recreation.

More effective speaking, reading, and writing should also be evident: (1) The student should have learned to listen for the flavor as well as the substance of what he hears. (2) He should have grown in power to hear sense-appealing words and apt comparisons. (3) He should have developed a personal system of mental or verbal note-taking which he can adjust to the organizational pattern of the speaker. (4) He should have learned what to do about unfavorable elements in the listening situation (light, temperature, extraneous noises, audibility of the speaker). (5) He should have learned to recall (with source) challenging ideas and to extend or to verify his aural memory of broadcasts, forums, dramatic presentations, and concert reading of parts of a book by relistening to recordings.[30] (6) He should have developed personally and socially acceptable ways of releasing his emotional reaction to a speaker in a living room, a class-room, an auditorium. (7) He should have an eagerness for experience which keeps his ears alert for new ideas, for new

[30] For information about available recordings, write the National Association of Educational Broadcasters, University of Illinois, Urbana, Ill., or call the local radio-TV station or public library.

ways of expressing familiar ideas, and for association of what he hears with what he already knows, believes, and enjoys. There are available tests [31] and devices for checking "How Well Do You Listen?" Perhaps the best, however, will be the one created co-operatively by students and their teacher after they have had exploratory experiences in listening together; have checked, in different kinds of listening environments, their purpose, the content, and the situation; and have identified individual and group needs for instruction in specific skills.

This chapter has reported successful experiences in bringing about improvement in students' listening and concludes with a bibliographic invitation to further exploration of the problem—developing competence in listening.

BIBLIOGRAPHY

Books

ACE, Goodman, *The Book of Little Knowledge* (New York, Simon & Schuster, Inc., 1955).

DeBOER, John J., ed., *Education and the Mass Media of Communication* (Urbana, Ill., The National Council of Teachers of English, 1950).

DUKER, Sam, "Research in Listening," a paper presented at a meeting of the American Educational Research Association and the National Conference on Research in English, Atlantic City, N. J., February 21, 1956 (mimeo).

HERZBERG, Max J., *Radio and English Teaching*, Monograph No. 14, National Council of Teachers of English (New York, D. Appleton–Century Company, Inc., 1941).

LaBRANT, Lou, *We Teach English* (New York, Harcourt, Brace & Company, Inc., 1951), pp. 187–201.

National Council of Teachers of English, Commission on the English Curriculum, *The English Language Arts*, NCTE Curriculum Series, Vol. I (New York, Appleton-Century-Crofts, Inc., 1952), pp. 328–373.

National Society for the Study of Education, *Mass Media of Education*, Fifty-third Yearbook, Part II (Chicago, University of Chicago Press, 1954), Chs. IV, V, XI, XII.

NICHOLS, Ralph G., and LEWIS, Thomas R., *Listening and Speaking*,

[31] American Educational Research Association, *Review of Educational Research*, Vol. XXV, No. 2 (April, 1955), pp. 130–131.

A Guide to Effective Oral Communication (Dubuque, Iowa, William C. Brown Company, 1954).

Periodicals

American Educational Research Association, *Review of Educational Research*, Vol. XXV, No. 2 (April, 1955), pp. 121–138.

BROWN, Don, "Teaching Aural English," *English Journal*, Vol. XXXIX (March, 1950), pp. 128–137.

BROWN, James, "Construction of a Diagnostic Test of Listening Comprehension," *Journal of Experimental Education*, Vol. XVIII (December, 1949), pp. 139–146.

Education, Vol. 72, No. 7 (March, 1952), "Communication Skills Number."

Education, Vol. 75, No. 5 (January, 1955), "Listening Number."

FREEMAN, Bernice, "Listening Experiences in the Language Arts," *English Journal*, Vol. XXXVIII (December, 1949), pp. 572–577.

MERSAND, Joseph, "Why Teach Listening?" *English Journal*, Vol. XL (May, 1956), pp. 260–263.

NICHOLS, Ralph G., "Listening Instruction in the Secondary School," *National Association of Secondary-School Principals Bulletin*, Vol. XXXVI (May, 1952), pp. 158–174.

WILSON, C. E., and FRAZIER, Alexander, "Learning through Listening —To Each Other," *English Journal*, Vol. XXXIX (September, 1950), pp. 367–373.

Recordings

(Available through National Council of Teachers of English, 704 South Sixth Street, Champaign, Ill.)

Dylan Thomas, reading his own poetry on LP. Two volumes.
Edgar Allan Poe, selections read by Basil Rathbone on LP.
Elizabethan Love Songs and Harpsichord Pieces. LP recording.
Everyman, LP recording starring Burgess Meredith.
Hearing Poetry, Chaucer to Milton (Vol. I) and Dryden to Browning (Vol. II). LP recordings.
Ogden Nash, reading his own poems on LP.
"The Pit and the Pendulum," LP recording by Gilbert Highet.
Robert Frost, reading his own poems. Two LP records.

PREVIEW OF CHAPTER 9

The Rewards and Demands of Writing

Real Purposes and the Kinds of Writing They Demand

Personal Writing

Evaluation of Personal Writing

Formulation of Opinion

The Presentation of Facts

Letter Writing

Service Writing

The Importance of Words

Development of Skills

Caring for Individual Differences in Writing

The Problem of Handling Papers

Conclusion

Bibliography

CHAPTER 9

Meeting Youth's Needs through Writing

TEACHING WRITING is both difficult and rewarding, demanding much but offering much to teacher and student.

THE REWARDS AND DEMANDS OF WRITING

Anyone who has ever guided the written expression of ideas knows the joy and the challenge of discovering the widely differing young minds and the placid and stormy emotions awaiting release through writing. Such release is the real function of teaching personal expression. Faced by a group of doubtful, hopeful, expectant, reluctant individuals, the teacher must create out of them "a symphony orchestra," as Louis Adamic terms the ideal United States. The tragedy would be to make them a melting pot where all creative individuality, all independent thought, would be merged into one drab following of patterns set by teacher or by text.

Knowledge of One's Self and Others

Sharing ideas or experiences through writing is one way of learning to know one's self and to enrich one's personality. Many students and adults have told how they "wrote themselves clear" before participating in a discussion or deciding on a course of action. In a senior class in Seattle, the conversation concerned mature and immature ways of dealing with anger. "I have learned my method from my mother," said

293

one girl; "I write a fiery letter—and then tear it up." "I write about things I like," said another, "things like rain on the windows, wind through my hair, hiking in the mountains; doing so makes me enjoy them more." "Since I started to write about television construction," said one boy, "I have learned much more about it." Said another boy, "I like the way we write down our thoughts and then compare them. Every time we do so, I learn something new and change my own thinking a little." "Writing has made me understand myself better," said a girl.

Often the most promising pieces of writing are those which students bring in shyly, saying, "You read this, but don't read it aloud or let others see it."

Writing is also a means of learning to know others. "Writing stories about people has made me notice other persons more," said one student, "and try to understand them." Karen wrote at length on "The only way to heaven"—*her* way. Before asking her to read her paper to the class, the teacher read excerpts from Mrs. Fitch's *One God: The Ways We Worship Him,* a book which presents fairly and sympathetically the Jewish, Catholic, and Protestant religions. Other students offered to write about the symbols, practices, and beliefs of their religions. The teacher felt repaid for his efforts when Karen exclaimed, on presenting her ideas to the class, "I think my religion is best, but I can see how you would all think that about yours, too. It makes me respect what others believe."

Respect for the Thinking of Others

A class where thinking is shared through writing is likely to become a closely knit class. Working relationships are good. Often the members form lasting friendships. Differences of opinion and point of view are not necessarily removed; they are integrated. A frequent remark is some variation of "I can't agree with his views on that subject, but I respect his thinking."

If some of the student's statements are disapproved of, others are applauded. Gradually, as he becomes aware that his own thinking is received courteously and thoughtfully, he learns to respect the thinking of his classmates. He realizes also that a difference in point of view is not a fighting matter but a topic for absorbing discussion.

In ways such as these the high school program introduces the young person to experiences in writing suited to a democratic society where freedom of press and of speech (as well as writing) are treasured rights. The young person, protesting in his school editorial some administrative policy, should become aware that he is using a national right, and that his classmates, in arguing or disagreeing frankly, are making use of the same privilege.

Observation and Organization of Experience

Even on an elementary level, writing should help the young student to observe and to organize his experience—in other words, to think. He says, for example, that he has "nothing to write about." Through illustration and suggestion, however, the teacher helps him to focus on one of the many experiences he has had: the remodeled house along the way to school, signs that winter is over, the steps in building a camp fire, how his father folds a newspaper, the antics of a younger sister, the way one answers the telephone, what is recalled about an outing, resentment against household tasks, the idiosyncrasies of a relative, and so forth. The student with nothing to say is merely someone who has failed to look closely at his own experience and see it related to those interests and events which make up the lives of his friends. It is the job of the classroom to open his eyes.

Obviously, the teacher who guides such writing must have his own eyes open. He must be the kind of person who invites confidences, who can direct thinking, and who holds up standards of performance both in thought and in the use of language which young people learn to respect.

Hard Work Involved in Grappling
with the Expression of One's Own Ideas

Writing of this kind is hard work. Sincerity, not glibness, is its aim. Schools are sometimes guilty of encouraging superficiality, urging the student to "express himself" when he is far from ready for expression. "Write something," the teacher has been known to say. "Here are three subjects; surely you can say something about at least one of them." Good writing, communication of thought, just does not come about in that way. Before anyone writes, as every student should know, he should have some observation, experience, question, or conflict which he is interested in communicating. He must know what his purpose is, to whom he is speaking, what point of view dictates his expression.

Students must often plan writing a long time in advance of sharing their ideas with others. As the writing proceeds, they must have time for suggestions from the teacher, for discussion with their classmates, and for help with matters of form and content. The assignment to get out paper and pencil and begin at once assumes a product of little value. Teachers have been known to chide the student who failed to respond: "What, fifteen minutes and nothing written yet?" Important ideas may be working in the student's mind for several days before they are put down. Delay may indicate good judgment. A hasty or superficial assignment may negate what has been taught about correctness and effective presentation of ideas.

Jacques Barzun insists that students hand out to teachers the kind of "second-rate hokum" they give evidence of expecting by the superficial methods they often use. Good, hard thinking on the part of both writer and reader, he believes, is necessary if students are to be "ready to follow athletically on the trail of articulate thoughts, rather than look for the soapy incline to muddled meaning." [1]

[1] Jacques Barzun, *Teacher in America* (Boston, Little, Brown & Company, 1945), p. 50.

Ability to write can never be achieved incidentally through the indirect process of exercise-doing. The very nature of writing indicates that it must be learned through actual experience in putting words together to express one's own meaning. One does not learn how to create a sentence by adding or subtracting words and punctuation marks in the sentence someone else has created. Composing a paragraph or an essay is a closely knit operation, and playing with the pieces will not substitute for making the whole. Learning to write therefore calls for writing by the student and direct teaching by the teacher. There is no other way, and time-consuming though it is, the task is there if young people are to learn to express their ideas effectively in writing. Obviously there is a degree of discipline in written composition to which both young people and their teachers must be willing to submit if worth-while results are to be attained.

REAL PURPOSES AND THE KINDS OF WRITING
THEY DEMAND

Real purposes are basic to good writing. If one is to plan a useful program for high school students, therefore, he must examine carefully the purposes for which adolescents write and the forms which their written expression habitually takes.

Personal Writing

Personal writing gives young people a chance to express their feelings, to share their emotions. It gives them an opportunity to observe, to reflect upon, and to reveal experience in writing for others. It permits enjoyment of humor and flights of fancy. Usually such writing takes the form of personal letters, stories, essays, and poems, or of straightforward presentation of one's thoughts or feelings in material written for the purpose. It also involves such social communications as invitations and replies, letters of condolence or congratulation, and notes of thanks for gifts or favors received.

Clarification and Expression of Ideas

A second type of writing which plays a large part in life both in school and out involves the clarification and expression of ideas and the gathering, organization, and presentation of information for some specific purpose—arguing, for example, for a new set of tennis courts for community use, or presenting to one's classmates a report on the recent televised performance of a Shakespearean play.

Doing Business by Mail

A third and important purpose for writing is doing business by mail—announcing meetings, ordering goods, soliciting funds or support, selling or advertising the high school annual, seeking a job or asking for a recommendation. The conventions of business writing are fixed, and mastery of them in high school will free many a young person for attention to matters demanding increased maturity as he moves on to college or out into business.

Finally, service writing of various kinds is used constantly throughout high school years—posting written notices of meetings, keeping minutes, thanking a speaker for an assembly talk, or congratulating a fellow student upon his success in dramatics or sports. All these furnish occasions for teaching courtesy and completeness in writing and attention to appearance and correct forms.

PERSONAL WRITING

The writing of personal experiences persists throughout life. Each sharing of experience is a step toward self-realization. It is a part of growth toward maturity. Writing of this kind forms a continuous thread in the writing program from the seventh grade through the twelfth. Such experiences, shared through simple stories and poems in the junior high school, are often communicated through the essay, play, or more literary poem in the upper years. The urge to exchange experience is common to normal persons, and the range of material should be as varied as the students themselves. In consequence, this writing offers an almost ideal basis for dealing with the habitual structure and usage of the student and for relating these matters to life experience. Increased skill in use of language comes most easily to the student who is concerned with making his thoughts and feelings clear to others. Since his purpose is to communicate something he considers important, he is eager to use a style suited to the thought or feeling he has to convey and is willing to make corrections or changes when he fails.

Initiation of Personal Writing

The first business of the teacher of writing is to create in the classroom an atmosphere in which sharing personal experiences comes naturally and where each person, because of his "journalist's eye," is alert to the novel and to the significant in what is heard, seen, read, or done alone or together as a class group. In such an atmosphere, each person can feel free to share his experiences and to express his questionings, convictions, even prejudices, knowing that they will be considered respectfully and honestly.

Younger students, of junior high school age or even the emotionally young in the senior high school, will frequently write on very simple and objective experiences: the care of a pet or its clever tricks; family affairs (such matters as getting down to breakfast, going to a show, entertaining the unexpected guest, and so forth). Often such seemingly trivial writing has real significance to the writer and is indicative of larger matters. A twelve-year-old boy, for example, wrote about his grief at being refused a dog and set loose a series of excited comments on the selfishness of adults; a girl described her struggle to hear a certain radio program and opened a discussion of conflicts between adult standards and youthful desires.

Stimulation of Thought and Recollection through Discussion

In introducing personal writing, it is well to give ample time for discussion in order to stimulate thought and recollection about one's own experience. For example, one student's ideas on daydreams brought a flood of discussion. Some of the students had been vaguely troubled because they daydreamed. They were relieved that others had the same habit. The transition to the next step came naturally. What are the values of daydreaming? What are the dangers? What kind of daydreaming is valuable? How can daydreams be translated into creative activity? The person who can write of his questionings and can share these with others has taken a long step toward social consciousness and maturity. "What things happen to us," the teacher asks, "that are worth telling?" Too often, perhaps influenced by our mass media stories of murder, spying, and adventure, the student is likely to avoid the simple and common experience. A little help will lead to understanding what makes the really "interesting" story. Perhaps the teacher will read from a collection of stimulating student-written pieces collected from other classes, each chosen because it illustrates a point of view or a situation which is likely to touch off writing or discussion by members of the class.

Guidance in Writing about Personal Concerns

It is likely that throughout the high school years many boys and girls will write about family life, since gradual growth away from family restraints is one of the problems of youth, and balancing independence and consideration is a difficult matter.

An eighth-grade boy in a slum area wrote:

I wish I had a *bycycle* and could go places, my mother and my father think I would get hurt and they won't let me save my *mony* for the bike. I would be *carful* and know enough to keep out of the way of trucks and such, they think I'm still a baby.

Marking such a paper calls for thought and tact. The ideas are actually clear to any reader, but errors need to be corrected. The teacher who received this paper wrote the following comment on it:

I am sure almost everyone in the class has had this kind of problem. It is hard to match what we want with what others think is best. I understand why your parents would worry, but I know too that you want the bicycle very much. This paper seems to me to have such an important idea that you should put it into perfect form and perhaps post it for comments. I have put a check under words that are misspelled. You can correct those at once. Then read the story over aloud, to find where you have used commas instead of periods.

When you have made the corrections, check them with me and then make the correct copy. You might compare what you have written with what Jean wrote last week. See if you can discover why I think your ideas are alike. (Note: Jean wrote about wanting to go to a picture show of which her mother disapproved.)

An older boy in the eleventh grade revealed his concern with the same problem:

There is one reason which though it doesn't deal directly with school, it plays a large part in my dislike for school. It is that in eighth grade I had a chance to go to a dancing class with others of my class, which would mean that I could have broken into social activities with others of my class. But my parents said no. Because of that I now find it very hard. . . .

Here is the struggle for social status paralleled by the struggle for expression. As with the younger boy, there is need for understanding and for help with the actual wording of his statement. The sincerity of the material indicates its importance to the writer.

Following are two papers showing growth in maturity in both ideas and writing:

Family Crisis

It just happened last night. I was sitting at the dinner table when mother told me the bad news. Daddy had gotten a disease in his right leg and it had spread to his right arm. Well, this had happened before, so I didn't think much about it. But when she told me he might have to have his leg amputated, it was a shock. Such a shock it was, suddenly, that nothing else mattered except how to help daddy. He came home that evening. But he was a different man. I was surprised. He was laughing and joking with everyone. He did not act like a man whose leg might be taken from him soon. He acted like a man who had everything to live for.

Sometimes in everyone's life a crisis comes. A person thinks nothing could happen to him or to his family. But it does. It happens to the Joneses next door, to the Browns up the street. It happens all over— but it never seems very real until it strikes one's own home and family.

JACK

For Sale

FOR SALE—lovely grey stucco home; nice district near school and shopping center; four large bedrooms; knotty-pine party room; spacious living room; modern kitchen and bath; patio with out-door fireplace. Owner transferred; must sell immediately.

The advertisement was hard to find among all the others, stuck away down at the bottom of the page, and I felt glad when I couldn't find it at first. Other people might not see the ad either, and then they wouldn't come to look at my home. But I know I'm only dreaming; someone will see it and come. The strangers will decide the stairs are too steep, or the closet is unhandy, or maybe something won't suit them. Finally, though, they will buy my home anyway. The advertisement is so small and average-looking that anybody might not give it a second glance. But it isn't small and average to me; to me it is my whole life, all my sixteen years, tied up in a few words. But how can anyone put a life into just a few words? How can he show how important those words are? How can anyone put all my hopes and ambitions, all my childhood and all my growing up into a sentence or two for people to skim over and then forget?

"Lovely grey stucco home; nice district near school and shopping center. . . ."

"Lovely home . . ." but it's not just a home, it is comfort and security and love. It is that warm feeling I have when I walk up the familiar red steps, always stumbling a little on the third one that tips. It is looking in the old mailbox to see whether there might be a letter for me.

"Nice district near school and shopping center. . . ." But how can people know how refreshing it is to walk down to the store on a rainy fall day with the wind blowing through my hair and all the neighbor kids shouting "Hello!" How can they know how soft and green the birches are, out in front, and how little and tender the buds look in early spring? Will the new people be very careful not to frighten the birds that build their nest outside the dining-room window, and raise their babies? They are always such scrawny, hungry babies; and they open their mouths so wide that I'm always afraid the current Mrs. Robin will fall in. And will the new folks ever know how luxurious it is to stay in bed until quarter after eight, even though it is necessary to scurry like mad, then, to get to school on time? Will they ever appreciate the chance to come home where it is quiet for lunch, so they can study their history chapter they didn't review the night before?

"Four large bedrooms; spacious living room; modern kitchen and bath; knotty-pine party room . . ."

Can anyone ever know the thrill I had when Mom surprised me by redecorating my room while I was at camp?

It was perfect, all pink ruffled bedspreads and pale green wallpaper fresh as springtime. I even promised to keep it picked up but somehow after those first few weeks, I forgot. Then I'd have to stay in on Saturdays until it was cleaned.

And there is the living room where I had my party celebrating the graduation of my class from grade school. We rolled back the rugs and danced in our stocking feet so we wouldn't scratch the gleaming floors. That was before we added the recreation room, the room Dad built all by himself. He was so proud of his work, so proud of the built-in bookcases he had made with so much trouble, and the tile floor he put down so we could dance. I'll always remember the parties we gave especially after the football games when we were freshmen. We would drink cokes, and eat cookies, and dance or listen to the radio, or maybe just talk.

"Modern kitchen and bath . . ." Vivid in my mind is the summer Mom decided I should learn to cook. She was so calm and patient, even when I stormed and cried and wailed that I could never learn. I finally did learn, though, and that first meal I planned made Dad beam from ear to ear. The chops were a little under-done, and the cake was soggy, but it didn't matter.

"Patio with out-door fireplace . . ."

Those few words can never show the wonderful times we had, the burnt wieners, the marshmallows that caught on fire, the sultry summer days when I rocked in the porch swing, sipping lemonade and swooning over movie magazines and Frank Sinatra.

Then, there is the bulkhead between our driveway and Mary Jane's house. We used to scrap over who really owned it. Our tempers would flare, and we would stalk away from each other with our noses high.

"Owner transferred; must sell immediately . . ."

So we will move to Spokane, and buy another place, and soon we will be all settled. But will I feel as though I belong? Somehow, I know things will never be quite the same to me. This home can never be replaced; it holds my childhood.

ROBERTA

In comparing these two compositions, older pupils can sense the surface quality of the first, the announcement rather than the revelation of feeling, the pronouncement of a moral at the end. The chronology is clear. The sentences need variation, and concrete terms should be used.

The clarity of design in "For Sale," the stream of consciousness technique contrasted with the matter-of-fact description of the advertisement, helps the reader enter into the feeling of the author. The unity of tone and purpose kept throughout is enhanced by the excellent diction, the suggestiveness of the language used. The strong concluding sentence acts almost as a summary of both feeling and events.

The Importance of the Expression of Emotion

Emotion plays a large part in the experience of youth; personal writing, therefore, should express emotions.

The imaginative story. Often students prefer to use the imaginative story or poem as a cloak for personal emotions and concerns which they are not ready to reveal or which they know involve family relationships better kept as private. Few, however, can achieve the artistry and restraint of "The Pinball Machine."

The Pinball Machine

The street ball came out of the chute on the right side of the machine, rolled around the top, rebounded off the bumper on the side, and began to roll down the board. A half dozen pairs of eyes followed its progress as the lanky youth pushed and tugged at the pinball machine, guiding the ball, striving to make it fall into the hole near the bottom marked, "Super Special When Lit."

The ball hesitated against a light, rolled to one side, and then glanced off the protecting bumper and into the hole. The machine began to hum and click, and the number in the space marked "Free Games" mounted higher and higher.

"Holy smoke! George's got ninety-five games!" exclaimed an onlooker.

The rest of the crowd of youths pressing around the machine stood silent, watching reverently. George smiled happily and pushed in the coin slide to begin another contest with the gaudily lighted machine.

He was keenly enjoying his triumph. Until he left the machine,

George was the hero. He was a man who had done the impossible. The moment belonged to him. He must savor it and prolong it to the extreme.

Again he won, and his score went up over the hundred mark. "Five bucks," someone whistled. "Gee, would I like to do that!"

George's face glowed with pleasure. The remarks of his friends relaxed and warmed his body and sharpened his skill. He played as if in a trance, concentrating solely on the game. Every comment, however, brought a flicker of a smile to his face.

Interest began to wane. The impossible had been witnessed and now the moment was over. Slowly the crowd thinned. Finally George cashed in and left the café.

It was already dark as George walked down the street toward the big house where he lived. Climbing the stairway to the front porch, he unconsciously slowed his steps. Before he reached the door, he hesitated a moment and then went in. He walked into the kitchen.

"Hello, Mom. We eat pretty quick?"

"As soon as your father gets back. I had to send him to the store for whipping cream. What've you been doing all day?"

"I went down to the luggage factory this morning, but they didn't need any help. I earned some money today, though. Helped a guy paint his garage, and he gave me five bucks. How about keeping some of it for me?"

He reached into his pocket and took out three dollars. The mother put down her work and came over to take the money.

"Maybe you can get yourself a new shirt with this. You better go wash up for dinner now."

Later, as George sat reading the evening paper, he heard his father return from his errand to the store and begin talking to his mother. The murmur stopped suddenly.

"George, come in here." It was his mother's voice.

Reluctantly, the boy put down the paper and walked into the kitchen. His father was seated by the table. One hand was in a tight fist in his lap. The other was spread out on the table alongside the three dollars George had given his mother.

"George, where did you get this money you gave me tonight?"

"I helped a guy paint his garage," he answered, eyeing the money and then his father.

"You're sure, George?"

"Yes, I was with some fellow living over on Tenth. We painted the garage white with a green trim."

"You weren't in Chet's place at all today, were you?"

"I had a cup of coffee in there on the way home. Took about twenty minutes. That's all today, though."

"That's a lie!" His father's voice exploded hard and harsh. "You were in there tonight playing that pinball machine, and I saw you myself!"

George looked at the floor and said nothing. His mother put her hand to her face and nervously chewed her little finger.

"Well, weren't you?"

"Yes, I guess so."

His father rose to his feet triumphantly.

"Lying again. A fine son I got! Take your gambling money. Your mother don't want it!"

He threw the money against George's chest. Without lifting his eyes, George bent over and picked up the bills. He continued to stare at the floor after he had straightened up.

His father sat down.

"Look, George. Why do you have to keep on doing these things to your mother and me? Haven't we been good to you? You have a nice home here. I've offered you the same chance your brothers had to go to college, and I've given you almost everything you've ever wanted."

George kept silent. After a while, his father went on.

"All we ask, George, is that you get a job and quit this hanging around street corners and hamburger joints with those lazy bums. All you have to do is say the word and I'll pay your tuition right now so you can go to college. Or you could come down to the foundry tomorrow with me and go to work."

"I'd rather get a job on my own." George's voice was low.

"On your own! If you're going to get a job, you have to get out and hustle. You know there's only one thing I can decide. It hurts me to say it, but I'm beginning to think you're nothing but a lazy bum. You'll never be anything but a lazy bum, sponging off your old man."

George turned suddenly and ran out of the room.

Down at the lunch counter George slid onto a stool and said, "Give me a hamburger steak, Chet."

"Okay, kid. Back pretty soon, aren't you? Trouble at home?"

George didn't answer. When Chet brought the steak, he ate fast and silently.

Three hours later, George opened the front door of his home and slipped in. His mother was sitting in the front room reading a newspaper by the dim light of one lamp.

"Hello, Mom." His voice was careful and shallow.

"Hello, George. Where've you been?"

"Oh, I was walking around."

"Well, you'd better go to bed now."

"Okay."

"And your father's sorry he said what he did tonight. He was tired out. Only tomorrow, George, will you try to get a job? And stay away from Chet's, too. Maybe tomorrow evening we can all have a little talk."

"Sure, Mom. Good night."

"Good night." In his room, he heard his mother turn off the light and slowly follow him up the stairs.

JASON

The place of verse. Often, a student's writing about his personal concerns is in verse—sometimes mere doggerel. Rhythm and rhyme may reveal either excessive feeling or the effort at restraint. Whatever the resulting verses, merely producing some kind of "poetry" gives great satisfaction to the young writer and often status in the eyes of his fellows. Cautious in his criticism, the teacher nevertheless finds in the situation an excellent opportunity for developing sincerity, for pointing out that the meaning and feeling of a word are of more importance than its form, and that the good writer *uses* form, but is not *used* by it. Humor, too, frequently becomes a cloak to cover the serious intent of the writer when he fears opposition or contempt.

The selections below were all written spontaneously during a class hour in which each student agreed to convey to the others his reactions to something or some incident which had recently impressed him. The first quoted here, "There Is Nothing Like a Band," was written after a "pep" assembly in which the school band played an important part. It is obviously a parody—perhaps unconscious—of "There Is Nothing Like a Dame," yet it reveals the conflict between independent thought and expression and the desire to use the symbols and methods of the adult world.

There Is Nothing Like a Band

There is nothing like a band,
Nothing like the shrilling trumpets,
Nothing like the thund'ring drums.
Oh, I think the music's grand!
There is nothing like a band.

I love the smashing, clashing, crashing of the cymbals,
I love the pounding, sounding of the drums,
And more than anything I love
    The even beat
    Of marching feet
    As the band goes onward down the street.
Oh, I think the music's grand;
There is nothing like a band!

HELEN

Another parody, doubtless, "Take It from Me, You're in Love," is in marked contrast to the restraint of "The Flame":

Take It from Me, You're in Love!

If your knees feel wobbly,
And your heart flip flops,
If your hands are quivery,
And your blood pressure drops,
Take it from me, you're in love!

When you feel light-headed,
And you just can't eat,
When your eyes go blurry
And your heart skips a beat,
Take it from me, you're in love!

When blue looks purple,
And purple looks pink,
When you're really a genius,
And yet you can't think,
Take it from me, you're in love!

This poem may sound goofy,
But your patience renew,
And bear with me, brother,
'Cause I'm in love, too.

JAN

The Flame

He comes to me in the dark calm of the night.
He comes like the flame on a candle.
He is warm, glowing, fierce and beautiful.
I reach out for him
And like the candle, I am burned;
For everything that touches him is hurt.
But I remain true to him
For in my heart
There is a spark from the candle
That never dies.

It will be there forever living inside of me,
Burning its way deeper and deeper into my heart.
And then he speaks
Things that I remember him saying, long ago—
Little things that to him mean nothing,
To me, the world.

Then I see his face,
With that smile I remember so well.
Standing there in the darkness.
But then, as suddenly as he came,
He vanishes!
As if someone had blown him out.

All is still once more.
Reality is again upon me.
I will never let the flame go out in my heart.
I will never forget.

The junior high school product. Junior high school students, in writing for amusement, often specialize in punning, parodies, misuse of words, malapropisms, and so forth. These are interesting topics, with good language theory underlying their interpretation. Youngsters in Grades 9 and 10 are usually delighted with the unexpected ending—the thrill that was really a dream, the dear feminine friend who turns out to be a boat, the terrible danger that proved to be merely a cat in the attic. These should not be scorned. Great writers have used the same basic devices, and youngsters are not to be denied this pleasure.

Personal experience in writing, then, can be a source of entertainment or revelation for the reader, an outlet for personal feeling and emotion for the writer, an avenue of deeper social sympathy on the part of both.

Evaluation of Personal Writing

Evaluation of writing must invariably take into account the writer's purpose. What was the writer trying to do? How well did he succeed in doing it? Merely calling a paper "good" or "bad," "interesting" or "uninteresting," does not get at the basic question of how to attain a desired result. Did the writer say something worth saying? Since most writing is addressed to the class, audience reaction is a natural means of measurement. If the writing is a story of personal experience, was the progress of events clear? Did the reader come to know the writer or the characters in the story? If the writer had a particular mood to reveal, did he do it well? Did his choice of words help him to accomplish his purpose? Did the conversation sound real?

Help from the class. The ninth-grade paper which follows illustrates the points proposed for evaluation. "The Fire" was an exciting experience to Elaine. She keeps the story moving and handles the threads well. The conclusion is particularly good. The reader enjoys the summing up in good mathematical fashion. She makes the reader share her admiration for her uncle.

The class will note these qualities. The writer knows she has accomplished her purpose.

The Fire

This story took place on Thanksgiving Day in 1945. We were at my grandmother's house. She had prepared a big dinner and we were waiting for one couple to arrive so that we could begin the meal. My grandmother was in the kitchen making last minute preparations when we heard her shout that she smelled smoke! Some of the men investigated and found that a small fire had broken out on the back porch. Someone called the fire department while Grandma and all her guests evacuated the house. We kids were all put in someone's car that was parked in front of the house. About ten minutes later while the fire was merrily burning the back porch down to ashes, a light dawned on my mother and she suddenly shouted "Where are the kids?" It was a good thing someone else thought of us before my mother did.

Grandmother's back porch was located very close to the kitchen. My uncle had a heroic thought and went to rescue the turkey as it had forgotten to evacuate when the rest of us did. As he entered the house, the fire department arrived. They went to work quickly. They turned on their hose and accidentally aimed at a window connecting the back porch to the kitchen. The force of the water broke the window and glass flew in the kitchen. My uncle, at this moment, was busily saving the turkey, etc. His face was cut rather badly from the flying glass. Just at this moment the last couple arrived for dinner. I imagine they were rather surprised at the scene which confronted them. After a few details they quickly drove my uncle to the nearest hospital. Meanwhile the firemen wiped up most of the water and cleaned up the glass etc. The fire was out and the results were: 1 badly burned porch, 1 badly cut up uncle. The firemen had a snack and left. My uncle came back in a short while with his face covered with bandages, which incidentally didn't prevent him from eating a good portion of that turkey which he tried so hard to preserve.

ELAINE

The need for revision. Increasingly, writing involves re-writing. What should be the direction of improvement? The story is told in four scenes, but there are only two paragraphs:

Scene I—Grandmother's last minute preparations.

Scene II—The discovery of the fire and the protection of the children.

Scene III—Uncle's (does he need a name?) heroic act and its consequences.

Scene IV—Thanksgiving dinner with the triumphant uncle.

How much would conversation add to the story? What was Grandmother saying to herself in Scene I? Where else would conversation help? Could the secret about where the children are be kept from the reader, too? How could the title be made more alluring?

Fellow classmates can make suggestions of this sort. If the writer wishes, a small group may help her build up each scene. A poster on the wall may show her how to paragraph and punctuate the conversation. This story is good enough to be made even better.

Help from the teacher. Finally the teacher adds his comment, which serves more than one purpose. It should:

1. Give evidence that the teacher respects the effort made.
2. Stimulate further writing.
3. If possible, extend the writer's understanding of his theme; relate it to other experiences; indicate larger implications if they exist.
4. Suggest needed changes.
5. Indicate errors.
6. Note gains if any exist.

Help through comparison with other writing. Sometimes the value of more succinct telling and a more vivid and imaginative use of words can be illustrated through reading the work of a gifted writer who deals with experiences which we all have. Frances Lester Warner, in *The Pleasure of Your Company,* gives the reader great delight in such an ordinary incident as a husband's helping his wife to close the dining table after extra leaves used for a party the night before have been removed: [2]

> While she was placing the spare leaf against the closet wall, he bent over, stretched himself almost flat, reached with his long arms to the far end of the table, and snapped the two halves together.
> The trouble was that when he leaned over, the end of his necktie slipped its moorings and dangled into the gap where the extra leaf had been. When the two halves snapped together, they took his tie in their bite. This table was equipped with a patented snap that locked securely.
> When the housewife returned from putting away the extra leaf, she found her husband tethered by his own necktie, his face mirrored in the polished surface beneath his chin.

Choice bits such as this will help pupils see the value of just the right words to describe an everyday experience. The rhythm and variety of sentences also help.

Adapting criticism to the level of the pupil's attainment. But not all ninth-grade writing is as good as "The Fire." Edwin has many more problems than Elaine. He, too, has a clear idea of the progress of events, but he needs much more assistance with making paragraphs help him indicate the divisions of his story and with keeping all parts of his sentences together. His revision may well center on these two things. The pupils and teacher will want to compliment him on those sentences which are truly dramatic. They will also help him with his spelling and with his one or two slips in grammar.

A Cold Game

December 9, 1948. The time was 7:oclock, it was dark and windy. It was time for me to go to my team basketball practice. Out of the house I ran. I ran about ½ of a block and had to stop, I was puped. I cut through the ally and two houses, and across Lincoln field, and there I was at the basketball court. Up the cement stairs and through the glass door. No one was in the hall so down the cement coradoor I went.

[2] Frances Lester Warner, *The Pleasure of Your Company* (Boston, Houghton Mifflin Company, 1940), p. 43.

Each step I took could be herad nice and louged. Throw the doors marked Boys Locker. The gray wall were the same last year, 2 years ago, and two years before that and goodness only knows how many years before that. The locker were the same and so was everything else. I went up to a locker and took off my coat and put it in. Next was the shirt and the paints and the next second I was naked, it was cold, brr!! Quickly I put on my "T shirt" and shorts. And once agin I started to run, up the 20 old stairs to the gym. It wasn't much warmer here. None of the players were here so I sat down and watched a teame practice. One by one the members of my team came in. I begin to feel more at home. The clock struck 8 bells and we went on the floor. The dark brown walls of the gym got to look more happyer. After 30 minets of playing I had scored 4 points and was very tried. Will time flew by and it was nine oclock and time for another team to take the floor. We were all very tried. So down the 20 old stairs to the gray locker room. The boys sat around speek about the game and girls.

Within the next 10 minets I was crossing Lincon field, between two house, and through two houses and I ran that ½ block and was home, "Thank God!"

The End

EDWIN

FORMULATION OF OPINION

Writing to formulate opinion and to influence others is one of the most important writing activities of our time. Illustrations are multiple in the adult world: a letter urging a relative to come for a visit; a note to the local paper protesting the action of some group or the position taken by the paper; a motion or petition or resolution prepared for some club, union, or association; a paper written for a club program or the P.T.A.; articles in magazines; books; editorials; and so forth. In reverse, adults listen to and criticize or agree with countless statements of opinion designed to influence their votes, their attitudes on national and international concerns, their interest in health and educational programs, or their behavior in national defense activities. Whatever the objective, one method in a democracy is the formulation and criticism of opinion.

Facing the Facts

Students, therefore, not only face abundant need for understanding such procedures, but come to school accepting them as normal ways of behaving. Eager as they are to imitate and use the methods of the adult world, they are ready to formulate their own opinions at an early age. Indeed, one problem of the teacher of junior high school students is the eagerness of these youngsters to make pronouncements on almost any question without much basis for their beliefs. They will state firmly what the government should do on the most complicated of issues, repeating stoutly the conclusions they have heard at home or from neighbors. One aim, then, in this field of writing is to teach the basis for formulation, the need for facts underlying judgments, and the complexity of seemingly simple issues.

There are many topics within the range of seventh-grade youngsters. They are daily acting on the basis of their beliefs concerning radio and television programs, the right of an individual to choose his friends, the proper behavior for one at their age, the limitation of adults' right to exercise authority, the importance or unimportance of school work, and on through an endless list. In one study of the primary interests of a seventh-grade class, it was found that problems concerning the selection and care of pets, relations between members in the same family, how to make friends, and school success were paramount. Around these problems were beliefs with varying degrees of firmness. Often, indeed, along with expression of opinion goes expression of doubt or question.

With a little encouragement, students will write out these opinions, beliefs, or doubts. One boy, for example, led off in an eighth-grade class with an attack on the girls of the grade who failed to support local ball games. The topic proved of great importance to both boys and girls. Even these young students raised such questions as: Should boys expect girls to be mere encouragers? Is the game for the players or the watchers? Why don't boys watch the games of girls?

Substantiating Beliefs

One teacher with a group of poor writers, boys who thought they could not and did not want to write, set up a plan whereby one or two students each day wrote on the board a sentence formulating a belief. These ranged from convictions about the best ball team in town to matters of race or nationality. "All Germans are tricky," "X-program is the best program on the air," "Mexicans ought to stay out of our state," and so on, ran the statements. Each writer was asked to stand discussion. Other members of the class challenged the statement, asked for illustrations, the basis for belief, and so forth. After a full discussion, the student had a day or two in which to write out his resulting convictions. It was assumed early that discussion might change one's ideas, and commendation was given for acceptance of new evidence. Gradually the habit of substantiating opinion with evidence and of admitting the possibility of error became established. The statements were usually brief and were revised until they met standards of clarity and correctness. They were carefully dated, since it was understood that what one believed in 1956 might not be his opinion a year hence. After hearing his statement, "All Italians are mean" discussed by the class, and discovering that two members were themselves Italians, one boy wrote:

I said that all Italians are mean. That is not the good way for an American to talk. Some Italians are honest and clean and you can like them. Some are not that way. I still know two who are mean.

This represents no high level of literary excellence but does stand for great effort and struggle with prejudice.

Handling statements of opinion often tests the teacher's skill and knowledge. Simple questions such as "Will you give us the source of your information?" "On what do you base this? Help us by telling your facts." "When did this happen?" "How many people are like this?" "Do you know any witnesses?" and so forth, are tactful ways of finding out what lies behind a statement and of suggesting that opinion is sound when it is based on reliable data.

Frequently it is important and interesting to encourage students to write around some central theme. This may be some question of school policy, a focus for personal problems, such as Understanding Each Other, or a book or other common experience. In cases of this kind it is important to see that the following learnings are clear: that where information is available it should be used; that gaps in information should be admitted and recognized; that, although all available facts have been gathered, there is still room for difference of judgment. Even when discussing questions of policy, students should not be divided into "pro" and "con" groups; that is, the yes-no, black-white kind of argument should be avoided.

Seeing from More Than One Angle

One teacher stimulated the expression of personal opinion under the heading, "From My Angle." In order to know each other better, a twelfth-grade group decided that each would write about a specific experience, showing a general belief. Topics were varied and included the following:

1. My father is a day laborer. I know what hard work and loss of a job mean.
2. My father works for a salary. In spite of increased costs of living, our income remains the same.
3. There are many problems and responsibilities for my father, who is an employer.
4. I've been brought up in the Catholic Church. Our religion is dear to us.
5. We Jews love others too.
6. I'm a newcomer in this district. I can look impartially at your cliques.

How to build up or expand such an idea by illustration, by added detail and information, was a real problem for these students. Examples in current magazines and in the textbooks available in the classroom were used to stimulate both variety and fullness of development of the topic selected.

Compositions were read in class groups, and each group selected as best the one which seemed most genuine and sincere, and the most fully developed presentation of the individual's feeling. These selections were then read and discussed by the whole class.

Getting Order into Thinking

Grappling with the expression of ideas is valuable preparation both for life and for college freshman English. Examination of one's own thinking, breaking an idea into its parts, and expanding each in turn logically and completely are extremely important activities in the development of mental maturity. One teacher began by asking students to give three reasons for sponsoring a candidate for the presidency of the School Council. Each person wrote one clear topical sentence, keeping parallel ideas in parallel form: I believe we should vote for Bill because *he has already shown qualities of leadership in various activities of the school, he is a good speaker and can influence public opinion,* and *he is a hard worker and gets things done.* The next problem was to develop a paragraph proving each point that had been made, sometimes by anecdote or illustration, sometimes by means of factual information. Results showed that specific attention to clarity of statement and organization paid dividends. Students recommending the same candidate met together in groups and selected the best statement written to be mimeographed for distribution throughout the school.

The editorial column of the school paper or the section on timely topics offers an outlet also for those who wish to comment on questions being discussed at the moment.

Evaluating Expository or Persuasive Writing

It is clear that for expository or persuasive writing, even more than for personal writing, class discussion is the best means of testing success. The questions needed have already been brought out in the description of the teaching problem:

1. Is the writer's purpose clear? Is the statement of his thesis easily understood?
2. Do his main points stand out?
3. Is each one clearly developed and supported by acceptable evidence?
4. Are the writer's points presented in logical order?
5. Is his thinking fair or one-sided?
6. Has he won you to his idea? If not, is the fault yours or his?

THE PRESENTATION OF FACTS

The Formal Report

Some students find it profitable to gather and organize source materials around topics of interest.

Relation to broad units of instruction. For example, in the unit on *Back-Country America* (Chapter 4), students did considerable research on aspects of life among the people about whom they were reading. Valuable illustrative anecdotes came from novels and short stories. Other material, largely informative, was found in a wide variety of sources—books like *The Ballad Tree* and magazines such as *Holiday,* the *National Geographic,* or the *Saturday Review.* Biographies of authors also contributed much. The information was worthy of being set down in permanent and organized form —hence the written reports prepared by the class.

Help in pursuing topics of personal interest. Some years ago, young people were the object of pity because there were "no more frontiers to be conquered." A group of high school juniors set out to disprove the assertion and, incidentally, to investigate careers in which they had some personal interest —the bookmobile, the textile industry, the sulfa drugs, highway construction, housing projects, social service, soilless farming, teaching, dress designing, occupational therapy, the paperback-book industry, and the like. Skills of library research, selective reading, note-taking, and organization of ideas were taught as students summarized and sorted information under the teacher's direction in the classroom. Illustrations were verbal, for the most part, representing the skill of the individual in the pictorial use of language, ability to paste pictures being discounted as a goal of the teaching of English. It was also emphasized that pictures are more valuable left in the school's encyclopedias and magazines than cut out of public property and pasted into a personal report, thereby depriving hundreds of other readers of their use.

Problems of selection, organization, and form. Time for careful writing and revising after first drafts are written brings results in more simple, natural sentences and in broadening one's own ideas by consultation of many sources before attempting to express these ideas for others. Repetition, lack of sequence, and use of extraneous material can be avoided if time is given for careful supervision of the work done in the classroom.

Problems that appear constantly in this kind of writing are (1) distinguishing the relative value of sources, including date and authoritativeness; (2) furnishing in adequate bibliographical form a list of sources used; and (3) giving credit for quoted passages.

Unfortunately, there are times when assignments made in the classroom are actually beyond honest treatment by the students, who therefore resort to undigested quoting and to paraphrasing which almost quotes, not infrequently finding that these practices are accepted and labeled "research." In many instances, however, students are merely uninformed as to how to indicate their indebtedness to sources. There are at least three procedures from which the writer should learn to choose. He may give his own conclusions, not utilizing any borrowed phrases; he may make a statement beginning with X *tells us that* . . . in which no quotation marks are needed; or he may use an exact quote: X *says,* ". . . ." These distinctions need to be worked out with the student in specific situations.

Whenever a student has an inspiring experience in listening, in looking, or in reading, he captures something of the substance and flavor of the other person's experience. Without realizing it, he may absorb the speaker's or writer's words.

Remembering sources, as well as winged words, is an easy habit to develop if all teachers from the beginning of a student's experience with literature and with life encourage him to tell where he saw or read something he enjoyed and who said or wrote what he is repeating.

Developing originality in thought and in expression is also important. To encourage creative writing, a teacher needs to lead students to identify themselves emotionally with professional writers who have the gift of language. Having created readiness for writing, the teacher lets the students write themselves out. Then in the rereading and discussion stage of revision, the teacher invites the students to consider and to quote the persons or authors whose words they *may* have leaned upon in trying to communicate their personal experience. This kind of searching the soul for sources of inspiration and of actual words puts in proper perspective the problem of honesty with words.

As students mature, they can be taught to look at quoting sources from the angle of *infringement of copyright*. This concept is readily understood by secondary school students who have been trained in the elementary school to experience *pleasure in finding an author* who says effectively what they—the readers or listeners—feel and also to remember and acknowledge the source by giving the author's name and the title of the book or periodical, of the television or radio show, or of the movie or stage play in which the words were read or heard.

Writers influence each other's style. Young writers learn to find their own style by imitating, consciously or unconsciously, the style of other writers. Personal integrity and copyright laws require that the speaker or writer know when he is using his own words and when he is quoting the words of another writer or speaker.

Limited value of formal reports for some students. With the increase of core programs and of broad units in the language arts, more and more occasions arise for formal written reports. It should be remembered, however, that many students—probably the majority—profit more from a series of brief experiences in writing than from such formal, lengthy, and involved procedures.

Brief Presentation of Facts on a Limited Topic

Ability to write a well-developed paragraph or two or three related paragraphs of information on a single topic, somewhat limited in scope, is of fundamental importance to the average boy or girl as well as to most adults. Sam, for example, in his discussion of *How Radio Sound Effects Are Made,* shows that he has mastered this skill. His explanation is direct, interesting because of its concrete illustrations, and simply organized. It is clear as to purpose and captures the interest of the reader by its direct questions. It has a brief, pointed introduction, a well-rounded conclusion, and a content selected with the interest of the reader in mind.

How Radio Sound Effects Are Made

Have you ever wondered how they can make things sound so real over the radio? I have, and working on this topic has given me a chance to find out.

Rain is represented by the crinkling of cellophane or by the pouring of bird seed on paper. Pounding a metal drum with tympanic sticks gives the effect of thunder. Roaring surf is nothing more nor less than peas rolling on a mirror.

Did you ever hear horses galloping furiously, their harnesses jingling as they go? If you had been in the studio instead of in your parlor, you might have seen a large man pounding rubber plungers against his chest and another jingling keys on a metal chain. Perhaps the galloping was accompanied by the rush of wagon wheels along a cobblestone driveway. This noise is often made by turning a wheel with an iron rim over iron rollers set at different distances apart to make the sounds of different kinds of wagon wheels. In the same way, the effect of people walking on gravel is created by having someone walk about in a shallow box filled with gravel.

Does a murder mystery sound particularly gruesome to you over the radio? If so, you should see the harmless way in which it is done. A distant gun shot is represented by a quick spring of an eyeglass case or by slapping a pine board against a leather cushion. The squeaking of a heavy door is as harmless as a violin bow drawn across a berry box, and the silent murder itself is committed by thrusting a knife into a potato.

I think you will agree with me that it takes a great deal of ingenuity to be an "off-stage noises" man in a radio station.

SAM

Percy, on the contrary, presents a mere aggregation of facts about *aviation,* too large a subject, to begin with. He doesn't know what he aims to do and, consequently, neither does his reader. His first sentence, which gives the impression of being his topic, is misleading. No later sentence bears upon it.

Aviation

Airplanes play a very important part in transportation, war, forestry and many other things. The fastest time ever traveled in a plane on the level is 460 miles an hour, made by a French army man. He also has the record for the fastest in a dive, 600 miles an hour. The army has many planes, all of which have two bladed propellers.

Recently the army had planned to have three bladed propellers, but the machine guns are not timed right for three blades.

The average passenger planes carry from thirty-eight to forty-two passengers. Some planes carry seventy-two passengers, but there are not very many. There is a plane which carries a cannon and four machine guns, and goes two hundred and fifty miles an hour. By moving a flap on the wings the pilot can apply brakes to the ship while gliding to a landing.

In Montana there is an eight place monoplane being used as a roadside lunch room. It still has its motor in it. Altering the wings on a plane will increase the speed and lifting power. Some of the bigger planes carry their crew in the wings.

In the future they plan to have the airports on top of the large buildings. Also there will be more planes than ever.

PERCY

The pupil has gathered a fairly good collection of facts. He should be helped by the teacher to determine what aspect of aviation he really wishes to discuss and to select and organize his data accordingly. When these reports arise out of class discussion, they are usually better focused.

Application to All Subjects of Study

The techniques of formulating opinion and of reporting information have a place in many subjects of study. In science and social studies, the gathering and discussion of data lead naturally to the summarization of what has been learned. With the aid of class discussion, youngsters are able to sense relationships of cause and effect and profit from recording conclusions in their own words. Occasionally, too, such discussion leads to individual study of topics of personal interest. Consideration of the best methods of assisting students to make such reports brief, clear, and of functional value to listener or reader may well be the subject of discussion in faculty meetings.

Making students articulate in many areas of learning. A national engineering society has recently complained that college graduates in engineering cannot make their projects clear to the public because of lack of training in simple exposition. A scientist remarked not long ago that science students in the freshman year of college cannot write well enough to summarize the results of their experiments. If this is true (though it is reasonable to question the sweeping nature of the pronouncement), no English teacher can remedy the situation. Only a scientist can make students articulate in science. Only an engineer can bring simplicity out of the intricacies of an engineering problem. Hence, writing up experiments and explaining, orally or in writing, scientific or social studies problems are among the important concerns of the science and social studies departments.

Using the subjective examination. The subjective examination, also, might well be re-established to test outcomes which cannot be touched by the objective test, useful as it is within a limited area of measurement. Whether in English or other subjects, such a subjective examination should be given in unhurried fashion on a different day from the objective one, with the recognized purpose of testing ability to select, organize, and present ideas in each area of learning. Such skill is a legitimate expectation in any subject of study.

Improvement of boys and girls in these skills may well be the object of concerted action on the part of all teachers of the school.

Selecting, organizing, and presenting facts. The paper based on reading makes large demands when it comes to the first step of "discovering and recognizing material." Here the student needs to apply what he has learned about the card catalog, indexes to periodicals, encyclopedias, atlases, almanacs, dictionaries or biographies, books of quotations, and the vertical file of pamphlet materials. Qualified teachers of science, social studies, art, music, and foreign languages know the "finding tools" in their specific fields and can reinforce and supplement the training which the student has received from his English teacher and school librarian.

In attempting to locate revelant materials, the investigator has a set of questions he wants answered and must constantly decide which of the materials he finds are pertinent. He may, with a general interest in a topic, be organizing his findings around proposed questions even as he reads. The less expert person reads, makes too-abundant notes, and finds himself with merely a mass of material. Students need much help at all stages of this process.

It often happens that all three steps occur in the order just given; but in many cases the three steps overlap, and sometimes the order may be changed. For example, one may want to write about the settlement of his home town and the still existing signs of that settlement. He may know that he wants to write about:

a. Reasons for the first settlement.
b. Extent of the first building.
c. Present remnants of the old town.

He may thus have worked out the step, "organizing thought," before he discovers and recognizes his material.

In another case, in attempting to formulate, for instance, one's belief on a local issue, a writer may find it helpful to begin by writing down some of his ideas and convictions as a stimulus for organizing his thoughts. Indeed, it often happens that a first step in formulating an opinion is exploratory —setting down random statements which in themselves help the writer to think. It should also be emphasized again that the process of writing itself is a stimulation, and that the best of outlines often, in fact usually, needs to be changed as the topic develops in the hands of the writer.

Many of the brief papers written in the junior high school, or even in later grades, will follow a simple sequence of the events narrated. Sometimes the plan for the paper is so obvious and so easily carried in the writer's head that he does not need to write down an outline. With more elaborate papers he will need a written plan to follow. Statements of opinion usually require very careful organization—and reorganization. (In dealing with outlines care should be taken that the outline remains a *means* and *not an end*.) A form of outline for this kind of writing should be agreed upon throughout the school so that requirements will be uniform. Always, however, the problem must initiate the outline, not the outline the search for a problem. No better basis for outlining has been found than the question, "What does the reader need to know, and in what order should I proceed so that he will follow my thinking?"

Often good teaching of organization will come in comments after the first draft has been submitted. Questions such as "Why did you put this section first?" or "What is the order of your points?" will be effective. A suggestion to go over the paper and put together related parts, perhaps clipping and pasting as an intermediate step, may show the value of a *preliminary* plan. Eventually, students should learn to make for themselves really useful outlines or plans.

It should never be necessary to hand in an outline in order to show that the paper had a plan; the plan should be obvious in the quality of the paper.

In addition, attention must be given to proper bibliographical style, which also should be uniform throughout the school.

Evaluating Outcomes

Evaluation will include the skills just discussed. It should be done first by the writer, then by a group of his classmates, and last by the teacher. As a means of summarizing the skills involved, the students may set up some such bases as the following for purposes of evaluation:

1. Are the ideas and information interesting and well suited to the writer's purpose?
2. Is his outline clear and easy to follow? Do main ideas stand out from subordinate ones or illustrations?
3. Are his paragraphs well developed and his transitions clear?
4. Are his sources authentic and his quotations well integrated into his own writing? Has he used acceptable bibliographical form for acknowledging his sources?
5. Are his sentences clear and well formulated? Are they punctuated so as to make them easy to read?

LETTER WRITING

Letter writing is the most common form of writing used outside of school. It should therefore be the form most frequently and consistently taught in every grade from the seventh through the twelfth.

The Purposes of Letter Writing in and out of the Classroom

Young people write letters for the same reasons as adults: to visit by mail with absent friends or members of the family; to send, accept, or refuse invitations; to express sympathy, congratulations, or thanks for gifts or entertainment. They also do business by mail: ordering, inquiring, furnishing information or explanations, conducting the affairs of clubs or student government, influencing votes, or selling the school annual.

What is taught in letter writing should be determined by the needs of the student of a given age or class. One seventh-grade teacher utilized a wide variety of situations which came up weekly in her classroom to stimulate improvement in letter writing and also to teach the occasions on which it is appropriate to write letters. Her class carried on an extensive correspondence with another seventh grade in a neighboring town. They sent for free and inexpensive materials related to a hobby project, many of the children bringing ads from magazines at home for the samples or other trivia for which they are in the habit of writing. The pupils wrote invitations to programs in their classroom and in the school as a whole. For any act of kindness or of service to the class or one of its members, someone was delegated to write a letter of thanks. When the shipment of books from a children's book club did not arrive on time, a committee prepared and sent a letter of inquiry. Any member of the class who was forced to remain at home for a few days because of illness was sent a letter by each of his classmates.

A ninth-grade teacher stimulated class members to keep notebooks of letters thus written, writing beneath each example a list of the qualities which he had tried to achieve in this kind of letter. These notebooks were kept on display for a while and then were filed for future reference in case any one of the seven types of letters was to be used again.

Any teacher alert to the activities of home and school can find real occasions for letter writing. If a school system wishes, however, to allocate certain letters to certain grades in order to make sure that they are taught, it can readily do so on the basis of a survey of the letter writing needs and opportunities characteristic of each grade. For example, at the seventh-grade level these are commonly used: news letters to absent friends or members of the family, invitations, thank-you notes, letters of congratulation, letters asking for information, or letters requesting a sample or a favor. Seniors, on the other hand, find useful also the letter of inquiry, the letter asking for a recommendation, the letter of application for a job or for admission to college, and an advertising or promotion letter related to school activities.

Application of the Principles of Personal Writing to the Friendly Letter

The writer of the effective friendly letter is the person who has taken in sensory impressions and has reflected upon his experience, selecting what should be told to the reader, organizing suitably, and using sense-appealing words to recreate the experience. The result is usually miscellaneous in content, without any general unity except that of close writer-reader relationship.

Illustrations. Often student committees can collect or find in books letters which effectively illustrate these principles. One committee, for example, chose Theodore Roosevelt's letter to his daughter Ethel while he was on a hunting trip in Colorado as an excellent example both of projecting one's own personality into a letter and of keeping in mind what would interest the reader.[3] Good letters of invitation, for example, written by class groups should be filed and used later for purposes of illustration.

Help from texts and etiquette books. Textbooks often help by presenting examples of good and poor letters from which students may draw generalizations concerning the necessary content and tone of different kinds of correspondence. Etiquette books, which young people pore over constantly, often give much help with what to include in social and business letters, what tone to employ, and what form to follow. Students can look for a variety of ways of opening a thank-you letter, for simple and unstilted ways of saying, "I'm sorry" or "I'm glad," and so on. The effort to write in a

[3] Joseph Bucklin Bishop, ed., *Theodore Roosevelt's Letters to His Children* (New York, Charles Scribner's Sons, 1919), pp. 23–24.

formal, set, or ornate fashion is often associated (in the mind of the adolescent) with reaching for adult modes of expression. The importance of conversational tone and simple sincerity should be emphasized. A letter to Joel Chandler Harris, for example, thanking him for a copy of *Nights with Uncle Remus*,[4] one which came also from *Theodore Roosevelt's Letters to His Children*, greatly delighted a junior high school class. The only trouble was that for weeks afterward, these pupils began every thank-you note with, "It was worth being (sick), and so on, to receive. . . ." That was a change, at least, from "Thank you very much for. . . ." The quest for variety is never-ending.

Prevention of error by preteaching. As in other kinds of composition, prevention of error and build-up of interest and method *before* pupils write save hours of discouragement and boredom spent in later correction of errors which could have been avoided by specific teaching in advance of writing. One advantage of letter writing is, however, that the student recognizes the letter as his personal representative by mail, and he is more willing to revise and to copy than he sometimes is in other kinds of composition.

Application of Principles of Expository
Writing to the Business Letter

The longer business letter, perhaps explaining why people in the community should support the team or the band or buy the school annual, develops skill in expository writing, in which the gathering, organizing, and presenting of ideas differ rather markedly from similar techniques in the friendly news letter.

Greater informality in business letters. Doing business by mail is becoming more informal. Letters that used to begin, "Yours of sixth instant received. In reply will say," now read in straightforward conversational fashion: "We are happy to hear of your interest in our . . . and are glad to send you

[4] *Ibid.*, pp. 67–68.

detailed information about it." Few letters, even of application, today end in *Respectfully yours*. Even *Yours truly* is tending to give way to *Cordially yours, Sincerely yours,* or *Faithfully yours*—forms which used to be reserved for social correspondence.

A display of letters, for example, from publishing companies, may be examined by students to discover these changes: *Dear Sir* and *Dear Madam* now tend to be replaced by the more personal *Dear Mr. Breckenridge* or *Dear Miss Ensley*. The old dangling ending, *Hoping to hear from you soon,* is also gone because it demanded the formal *we remain* after it. Nowadays firms close with a simple, straightforward "We hope to hear from you soon" or "Let us know if we may be of further service."

Business letters may be judged for (1) courtesy, (2) clarity, (3) completeness, and (4) conciseness. After such an analysis of successful business letters, students are ready to list in their notebooks the qualities they wish to have in their own letters.

Practical reasons for conventional form. Conventional form in business letters serves real purposes, which youngsters may discover by visits to the post office or to a business house. The writer of a business letter files it under the name of the recipient, below which is the address of the receiver for future reference. The recipient files it under the name of the sender, and he uses the address in the heading. The post office asks that no abbreviations of cities or states be used because of constant confusion in some handwriting of *Miss.* and *Minn.,* of *Ia.* and *Ida.,* or of *Me.* and *Md.* Time lost in writing these words out may be saved by omitting punctuation at the ends of the line in heading and address because it serves no useful purpose. Knowing the reasons back of conventional letter form makes pupils less impatient of what may look to them like unnecessary formalities.

Order letters have items tabulated in columns to make the filling of the order easier. The letter of application must include certain details needed by a prospective employer. Since it is a long-range interview by mail, it must be neat and businesslike in appearance and it must give some impression of personality, just as one's appearance and personality stand out in a personal interview. One business school gave this somewhat humorous but important advice to its students: [5]

> If you'd for a job apply,
> Sell yourself
> Use some good strong reason-why,
> Sell yourself
> Estimate your merits high,
> BUT—don't aviate the "I"
> Till it hits the bloomin' sky—
> Quell yourself!

Relationship of tone to manner of expression. Too many sentences beginning with *I* give the wrong impression. Changing them will also lend pleasant variety to sentence structure. The college student who writes, "I shall be able to coach debate exceptionally well because I was on the famous debate team that won every debate last year" needs help with saying the same thing in a more circumspect fashion: "I should do my best to bring out a winning debate team, having had the privilege of working this year under Professor Albin, whose expert leadership has helped us to win over every opponent." *How* a thing is said counts tremendously in letter writing, because one cannot be there to see and correct the effect of one's words.

SERVICE WRITING

Service writing includes all those forms of practical writing which are necessitated by the daily activities of school and classroom. Unless a teacher has made a careful analysis of such opportunities for the improvement of writing, he

[5] John B. Opdyke, *Business Letter Practice* (New York, Isaac Pitman & Sons, n. d.), p. 161.

may not know how rich the field of service composition may be.

Surveying the Field

As a preliminary step in working out a curriculum, the teacher may well keep a record for a semester or year of all the writing done in relation to the work of the school and classroom and allocate the assignments to the various classes.

One teacher who made such a list for a ninth grade found over one hundred items such as bibliographies, announcements of trips and arrangements for them, assembly programs and committee notices, lost articles, regulations for games and public performances, requests to the office, letters of condolence, invitation, and thanks, legends for work to be displayed at parent-teachers' meetings, and minutes of club meetings. All these demanded neatness, clarity, simple organization, and consideration of the varied audiences. All opened the way for teaching language skills in relation to the needs revealed. Many of these notices might have been prepared by the teacher; many might have served the purpose though carelessly done. All were better done well and constituted appropriate responsibilities for students to take.

Teaching in Relation to the Needs Revealed

In handling these services, the teacher is sometimes tempted to depend upon two or three competent (and neat) students, often girls. Indeed, the idea may easily grow that the only ones who attend to writing courtesy notes are a half dozen or fewer little girls. The tendency is, however, easily broken up. Who is the appropriate person to write this letter, a boy or a girl, a friend or slight acquaintance? What does the class as a whole want to have said? What do the writers need to know about their roles?

When a secretary keeps minutes for group meetings, there is no need to assume that secretaries are born and not made. The class members may, in the learning stage, take turns at keeping minutes; or a different group may keep notes for minutes at each session, and compare results.

If a letter is to be composed, several students with different styles and approaches may all attempt the task, their results may be compared, and a final draft drawn later.

There are sometimes teachers who object to the time required for such detail as has just been suggested. It takes time, they may say, from the regular work of the class. What is the "regular work of the class"? In English, it is learning to write well enough to carry on the varied business of life. Obviously, there are many writing tasks in every school. Doing these well as they occur would seem to be the most appropriate way of learning that writing should be well done. If such opportunities fail to appear, the teacher should question the quality of his course.

THE IMPORTANCE OF WORDS

One may use clearly constructed sentences and well-organized paragraphs and yet be deceptive, or dull, or unintelligible because of his choice of words.

"People talk past each other," said an eminent linguist, because the experience of each of them has given different meanings to the same word. An American woman wrote to relatives in Britain proudly describing her "cabin" on the shore of Lake Superior. The reply came back assuring her of their interest in her "lakeside hut." Churchill tells of misunderstanding between British and American leaders during the war, the former wanting to "table" a matter of great urgency. "Tabling" in England meant to put it on the table before the presiding officer for consideration; in America it meant postponing it indefinitely.

The Personal Element in Meaning

An eighth-grade teacher made pupils conscious of the different emotional tones which past experience gives to words by asking for a discussion of favorite Christian names. Much nodding and shaking of heads indicated a wide range of association with the same name—Jack, for example, or Jane, or Bridget, or Isaac. Even parallel forms of the same name brought different reactions:

Jean, John, Ivan, Johannes, Jan, Hans, Chan
Theodore, Tad, Ted, Dode, Teddy

On examining the reasons for their strong likes and dislikes, pupils discovered them in national or family backgrounds and often in a generalized emotion resulting from acquaintance with one person—beloved or disliked—who bore the name.

Richard Altick provides an excellent example of how past experience and emotionalized attitudes enter into the interpretation by two different individuals of the same speech in a political campaign, a result which always follows the use of glittering generalities: [6]

The Candidate: "We must protect our sacred heritage, our American way of life."

First Listener   (a mechanic): "Good stuff! American way of life—high wages, profits of big business limited by taxation, monopolies forbidden, labor unions protected by law, equal opportunity for all, nobody too rich, nobody too poor. . . . I'll vote for him!"

Second Listener (owner of a small factory): "My sentiments exactly! American way of life—government keeps its hands off business, no excess profits tax, labor unions kept in hand by restrictive laws. If a man has the brains and the aggressiveness he can make a million dollars and it'll be his own. . . . I'll vote for him."

Who is going to be disappointed after the candidate takes office and begins making his decisions? He cannot serve two masters; yet both voted for him because he favored what they favored—a vague phrase which was bound to please them so long as it remained undefined.

[6] Richard Altick, *Preface to Critical Reading* (New York, Henry Holt & Company, Inc., 1946), pp. 22–28.

The Emotional Content of Words

Students also enjoy guessing the emotional tone or attitude of speakers revealed in the different words they use to describe the same thing. Why, for example, does one call a friend's pet "a dog of mixed breed" and not a "mongrel"? Why does a store advertise "an economy sale" and not "cheap goods"? What attitude of mind is revealed by the people who call a boy each of these names:

| kid | lad | brat | future citizen |
| boy | urchin | young person | member of the rising generation? [7] |

If one lives in a small town, does it matter whether a friend refers to it as:

| village | whistle stop | Podunk |
| community | rural settlement | jerkwater town? [8] |

What is the difference between an *accomplice*, a *collaborator*, a *colleague*, and a *crony?*

Recently a newspaper hostile to the United Nations began a news story on radio programs for United Nations Week with these words: "This week the radio stations of the Chicago area will *blast the ears of the public* with the story of the *remarkable* accomplishments of the United Nations." [9]

Still another influenced certain elements in the community to vote against a young man who, though a person of wealth and privilege, wished to distribute wealth more equitably throughout the nation:

A fabulously rich playboy, who got tired of his ponies, got the idea that he would like to repudiate the free enterprise that privileged his grandfather to endow him with so many million dollars he could never hope to count them.

Language has great power both to reflect the emotional tone of the speaker and to affect the emotions of the reader.

[7] *Ibid.*, p. 59.
[8] *Ibid.*, p. 59.
[9] *Ibid.*, p. 59.

Well used, that power gives to great literature one of its chief claims to distinction. Constant use of literature and of effective writing in current books and magazines in the class where students are writing helps young writers grow in power to influence others in legitimate ways.

Older students under the direction of an interested teacher may move from this kind of approach to consideration of the relation between the word and reality which is exemplified in Wendell Johnson's simplification of Korzybski's diagram of the process of abstraction.[10]

Increasing Awareness of Words

In addition to these semantic problems, young people should be led through their writing to a greater awareness of words—the wealth of words available and the power that comes from use of the exact word, the pictorial or imaginative word, the word which suggests sound or mood.

Frieda Radke in her little book, *Living Words,* presents an interesting diagram of possible specific substitutes for the general word *rich:* [11]

VARIATIONS OF *rich*

Soil	fertile, productive, fruitful
Voice	resonant, full, mellow, deep
Material possessions	wealthy, opulent, prosperous, affluent
Vocabulary	extensive, colorful, varied, copious
Food	luscious, greasy, highly flavored, highly seasoned
Color	vivid, deep, striking, brilliant
Harvest	abundant, bountiful, copious, plentiful
Clothing	costly, luxurious, splendid, sumptuous

As suggested later in the discussion of spelling, older students should learn to use such reference sources as Roget's *Thesaurus* to aid them in finding the exact word to express what they have to say.

[10] Wendell Johnson, *People in Quandaries* (New York, Harper and Brothers, 1946), pp. 112–142.
[11] Frieda Radke, *Living Words* (New York, Odyssey Press, 1940), p. 89.

Development of a wealth of words suited to the varied purposes of communication is one of the chief functions of the teaching of writing. Recognition of the emotional tone of words and the danger of falsely generalized meanings is a major contribution of the writing class to the preservation of the processes of democracy.

DEVELOPMENT OF SKILLS

All the manifold details of written form, of spelling, of grammatical usage, and of vocabulary development arise to plague the youngster who tries to record his experiences in writing. If he has a real purpose for such activity, he recognizes the value of accuracy in these matters—of knowing the rules, so to speak. This is a major argument for motivation of writing through the student's own needs.

Use of Self-Help Devices in Sentence Structure

Problems of grammar and spelling are discussed in a later chapter. Often teachers find it helpful to develop with a class from the examination of their own writing, questions by means of which to judge their sentences. These, for example, are suitable for the junior high school years:

TESTS OF EFFECTIVE SENTENCES

1. Have I said what I mean?

   Mollie was the horse's name I was riding.
   The road was narrow and sharp curves.
   This is another important feature of 4-H Club work, giving the members control of the activities.

2. Have I used exact words to make my meaning clear?

   Geysers were sending their *magnificence* into the air.
   Here is a series of objects described by omnibus words:
   wonderful—food, bears, geysers, views, sequoia trees
   swell   —drives, dinners, air, inns, hikes
   sweetest —waterfalls, cottages, colors, mountain flowers
   What words would more exactly describe each?

3. Have I repeated words unpleasantly?

We stayed two days at Old Faithful Inn and could see Old Faithful from the roof of the Inn.

Your packages came just when Marion and I were packing, so we packed them right in.

4. Are all modifiers (time, place, descriptive) in the same sentences with the words which they modify?

When the bell rang. We all ran into the school.

It was the most beautiful house in the village. Which everybody enjoyed visiting.

On the porch. A big St. Bernard dog guarded the doorway.

They had three kinds of displays. One of rocks; one of leaves; and one of fungi.

5. If they are in the same sentence with the words which they modify, are they next to them?

6. In sentences where I am talking about two different people, have I used the same pronouns (substitute words) to refer to them which I should have used for each one separately?

He went. I went. He and I went.

She gave it to me. She gave it to Bill. She gave it to Bill and me.

She gave it to us. She gave it to boys. She gave it to us boys.

Others are especially suited to the more complex sentence structure of Grades 10–12:

1. Do pronouns substitute for words clearly indicated in the sentence or in previous sentences?

One day's work didn't seem very encouraging, but it helped to be able to put it down.

Ever since I was old enough to hold a jackknife, I have carved out wooden figures and made it my hobby.

2. Are my connecting words well chosen to show the exact relationships in the thought? Or would the sentence be better without a connecting word?

Overuse of *and so:*

    It was raining and so we stayed home.

    Many people were out of town and so the audience was small.

Use of *and* where no connective is needed:

    We had gone to the circus early that morning and the circus tents were already up and we got to see the men eating their breakfast in one of the big ones.

Use of *and* to express relationships which are not additive:

    My uncle was very ill and we did not go into the room.

    My teacher has been to Europe and she tells us interesting things about the countries she visited.

3. Are parallel ideas expressed in parallel form?

We had ice cream before we left town, went out to the arena, and the Ice Follies were enjoyed by all.

We enjoy hiking, fishing, and when we go swimming.

4. Have I tried to be ornate rather than straightforward in my expression so that what I have said really means nothing?

I seated myself and proceeded in a vain attempt to look as wise and as nonchalant as my picture of a typical university student should.

In selecting this as a very significant experience I am guided by many factors which tend to construct a very worthwhile and pleasant accomplishment.

A college that rests on a firm financial foundation has the greater ability to unleash the minds of its students.

5. Are my comparisons incomplete?

I get more enjoyment out of playing for myself whenever I feel like it than anything else.

6. Have I left an expression uncompleted?

I have never and probably will never regret my choice.

Capitalization and Punctuation as Aids to Communication

The day of sixteen rules for the capital letter, taught so many each year in isolation from the need of the rules in writing, is gone. Personal writing and social letters invariably raise the question, "When should one capitalize *mother, father, uncle,* and *aunt,* and when should one not?" Letters from the class to a business firm demand proper capitalization of the name of school or firm, of street, city and state. The unit on *Back-Country America,* in Chapter 4, brought up the necessity of capitalizing specific geographical names and sections of the country, but not directions. Capital letters, then, are approached in relation to the problems of actual communication, and are reviewed as often as the need for them arises.

The same thing may be said of punctuation, which is now being related to patterns of thought and expression. Marckwardt, in the introductory essay in the *Thorndike-Barnhart Comprehensive Desk Dictionary,* divides the problem into punctuation that (1) terminates, (2) introduces, (3) inserts, and (4) unifies. Then he adds the punctuation of series, indication of exact speech or of possession, and finally, certain minor special usages.[12]

Some marks of punctuation, like the semicolon, are seldom used except in exceedingly mature writing. Examination of articles in *Life, Time, Harper's,* and the *Atlantic* for use of semicolons and other marks of punctuation is an enlightening enterprise. The results make one wonder why a semicolon should be mentioned at all in the junior high school.

Younger pupils write considerable conversation. They need to have before them examples of how to punctuate and capitalize alternating remarks, the name of the person spoken to, simple series, and appositive modifiers. Mastery of these matters, plus the apostrophe in contractions and to show possession in nouns but not in pronouns, should be the aim, leaving more intricate and mature problems to the senior high school.

In the senior high school, as ideas become more complex and modifiers are needed to show exact relationships in thinking, the use of the comma for long introductory modifiers, for modifiers which interrupt the main thought, and for long appositives needs to be added. No detailed and involved grammatical classifications are necessary. As noted in Chapter 10, Dr. Kaulfers'[13] sentence from "Grammar for the Millions" is a case in point: "When *but* means *except,* no comma is necessary before it." Articles by Rachel Salisbury[14] and Helen Rand Miller[15] are very helpful in this connection.

[12] Albert H. Marckwardt, "Punctuation," *Thorndike-Barnhart Comprehensive Desk Dictionary* (New York, Doubleday & Company, Inc., 1951), pp. 21–24.

[13] Walter V. Kaulfers, "Grammar for the Millions: If Not Formal Grammar, Then What?" *Elementary English,* Vol. XXVI (February, 1949), pp. 65–74, 107.

[14] Rachel Salisbury, "The Psychology of Punctuation," *English Journal,* Vol. XXVIII (December, 1939), pp. 794–806.

[15] Helen Rand [Miller], "Grammar through Traffic," *English Journal* (High School and College Edition), Vol. XX (September, 1931), pp. 557–562.

Other Self-Help Procedures

Many of the problems of sentence structure and punctuation can be eliminated by teaching students to read aloud what they have written, listening for unpleasant repetition, for omissions, for clarity or lack of clarity in their sentences, for the rhythm or flow of ideas, and for sentence completeness or interruptions to the thought.

Such self-help procedures might well include a listing and mimeographing on a single sheet of those few matters of punctuation and capitalization which come up again and again in the writing of each grade. Both teacher and students may refer to these items by number and use them as a checklist against which to evaluate both single pieces of writing and progress over a period of time. Stock-takers' reports written by students themselves on the basis of such checks help greatly to establish the direction of progress. As usual, a few mistakes made over and over again make up the bulk of the errors.

CARING FOR INDIVIDUAL DIFFERENCES IN WRITING

Degrees of success in the writing of individual students have been less widely publicized than those in reading; yet they are equally great.

Attention to Differences within the Same Class

Fortunately, different people may approach personal writing, the formulation of opinion, the reporting of facts, and letter writing at very different levels and still have the mental stimulation of a common task and a unified group discussion. Each piece of writing is judged both on its merits and in relation to the abilities of the learner. The teacher's comments are addressed to individuals, and class members may work as individuals or in small groups on remedial materials individualized so that each student may do what will help him most. These are techniques most commonly used to care for individual differences within the same class.

Use of Writing Laboratories

Similarly, the writing laboratory, giving opportunity for writing in the classroom, makes possible the teacher's moving about the room to help individuals. Small groups can also get together to share their work on similar difficulties.

Some schools appoint committees of superior students to act as clinicians for those who seek consultation services. Mrs. Rideout of the La Crosse Junior High School in La Crosse, Wisconsin,[16] describes such a plan. The doctor and his clinical staff, each a specialist in some particular ailment like misspelling or misuse of the comma, have an office in one corner of the room to which those in need of help take their papers.

Certain junior colleges have developed writing laboratories to which students may take their writing problems from all subjects of study. The scheme sometimes permits referral of a student to the laboratory by any teacher who finds him in need of special help.

Elective Courses in Writing

Elective courses in creative writing and journalism for those with special gifts or interest in writing are common throughout the country.

Portland's program for the gifted. The schools of Portland, Oregon, for example, are co-operating in a special research study of the education of the gifted. Miss Jean Caryl Severeide describes the program as it operates for children up through the eighth grade in the George Atkinson School:

[16] Irna Rideout, "Clinic Solved Our Punctuation Problem," *Elementary English*, Vol. XXX (October, 1953), pp. 341–342.
See also Dorothy E. Sonke, "English Workshop," *English Journal*, Vol. XLIII (October, 1954), pp. 363–366.

In the fall of 1954 a series of screening tests was given to the intermediate and upper grade students to determine whether creative writing talents might be uncovered. These tests consisted of phrase, paragraph, and story development. The topics concerned animals, humorous incidents, and interesting experiences.

After careful evaluation by individual teachers, the children were chosen for a special seminar class. The youngsters were selected as to interest, I.Q., or writing ability. In the final analysis, however, those chosen were above average intelligence and possessed interest and capabilities in writing as well as in other creative areas.

The students were grouped according to grade levels, and each group elected a chairman and steering committee. The committee considered the "areas of writing interest" of each student. The agenda of the discussions were then planned. Writing took place before the weekly discussion, and there was critical evaluation of the material which was read to the group. Any story or poetical expression which was considered outstanding by all was read by the teacher and writer for grammatical and spelling errors. The material was then typed, illustrated, and placed in a permanent scrap book.

One activity which was enthusiastically tackled by the upper grade students was the writing of a story for the primary level children. The youngsters discussed the interests of such readers (animals and fairy tales) and, at the next group meeting, shared the material they had written. It was decided that the stories should be read in the primary classes where criticism of the children would be invaluable. Each writer was enlightened by the reactions of the listeners.

The embryo writers discovered that creative writing is mainly concerned with a flow of ideas. After the idea is developed, sharing the material becomes essential. The proofreading is never omitted but is not of primary concern.

The goals of the students and teacher are closely allied in these activities: they are striving to make a critical analysis of their own writing and that of others; they are endeavoring to form judgments about their writing and the worthwhile writings of the past and present; they are attempting to improve their powers of observation along with their skill in oral and written expression. In the achievement of these desired goals they are finding enjoyment and a worthy use for their leisure time.

The ultimate aim of the teacher is to have this seminar take place in every classroom and thereby enrich the home-room activities of all students.

Enthusiasm spread similarly in the Ainsworth School under the direction of Nadine Ellis:

As an experiment, a special-interest group in creative writing for seventh- and eighth-graders was tried for a year in Portland, Oregon.

The school realized it had a large group of students high in verbal factors of intelligence who were artistic and showed an interest in writing. These pupils were allowed to meet twice a week in a laboratory situation.

The group discovered that writing *can* be fun. They called their class listening, reading, telling, writing—just for fun. The purpose was simply to give the members extra chances to express themselves. Getting one's idea on paper in the fleeting moment before it's gone was the main concern.

Many different kinds of motivation were tried for those who needed an inspiration—weather, jumbled picture words and phrases, music, abstract art objects, unfinished stories, and the like. Several times simply a sentence such as "The boy walked down the street," or "The room was left in wild disorder" was enough to start the pencils moving.

Everything the group tried to do could be done perhaps even better in a homeroom situation; and the surprising result of this experiment with a special interest group was the general effect it had upon the homeroom experiences for all the children. The enthusiasm of this group was so contagious and the results of their writing were so stimulating that at the end of the year the faculty decided the special group was no longer needed. They wanted to have creative writing in *their* classrooms.

The original aim of helping these children express themselves with more ease, confidence, and enjoyment was adopted by the entire school.

A core course in the high school also co-operates in the experiment. It is under the direction of Charles K. Sapper.

Here at Grant High School an experiment in meeting the needs of gifted children has given us an exciting opportunity to explore unusual perceptions in creative writing at the ninth-grade level. This program has held the number of pupils per class to a maximum of twenty-five, and probably classes average closer to twenty students. Experimentally we have grouped some of our superior students in homogeneous classes; some in heterogeneous classes. Furthermore, we enjoy all the advantages of time and flexibility inherent in a fusion of language arts with the social studies in a double period combination.

To stimulate imaginative thinking and writing our hypothesis is that anything within the range of the student's imagination can serve as the link between the student and his theme. As one of the primary purposes for combining English and social studies is the opportunity thus created for applying fundamental English skills to a subject matter field, much of the stimulus for writing comes from social studies experiences. Some of the more successful have been: "My daily life as a Japanese (or Chinese, Malayan, etc.) teen-ager," "My first million years as a fossil," "How I would persuade an American P.W. who wished to remain with his captors to come home." Other stimuli include replies to "letters to the editor" column from the daily newspapers, imaginative personifications, creative interpretations of ordinary experiences, and responses to "mood music."

For the student himself, whether average or superior, probably one of the most important values to be derived from these activities is the realization that he can "create"—that he can pick and choose from the myriads of vague images in his mind and become more adept at clarifying perceptions in an orderly arrangement on paper. A bonus value growing from this realization is an ever-expanding usable vocabulary. The emotional catharsis inherent in the student's being able to express what he could not say before is another result of this use of creative writing—indeed, perhaps the most important because of its far-reaching effects on his total personality.

Los Angeles' senior high school program. Like many other cities, Los Angeles has a highly developed program of electives in creative writing for those particularly gifted in such work. All of the courses emphasize an awareness of experience and the recognition of aesthetic values in the re-creation of it in literature. All combine writing with appreciative reading of poetry, essay, and fiction. The writing done involves these and other forms. "In prose," says Miss Garrison of Dorsey High School, "we work from the informal essay to descriptions, incidents, and finally into a real short story. The short story is the hardest thing we do, but the class always has a wonderful time reading aloud and listening to the stories. The oh's and ah's are reward enough for the weeks of planning and writing." Dorsey High School publishes a yearly magazine of student writing, called *Trial Flights.* Manual Arts High School has an annual Creative Arts Program in which art, music, and creative writing groups share the best work of the year with the students and their parents.

A summary statement concerning the total program in high schools throughout the city sets up as the goals these discoveries by each student participating: Discovery of

1. An interest in, and the value of, reliving past experiences.
2. The fascination of discovering meanings, motives, and ideas through the process of writing.

3. A growing consciousness of one's own capacities, characteristics, and thought patterns together with those of others.
4. A love for, and appreciation of, good literature.
5. A deep and lasting satisfaction in one's growing ability to use language effectively.[17]

Evanston's course in journalism. In Evanston, Illinois, students interested in journalism are able to combine work in that area with English. The program is summarized by Clarence Hach, head of the Department of English and a former president of the National Association of Journalism Directors of Secondary Schools:

Because we believe that good journalism is good English, we make it possible for our students to elect journalism as an English course in the junior year. We thus eliminate the problem common in many schools that students with a journalism interest can't elect the journalism course because of a full schedule.

The English J course may be elected without a permit by those students who have A or B averages in Sophomore English. Students with a C average in English 3 may take the course upon recommendation of their Sophomore English teacher and the approval of the chairman of the English Department. We do not believe in limiting the course to better-than-average students, for we have often found that through the medium of journalistic writing, many students of average writing ability in regular English classes become interested in writing and extremely adept at it. We have found this to be especially true of boys who "find themselves" in sports writing. We do not accept students in this special interest class who are below average in their regular English classes, for we have found that they are usually the ones weak in "mechanics," sentence structure, and the like and that because the course is a combined English-journalism one, we can't afford the time to concentrate on more elementary matters.

The course gives English credit. The English J students have all of the required literature, all of the required non-journalistic writing, all of the program in grammar, spelling, and punctuation. In addition, they have all of the journalism necessary to produce a school paper. They have much more writing than students do in the regular classes. They don't get as much literature, but they get a great deal. The course is a full one, but because of the special abilities of the students and their interest, we can cover material more rapidly than other classes can.

The students who take the English J course serve as the reportorial staff for *The Evanstonian.* After six weeks of class training in tech-

[17] The English Department of Mt. Vernon High School in Mt. Vernon, New York, publishes a booklet describing its program in creative writing.

niques of interviewing and the fundamentals of newswriting, they are assigned to senior editors (students who have had the course) and work under their supervision on various beats: music-drama, sports, features, and so on.

The paper is really a student activity—run by the senior staff who have had the course and have, in addition, gone through a special training period toward the end of the school year. In this period, those students interested in trying out for the senior staff attend an after-school class one night a week. Here they learn about the more technical aspects of newspaper production which we don't have time to teach in the combination course and which really aren't necessary for those students not interested in going on with the paper in their senior year. During this period, too, the juniors work as assistants to the senior editors, eventually putting out two tryout issues of their own. After staff election, the new staff, who are still juniors, produce the final issue of the year completely on their own. Then, when the staff returns in the fall, it can prepare the first issue without any difficulty and of as good quality as any other during the year. This interlocking system, I believe, helps to explain the high quality of *The Evanstonian* through the years.

Some students prefer to work on the yearbook rather than on the paper. They may do this their junior year and then try out for senior positions on the yearbook staff. The method used is similar to that for the paper. Another teacher, however, sponsors the yearbook.

Journalism in a small high school. A similar program in a small high school is described by E. L. Powderly of Red Wing, Minnesota, where the school enrolls 450 pupils.

Journalism in Central High School in Red Wing is made up of a two-year, four-semester course offered as an elective for juniors and seniors. The prerequisite is a B average in social studies and English courses although in some instances this a waived. Class size has been limited to twenty-five students when the occasion demanded, but the average enrollment has been from fifteen to twenty students.

Class work the first year for the juniors includes a study of the school. This covers the administration, policies of the board of education, curriculum, course of study, co-curricular activities and their place in the educational program. Evaluative study of current affairs, theater arts, music, books, radio and television is also a part of the course materials. This goes along with the usual study of newspapers and their functions and history.

These topics are used for writing practice in the various journalistic forms and sometimes for creative writing. The desired objective in the writing is to be clear, concise and mature. The chapters on varieties of English, good English, and the qualities and meanings of words from the English textbook in use provide a basis for enlarging on mechanics already learned. Books on language such as *Language in Action* by Hayakawa are required reading.

The staffs of the school's publications consist of those electing the second year of the course. (Some seniors electing this class without credit in Journalism 1 are admitted.) This group of seniors in a regular laboratory class session edit and publish the school newspaper and the school yearbook as well as operate a press bureau to cover school events for the local press and radio. This year an added venture in journalism for the seniors has been the development of a regional radio news program. Correspondents from twelve neighboring schools send news to our staff to be prepared and presented, by a staff member, in a weekly news program from the local radio station.

In all of the work of the senior journalists every opportunity is given to develop full responsibility for writing, editing, and publishing without any censorship. The development in the students of initiative, of respect for truth, of standards of good taste and good judgment, as well as of good writing, is the aim of the publications.

THE PROBLEM OF HANDLING PAPERS

How much should students write? No one knows the answer to this question, but there is a universal feeling that they should write more than they do. Some teachers plan a substantial piece of writing every fortnight. Some manage brief bits of summary or personal reaction every day. Others hope for some carefully formulated report or narrative every week.

Reduced Loads for English Teachers

With large classes, and many of them, teachers have become thoroughly discouraged. Committees like the one in California are seeking reduced loads for English teachers.[18] The outlook is not promising. With the shortage of teachers and mounting enrollments such an approach to the problem looks all but futile. Moreover, research has been unable to

[18] William J. Dusel, "Report to California Secondary School Administrators on the Teaching of English in California Secondary Schools—A Study Recently Conducted by the California Council of English Associations, California," San José State College, September 26, 1953 (mimeo.).

prove that meticulous correction of papers pays dividends. More research comparing different methods of securing results in writing is urgently needed.

Schemes for Reducing the Paper Burden

In the meantime, certain courses are open to the teachers. One is to do more stimulating and more building up of ideas *before students write* so as to make less correcting necessary after they have written. A second is *to devise all possible methods of self-help* for students to use in the final editing of their own papers. The punctuation of conversation and the form for business letters can be mimeographed on individual sheets for use as examples. Some of them can be placed on large sheets of brown paper and hung on easels where students may consult them. Brief guides to punctuation, capitalization, and usage can be prepared from common errors revealed in the students' writing and used as keys for correcting. If the students help make the guide, they will understand its use.

But editing implies more than mere proofreading. Young writers will be better able to detect mechanical errors than to evaluate the worth and clarity of their ideas, the adequacy of their organization, and the appropriateness of their diction. Often, for example, they may see that an explanation lacks clarity but cannot spot the omitted step or the illogical arrangement of their ideas. Lack of felicity in diction may be still harder to detect. They may fail to sense the need for conversation, for building up one incident or for reducing another, and for clearer and more adequate structure within a paragraph.

Students can be taught that mere proofreading is not enough. They may develop a series of questions relating to paragraph organization and development, to the need for transitions, to clarity and order in the whole composition. They may build for themselves from their reading of successful narratives a series of standards for judging a story, for using sense-appealing words or precise and exact expressions. They may learn to use the dictionary of synonyms, as well as books on current usage. Teaching independence in the evaluation of the individual's own writing and giving guidance for improvement are necessary parts of instruction in composition.

Evaluation by the learner can never replace the teacher's judgment; yet it is imperative that students assume responsibility for doing all they can to improve their own writing and that of their classmates before they ask the teacher to lend a hand.

First of all, then, the student himself must evaluate his own paper. After that he may share it with the class or with a small group within the class to see how well his ideas have been communicated. Often, as has been demonstrated throughout the chapter, class discussion of the paper ensues. After that, the teacher gives the final evaluation. The job should be two-thirds done before the teacher enters the picture except as he has stimulated ideas and prevented errors by pre-teaching and has answered questions and furnished help to individuals while they were writing.

CONCLUSION

To go back to a statement made at the opening of this chapter, learning to write is hard work. It calls for constant writing by the student and direct teaching and evaluation by the teacher. There is no other way, and time-consuming though it is, the task is there if there is to be a population able to express ideas clearly, effectively, and with integrity.

BIBLIOGRAPHY

Books

Applegate, Mauree, *Helping Children Write* (New York, International Textbook Company, 1948).

BROWN, Ivor John Carnegie, *No Idle Words* and *Having the Last Word* (New York, E. P. Dutton & Co., Inc., 1951).

COUSINS, Norman, ed., *Writing for Love or Money;* 35 essays reprinted from *The Saturday Review of Literature* (New York, Longmans, Green and Company, 1949).

ERNST, Margaret S., *Words: English Roots and How They Grow,* 3rd ed., rev. (New York, Alfred A. Knopf, Inc., 1954).

FRIES, Charles Carpenter, *The Structure of English; An Introduction to the Construction of English Sentences* (New York, Harcourt, Brace & Company, Inc., 1952).

GURREY, Percival, *Teaching of Written English* (New York, Longmans, Green and Company, 1951).

HAYAKAWA, S. I., in consultation with Basil H. Pillard, *Language in Thought and Action* (New York, Harcourt, Brace & Company, Inc., 1949).

HEATH, Eric, *Writing for Television* (Los Angeles, Research Publishing Company, 1950).

Kansas State Department of Education, "Suggested Standards in Composition for High School English," *Bulletin of the Kansas State Department of Education and the Kansas Education Association* (Topeka, Kan., The State Department of Education, 1948).

LABRANT, Lou, *We Teach English* (New York, Harcourt, Brace & Company, Inc., 1951), pp. 143–170.

LEACOCK, Stephen, *How to Write* (New York, Dodd, Mead & Company, Inc., 1943).

MIRRIELEES, Lucia B., *Teaching Composition and Literature in High School,* rev. ed. (New York, Harcourt, Brace & Company, Inc., 1952).

MUNSON, Gorham Bert, *Writer's Workshop Companion* (New York, Farrar, Straus and Cudahy, Inc., 1951).

———, *The Written Word; How To Write Readable Prose* (New York, Creative Age Press, Inc., 1949).

National Council of Teachers of English, Commission on the English Curriculum, *The English Language Arts,* NCTE Curriculum Series, Vol. 1 (New York, Appleton-Century-Crofts, Inc., 1952), pp. 302–327.

New York City Board of Education, *Developing Children's Power of Self-Expression through Writing* (New York, The Board, 1953).

New York State Department of Education, *Supplement to the Language Arts for the Senior High School* (Albany, N. Y., The State Department of Education, 1955).

PALMER, Osmond E., and Diederich, Paul B., *Critical Thinking in Reading and Writing* (New York, Henry Holt & Company, Inc., 1955).

PYLES, Thomas, *Words and Ways of American English* (New York, Random House, Inc., 1952).

RALEIGH, Walter, *On Writing and Writers* (London, Edward Arnold & Co., 1926).

SHEPHERD, R. A., *Creative Writing Based on Reading* (Urbana, Illinois Association of Teachers of English, 1954).

SMITH, Dora V., *Communication, the Miracle of Shared Living* (New York, The Macmillan Company, 1955), pp. 78–94.

THOMAS, Cleveland A., *Language Power for Youth* (New York, Appleton-Century-Crofts, Inc., 1955).

THOMAS, E. S., *Evaluating Student Themes* (Madison, University of Wisconsin Press, 1955).

Periodicals

BENNETT, Paul L., "Reading and Writing Program for the Talented Student," *English Journal,* Vol. XLIV (September, 1955), pp. 335–339.

BROWN, John Mason, "Blue Pencil to Parnassus," *Saturday Review,* Vol. XXXIII (April 8, 1950), pp. 7–8+.

———, "New Voices and Old," *Saturday Review,* Vol. XXXIV (January 13, 1951), pp. 48–49+.

———, "Pleasant Agony," *Saturday Review,* Vol. XXXII (June 25 and July 9, 1949), pp. 27–29, 36–38.

———, "Two Fronts," *Saturday Review,* Vol. XXXIII (August 12, 1950), pp. 6–7+.

CATHELL, Dorothy, "Honors English: Break for Bright Students," *Clearing House,* Vol. XXIX (February, 1955), pp. 331–337.

COOK, Luella B., "Fundamentals in the Teaching of Composition," *English Journal,* Vol. XXX (May, 1941), pp. 360–370.

———, "Reducing the Paper Load," *English Journal,* Vol. XXI (May, 1932), pp. 364–370.

COUSINS, Norman, "Don't Americans Read or Write?" *Saturday Review,* Vol. XXXIV (July 14, 1951), pp. 24–25.

DE BOER, John J., "Oral and Written Language," bibliog., *Review of Educational Research,* Vol. XXV (April, 1955), pp. 107–120.

DuBOIS, G., "Get Out the Opaque Projector," *Educational Screen,* Vol. XXXV (March, 1956), pp. 99–100.

DUSEL, W. J., "Some Semantic Implications of Theme Correction," *English Journal,* Vol. XLIV (October, 1955), pp. 390–397.

GROMMON, Alfred H., "Preparing High-School Students for College Composition," *California Journal of Secondary Education,* Vol. XXVIII (February, 1953), pp. 113–118.

HACKETT, Herbert, "Make the Reader See It!" *Education,* Vol. 76 (April, 1956), pp. 487–490.

———, "The N-V Line: The Strength in Writing," *Education,* Vol. 76 (April, 1956), pp. 490–491.

———, "The Opaque Projector: Focus on Problems," *Education,* Vol. 76 (April, 1956), p. 493.

————, "Organize Your Thinking So the Reader Can See It," *Education*, Vol. 76 (April, 1956), pp. 491–492.

HAYAKAWA, S. I., "Recognizing Stereotypes as Substitutes for Thought," *Progressive Education*, Vol. XXX (March, 1953), pp. 150–151.

HAZARD, Patrick, "I Know What I Like, I Think: Writing and Clarification of Values," *Education*, Vol. 76 (April, 1956), pp. 502–507.

HERZBERG, Max J., "It's No Fun to Write," *English Journal*, Vol. XLI (March, 1952), pp. 127–131.

HOOK, J. N., "Suggestions for the Use of Ideaform," *English Journal*, Vol. XLV (January, 1956), pp. 33–34.

KEGEL, Charles H., "Specificity in Words and Ideas," *Education*, Vol. 76 (April, 1956), pp. 484–487.

LABRANT, Lou, "Inducing Students to Write," *English Journal*, Vol. XLIV (February, 1955), pp. 70–74.

————, "Writing and Structure," *Education*, Vol. 76 (April, 1956), pp. 468–471.

LAWSON, R. H., "Composition for Seniors," *English Journal*, Vol. XLI (February, 1952), pp. 82–85.

LEPS, Fannie B., "What Comes before Revision," *Baltimore Bulletin of Education*, Vol. XXVII (March, 1950), pp. 36–37.

LOUGHLIN, R. L., "Think before You Ink," *High Points*, Vol. XXVII (February, 1955), pp. 16–27.

McCARTHY, A., "Teaching Slow Learners to Write," *Bulletin of the National Association of Secondary-School Principals*, Vol. XXXIX (September, 1955), pp. 106–110.

MARY CORONATA, Sister, "Expressional Writing in High School," *Catholic School Journal*, Vol. LV (February, 1955), p. 47.

MUNSON, Gorham Bert, "Condition of the Writer," *Saturday Review*, Vol. XXXV (February 16, 1952), pp. 11–13+.

————, "Workouts for Writers," *Saturday Review*, Vol. XXXV (April 5, 1952), pp. 18–19+.

SHERIDAN, Marion C., "Can We Teach Our Students to Write?" *English Journal*, Vol. XL (June, 1951), pp. 320–324.

SMITH, Hyrum M., "Dynamic Ventures in Creative Expression—An Integrated Program," *Education*, Vol. 76 (April, 1956), pp. 478–483.

THOMAS, Cleveland A., "Improvement of Language Instruction in Secondary Schools," *School Review*, Vol. LXIV (January, 1956), pp. 23–28.

THORNLEY, W. R., "Case for Creative Writing," *English Journal*, Vol. XLIV (December, 1955), pp. 528–531.

THORNTON, Helen, "English for Technical Students," *English Journal*, Vol. XLIV (September, 1955), pp. 343–346.

PREVIEW OF CHAPTER 10

I. GRAMMAR AND USAGE

Difficulties in Discussing Grammar

The Importance of Teaching the Facts of American English

Basic Considerations in Developing a Program in Grammar

Elements Requiring Instruction

Problems of Teaching Method

The Effort to Evolve an Adequate System of English Grammar

II. SPELLING

Common Attitudes toward Spelling

Functions of the Spelling Program

Selections of Words to Be Taught

Need for a Method of Attack on New Words

Diagnosis and Overcoming of Difficulties

The Importance of a Positive Approach to Vocabulary Building

Summary

Bibliographies for Parts I and II

CHAPTER 10

Developing Competence in Grammar, Usage, and Spelling

I. GRAMMAR AND USAGE

THE TEACHER of English who would do the best possible teaching of grammar in the secondary schools, in common with anyone who would discuss the subject intelligently, must reckon at the outset with three special difficulties.

DIFFICULTIES IN DISCUSSING GRAMMAR

The Ambiguity of the Word *Grammar*

The first difficulty is that the word *grammar* is ambiguous. Sometimes it means good usage. Thus, if one hears Mr. Smith say, "John, when he talks, doesn't use very good grammar," one knows that Mr. Smith probably means that John does not have a very good command of conventional English usage, at least on the more formal levels. John has said, perhaps, that he and Bill "ain't going to do this job, because him and me is going to quit." When "grammar is taught" in this sense, an effort is made to improve the student's ability to use certain English constructions.

On the other hand, sometimes the word *grammar* is used to mean *systemized knowledge or theory* of the structure of the English language, and especially of the English sentence. Thus, if Mr. Jones says, "The trouble with high school students today is that they don't know their grammar," he probably means that they have not acquired a conventional body of grammatical knowledge or theory. When "grammar is taught" in this sense, the purpose is to help students understand the general relationship between subjects and predicates, for example, or pronouns and their antecedents.

The point is that English usage (accepted constructions) is one thing and grammatical theory (descriptions of the word forms and the word order which express the relationships among words) is another. *Usage and grammar raise different kinds of teaching problems and should not be confused just because some individuals use these terms synonymously.*

The Lack of a Universally Accepted Description of English Grammar

A second difficulty arises from the fact that there is not, at present, one universally accepted system of describing English grammar. On the contrary, for more than a generation, linguistic scholars have been examining critically the shortcomings of the present system of analysis, which was organized in the eighteenth century by analogy with the grammar of Latin. These scholars have been attempting to develop a new, more scientific analysis which will describe more accurately the facts of the English language. Further on in this chapter this difficulty is discussed in greater detail. The point at the moment is that the teacher of English who is honestly trying to do the best possible teaching of grammar in the secondary schools cannot rely securely on the grammatical analysis which he was probably taught any more than the teacher of physics can rest content with teaching the physics he learned a decade ago.

The Question of a Relationship between a Knowledge of Grammar and Ability to Speak and Write

Even if the scientific knowledge of grammar were at present all neatly bound up in a systematic package, with no more questions to be asked, a third general problem would still remain. What is the relationship in the secondary schools between the teaching of English grammar and the development of the students' ability to use language well? The teaching of systematic English grammar to a student does not automatically result in his speaking and writing better. On the other hand, the teaching of grammar cannot be ignored, for through a functional knowledge of the basic structure of the English sentence and of the terms used in identifying language forms, an intelligent student can be assisted in the revision of his writing and in the self-analysis of recordings of his speech.

In brief, anyone who wishes to teach English well in the secondary schools must (1) keep in mind the distinction between English usage and systematic grammatical knowledge, (2) understand that the systematic English grammar which is now available for use in the schools is not adequate, and (3) recognize that the relation of the teaching of grammar to the development of ability in writing and speaking (as well as in reading and listening) is a practical problem with which the teacher will probably keep working as long as he remains a teacher.

THE IMPORTANCE OF TEACHING THE FACTS OF AMERICAN ENGLISH

The teaching of grammar to students in American secondary schools should be soundly based on the facts of *American English*. This statement recognizes that the English language has many varieties, and that the study of *American English* is appropriate in *American* schools. The more learned one is in English, the more interested he is in the variations of the language; and the more learned one is in American English, the more interested he is in the various "levels" and dialects, or regional varieties, of which it is composed. Here, incidentally, is common meeting ground for the high school student and the scholar. They both find interesting the ways in which people in different localities talk.

Observation of Current Usage

First, the student should be encouraged to observe the way all of the people around him actually use the English language. He should be encouraged to notice English as it is spoken and written. If by any chance the grammar he is being taught cannot explain the acceptable usage which he hears and reads, to that extent the scheme of grammar is inadequate.

For instance, consider the sentence, *The bandit held up the train.* In conventional grammatical analysis, *up* is either a preposition (and *the train* the object) or *up* is an adverb. But neither of these makes any sense. The bandit did not hold the train, and certainly he did not hold it aloft. *Up* is best thought of as part of the verb, *hold up,* with its complement, the *train.* A similar use of *up* can be observed in *He called up Mary,* and somewhat less clearly in *He thought up an excuse.* Since *up* here functions as part of the verb we need not hesitate to call it part of the verb, although it does not usually appear as a part of verbs in the dictionary, nor need we quail if a textbook says that auxiliaries always precede the verb. Similarly, although there is sometimes objection to putting a so-called preposition at the end of a sentence, we need not object to *He put the cat out.* One usually puts out a light but does not put out a cat. The truth seems to be that the verb in English is complicated and not usually well described in the texts now available.

It should be noted, however, that whatever one's classification of the words *up* and *out,* it in no way affects his use of them in the sentence, a fact which helps to explain why no clear relationship has been established between grammatical knowledge and the use of language.

As another illustration, it can be noted that the tenses of the verb as described in most texts do not picture accurately the American use of verbs. *I go to school* is likely to be called simple present; but obviously it is not, if by simple present we mean that the verb form refers to a single, present action. *I go to school* might better be called something like *present durative*, since it implies that the student is going to school, has gone to school, and presumably will continue to go to school. In the expression, I am going, *am going* is not necessarily progressive, but comes much closer to being simple present. On the other hand, the so-called simple present can serve for the future, as in *I go tomorrow*. Similarly, the so-called past usually implies the perfect, and the so-called perfect is more frequently simple past. And so with most of the other recognized "tenses." Furthermore, most verbs do not very closely resemble the recognized forms. What, for instance, are the verb and the verb form in the following sentence: *I have it in mind to initiate a series of experiments calculated to so alter production methods as to revolutionize the packaging of breakfast foods.*

Such classifications, again, bear little relationship to one's use of language. The purpose here is not to encourage detailed classification but rather to urge the importance, if one attempts such generalizations, of making one's teaching square with the known facts of English structure.

A grammar that describes the future tense of verbs as being formed with "shall" and "will" does not adequately explain such facts of American English as "We leave tomorrow" and "I am going after a while."

Such a construction as, "The reason I chose this dress is because I prefer green to red," defies logical grammatical analysis, but is nevertheless a sound and acceptable English construction. It was used by John Locke as early as 1690; it is to be found in standard literature since that date, and is found in literary writers of today. Hence to condemn this structure as ungrammatical is to use "grammar" in too limited a sense.

When a baseball is hit into right center field and the right fielder, who is set to catch it, observes that the center fielder is charging in his direction, the universal expression is "I got it." The formally correct statement, "I shall catch it," would not be appropriate for that time and place.

Recognition of the Changing Nature of Language

Second, the student should be helped to understand that the language he uses is in process of change. The change may seem to him extremely slow, except perhaps as he becomes momentarily entranced by a new bit of slang, but he should be encouraged to accept the process of linguistic change as a matter of course. The language of yesterday or of tomorrow, of Shakespeare's day or of his own, should not be presented as "the right way" of using language, but rather as the *actual* way a changing language was used or is being used at one place and moment in history. Although he should be encouraged to accept linguistic change as normal, the fact of change should not be so overstressed that he gets the notion that there is no preferred way of speaking or writing in a specific situation today.

On the contrary, he should be taught that there is a choice between alternative ways of expressing an idea and that an expression may be judged to be acceptable or unacceptable in *any particular situation.* In fact, the point should be very strongly emphasized, week after week and year after year, that the best use of English is that which is *most appropriate for the particular situation in which it is used.* The student should be helped to see, first of all, that language is always used *in a particular situation.* A student speaks to a teacher in a classroom; a girl talks to a boy at a party; a coach talks to a team on a football field; John writes the minutes of the last Photography Club meeting; Jane asks a camp director for a summer job. "Good English" is the English appropriate for the particular occasion in which it is used. In one sense a man may have a general ability to speak or write English well; but in a truer sense this ability consists of being able to choose the right words to say the right thing on any particular occasion. A comparison may be made with the ability to play baseball well. Playing baseball well depends not just on general ability but on being able to do what is appropriate in a particular situation. When a grounder is hit to a shortstop, for example, the right thing for him to do depends on whether it is the latter half of the ninth inning with the score tied and one out, with a slow runner on first and a fast runner on second—or whether some entirely different situation exists.

The student must be helped to recognize both that words are always used in a particular situation and that there are more effective and less effective ways of expressing his thoughts in that situation. Assuming that, in English, prepositions should always precede their objects and never end sentences is like assuming that there is only one base to which the shortstop should always throw the ball.

The Meaning of Levels of Language

A realistic analysis by a grammarian or by a high school student of the way words are actually used in English sentences will lead him to recognize the existence of many different "levels" of usage. These levels [1] include an illiterate level, a homely level, an informal standard English level, and a formal standard English level.

The term *levels of usage* has become familiar in recent years and is valuable. It calls attention to the fact that there are several different kinds of usage in English. Words are used in one way in a newspaper editorial, in another way in a machine shop, and in another way on the playground. Two weaknesses in the metaphor of "level" should be noted, however, to avoid misinterpretation. One misinterpretation is that the "levels" are arranged in a descending hierarchy from

[1] Charlton G. Laird, *The Miracle of Language* (Cleveland, World Publishing Co., 1953).

Robert C. Pooley, *Teaching English Usage* (New York, Appleton-Century-Crofts, Inc., 1946), Ch. III, pp. 16–24.

best to worst—that the language of a *New York Times* editorial, for example, is "the best" way to use words and that the language of the baseball field is much poorer. The various "levels" of usage perhaps do correspond more or less roughly to existent American social hierarchies; but students should not be encouraged to believe that the language of one "level" is necessarily better or worse than that of another. Rather, to repeat, students should be taught to ask themselves: "Is this level of usage appropriate to this particular occasion?" Second, the levels of usage are not sharply defined and clearly distinct one from the other. On the contrary, they overlap in many ways. For example, a president returning from an international conference told a formal session of the Congress of the United States of America that he did not "expect to make a hit every time he went up to bat," and this mixing of the formal language of government and the jargon of baseball is a normal overlapping of language levels in contemporary American English.

With these warnings about possible misinterpretation, however, it should be stressed that an understanding of the various kinds of dialects and levels of usage in American English should be developed in students. Very often a student's ability to choose the right expression in a particular situation will depend upon his sensitivity to various kinds of English. To develop such sensitivity, there are many kinds of listening experiences readily available in the school day. One good learning assignment is to invite students to listen [2] to the "chummy" or "homey" way in which broadcasters speak during breakfast programs and farm programs. This experience can alert students to the deliberate use of a "level" of language which the speaker has assumed to be the "level" of his audience. Sensitive appraisal of "levels of language" can also be developed by directing students to listen from this angle to adult and student speakers at school assemblies, club programs, home-room periods, and over the

[2] See also Chapter 8.

public address system. Another useful teaching device in this connection is to encourage students to find different levels of usage to express the same general idea: for example, "What are you trying to do?" "What's the big idea?" "What you think you're trying to do, Bud?" or "The book was excellent." "The book was tops." "The book was a wow." Divided usage is easily illustrated by such current expressions as loan (lend), 3 + 2 is (are) 5.

In sum, it is the grammar and usage of *American* English with which the secondary school teacher in America is primarily concerned. Like earlier stages of the language, American English is in process of historical change; it has various overlappings in levels of usage; and the best way of using it is the way most appropriate in a particular situation here and now.

BASIC CONSIDERATIONS IN DEVELOPING
A PROGRAM IN GRAMMAR

Discovering the best relationship between the teaching of English grammar and the development of the students' abilities to speak and write is no easy task.

Tenable Assumptions Underlying the Program

It may be safely assumed that in the secondary school the major objective of the English teacher in this connection is to help students to listen, to speak, to read, and to write better, and that he is trying to discover the best way of teaching grammar to achieve this end. Alternative assumptions—for example, that systematic grammar is an entertainingly intricate game, like gin rummy or bridge or chess, which should be learned just for the fun of playing it; or that grammar is a painful but wholesome form of "mental discipline"; or that grammar is an ancient and honorable discipline which automatically improves a student's ability to speak and write; or that knowledge of the structure of the

English sentence is an obsolete fad which is worthless in modern schools—all of these assumptions are erroneous and unacceptable.

Appropriate Timing in Relation to Growth and Need

The question, then, is when and how grammar should be taught. The best answer is found by the teacher who knows the facts of linguistic science and also the research findings in language growth and development. Such a teacher—informed about language and sensitive to the student's learning processes—can decide *which grammatical concepts* will help an individual student (or a group having similar characteristics) to write and to speak more effectively and correctly. Such a teacher also readily senses *how and when to teach these concepts* and *how to encourage the student to apply his grammatical knowledge in revising his writing or in appraising his speech* when he listens to a recording of it.

Traditionally, English grammar has been taught too early and too fast. Although readiness will differ for individual students, it may be assumed that structural grammar, that is, the various parts of speech, the special functions of different sentence elements, and the like, need not be taught prior to the seventh grade.[3] To some students it may not be taught at all. Language instruction in the elementary grades [4] should properly concentrate upon growth in communication itself, including direct teaching of usage, and leave analysis of language elements until the child reaches greater maturity.

Informed teachers know that the same amount of grammar cannot be learned by every student in a certain period of time. Nor can grammar be taught "all at once" or "once

[3] For a fuller treatment of this point, see Robert C. Pooley's "Forever Grammar," *Bulletin of the National Association of Secondary-School Principals* No. 30 (February, 1946), pp. 45–49.

[4] National Council of Teachers of English, Commission on the English Curriculum, *Language Arts for Today's Children*, NCTE Curriculum Series, Vol. II (New York, Appleton-Century-Crofts, Inc., 1954), Ch. 7 and especially pp. 238–241.

for all." A teacher cannot teach a student in the seventh grade all the grammar he will ever need to know about the sentence and then forget the problem thereafter. Such teachers also recognize that postponement of instruction in grammar until the twelfth grade would deprive some students, during earlier years of their high school life, of grammatical knowledge which, normally, they need.

A case is sometimes made for teaching systematic grammar "once and for all" in the seventh or eighth or ninth grade, on the grounds that the students by that time have sufficient ability to grasp and apply linguistic generalizations, have an adequate vocabulary of linguistic terms, and feel a need to understand the more complicated sentence patterns which they are beginning to use. But here again the same objections are relevant. *A knowledge of grammar cannot be learned "all at once" or "once and for all."* Neither can it be effectively acquired apart from a situation in which the pupil is grappling with the specific improvement of his own writing and speaking. *Therefore, it is important that the teacher understand the relationship between direct instruction in grammar and attentive, motivated practice in correct usage.*[5]

The more one analyzes the problem, the more it becomes clear that the teaching of grammar cannot be relegated or confined to one term or one year. This is true primarily for two reasons. First, the student is growing during his school years from early childhood to late adolescence; he cannot learn all he needs to know about grammar at the beginning, and he must not wait until the end of his schooling for instruction in many of the things he needs to know along the way about the language he is learning to use. Second, the intelligent student's need for some systematic understanding of the language he is using increases as he grows older; his

---

[5] National Council of Teachers of English, Commission on the English Curriculum, *The English Language Arts*, NCTE Curriculum Series, Vol. I (New York, Appleton-Century-Crofts, Inc., 1952), pp. 297–300.

experiences and ideas become more complex and his need for clarifying them and expressing them in more complex linguistic forms becomes more urgent.

Many of the concepts involved in certain aspects of grammar require more maturity than an elementary school child possesses and than many seventh- and eighth-graders have. The maturity of the individual, as well as that of the class group, is a clue to the teacher as to where to introduce a direct, but always functional, study of grammar. In the fifth grade, for example, or even in the seventh or eighth, most students do not use very complicated sentences and could learn the grammar of the compound-complex sentence only in the most parrot-like fashion. Such students frequently have been rushed through concepts before they have had time to assimilate them in daily experience. A few concepts slowly and patiently taught will bring about greater mastery and greatly improved attitudes toward grammar.

If grammatical analysis, for example, is begun in the seventh grade, the work of that grade might be confined to establishing the fundamental concepts of subject and predicate only, in frequent but short periods of instruction until all reasonably able students can locate and name the subjects of simple sentences which they write, and with equal confidence can locate the predicates and point out the predicate verbs. The purpose of this instruction is to develop that feeling for the grammatical structure of written English generally called "sentence-sense" so that students will write grammatically complete sentences. In the eighth grade this slow, patient teaching might establish thoroughly the complements of the simple sentence: the predicate noun and predicate adjective, and the direct object. Thus, at the end of the eighth year the student would have full command of the basic structure of the simple sentence. If he does (and most reasonably able students can with such patient instruction), it will be no mean accomplishment. By the time students have reached senior high school, they may find real need for some systematic understanding of the ways in which subordinate elements in the sentence convey subordinate ideas and how connectives can tie ideas together.[6] This problem is treated at some length later in the chapter.

It becomes clear, then, that the teaching of English grammar should be in relation to (1) the student's ability to understand the point of grammar being taught, and (2) his need for understanding and using this particular point in connection with his own problems of listening, speaking, reading, or writing. There is far more chance of teaching a grammatical point—the relation of pronouns to the words for which they stand, for example—in such a way that the student will actually learn it and use it effectively, if it is taught when he has demonstrated a real need for it—when, for instance, he is using a pronoun so unclearly that the reader is not certain what it stands for. It also implies that the teacher should be alert to recognize the student's need for grammatical knowledge and should know enough grammar and psychology to assist the student at his stage of readiness.

Obviously, to carry out such a program of instruction calls for curriculum planning by teachers at all levels of a school or school system. The scope and sequence of grammatical material must first be agreed upon; then each teacher must do thoroughly what is appropriate for each individual within his class group. No teacher should criticize the previous teacher of any student for a failure to teach grammatical elements which were not appropriate for that student at his level of attainment.[7] The adoption of a cumulative program will require careful planning by teachers and curriculum workers and discriminating use of the language textbooks which include more grammar than is needed for most students.

6 *Ibid.*, pp. 292–293.
7 Robert C. Pooley, *Teaching English Usage* (New York, Appleton-Century-Crofts, Inc., 1946), pp. 223–226.

Different Approaches for Different Students

Knowledge of systematic grammar is likely to prove most useful, not to the less able students, but rather to the more able. To *learn* systematic grammar, the student has to grasp the principles involved. To *use* systematic grammar, he has to apply the principles to his own speech or writing and to the speech or writing of others. Such ability to grasp principles and to apply them readily to new sets of facts is stronger in some students than in others. In the brightest student, this ability is often his most noticeable characteristic; in the dullest student, such ability may be almost non-existent. As the brighter students in high school are usually those who read most and have the most extensive linguistic experience, they are usually the ones who have least trouble with problems of good English usage. Thus, ironically, the students who learn grammar most easily are those who, in one sense, have the least need for instruction in it.[7a] The students who have most trouble using English are those who find systematic grammar too difficult to learn even though a very gradual and concrete approach is maintained.

The slower the student is, therefore, the less reliance should be put on grammatical generalizations and classifications as a means of improving his understanding or use of English. He is likely to profit more from direct teaching and habit formation of a particular detail of good usage. It does little good to remind John of a rule concerning agreement of subject and predicate if he is still unable to identify predicates and has no concept of agreement. Much teaching done by gifted verbalists is completely lost on students of limited verbal ability who have little appreciation of the meaning of grammatical rules or who do not recognize an example as a violation of a grammatical rule which has been formally stated by the teacher or the textbook.

[7a] See recent statements from the colleges (Chapter 12), indicating greater need for practice in the expression of ideas.

Again, in traditional teaching which has been altogether too deductive, a student is told that "an adverb is a word that modifies a verb, adjective, or another adverb." He commits this definition to memory and is then supposed to be able to identify adverbs by applying the rule. It would be an understatement to say that he is often unable to do so.

In inductive teaching of the adverb, the teacher presents a number of language situations in which the verb (a concept already learned) is qualified by accompanying words. John ran slowly; quickly the cat jumped; the train glided smoothly, and the like. Attention of the students is centered upon the effect of such words as *slowly, quickly, smoothly,* on the verbs which they accompany and therefore on the thought of the sentence. Students are asked to create new sentences in which verbs are similarly qualified. In time, the teacher will ask, "Does anyone know the name of such words as *slowly, quickly, smoothly,* as they are used in these sentences?" Some student may supply the name "adverb," or the teacher may supply it. The teacher then asks, "What general statement can we make about adverbs from these sentences?" Each student is encouraged to "make up" his own rule for class evaluation. With patient leading, the teacher can secure from students the observation that adverbs qualify or modify verbs and therefore contribute a new element to the idea being expressed. This much should be written down as a principle derived from experience. In a similar manner the modification of adjectives and other adverbs will be developed. Ultimately (and note that this procedure takes time and must not be rushed) the class will have derived a rule from their own observation that adverbs are words that modify verbs, adjectives, and other adverbs both structurally and from the point of view of meaning. This method avoids all difficulty in classifying, independently of their use in a sentence, such words as *home, mile, year.* Observation will show that "I walked *home*"; "John ran *a mile*"; "The birds stayed *a year*"—all illustrate verbs qualified by accompanying words, which must therefore be adverbs. There are, however, many modifiers which cannot be distinguished as either adverbs or adjectives. Sentence modifiers can usually not be so distinguished.

The rhetorical value of the adverb is thus established. So also is the traditional grammatical reason for saying *Run quickly,* instead of *Run quick.* Usage again, however, supersedes the rule in such expressions as *Drive slow,* which is now acceptable. Only by looking the word *slow* up in a recent authoritative dictionary or handbook of current usage can the student discover that in that situation *slow* is acceptable when used as an adverb. Linguistic authorities point out that the cadence of the sentence rather than grammatical rule governs the usage in such sentences. Students should be taught to observe the usage of those around them and to compare it with that of the dictionary or handbook.

The teacher should induce the student to decide what he wants to say, and then to say it by choosing his main idea as a subject. That is, teaching sound sentence structure, as opposed to correcting faults in sentence structure, is important.

It is always possible that any particular item of grammatical knowledge will be helpful to a particular student long before most of his classmates can even understand it—or years after most of them have grasped it. Individual students as well as groups vary widely in their rates and directions of linguistic growth.

It is, therefore, the responsibility of each teacher to work out his own method of presenting the grammatical knowledge that will meet the language needs of his students in direct connection with their own speech and writing. How some teachers have approached this problem is described in the section of this chapter devoted to teaching methods.

ELEMENTS REQUIRING INSTRUCTION

In general, the needs for grammatical knowledge on the part of those capable of applying it to speech and writing will be related to six problems: sentence structure, modification and subordination, agreement, noun and pronoun, verbs, and adjectives and adverbs.

Sentence Structure

Students have learned to use simple sentences, more or less ably, by the time they enter school, and they have acquired some immediate, almost automatic understanding of, as distinct from systematic knowledge concerning, subjects and predicates and objects. They know, for example, when they hear *The man ate the bear,* who ate and who was eaten, and that *The bear ate the man* means something different. As they grow, however, they need help in understanding the operation of an effective sentence. They need practice in writing and in appraising sentences which are complete, clear, and varied. They need to learn about subjects and predicates and whatever tenable distinctions can be made in thought or in structure between sentences and fragments of sentences. They need to understand how punctuation clarifies meaning and is a part of the form of the sentence. The mature students, whose thinking becomes increasingly complex, can apply their grammatical knowledge in self-appraisal and revision of their writing and of their speaking (when they listen to recordings of their talks and of their participation in class discussions).

Modification and Subordination

As students grow and their experiences and ideas become more extensive and intricate, and hence potentially more tangled and confused, they need to clarify for themselves and to express to others increasingly subtle modifications of thought and increasingly complex relations of ideas. Then it is that grammar becomes increasingly useful in helping the able students to understand the general ways in which words and phrases and clauses can modify each other and indicate directly or indirectly degrees of primary or subordinate importance. At this stage students also need instruction in the use of appropriate connectives to tie ideas together and of internal punctuation to make their meaning clear to the reader. The aim, however, will always be improvement in expressing meaning rather than mere classification of grammatical forms.

Agreement

The problems of grammatical agreement in modern English are much simpler than those which arise in a more highly inflected language like Greek or Latin. In most instances, the arrangement of the words in the English sentence has replaced inflectional endings as the device for indicating relationships of meaning. Thus, the speaker does not have to say *The bear ate the man-um* (or *The man-um ate the bear*) if man is the object, or *The man ate the bear-em* if the bear was eaten by the man. There are, nevertheless, still a number of words in English which require a change of form to indicate a change of relationship to another word, for example, *You sing,* but add an *s* if the subject is *He* (*She* or *It*), as in *He sings;* and in such sentences as *There is one* in contrast to *There are two.*

Further, in speaking or writing there tends to be confusion concerning a number of problems of agreement, especially when the words which should agree are some distance from each other, as in the sentence, The *character* of Hamlet, as is true of the characters of most men and women at all times and in all nations, *stands* by *itself.* A student learns sentence patterns unconsciously. He *also* learns sentence patterns by *example and illustration.* Out of what he has absorbed from good reading and alert listening in the classroom and in school assemblies, as well as on TV and radio, he can be led to develop inductively grammatical facts. These he can be encouraged to apply in handling the problems of agreement which he encounters.

There will be frequent needs both in school and in adult life to consult reliable sources of information on current usage. It is, therefore, important that the teacher develop in every student an attitude favorable to consulting such handbooks. The student needs training in selecting up-to-date and responsible authorities and in using the information in the handbook with respect to the meaning he wishes to convey. Some problems of agreement can be solved only by the writer's own determination of what he means. Knowing what he means he can verify in a handbook the usage which is acceptable in that particular situation.

Noun and Pronoun

The need for a grammatical framework for nouns and pronouns is not nearly so great as if English were a highly inflected language. The need, nevertheless, exists in a number of instances, primarily in relation to pronouns. Pronouns are still highly inflected (*I, me, my, mine; we, us, our, ours,* for example). Since pronouns usually stand for nouns, their grammatical form is often determined by the nouns with which they agree (*The men gave John* THEIR *books; John gave the men* HIS *books*). Clarity of speaking and writing depends to a considerable degree on clarity in the reference of pronouns. For these reasons, the student should have much practice in the accurate use of nouns and pronouns.

As was pointed out in *The English Language Arts:* [8]

[the] formation of plurals of nouns is not primarily a grammatical problem. It can be dealt with more simply as spelling. Showing possession in English is a matter of recognizing the *fact* of possession and adding ' or *'s*. The problem needs no formal classification as grammar. . . .

Case uses of the pronoun cause trouble chiefly in compounds which can be determined by reference to usage. Fries's statistical confirmation of the linguist's statement that in standard English, position in the sentence is tending to substitute for case is a significant one. *Who* did you ask? To *whom* did you send the invitation? and It is *me,* are examples of the use of the nominative forms for nominative positions in the sentence and objective forms for objective positions, often regardless of which is subject and which is object or predicate

[8] *Op. cit.,* p. 295.

pronoun. The fact that pronouns have special forms to show possession, without use of the apostrophe, needs emphasis. This is *your* book. This book is *yours*. This is *their* book. This book is *theirs*. Contractions can and should be mastered early by most pupils.

Usage needs to be examined as it varies from singular to plural according to meaning with such pronouns as *each, everyone, anybody,* and the like, and with collective nouns like *team, crowd,* and *flock*.

Verbs

The student needs to use accurately not only one-word verbs, like *sing,* but also verb phrases, like *will have sung* or *was going to sing.* Whether he is telling a story or writing a report of an activity, he must select an appropriate way of expressing *present, past,* and *future time* and must keep the time sequence consistent within a given story or report. Often he must choose from among different verb forms the one which will agree with the simple subject of his sentence. A grammatical study of verbs, when checked continuously against the meaning of the experience under discussion, can develop the student's awareness of what is acceptable and effective in a specific situation and can lead to his formulating useful and sound generalizations.

Though systematic knowledge of the grammar may be helpful for certain pupils, it is nevertheless true that many of the most stubborn problems which students have to face in relation to verbs cannot be readily solved by such grammatical knowledge. These are often problems of the strong verbs —not *I seen him* but *I have seen him* or *I saw him.* This is a good place to remember the distinction between teaching *correct usage* and teaching *systematic grammatical knowledge* or *theory.* Both logic and teaching experience indicate that direct practice of the correct pattern, with little if any regard to grammatical framework, is usually successful in connection with teaching the proper use of strong verbs. For the student who has trouble with *I seen it,* for example, teaching him that the verbs involved are past participles and not proper past tenses will probably not improve his usage of these forms. Likely to be far more effective is directing his attention to the fact that *seen*, when it is expressing the main action of the sentence, should usually have *had*, *has*, or *have* with it, as in *I have seen it, He has seen it, They had seen it*. Having the students repeat many times orally and in writing the same correct pattern establishes it. This can be accomplished without boredom to the students or teacher if both seek interesting sentences in the students' speech and writing and in magazines and newspapers. Reference to recent dictionaries and to handbooks of current usage should supplement the students' observation of the language in use today.

Adjectives and Adverbs

Many problems of choosing the right adjective or adverb are good-usage problems, in which direct memorizing is worth while; but many others are problems in which grammatical knowledge can be helpful. Perhaps most important among the latter is the use of adjectives and adverbs in making comparisons. Expressing comparisons within the students' experience is more useful than labeling forms.

PROBLEMS OF TEACHING METHOD

The fact that the teaching of grammar is treated in a separate chapter in this volume does not imply that grammar should be taught apart from speech and writing in the classroom. The practical problem which the teacher continually faces is how to present principles of grammar and elements of usage so that they may affect directly the speech and writing of each student.

The following suggestions for handling this problem have come from successful teachers and from the known results of research.

The Need of Relating Instruction
Directly to Speech and Writing

The teacher should determine by analysis of the speech and writing of his students what grammatical usages and principles they have need of learning. He should teach these principles by direct application to the effective and ineffective expression of the pupils themselves and should measure growth in terms of improvement in speaking and writing. He should at the same time teach his students to recognize such effective and ineffective expressions in their own efforts at communication, to set up goals for improvement, to seek methods of developing better habits of speech and writing, and to propose standards by which to judge their success. Illustrations of this technique appear in Chapter 9 in relation to the improvement of sentences.

Students should be encouraged, also, to make up sentences of their own as illustrations of grammatical facts being presented, because ability to create such sentences demands a practical grasp of the concepts involved. For example, when the students have taken the first steps in learning about subjects and predicates, they may be given interesting subjects for which to create predicates or lively predicates for which to make good subjects. Or they may be given fragments, consisting of subjects *without* predicates or predicates *without* subjects which are punctuated as sentences, and be asked to find out what is wrong with them and to make them right. A discussion of the students' corrections will reinforce the grammatical fact being studied.

The Value of an Inductive Approach to Rules

The inductive method (discovery of a generalization through the study of many specific illustrations) should for the most part be used in introducing a new grammatical point. Although there is nothing wrong with stating a grammatical principle first and then illustrating it, a more effective procedure, usually, is to have the student find for himself from the analysis of a number of carefully prepared sentences the principle for which he has need. The important point here and elsewhere in the teaching of grammar is that the student shall not be tempted to memorize a statement instead of developing a clear concept. He must be helped to see that grammatical knowledge is a useful framework for analysis of the language he is using every day in speaking, listening, writing, and reading. For instance, the generalization that commas are used to set off parenthetical elements should be taught when such expressions appear in the students' spontaneous speech and personal writing. Other interesting examples may be found in magazines and books, including language textbooks. The observation that change of intonation and pauses in speech serve as clues to the listener, just as punctuation in written English helps the reader, gives meaning to generalizations about accepted practice.

Illustrating the rhetorical and meaning value of modification in a discussion of their own writing may be used to motivate students to look at the grammatical facts of modification. A series of sentences built around the same simple subject and simple predicate may likewise be used to show how the modification of a basic idea can alter its meaning; for example, *The old man sat down, The old man in the blue overalls sat down on the pile of hay, The old man in evening dress sat down in the speaker's chair, The young man who was wearing a Brooklyn Dodger's uniform for the first time sat down on the players' bench.* Discussing students' campaign talks for student officers, revising scripts for timed radio talks, and condensing copy to fit space limitations in the school newspaper are examples of genuine opportunities for teaching students how to determine which of their ideas are co-ordinate, which are subordinate to others, which can be effectively given in a single word, which need a phrase, which a clause.

The importance of teaching sound sentence structure as

opposed to correcting faults in sentence structure should be emphasized in this connection. The teacher should induce the student to decide what he wants to say and then discover in the effective expression of his idea a subject and a predicate. Much faulty sentence structure results from heedless beginnings, which in a distributive grammar like English become automatically faulty subjects, which, in turn, lead to faulty use of the passive voice, which encourages loose reference, and so on and on.

The Avoidance of Mere Definition or Identification

Mere definition or identification is of minor use in the teaching of grammar; in fact, if grammatical classification is pursued as an end in itself it can become positively harmful. Though it is important for a student to learn to say, "The book was given to John and *me*," it really does not matter much whether he can or cannot identify *me* in the sentence as a "retained object" or define a transitive verb as one which must have a direct object or, if used in the passive, may have no direct object. Undue emphasis on such points in the secondary school can give students a fundamentally wrong impression of the nature of grammar and why they should be interested in it. The real evidence of a student's grasp of grammatical concepts lies in his ability (1) to write good sentences, (2) to manipulate parts of sentences easily, and (3) to improve sentences which need improvement.

Provision for the Needs of Individuals

It has been demonstrated earlier in the chapter that the native endowment of students affects in large measure their ability to profit from the study of grammar. Weaker students find it difficult either to grasp or apply generalizations concerning linguistic forms and their uses. The big question which remains is, What can the teacher do about these differences in the classroom?

Segregation of classes according to ability or according to

educational objective, while making it easier for the teacher to adapt his program to students having varying levels of ability and differing educational goals, interferes with the development of certain powers of communication exceedingly important in a democracy.

This volume does not recommend such segregation, for the Commission believes that the major purposes of teaching communication may be served better in groups which represent a range of abilities and interests. A further reason is that too frequently teachers of segregated groups have not differentiated instruction to fit the specific abilities within the class. Occasionally, when an entire school system has segregated English classes for the purpose of giving weak students more time for grammar, the program has become monotonous and futile in the absence of real communication.

Enough research is available to help teachers determine what a useful program for weak pupils would be—ample opportunity to speak, to exchange ideas with others, to record simple, well-organized, and clearly expressed ideas in writing. Habit formation is the aim with stress upon acceptable usage at a conversational, not a formal, level. Illiteracies must be tackled first: I *seen* it. He *done* it. *Them boys. That there.* Sound is an important element in establishing habitual use of the accepted form. Many of these less able pupils fail to hear the *ed* on words like *helped*, and therefore they write, "He help me do yesterday." Such students need much oral practice in expressing their ideas simply, clearly, and logically.

Some of them, even in the twelfth grade, will profit from the kind of patient presentation of simple sentence elements recommended on page 366 for the seventh and eighth grades. They may be expected to do some things much later than other students—and some things not at all.

In order to adjust the program to individuals, the teacher must discover at what level students are performing as they write and as they speak to the class. A good usage test which keeps close to the actual speaking and writing experiences of young people and measures currently acceptable usage will also reveal what the students need to learn. In the light of evidence from these actual communication situations and from these tests, the teacher may determine what matters need to be stressed with the entire class, which may be presented to small groups having similar difficulties, and which must be worked upon by individuals. Grouping of this sort within the class will always remain flexible according to the needs of the moment.

Some teachers have developed sets of cards presenting explanations and drills on the usages which cause most difficulty, for which reference numbers may be placed on papers written by individual students. Some keep card notes of difficulties individuals reveal as they speak. During supervised study periods, class members may work on these cards as the teacher goes about the room helping individuals or groups as the need arises.

Personal records and plans kept by the students themselves are useful as means of checking progress, especially for more able students, who should be encouraged to set goals for themselves and to plan their progress toward them. These students should be encouraged also to determine from their reading, from listening to adults over the radio and to speakers on the public platform what constitutes maturity and what are reasonable goals toward which they should be striving. Personal responsibility for growth should be emphasized with these more gifted young people. They should be held to a high standard of performance and to constant applications in their own speech and writing of the grammatical generalizations which they have mastered.

Use of reference sources, such as a thesaurus or dictionary of synonyms, handbooks of usage followed by reputable publishers, and other handbooks of grammatical usage available in the school library, should be a part of the students' program for striving toward maturity. They may also read with pleasure and profit some of the discussions of the English language and current controversies concerning it which are listed on page 384.

The Measurement of Results

If "the proof of the pudding is in the eating," the test of the student's mastery of grammar is in his speaking and writing. Both teacher and class should seek positive evidences of growth through examination of the speech and writing of students for such factors as the following, which may be set up by the students themselves in class discussion:

a. Use of grammatically complete sentences.
b. Increasing accuracy of agreement between verbs and their subjects and between pronouns and their antecedents.
c. Growing variety in sentence order by increased use of modifiers at the beginning of the sentence.
d. Gradual growth away from compound sentences using *and, but, so* for co-ordination to complex sentences using connectives such as *when, where, as, since, who* to indicate more exact relationships between the ideas expressed.
e. Effective use of other subordinating elements to build up the idea of the sentence.
f. For some, at least, growth in balance and emphasis in sentence structure by the employment of varying lengths of sentences and the skillful use of parallel structure.

THE EFFORT TO EVOLVE AN ADEQUATE DESCRIPTION OF ENGLISH GRAMMAR

As was pointed out at the beginning of the chapter, there is at present no one universally accepted description of English grammar. On the contrary, a grammatical revolution is under way. As is normal in revolutions, many of the symptoms are warlike. A defender of the traditional faith asks, Who killed grammar? A professor commenting soberly on the topic reports to a professorial meeting that the new scientific linguists "violently object" to misstatements about language.[9] The warlike symptoms are interesting and perhaps healthy as a sign that the subject is being taken very seriously, and teachers of English should try to understand them; but the symptoms should not distract attention from the basic change which is taking place.

Critical Analysis of the History of Traditional English Grammar

The change began with critical analysis of the history of traditional English grammar. An historian of the subject has summarized as follows the way this grammar came into being: [10]

Western grammar starts as a phase of Greek intellectual exploration. It is a late phase, a part of the dusky Hellenistic afterglow, and is inadequate even as an analysis of Greek. Its adaptation to Latin weakens it, it is confused with philosophy in its transmission to modern Europe, and for us it finally becomes the basis for a rigidly prescriptive treatment of English. This astonishing transformation of a speculative intellectual exercise into an almost universally accepted pedagogical device came about because of the enormous prestige of the classical tradition, the great age of that tradition, and the almost complete ignorance until very recently of what we now call linguistics. Grammar became so integral a part of Western educational practice that a faith in it was acquired with the education itself. It is hardly strange that as part of our educational experience we should all have acquired an implicit faith in grammar just as all our ancestors a few centuries ago accepted the Ptolemaic description of the sun revolving about the earth. The Ptolemaic hypothesis, not much younger than Greek grammar and a product of the same Hellenistic culture, maintained its hold on Western thought for much the same reasons that Western grammar still does.

It was pointed out by Dykema that traditional grammar was developed to explain the structure of Greek and Latin and does not provide a very good description of the English language. Its emphasis on case, for example, arises because

---

[9] James B. McMillan, "Summary of Nineteenth Century Historical and Comparative Linguistics," *College Composition and Communication,* Vol. IV (December, 1954), p. 149.

[10] Karl W. Dykema, "Historical Development of the Concept of Grammatical Proprieties," *College Composition and Communication,* Vol. V (December, 1954), p. 139.

of the importance of case in Greek and Latin; case is much less relevant in English. In Latin there are actually five cases of the noun—the Latin word for *king* has in the singular the forms *rex, regis, regi, regem, rege,* for example—but in English there are only two, *king* and *king's.*

Further, the traditional grammar was criticized as essentially prescriptive or authoritarian in nature. Not only did it not give a good description of the English language; it attempted to tell people what the English language *ought* to be and how it *ought* to be used. Often arbitrarily, the critics insisted, it classified usages as "right" or "wrong."

Perhaps still worse, its authoritarian insistence on what the English language *ought* to be, kept grammarians and other students of the language from studying English objectively and scientifically to find out what its structure actually is.

Two Results of the Criticisms of Traditional Grammar

These and other criticisms, for the most part valid, of the traditional grammar have led to two general results.

One result has been an effort to improve it by avoiding its major weaknesses. Thus, grammarians have tried to pick out the parts of the traditional grammar which were "functional" in modern English. Definitions have tended to become somewhat less metaphysical and more descriptive. Parts of speech are defined in terms of the use of words in sentences, and so on. Emphasis has been put on grammar as a reasonably good description of the way words work together acceptably in sentences rather than on grammar as prescriptive or authoritarian.

The second general result has been much more radical and fundamental. Beginning in the nineteenth century and continuing very actively in this generation, a significant group of linguists has been studying the structure of the English language freshly and scientifically. They have not been trying to remold or refine the traditional description of grammar, but rather to look at the facts of the English language themselves and see what the facts tell them. Much of this work has been published only within the last twenty years. Professor Donald J. Lloyd says that "we must not forget the rawness or recency of our present knowledge of English speech," [11] and lists these books as recent "monuments": Bloomfield's *Language* (1933), Fries's *American English Grammar* (1940), Bloch and Trager's *Outline of Linguistic Analysis* (1942), Nida's *Synopsis of English Syntax* (1943), Pike's *Intonation of American English* (1945), Trager and Smith's *Outline of English Structure* (1951), and Fries's *Structure of English* (1952).

The scientific linguists emphasize the primacy of the spoken language rather than the written, the paramount importance of current usage, the existence of various dialects within a language, and the necessity of objective description and analysis based on form. Their purpose is to reveal the actual means by which the relationships of the words in sentences are indicated. These means are not only grammatical inflections of a few words, but pauses, intonations, and an intricate system of word arrangement by which the subjects, predicate verbs, objects, modifiers, and so on, in the sentences are recognized in speech. These are, therefore, what need to be studied. As with any theory or system of knowledge, the new structural grammar has its own terminology, which is largely meaningless except to one who has studied the system. This is true also of the traditional grammar. Hence it is impossible to give an adequate explanation of the new structural grammar in a few paragraphs. Its key terms include *signals of meaning, phonemes, morphemes, function words, junctures, structure, pattern* and *form classes*, and much stress is put on *levels of pitch* and *intonation*. The new structural grammar of English is historically just at the place where it is being fully organized as a scientific system, and it is now being adapted for use

---

[11] Donald J. Lloyd, "Grammar in Freshman English," *College Composition and Communication*, Vol. V (December, 1954), p. 162.

in the schools. Further refinement and critical analysis of the new system, and experiments with adapting it for use in secondary school classrooms may be expected. In 1954, Professor Lloyd reported the use of the system in his teaching of college classes at Wayne University, but regretted "that there are so few other teachers trading information with me about the practical everyday conduct of this kind of class." [12]

In summary, traditional English grammar, which at the present time is the grammar of English that has been adapted for use in secondary schools, has been justly criticized as not a scientific analysis of the English language, not adequately descriptive of the English language, too prescriptive and authoritarian in attitude, and tending to interfere with careful study of the actual structure of English. Such critical analysis has led both to the attempt to improve the traditional program of grammar and to the formation by students of linguistics of a new, scientifically based structural grammar. At the present time, there is no one analysis of the grammar of English which is universally accepted. In the years immediately ahead there will be seen (1) further attempts to improve the traditional description of grammar, (2) further critical analysis and refinement of the new structural grammar, and (3) experimentation with the adaptation of the new structural grammar for the secondary schools. The effort is not to avoid grammar but to find the most truly descriptive grammar of English.

II. SPELLING

COMMON ATTITUDES TOWARD SPELLING

The conventions of spelling, like those of grammar, have their real value in what they contribute to the effectiveness of expression—in this case, of writing. The tradition of the spelling bee early divorced spelling both from written ex-

[12] *Ibid.*, p. 166. See also Paul Roberts, *Patterns of English* (New York, Harcourt, Brace & Company, Inc., 1956).

pression and from communication in the minds of many people in this country. The pioneers sought entertainment which required little equipment, and one blue-backed spelling book was good for a whole winter of Friday evenings! The premium was on spelling the most outlandish words. He who could spell *syzygy* stood up longest and became the hero of the community. The procedure may have been good entertainment, but it was bad pedagogy. Everyday words were ignored. The person who needed the most drill sat down first. Everyone was exposed to an identical list of words. Spelling as a *writing* skill was forgotten, although more errors in spelling are occasioned by careless handwriting than by any other single cause.

In general, there is little correlation between intelligence and ability to spell. Perhaps that may be one reason why so many people in the community feel competent to criticize the results of teaching spelling! Recently in response to such protests, the administration in a large city system ruled that every student in the schools should learn twenty-five spelling words every Friday; yet neither the community nor the administration thought to inquire whether the pupils were ever asked to write. In this type of situation, the superior professional knowledge of the staff should override the shallow, unpsychological solutions offered to correct problems distressing to both school and community.

Frequent experiences in writing are basic to any program for the improvement of spelling. Recent research in Minneapolis and elsewhere has proved beyond a doubt that increasing the amount of writing done by students and *giving direct attention* to words misspelled stimulate greater progress in spelling than learning set lists of words, so many each week.

FUNCTIONS OF THE SPELLING PROGRAM

There are at least five important aims for the teaching of spelling: (1) mastery of the most commonly used words;

(2) consciousness of how words are built; (3) adequate methods of attacking the learning of new words; (4) independence in the use of the dictionary; and (5) individual acceptance of responsibility for spelling correctly words used in writing.

SELECTION OF WORDS TO BE TAUGHT

Years ago, the number of words commonly appearing in spelling books used in the first eight grades varied from six thousand to ten thousand.

The Search for the Most Commonly Used Words

Today it is known on the basis of actual counting of words in personal and business letters, in issues of the Sunday paper, and the like, that between two and three thousand words make up, roughly, 97 per cent of all words used by the average person in writing. It is clear, also, from research that some college graduates at work in various professions use three hundred times as many words as do persons who left school at the end of the third grade. In addition to extending the writing vocabularies of the gifted, the schools have an obligation to give everybody, insofar as his learning capacity will permit, a mastery of the basic two or three thousand words. These appear in most printed series of spellers. Cities like New York have grouped them in small multigraphed spelling dictionaries, according to their usefulness for the writing of children in each grade.[13]

Some schools teach these words in the order of their appearance in the commercial spelling book, an order usually substantiated by research. Others insert them into the units of instruction where they are most likely to be used. This latter procedure recognizes the research basis of the lists but combines such evidence with the need of pupils, within a particular class, for using the words.

[13] New York City, Board of Education, *Manual to Guide Experimentation with Spelling Lists A, B, and C* (Brooklyn, The Board, 1951).

Use of Unit and Personal Words in Spelling

Two other sources of spelling words are important: one is the teaching unit in progress in which words peculiar to the unit, such as *pioneer* or *covered wagon, classical* or *romantic, science* or *fiction, local color* or *verisimilitude, adolescence* or *marriage,* or *recognition,* are repeatedly used as young people write about what they are studying or reading at the moment; the other is in the personal words required by each individual because of his own unique experience. Words needed, for example, by students who have spent the summer in the Rockies will be very different from those needed by a boy who has driven a truck to a wharf. Such words might well be kept in a special place in each pupil's notebook and be studied independently by each individual, using the methods learned in the presentation of the two or three thousand words taught to all students in common. Once in two weeks, class members may choose partners and dictate their personal spelling words to each other.

In all spelling it is obvious that individuals vary widely in the words they need, in their methods of attack on new words, and in the speed with which they can learn. Hence, grouping into small groups within the class and emphasizing words needed and misspelled by each individual, whether in his own writing or in a pretest, are imperative if economical learning is to take place.

Constant Emphasis upon Commonly Used Words

It cannot be emphasized too frequently that pupils, regardless of the grade in which they are enrolled, should learn the simple, most used words first. Some spelling series, by adding so many hundred words annually to the list, present in the eighth grade words for which few pupils will have any use. Twelve- and thirteen-year-olds once faced a seventh-grade spelling list which presented for mastery such words as *interdenominationalism* when they couldn't spell *can't* and *already*. All research into the words which junior high school students misspell suggests a need for review of the simple words most misspelled in the writing of intermediate-grade children. James Fitzgerald has an excellent list of the 222 words most frequently misspelled in the writing of Grades 4, 5, and 6.[14] The word *across* proved to be the most persistently misspelled word throughout the junior and senior high schools of a Middle Western city. Dolch has a list.[15] Guiler studied the words most misspelled in the seventh and eighth grades.[16] Jones' one hundred spelling demons are still useful.[17] Fred Ayer has recently produced a list of more difficult words which are commonly used and misspelled in the senior high school.[18] Pollock did a similar study of words misspelled by college freshmen.[19] The suggestion is not that all these lists be used with high school students, but that some one or two of them be used as pretests to find out which words students should concentrate on first. They have value, too, in proposing methods which individual school systems or individual schools could use to advantage in finding out which words are most misspelled in the writing of their own students. After the giving of such tests and the analysis of the individual needs revealed in written work, teachers may group pupils for instruction according to the errors they have made on the most commonly used words. While weak spellers are at work on these simple

[14] James A. Fitzgerald, *A Crucial Core Vocabulary in Spelling* (Milwaukee, Wis., The Bruce Publishing Company, 1941). See also by the same writer and publisher: *A Basic Life Spelling Vocabulary*, 1951, and *The Teaching of Spelling*, 1951.
[15] Edward W. Dolch, *The Modern Teaching of Spelling* (Champaign, Ill., The Garrard Press, 1950).
[16] Walter S. Guiler, "Primary-Grade Words Frequently Misspelled by Higher-Grade Pupils," *Elementary School Journal*, Vol. XLIV (January, 1944), pp. 295–300.
[17] W. F. Jones, *One Hundred Spelling Demons* (Chicago, Hall & McCreary Company, 1913).
[18] Fred Ayer, *A Study of High-School Spelling Vocabulary* (Austin, Texas, The Steck Company, 1945).
[19] Thomas C. Pollock, "Spelling Report," *College English*, Vol. XVI (November, 1954), pp. 102–109.

words, pupils who have mastered them may work with creating new words out of old ones such as *active, activity, activate,* and the like, or study the more mature words which are giving them trouble in their own written work.

Use of Pretests to Determine Emphasis

The value of pretesting as a device for discovering individual difficulties in spelling has been clearly established by research. Most words do not have the same "hard spots" for all learners. Each student must find his own "hard spots" on the basis of the pretest and concentrate on the words and parts of words that caused him trouble. For example, a student teacher once labored with a class of ninth-grade children on the "hard spot" in *lilies,* changing the *y* to *i* and adding *es.* Next day one third of the students spelled the *ies* correctly but put two *ll*'s in the middle of the word. One thousand college freshmen once produced twenty-nine different misspellings for the word *collateral!* "Hard spots" for each individual must be determined by pretesting and mastered by each one in his own best way.

NEED FOR A METHOD OF ATTACK ON NEW WORDS

In general, research has found no one "best" method by which all students learn to spell. It has revealed, however, that the best spellers have a systematic method of approaching new words; whereas poor spellers commonly go at the task in a very hit-and-miss fashion.

Steps in Learning to Spell a Word

Learning to spell is a complex matter involving *seeing* the word distinctly, *hearing* it clearly, *comparing* what one sees with what one hears as in *often* and *pretty, recalling* the word, *writing* the word, *knowing the meaning* of it in the context of one's own written expression. Guiding pupils in these processes and grouping them in terms of the amount of specific help they need, are important techniques of *teaching* spelling. Too many students are not being *taught* how to attack new words. They are merely being *tested* by teachers who pronounce, for them to write, a certain group of words assigned for mastery. Most spelling books develop learning techniques carefully in presenting each lesson. Teachers can expand these methods as they study the needs of the class.

Developing Independence and Use of the Dictionary

Pupils should understand that independence in learning new words as they need them is one of the major aims of the study of spelling. It is impossible for anyone to learn in school all the words he will need throughout life. For example, between the last two editions of Webster's *New International Dictionary* one hundred and fifty thousand new words or new forms of old words entered the language. Twenty-two pages of words have come into English recently from the textile industry alone. Students should therefore never be allowed to think they have done their full duty when they have mastered only the words in a spelling lesson. They must go on to the mastery of many other words as they find need for them in writing.

Developing independence in the use of the dictionary, and with older pupils of such reference books as Roget's *Thesaurus*, is an important part of teaching a mode of attack on new words. It should be remembered, however, that no student can look up a word in the dictionary unless he knows how to spell the first syllable of it. Dr. Horn's famous example is the word *circumference*.[20] Shall a person ignorant of the beginning of the word look under *sir, ser, sur, cer* or *cir?* Teachers should never allow a fetish for having pupils take responsibility for looking words up in the dictionary blind

[20] Ernest Horn, "Rationalization in Spelling," *Elementary English Review,* Vol. VII (March, 1930), pp. 51–53.

them to their own responsibility for *teaching* how words are spelled. When students know how a word begins, they should become proficient in using guide words, in interpreting pronunciation symbols, in noting syllables and accents, and in copying the word correctly from the dictionary.

In this connection, it may be noted that the alphabet is the most important single reference tool. Under newer methods of teaching beginning reading, boys and girls learn first to sense the total configuration of a word, later breaking it down into syllables and letters. If any pupils reach the seventh grade without a mastery of the alphabet, they should be organized into a small group and given instruction in the order of letters. By the ninth grade, they should be alphabetizing by the second and third letter of a word. Making their own alphabetized lists of the words which they have difficulty spelling is a profitable exercise. They can then use this improvised and greatly abbreviated dictionary for the words which they write most frequently.

Development of Insight into How Words Are Made

An important aim of the teaching of spelling is to develop a consciousness of how words are built.

Children of all ages enjoy a game. Why not give them a chance to guess how words are spelled, helping them to see that it is more important to sense how words are made and then not have to study them at all than it is to "study hard"? The premium should be on the flash of insight into how words are built rather than on the number of minutes one studies per word! For example, few students have discovered that, in general, when one adds *ly* to a word, one does not touch the end of the word. There are exceptions, of course, the most common being *truly*. Think, however, of the number of words one can spell correctly if he remembers that fact: *really, sincerely, immediately, finally, actively, cordially, attentively,* and many others. Students should note that they did not double the *l* in *cordially, finally,* and *really;*

they merely added *ly* to a word which already had an *l* at the end of it. Testing pupils on their ability to spell the words after gaining insight into how they are built helps to demonstrate the lack of need for "studying spelling hard" in the sense of attacking twenty-five words every Friday.

Once pupils have mastered the rule, they often must add the learning of words which are exceptions to it. Words that end in *y*, they discover, change *y* to *i* before adding *ly* as in *happily;* and words that end in *able* change the suffix to *ably: probable, probably; acceptable, acceptably.* Playing with words is fun and should often supplant the so-called "spelling lesson."

Use of Selected Spelling Rules

Spelling rules, like other generalizations, have doubtful value for students of average ability or below. Learning to attack each word individually is probably a more useful procedure for most types of words. Two rules, however, have distinctly greater value than others: the one governing the adding of suffixes to words ending in an unpronounced *e*, and the one governing the same process in words ending in a single consonant preceded by a single vowel. It is probably wise to keep these two rules apart until considerable time has been devoted to each. Inductive procedures are probably more effective than handing out the rule to the pupils and asking them to find examples. Students make as many words out of the word *love*, for example, as possible, dictating to the teacher, who spells them correctly on the chalkboard, and drawing conclusions carefully, step by step, in the formulation of the rule for themselves. For instance, from *love, loving, lovely, lovable,* and *loved,* the pupils may distinguish the conditions and determine the rule:

love—a word ending in unpronounced *e*.
ing, able, ed—suffixes each beginning with a vowel.
ly—a suffix beginning with a consonant.
Drop the *e* before a suffix beginning with a vowel.
Retain the *e* before a suffix beginning with a consonant.

After the development of the rule, the boys and girls should be given a chance to try themselves out on a short list of words without studying them, testing each by the rule on the chalkboard: *hopeful, excitable, coming, racing, excitement.* Later, after these words are learned, students may discover what happens to the *e* after *g* and *c* before a suffix beginning with *a* or *o* as in *courageous, serviceable,* and the like.

Other Techniques of Seeing Words

For older students, attention to what happens when a prefix precedes the word also helps:

un necessary	un happy
dis satisfied	dis appear
mis spell	mis apply
col(con) loquial	con tour

There is no doubling of letters in these words. The juxtaposition of an *s* at the end of the prefix and an *s* at the beginning of the word, for example, creates the illusion of doubling.

For average and weak students such devices as the following are especially helpful:

there, which points out place, has *here* in it.
their, which shows possession, has an *heir* in it.
all right is two words, the same as *all correct* or *all wrong.*
Principle, meaning a rule of action, ends like *rule,* in *le.*
All other common meanings of *principal* are spelled with an *al.*

Spelling Contractions and Possessives

Constant review of the spelling of contractions is necessary throughout the junior high school. Written drill is important because the problem is one of visualization: *they are, they're,* for example. This is a simple problem, involving little intelligence, and therefore may reasonably be expected to be mastered early. It should be mastered, if possible, before possessive forms are introduced. The fact that a pronoun never uses an apostrophe to show possession may be emphasized later. Spelling of plurals of nouns should be stressed before development of the idea of possession. What is meant by possession needs very special attention to avoid having children put an apostrophe after every *s* at the end of a word. Sometimes it helps to list names of possessors, putting after each in a second column the name of the thing possessed:

John's hat
girls' dresses

After the process is understood, responsibility for proofreading one's own writing should be emphasized.

The Need for a Wide Variety of Methods

When all these rules and devices are taught, it is obvious what a small proportion of the words in the English language they cover. They are no substitute for seeing how each word is put together, for dividing it into syllables, for hearing it accurately, for writing it carefully, and for using it in context.

Accurate pronunciation is a vital adjunct to good spelling. Many words in English are spelled as they sound: *interdependent*, for example, and *democratic* or *democratically*. In long words, the second half of the word is often garbled, primarily because of haste or a feeling of nervousness about the length of the word. Careless articulation causes the omission, for example, of the syllable preceding *ly: fin*a*lly*, democrati*ca*lly*, prob*a*bly*. Pupils write *supprise* because they pronounce *surprise* that way; "I went over to Windsor on the *inerbin*," wrote one boy, meaning *interurban*.

The Limitations of Phonics

High school teachers frequently complain that students cannot spell because the elementary school has neglected phonics. In general, it is not true that the elementary school has ignored phonics. Reading experts have proved that phonics represent one valuable means of attack on new words, but only one, and sometimes a misleading one because of the lack of consistency in the spelling of sounds in English. Phonics help in spelling *man, can, than, pan,* or *send, lend, bend, rend;* but one may be wrong almost as often as he is right if he spells English words by sound: *pritty,* for example, *ofen,* or *skoot* for scoot. One of the best illustrations of the problem occurs in the following poem:

Our Queer Lingo

When the English tongue we speak
Why is "break" not rhymed with "freak"?
Will you tell me why it's true
We say "sew," but likewise "few"?
And the maker of a verse
Cannot rhyme his "horse" with "worse"?
"Beard" sounds not the same as "heard";
"Cord" is different from "word";
"Cow" is cow but "low" is low;
"Shoe" is never rhymed with "foe."
Think of "hose" and "dose" and "lose";
And think of "goose" and yet of "choose";
Think of "comb" and "tomb" and "bomb,"
"Doll" and "roll" and "home" and "some."
And since "pay" is rhymed with "say"
Why not "paid" with "said," I pray?
Think of "blood" and "food" and "good";
"Mould" is not pronounced like "could."
Wherefore "done," but "gone" and "lone"—
Is there any reason known?
To sum up all, it seems to me
Sounds and letters don't agree.

There are twenty-seven ways of spelling the sound *o* in English; for example, *so,* alth*ough,* tabl*eau,* chau*ffeur,* s*ew,* and kn*ow.* Why, when one removes the *k,* does *know* become *now;* and again, why is *sow* pronounced one way in relation to seeds and another in relation to pigs? Moreover, why do we say alth*ough,* thr*ough,* en*ough,* pl*ough,* and hic*coughs?* Teachers of English as a foreign language are continually having to apologize for the fact that in English "sounds and letters don't agree." When teachers recognize that fact, they learn to be patient with students who are trying to master the difficult art of English spelling.

DIAGNOSIS AND OVERCOMING OF DIFFICULTIES

Teachers find it helpful to analyze the types of difficulties encountered in spelling by individual students. Much has been done on this problem in elementary schools which high school teachers would find useful. Some pupils have not learned to associate sounds and letters; others overdo the association in nonphonetic words. Some make mistakes in adding suffixes, often in such specific problems as adding *ly*. Among some students, reversals are common; they write *saw* for *was*. Others anticipate letters to come by writing *converstation* for *conversation*. Some simply do not articulate clearly and write as they speak. High school teachers find it very helpful with individuals to use diagnostic materials prepared for the elementary school. Those which test visualization often include four misspellings of a word and one correct spelling, asking the learner to tell which *looks* right to him. Having the students write the word syllable by syllable as the teacher pronounces it gives an indication of his accuracy in hearing and in sensing what relationship exists between letters and sounds. In this case, saying the *syllable* and having the pupil write it is important rather than naming the letters, because the sounds of the names of the letters do not resemble the sound of the syllable.

Dr. Grace Fernald, at the University of Southern California, differentiated clearly in her clinic those who learned best by visual, auditory, or kinaesthetic methods (the feeling of the muscular activity involved in writing the word). In her chapter on remedial work in spelling in *Remedial Techniques in Basic School Subjects*,[21] she gives a helpful description of

[21] Grace M. Fernald, *Remedial Techniques in Basic School Subjects* (New York, McGraw-Hill Book Company, Inc., 1943).

the procedures used. Although authorities differ in their attitude toward her conclusions, her insight into what constitutes spelling difficulty for individual students offers much to teachers. Among other things, she believes the schools overdo the visual approach to words for pupils who would learn more readily by an auditory or kinaesthetic approach. She warns against confusing the learner who profits from an auditory approach by overdoing the naming of the letters like *d i s* instead of having him write the sound, *dis*. She urges teachers to cross out misspelled words in the writing of very weak students and to write in the correct spelling. She warns that students should never be asked to write a misspelled word ten times in a column. Her photograph of such a list from the work of a poor speller shows that he spells the word in four different ways as he proceeds down the column and copies his own errors as he goes. Her advice is, therefore, to have him write the word and compare it with the original, then cover up his spelling, write it again, and compare it with the original, continuing the procedure until he has written the word correctly three times in succession.

There is general agreement among experts that spelling "disability" is much less common than it once was thought to be. Much help is available to teachers for diagnosing difficulties faced by individual students. Discouragement due to repeated failure and lack of insight into their difficulties are major factors to be overcome in helping poor spellers.

THE IMPORTANCE OF A POSITIVE APPROACH TO VOCABULARY BUILDING

It cannot be said too often that instruction in spelling should be tied up constantly to the child's own writing and the needs revealed in it. Teachers should be careful, however, not to take a merely negative attitude toward spelling. Mere pouncing on words misspelled in writing leads to loss of language power as students substitute easy words for more mature ones for fear of misspelling the harder words. Penalties for misspelling are never so effective as positive stimulation of increased word power.

The Value of a Wealth of Words

Edward R. Murrow, on Winston Churchill's eightieth birthday, paid tribute to his command of English: "Winston Churchill," he said, "mobilized the English language and sent it into battle, to steady his fellow countrymen and to hearten those Europeans upon whom the long dark night of tyranny had descended. . . . He has enriched our language and fortified our heritage." A wealth of words is a treasure not to be despised in today's world. Books like Funk's *Thirty Days to a More Powerful Vocabulary*,[22] now available in a paper-backed edition, indicate the relationship between breadth of interests and alertness to words and a large working vocabulary. Pupils should find in magazines and newspapers columns by writers who show power in the use of words. They should make some of these words their own. Listening to such speakers as Edward R. Murrow and Eric Severeid, both of whom the nation respects for their use of the language, should arouse in senior high school students a consciousness of the fact that those men who exert an influence on their own generation often have a wealth of words at their command. Adding daily to the students' own writing and speaking vocabularies should be an aim of the program in spelling.

The Study of Word Origins and Meanings

Word origins are a fascinating study. Inventions are often named for their inventors—*ohm* from J. S. Ohm, Zeppelin from F. von Zeppelin; Ford cars from Henry Ford. Some things are named from their place of origin—*canaries* from the Canary Islands, *artesian* wells from Artois in France. Some words are created from the union of two others which

[22] Wilfred Funk and Norman Lewis, *Thirty Days to a More Powerful Vocabulary* (New York, Pocket Books, Inc.).

combine to give the desired meaning—*telephone, phonograph, telegraph,* and *television*—to hear sound afar off, to write down a sound, to send writing afar, to see something afar off. *Antiseptic* comes from two words meaning "to build a fence against"—in this case against disease. Words, too, have nationalities. A *mosquito* is Spanish, a *poodle* is German, a *piano* is Italian, but a *polka* is Polish. Some words come from mythology, like *herculean, tantalize, cereal, panic,* and *martial.* Other words have different stories behind them. A *candidate* was a man running for office who was dressed in white to symbolize the purity of his principles. *Turban* comes from the Persian word for "tulip," the shape of which it resembles. *Boomerang* was given to us by the Australian natives who carved a stick which, when thrown, would return to the sender. A *pedigree* originated in the branching lines of the foot of a crane. Place names have interesting origins like *Rushford, Butterfield, Edinburgh, Centerville,* and *Strathaven.* So also have family names like *Armstrong, Smith,* and *Dickenson.* New words enter the language constantly—*nylon, penicillin, atom bomb.* In our day, even letters are combined so as to have specific meaning—*DC-6, DDT, UNESCO.* An aroused interest in words is the constant accompaniment of a good spelling program.

SUMMARY

Spelling, then, is an integral part of the program in written expression. Its importance arises from the need to communicate effectively. Words for spelling practice commonly come from the needs revealed in the students' own writing, from research studies of the words most frequently used in life both within and without the school, and from the requirements of the teaching units in progress. In addition to mastering the spelling of specified words, children need constant guidance in methods of attack upon new words and in sensing how words are built. The aims are independence in the development of an extensive writing vocabulary and a sense of responsibility for spelling correctly all words used. Some children will ultimately need three hundred times as many words as others. A habit of effective use of the dictionary is imperative. Diagnosis of the spelling difficulties of each student leads to individualized or small-group activities in spelling. For everyone, stimulation of an interest in words and a recognition of the power inherent in a wealth of words are recommended ingredients of an effective spelling program.

BIBLIOGRAPHY

PART I. GRAMMAR AND USAGE

Books

BARROWS, Marjorie Wescott, *Good English through Practice* (New York, Henry Holt & Company, Inc., 1956).

BRYANT, Margaret M., *A Functional English Grammar* (Boston, D. C. Heath & Company, 1945).

CARROLL, John B., *Study of Languages: A Survey of Linguistics and Related Disciplines in America* (Cambridge, Mass., Harvard University Press, 1953).

FRIES, Charles C., *American English Grammar*, Monograph No. 10, National Council of Teachers of English (New York, Appleton-Century-Crofts, Inc., 1940).

———, *The Structure of English* (New York, Harcourt, Brace & Company, Inc., 1952).

GLEASON, Henry Allan, Jr., *Introduction to Descriptive Linguistics* (New York, Henry Holt & Company, Inc., 1955).

HOOK, J. N., *The Teaching of High School English* (New York, The Ronald Press Company, 1950), "How to Grow Sentences," pp. 274–310.

LAIRD, Charlton, *The Miracle of Language* (Cleveland, World Publishing Co., 1953).

MARCKWARDT, Albert H., and WALCOTT, Fred, *Facts about Current English Usage*, Monograph No. 7, National Council of Teachers of English (New York, Appleton-Century-Crofts, Inc., 1938).

National Council of Teachers of English, Commission on the English Curriculum, *The English Language Arts*, NCTE Curriculum Series, Vol. 1 (New York, Appleton-Century-Crofts, Inc., 1952), "The Modern View of Grammar and Linguistics," pp. 274–301.

POOLEY, Robert C., *Teaching English Usage* (New York, Appleton-Century-Crofts, Inc., 1946).

ROBERTS, Paul, *Understanding Grammar* (New York, Harper and Brothers, 1954).

SMITH, Henry Lee, Jr., *Linguistic Science and the Teaching of English* (Cambridge, Mass., Harvard University Press, 1956).

WHITEHALL, Harold, *Structural Essentials of English* (New York, Harcourt, Brace & Company, Inc., 1956).

Periodicals

ALLEN, Harold B., "The Linguistic Atlases: Our New Resource," *English Journal*, Vol. XLV (April, 1956), pp. 188–194.

COOK, Luella B., "The Inductive Approach to the Teaching of Language," *English Journal*, Vol. XXXVII (January, 1938), pp. 15–21.

FRANCIS, W. Nelson, "Revolution in Grammar," *Quarterly Journal of Speech*, Vol. XL (October, 1954), pp. 299–312.

FROGNER, Ellen, "A Grammar Versus a Thought Approach in Teaching Sentence Structure," *English Journal*, Vol. XXVIII (September, 1939), pp. 518–526.

KAULFERS, Walter V., "Grammar for the Millions," *Elementary English*, Vol. XXVI (January–February, 1949), pp. 1–11, 65–74.

KELLER, Joseph, "On Teaching the Grammar of English," *English Journal*, Vol. XLV (April, 1956), pp. 206–207, 215.

SALISBURY, Rachel, "The Psychology of Punctuation," *English Journal*, Vol. XXVIII (December, 1939), pp. 794–806.

SOFFIETTI, James P., "Why Children Fail to Read, a Linguistic Analysis," *Harvard Educational Review*, Vol. 25, No. 2 (1955), pp. 63–84.

SUNDAL, Lorraine D., "A Transition Program in Grammar and Usage," *English Journal*, Vol. XLV (April, 1956), pp. 195–200.

PART II. SPELLING

ARTLEY, A. Sterl, "Principles Applying to the Improvement of Spelling Ability," *Elementary School Journal*, Vol. XLIX (November, 1948), pp. 137–148.

AYER, Fred C., "An Evaluation of High School Spelling," *School Review*, Vol. LIX (April, 1951), pp. 233–236.

———, *A High School Spelling Vocabulary* (Austin, Texas, The Steck Company, 1945).

DOLCH, Edward W., *The Modern Teaching of Spelling* (Champaign, Ill., The Garrard Press, 1950).

FERNALD, Grace M., *Remedial Techniques in Basic School Subjects* (New York, McGraw-Hill Book Company, Inc., 1943).

FINCH, Hardy R., "Ideas on Teaching Spelling," *English Journal*, Vol. XLI (June, 1952), pp. 298–302.

FITZGERALD, James A., *A Basic Life Spelling Vocabulary* (Milwaukee, Wis., The Bruce Publishing Company, 1951).

——, *The Teaching of Spelling* (Milwaukee, Wis., The Bruce Publishing Company, 1951).

——, *The 222 Spelling Demons* (Milwaukee, Wis., The Bruce Publishing Company, 1941).

GATES, Arthur I., and RUSSELL, David, *Diagnostic and Remedial Spelling Manual* (New York, Bureau of Publications, Teachers College, Columbia University, 1937).

GUILER, Walter S., "Primary-Grade Words Frequently Misspelled by Higher-Grade Pupils," *Elementary School Journal*, Vol. XLIV (January, 1944), pp. 295–300.

HARRIS, Oliver E., "An Investigation of Spelling Achievement of Secondary School Pupils," *Educational Administration and Supervision*, Vol. XXXIV (April, 1948), pp. 208–219.

HILDRETH, Gertrude, *Teaching Spelling* (New York, Henry Holt & Company, Inc., 1955).

HORN, Ernest, "Spelling," *Encyclopedia of Educational Research* (rev. ed., 1950), pp. 1247–1264.

——, *Teaching Spelling* (Washington, D. C., Department of Classroom Teachers and American Educational Research Association of the National Education Association, 1954).

JONES, W. F., *One Hundred Spelling Demons* (Chicago, Hall & McCreary Company, 1913).

KYTE, George C., and NEEL, Virginia M., "A Core Vocabulary of Spelling Words," *Elementary School Journal*, Vol. LIV (September, 1953), pp. 29–34.

MARKSHEFFEL, Ned D., "A Spelling Improvement Program," *Elementary School Journal*, Vol. LIV (December, 1953), pp. 223–229.

McEWEN, Gilbert D., "College Spelling Clinic," *College English*, Vol. XIII (January, 1952), pp. 216–218.

New York City Schools, Bureau of Curriculum Research, *A Manual to Guide Experimentation with Spelling Lists A, B, and C* (New York City, Board of Education, 1951).

POLLOCK, Thomas C., "Spelling Report," *College English*, Vol. XVI (November, 1954), pp. 102–109.

RINSLAND, H. D., *A Basic Writing Vocabulary of Elementary School Children* (New York, The Macmillan Company, 1945).

TRIGGS, Frances and ROBBINS, Edwin W., *Improve Your Spelling* (New York, Rinehart & Company, Inc., 1944).

WENZEL, Evelyn, "Common Sense in Spelling Instruction," *Elementary English*, Vol. XXV (December, 1948), pp. 514–520, 534.

ZOLLINGER, Marian, "Planning a Spelling Program," *Elementary School Journal*, Vol. XLV (February, 1945), pp. 349–354.

PREVIEW OF CHAPTER 11

Seeing and Telling Reinforce Each Other

Chart of Current Practices

Inferences from the Chart

Using Pictures
Teaching with Films
Painting and Sketching
Using Advertising Art
Viewing and Listening to Television Programs
Listening to Records and Radio

Representative Programs

Book Fairs
Communication Arts in an Integrated Program of
    English and History
A Community Study
Variations in a Local Program
A Symbol Centered Program
A High School Humanities Program

Problems in Multiple Reinforcement

Evaluation of Programs
Varied Contextual Elements in the Programs
Concern with Symbols
Preparation of Teachers

Bibliography

CHAPTER 11

Making Communication Arts and Skills Reinforce Each Other[1]

In a school journalism workshop several summers ago the educational director of Eastman Kodak said that he had long been suspicious, as many an English teacher has, of the supposed Confucian axiom, "One picture is worth a thousand words." It was too pat for his purposes. So he carried on a little investigation. He found that Confucius' saying was better translated "One seeing is worth a thousand tellings."

[1] The materials in this chapter, edited by Lennox Grey, Teachers College, Columbia University, with the assistance of Albert Karson, Jacksonville Junior College, Jacksonville, Florida, and Ralph Brady and Francis Shoemaker, Teachers College, Columbia University, have been provided by Ida Besdesky, Ellenville Public Schools, New York; Richard Corbin, Peekskill, New York; Raymona Hull, New York State Agricultural and Technical Institute, Canton, New York; Louise Bennett, Atlanta Public Schools, Georgia; Lillian Clark, La Grange High School, Georgia; Bernice Freeman, Troup County Schools, La Grange, Georgia; William King and Dorothy Fargason, Henry Grady High School, Atlanta, Georgia; Mrs. A. Moore, Mountville, Georgia; Edythe Daniel, Training School, Platteville, Wisconsin; Earl Hutchinson, Wisconsin State College, Oshkosh, Wisconsin; Karen Johnson and Jean Hoard, Wisconsin High School, Madison, Wisconsin; Carrie C. Autrey, Pittsburgh High School, California; Elena Catelli, Lowell High School, San Francisco, California; Esmer Clark, Berkeley Public Schools, California; B. Jo Kinnick, Alexander Hamilton Junior High School, Oakland, California; Virginia B. Lowers and Gloria Sturges, Los Angeles Public Schools, California; James Squire, School of Education, University of California, Berkeley, California; Richard Worthen, Contra Costa Junior College, Martinez, California; Richard Montgomery, Lake Forest Academy, Illinois; M. Agnella Gunn, Boston University, Massachusetts; Amity Pierce, Grosse Pointe High School, Michigan; Peter Donchian, Wayne University, Detroit, Michigan; Stanley Wagner, White Plains High School, New York; Kenneth McPhaden, Vancouver Public Schools, Washington; Mary Crow, Liberty High School, Bethlehem, Pennsylvania.

SEEING AND TELLING REINFORCE EACH OTHER

But neither translation suggests what seems still truer to many high school students and teachers today—that seeing and telling may be better than either alone. For if one sees a scene or picture uncritically and unselectively, without words to identify the most significant points and patterns in it, he can lose the meaning of it, just as words alone may fail to capture what they are meant to describe.

Today there is remarkable reinforcement between language communication and communication through other media, not simply as incidental audio-visual aids but as strong and equal allies in the essential business of communication which underlies all distinctly human activities. Teachers of English are exploring many possibilities.

There is no basic novelty in such reinforcement in high school or college English classes, of course. Most teachers do a good deal of incidental interrelating according to their interests and enthusiasms. They relate photoplays to novels, music to ballads or to Shakespeare's plays or to Goethe's *Faust*, pre-Raphaelite paintings to pre-Raphaelite poetry, Poussin's landscapes to eighteenth-century poetry, Thomas Hart Benton's paintings to *The Grapes of Wrath,* Marin's thrusting impressions of New York and Gershwin's "Rhapsody in Blue" to Dos Passos' *Manhattan Transfer.* Many teachers of humanities courses systematically combine literature with other arts. Such courses are now appearing in high schools as well as colleges, thanks to the John Hay fellowships of the John Hay Whitney Foundation designed to encourage teaching of humanities at the secondary school level. Still more teachers are developing courses akin to the "American Humanities and Secondary-School English" described by Tremaine McDowell.[2]

[2] Tremaine McDowell, "American Humanities and Secondary-School English," *National Association of Secondary-School Principals Bulletin,* Vol. 30 (February, 1946), pp. 66–72.

Concerning skills, most teachers talk about the importance of *observing* and *visualizing* before *writing,* of learning to *listen* to good informal *speaking* as a clue to good usage and *idiom* in writing, of thinking about the needs of one's *listeners* or *readers* as one outlines a *talk* or a piece of writing. All these things are taken as fairly obvious and as a matter of course, just as the good teacher of classics used to deal with aspects of art, archeology, and history as well as with language. What is new, or relatively new, is the growing awareness of the extent to which television, radio, recordings, films, and pictorial graphics (comics, color advertising, reproductions of paintings) are reinforcing one another for good or ill in bringing "the arts" and "language" to young people, and of the need for more than incidental attention to, and channeling of, such reinforcement in school, whether in the name of English, language arts, communication arts, or humanities. For a variety of reasons, pictures are having a particularly strong impact—hence, the emphasis on them at the start of this chapter—but sound and motion are lending new dynamics also.

Such co-ordinations and reinforcements raise many questions of practice, and some of principle, and particularly of the size of the context in which English should be studied and taught. These may be answered by a consideration of some of the current practices in schools across the country.

CHART OF CURRENT PRACTICES

The accompanying chart is intended to give a fairly quick comparative picture of the practices in English courses in high schools and junior colleges located in various parts of the United States. One California junior college is included because in California junior colleges are officially classified with secondary education. The names of contributors are arranged by region to show methods used by teachers working in different regional situations. Four parts of the country

SOME PRACTICES IN MODERN ENGLISH COURSES USING VARIOUS ARTS TO REINFORCE ONE ANOTHER

School	OBSERVING, VISUALIZING, AND DEMONSTRATING													SYMBOLISM			LISTENING AND SPEAKING							READING AND WRITING						MISCELLANEOUS	TOTAL
	Pictures	Advertisements	Painting, Sketching	Films	Television	Maps and Charts	Displays	Scrapbooks	Colleges	Comics	Bulletin Boards	Posters	Audio-Visual	"Color"	Collages	Other	Records	Radio	Assembly Program	Oral Reports	Interviews	Discussions	Miscellaneous	Research Procedure	Descriptive	Mass Media	Novels	Poetry	Miscellaneous	Miscellaneous	
Ida Besdesky, Ellenville Public Schools, Ellenville, N. Y.	XX	X	XXX	XX	XXX	X	X		X			X	X					XX	X	XXX	X	X	X	X	XXX	X	XXX	XXX	X		33
Richard Corbin, 1226 Constant Avenue, Peekskill, N. Y.	XX	X	XXX	X		X	XXX		X			X	X	XX				X	X	X	XX	X	X	X	X	X	XXX	XX	X	X	30
Raymona Hull, N. Y. State Agr. & Tech. Inst, Canton, N. Y.	XXX	X	X	X	XXX			X		X		X	X	X	X	XXX	XXX	XXX	X	X	X	X	X		X	X	X	X			30
Francis Shoemaker, Teachers College, New York City, N. Y.	X	XX	XX	XXX	XXX		XX		X	XXX		XX		XXX	XXX	XXX	XXX	XX	XX	XXX	XXX	XXX	XX	X	XX	XXX	XXX	XXX	X		48
Stanley Wagner, White Plains High Sch., White Plains, N. Y.	XX	X	XXX	XX	XXX	XX	X	X	X		X	X	X	XX			X	X	XX	XX	XX	X	XX				XX				26
Mary Crow, Bethlehem, Pa. (12th Grade)	XX	X	XX	XX	X	X	X	X	X			XXX	XX	XX				X	X	XXX	XXX	XXX	X		XXX	X	XX	XX	X	X	37
Anna May Todd, Bethlehem, Pa. (9th Grade)	X	X	XX	XX	X		XXX	XXX				XXX	XXX	X				X		XX	XX	XX	XX	X			X	X	X		29
Louise Bennett, Atlanta Public Schools, Atlanta, Ga.	XXX																				XXX			XX							5
Lillian Clark, La Grange High School, La Grange, Ga.	XXX		X	X	X	X	X		X			XX	X	X				X	X	XXX	XXX	XXX	X	X	X	XXX	X	X	XX	X	35
Dorothy Fargason, Henry Grady High Sch., Atlanta, Ga.																						XXX		XXX							6
Bernice Freeman, Troup County Schools, La Grange, Ga.	X		X	XX	XX	X	XX	X	X			X						XX	XXX	XX	XX	XXX			X		XXX	XX	X	XX	30
William King, Henry Grady High Sch., Atlanta, Ga.			XXX																									XXX	XXX	XX	8

Rating/checklist matrix of 26 teachers. Individual teacher totals appear at the top of each teacher column; criterion totals (across all 26 teachers) appear in the "26 TEACHERS" summary column at right.

Teacher / School	Total
Mrs. A. Moore, Mountville School, Mountville, Ga.	15
Edythe Daniel, Training School, Platteville, Wis.	27
Jean Hoard, Wisconsin High School, Madison, Wis.	12
Earl Hutchinson, Oshkosh State Teachers Col., Oshkosh, Wis.	40
Karen Johnson, Madison Pub. Sch., Madison, Wis.	13
Amity Pierce, Grosse Point High Sch., Grosse Point, Mich.	61
Carrie C. Autrey, Pittsburgh H. S., Pittsburgh, Calif.	5
Elena Catelli, Lowell High School, San Francisco, Calif.	26
Esmer Clark, Berkeley Pub. Sch., Berkeley, Calif.	11
B. Jo Kinnick, Alexander Hamilton Jr. H. S., Oakland, Calif.	22
V. B. Lowers, Board of Education, Los Angeles, Calif.	18
Gloria Sturges, L. A. Public Schools, Los Angeles, Calif.	15
James Squire, School of Ed. Univ. of Calif., Berkeley, Calif.	26
Richard Worthen, Contra Costa Junior College, Martinez, Calif.	6

Criterion totals — **26 TEACHERS**:

41, 22, 36, 33, 15, 20, 14, 17, 12, 3, 21, 12, 29, 11, 7, 15, 23, 20, 12, 34, 31, 14, 11, 28, 15, 40, 33, 14, 20, 11

are represented: The Far West (California and Washington); the South (Georgia); the Middle West (Wisconsin, Illinois, and Michigan); and the Northeast (New York State). Three major headings, *Observing, Visualizing and Demonstrating, Listening and Speaking,* and *Reading and Writing,* cover the arts and skills with which the practices, arranged as column heads, are concerned. *Studying Symbols,* a fourth heading inserted in the center for reasons to be explained later, indicates a fairly new approach to the study of communication which was mentioned often enough to warrant its classification as a major head. Samplings from the great variety of projects not included elsewhere are shown under *Miscellaneous,* and include such activities as the construction of a model Elizabethan theater by students of William King and the use of the school public address system for a radio production in Amity Pierce's class. The number of *X*'s indicates the relative emphasis given to each practice.

The chart does not purport to give a complete description of each course. Rather, it shows "Some Practices in Modern English Courses Using Various Arts and Communication Media to Reinforce One Another." It takes its form from what teachers reported rather than from what the compilers thought should be there. In all but two instances the entries on the chart have been checked by the contributors.

INFERENCES FROM THE CHART

The chart indicates that English teachers call on many arts. In view of the widespread use of art in various media, and the responsiveness of boys and girls to music on radio and recordings, the comparatively few mentions of activities involving music deserve notice. The communication aspects of music are matters of "common feeling" for most people, rather than of idea or concept. Yet Suzanne K. Langer's conception of music as formulating a sense of time, and the place of music in films, radio, and television, may bring more attention to music as communication.

Advertising art is used extensively because of its frequent attractiveness, timeliness, and accessibility. The interest in painting and sketching, and the number of other production activities appearing under *Miscellaneous,* suggest that "composition" in more than one form seems important to teachers and students.

The lack of study of comics indicates almost certainly that teachers feel comics to be of doubtful value, and even harmful.

The emphasis on observing, visualizing, and demonstrating, along with other skills, recalls a statement made in *The English Language Arts:* "Third [of the types of writing courses required in the first two years of college] . . . is the combination in the so-called communication courses of instruction in reading, writing, speaking, listening, and occasionally, observing." [3]

Perhaps the phrase "occasionally observing" is attributable to the fact that observing, visualizing, and demonstrating are not commonly listed as communication skills today. "Visualizing" once was stressed in the study of literature, with a somewhat different meaning from what is commonly understood in "observing." According to Franklin T. Baker two generations ago, "Galton pointed out a number of years ago that the untrained mind thinks largely in terms of pictures. . . . Nor does the power of picturing what one reads ever lose its value for the adult. . . . The formation of the picture is, therefore, one of the first things to be looked to in teaching literature." [4] Repeated references to visualization are made by Charles Swain Thomas: "One of the best

[3] Commission on the English Curriculum of the National Council of Teachers of English, *The English Language Arts,* NCTE Curriculum Series, Vol. I (New York, Appleton-Century-Crofts, Inc., 1952), p. 147.

[4] George R. Carpenter, Franklin T. Baker, and Fred N. Scott, *The Teaching of English in the Elementary and the Secondary School* (New York, Longmans, Green and Co., 1927), pp. 171–172 (first ed. 1903).

ways to get pleasure out of poetry and rouse interest in it is to develop the pupils' power of sensualization. . . . Read to your pupils . . . a stanza of poetry or a paragraph of prose; then immediately demand that books be closed. Open a fusillade of questions: What pictures, class, are in your mind? Which of your senses have been appealed to? Sight? Sound? Feeling? Odor? Taste?" [5] And again, in referring to drama: "One of the first and chief purposes of every teacher of the drama should be to make the students visualize the action." [6]

Because modern pictorial media have made visualizing less of a problem than it once was for many students of limited first-hand experience, teachers may be less explicitly aware of the need for work with these three—visualizing, demonstrating, observing—in their direct, more conscious concern with reading, writing, speaking, and listening. But "be observant" has been a long-standing precept in high school and college composition work, at least as old as Simeon Strunsky's essay, "Rhetoric 21."

Using Pictures

A glance at the chart indicates that pictures drew more responses than any other medium listed there, more even than film in the area of observing. It is fair to assume that the easy availability and ready use of pictures have contributed to their popularity, as well as the great flexibility which is possible in the use of them. Ida Besdesky, Esmer Clark, and James Squire, reporting on a program in Oakland, California, use the series entitled "What's in a Picture?", published by *Life* magazine, to motivate writing. Virginia B. Lowers finds that pictures of places—Hawaii, Wake Island, Java—are excellent for use with retarded learners, to get them into the activity of writing.

---

[5] Charles Swain Thomas, *The Teaching of English in the Secondary School* (Boston, Houghton Mifflin Company, 1927), pp. 231–232 (first ed. 1917).
[6] *Ibid.*, p. 289.

Observation of pictures relates to skills other than writing, as shown by Esmer Clark's use of *Saturday Evening Post* covers to suggest "problem situations" for sociodrama. These examples represent a kind of "one-to-one" relationship between the media: observation of the picture leads to the activity of writing or to another of the skills.

Another approach that points up the connecting links between the arts and skills by analogy between pictorial "composition" and written composition is described by Lillian Clark. Selecting a landscape for the opaque projector, she invites students to observe with *all* their senses, to pick out the elements of dominance in order to become aware of the importance of the observer's position, noting that the picture changes with the point of observation. A comparable use is reported by Richard Corbin: a painting by Corot illustrates unity, coherence, and emphasis in "composition." Elena Catelli draws upon the resources of a local museum to provide displays of art and architecture as background for literature in an approach resembling that of high school and college humanities programs.

Teaching with Films

The considerable use of films by English teachers may be explained by the many ways in which the film can serve. Stanley Wagner relies on the informational value of such films as *Build Your Vocabulary, How To Study, We Discover the Dictionary*. At what may well be the extreme opposite of the informational film is that abstract exercise in color, rhythm, and sound, *Fiddle Dee Dee*, which B. Jo Kinnick shows to her students preparatory to a unit in the writing of poetry.

The film may also be central to a unit; it may be studied for itself, as in the program described by Richard Worthen, which "calls for reading, writing, speaking, intensive listening and observing, and the organizing of a paper." He points out that "the movie has a great potential for promoting personal growth or for manipulating the thoughts and attitudes of the public. Since the movie is primarily one-way communication, the viewer should develop some sophistication in evaluation and in understanding *how* the movie communicates in order to maintain his intellectual autonomy." He uses *Picture in Your Mind* for close analysis of techniques: rhythm, repetition, alliteration, triads, and the like, and *Odd Man Out* for a study of "symmetrical organization of the whole film." Two propaganda films—*Deadline for Action* and *Crossroads for America*—illustrate "use of American symbols to reinforce the two arguments." The insights which come through investigation of the motion picture medium are applied in a long paper in which the student "organizes and expresses one 'area' of his experience with the film."

Painting and Sketching

In addition to using materials gathered from the mass media and other sources, many teachers have their students engage in projects which develop new materials. Painting and sketching, according to the chart, are the media most commonly used by students in their projects. James Squire notes: "Charcoal sketching of characterizations and settings is a useful device for measuring and suggesting growth in an individual's comprehension and appreciation of fiction."

Jean Hoard, in a "Workshop English" course at Wisconsin High School, Madison, Wisconsin, incorporated a unit in working with the media of art; students experimented with color and with form, with finger painting, clay modeling, weaving, collage-making, and finally, work with oils. "Not only did the workshop students learn about color in the experiment, but they also became more critical of their writing vocabulary. They learned the necessity of clarifying an idea, of balancing the composition, of blending colors to obtain the exact shade of meaning, but best of all, they learned to write with the eye of an artist as well as that of a composer."

Amity Pierce provides many opportunities for students

to paint in connection with their work in English: some draw illustrations for their own work, draw versions of Chaucer characters as they might appear today, draw pictures of the meanings of vocabulary words. In Mary Crow's tenth-grade unit on reasoning "some talented pupils make models or paint scenes to illustrate literature read by the class . . . these are rated by the class as to the extent to which each piece gives an *honest* impression of the period, scene or character."

Using Advertising Art

Many teachers (about half of those reporting here) have taken advantage of the wealth of visual materials made available by advertisers. Often the uses of advertisements are the same as those of pictures generally, but advertisements may also be employed, as Richard Corbin has done, as the object of "propaganda analysis," or, as Peter Donchian, in his course in methods of teaching English, puts it: ". . . for the identification of symbols and in investigating how pictures communicate *within* and *outside* the culture." He emphasizes the need for avoiding random impressionism in the study of advertisements or of any of the media, discouraging students from doing things in a haphazard or sketchy way. When the various media are called upon to reinforce one another, the connections must be clear; random observation is meaningless.

Collages, or montages of collected pictures or symbols used by half a dozen teachers, have been made easily possible through the wealth of advertising art that surrounds students at home and elsewhere. More than one student has found through making a collage that he has as much symbolic perception as Picasso, if not Picasso's skill.

Viewing and Listening to Television Programs

In view of the recent concern with the impact of television and comic books upon students' habits and abilities, the responses on these two media are worth noting. The TV column suggests that this medium has not yet been widely used, partly because it has not been available in some areas. From the start teachers have been greatly concerned with and interested in television, as indicated by the results of a poll of National Council of Teachers of English affiliates in May, 1953, conducted by the NCTE Committee on Study of Television, Radio and Film. Among the responses received, the following are particularly significant:

Already half of the English organizations replying (58) are using television for home assignments, for classroom discussion, or even in production. As large areas of our country have not had television long, or even now have no stations, such evidence indicates the great concern for the medium in English instruction.

Teachers of English almost unanimously attest to the stake they feel they have in this educational medium. In their opinion, television instruction can be used in developing the specific language skills. Although speaking, listening, observing, and demonstrating are the skills most adaptable to television teaching, reading and writing are suggested as feasible for presentation.

Standards for language use and literary experience can be developed through television, according to the majority of our responses. . . .

Although only nine of the teachers whose responses are listed on the chart indicated a systematic concern with television in their classes, this is an increase of nine over the poll of the same persons taken two years earlier. They have devised varied ways of making use of this potent new medium whose advent has evoked in the minds of many those words of Benét about our machine civilization generally: "Say neither . . . 'It is a deadly magic, and accursed,' nor 'It is blest,' but only 'It is here.' "

The limited use of TV is apparently due to its newness. Where it is readily available, some teachers have been quick to utilize the multiple-reinforcing values of the medium. Ida Besdesky found that TV was the first choice among students as a field for exploration in a unit on mass media; all but two students in a class of twenty-five reported that they owned or had ready access to a TV set. TV was late in coming to her community, which is screened by mountains, but once TV arrived, facilities have multiplied at a very rapid rate. She has used television in several ways: commercials provide material for description and use of "sense appeal"; comparisons are made between radio drama and drama on TV, giving insight into the limitations of each; discussions arise from programs like "Hear It Now" and "You Are There." "Pupils were surprised and interested to find that the teacher watches some of the same programs. It has given us another common meeting ground."

Stanley Wagner in White Plains makes considerable use of television. The area of his school is richly served by TV channels. He lists some of the things done with the medium:

1. Organization of TV club, with after-school meetings. Projects include a school questionnaire, a publication recommending good programs to students, and a bi-monthly film or kinescope showing actual TV programs, followed by critiques.
2. Reference in class to literary works which appear on TV.
3. A daily listing of recommended TV programs for students to be alert to (listed on chalkboard).
4. A class bulletin board with TV information.
5. Class discussions of "good" and "bad" programs and what makes them good or bad.

Student enthusiasm for television is noted by Edythe Daniel in Wisconsin; though a minority of her students have had access to sets, there are enough to provide "snappy, comparative discussions with their radio-listening classmates." In students' estimation, TV's greatest advantage is its "continuity due to minimized narration. The narrator seems to be a cliché of whom they have grown weary." Her use of television ranges from the collection of magazine articles concerning programs that interest teen-agers to the development of student-selected criteria which are applied to programs. (Some student comments: "Dialog is trite." "The music fits the mood of the happenings." "The comedy plot is weakened by lengthy commercials.") Student responses give information about listening levels as well as experience in critical listening. Edythe Daniel believes that the communication media offer some of the "finest ways of enriching the language arts program."

As James Squire notes, the most widespread use of TV involves supplementary, out-of-class work, including assignments to view such programs as *Hamlet* or George Stewart's *Storm*, with subsequent panels, discussions, and reports like those on current movies or stage presentations. Analysis of scripts brings understanding of the limitations of the new medium. At the University of California Summer Demonstration School during the political campaign of 1952, students viewed the proceedings of the conventions on TV. In one tenth-grade class, student interest in the proceedings was channeled into a general discussion and analysis of communication. Part of the period between the two parties' conventions was spent in such analysis, so that students were prepared for a more intelligent viewing of the second convention.

Richard Worthen mentions the difficulty of obtaining kinescopes for classroom use. National studies are being made now to solve this problem. He believes that analysis of TV may be made comparable to that of the movie: "Any class work which would promote sharper analysis and greater appreciation of the film would apply pretty well to television."

Listening to Records and Radio

Mass media can provide some experiences first hand: hearing poetry read by the poet, or "John Brown's Body" rendered by Raymond Massey, Judith Anderson, and Tyrone Power. About half the teachers reporting indicated use of records or radio, or both, for this kind of listening experience. Teachers, with little or much equipment, can stimulate listening.

What motivates good listening? It may be the appeal of "expertness" suggested above, or it may be the same familiar kinds of interest that stimulate effective writing or speaking. Louise Bennett found that in an eighth-grade class the students combined lively "visualizing" talk with lively listening in the course of oral reports. Each member, in turn, described his stamp or insect collection, displayed a scrapbook on interior decoration or dress design, or illustrated the mechanics of a model airplane or railroad. Other students made group presentations: social situations at the local drug store; the blackboard as a movie screen where coming attractions are previewed; a radio skit called "Are You Grown Up?" "It is here that eyes sparkle, when even the most timid speak with authority on the dominant interest in their lives. By catching, holding, and directing interests, the school will have confident speakers, attentive listeners, and co-operative citizens."

Dorothy Fargason puts into practice the kind of "visualizing" so vigorously recommended by Charles Swain Thomas in connection with the reading of poetry. She reads Robert Frost's "Two Tramps in Mud Time," after discussing the poet and others of his poems. After listening to the poem, students describe the pictures formed in their minds by the lines.

Bernice Freeman describes how a project in listening developed in one class: "In a discussion of why people do not learn in school, one of the weakest students in the class volunteered, 'They don't listen.' That led to talk about how students can come to listen more intelligently." Four questions were worked out for group consideration:

1. What constitutes skill in listening?
2. What interferes with listening?
3. What factors make for better listening?
4. How can we test improvement in listening?

Reports by the separate groups showed an interesting range of considerations that embraced the observing of social life outside of school (and how it might interfere with good listening), mannerisms on the part of teacher and student that worked for or against good listening, and the difficulties of trying to test for improvement of listening.

REPRESENTATIVE PROGRAMS

Some of the programs reported by teachers participating in this sampling of practices could not be said to center upon one or another of the media listed, or even upon an area like *Observing, Visualizing,* and *Demonstrating.* Rather, they reach out across the whole range of skills, and many of the arts.

Such a program is described by Earl Hutchinson in the eighth grade of the Training School. The problem at the center of the program was that of "living together." Out of the considerations of this problem arose the motif, based on the popular TV program, "This Is Your Life." Collages were made to give plan and order to the students' thinking, and to "keep from writing first." Working with the tangible medium, selecting the appropriate symbols from newspapers and magazines, laying out the meaningful design, and observing the others in the class working on the purposeful task of self-analysis seemed to be most worth while. The collages later served as outlines for brief biographies. An opaque projector to throw the completed collages on the classroom "TV screen," and a tape recorder as vehicle for the recorded biographies, combined with "live" voices and action to weld the whole into a successful "television production." Technical problems, such as program planning, timing, and the like, assumed new meaning to the students; and, as Earl Hutchinson puts it, "at the same time we were very much involved with trying to improve our writing because it was to become part of the tape recording."

Valuable as this purposeful welding together of the communication arts and skills was to the students, the most rewarding part was not anticipated. "A number of students seemed to gain stature when they looked at their lives in a positive way as contrasted to what must have been their evaluation of a rather 'drab beginning.' "

Book Fairs

In the preparation and conduct of book fairs, teachers have used several communication arts to inform the community concerning good books for adolescents. An outstanding example of this kind of activity is the Boston University Book Fair, conducted since 1951 under the leadership of M. Agnella Gunn.

It all started in a university class composed of teachers of secondary English and librarians from several New England towns. The motive for the project was to discover among the increasing number of books being published for young and older adults those which would be appropriate for teen-agers in Grades 7–12.

When on Saturday, May 12, 1951, approximately 500 teachers, librarians, administrators, authors, and publishers assembled in Hayden Auditorium, they saw an exhibit of hundreds of textbooks and trade books assembled by the representatives of 24 national publishers and two large local distributors.

"Books for Young Americans," the theme of the exhibit, appeared in posters and displays created by high school students. The arrangement of the books invited browsing. Teachers and graduate students informed about the books were available at each display to discuss these books with interested visitors.

The late morning program included a discussion by panelists, representing different approaches to the young reader: a head of an English department, a librarian, a teacher of English, a reading-club director, a textbook publisher, a trade book editor, a reading specialist, a book seller, and a book reviewer. The afternoon program was an informative and delightful talk by author Carl Carmer.

A co-operative evaluation following the first fair led to long-range planning for the next. Involvement of more high school students and their parents and greater use of student-created art were elements in the expanded plans. These all paid off when more than a thousand adults gathered for the Book Fair and Exhibit on April 26, 1952. Extensive exhibits were again assembled by publishers and distributors of textbooks and trade books. Original book posters designed and executed by students in the Boston Public Schools attracted visitors to look at the books.

Arranged to interest both elementary and secondary students, the 1952 Fair opened with a morning program, "Books for Today's Readers." At this session, boys and girls from elementary schools heard Thornton Burgess and David McCord and saw Virginia Lee Burton demonstrate with charm and humor how she drew the illustrations for her books.

The afternoon program was directed to the more mature reader. Junior and senior high school students and their teachers listened to illuminating talks by authors Gladys Hasty Carrol, Esther Forbes, Eric Kelly, Marion Lansing, and Marjorie Medary and participated in a provocative discussion by Clifton Fadiman of the most significant publishing events of the year.

Communication Arts in an Integrated Program of English and History

Unusually rich opportunities for using several communication arts were afforded twelfth-grade students through an integrated English and history course scheduled daily in a double period and conducted by Grace D. Broening [7] at the Forest Park High School in Baltimore. The students, with the teacher, discovered the interplay of civilizations,

---

[7] Grace D. Broening, "Integrating English and Social Studies," *Baltimore Bulletin of Education*, Vol. XXV (December, 1947), pp. 112–114, 143, 151.

as expressed in their institutions, traditions, laws, and government; in their literature, art, and music; and in their sports and pastimes.

During an informal group discussion on the first day, the students set as their goal to understand why people are acting the way they are in the twentieth century by discovering relevant patterns of thought and action in the seventeenth, eighteenth, and nineteenth centuries.

A quick view of obvious elements in the present-day world scene raised several questions which challenged a study of the revolutions of the eighteenth century. A canvass of the ways in which the peoples of the past have left their imprint on the present brought to light how periods of expansion or suppression ended in revolution: the English revolution after the breakdown of the dominance of agriculture; the French revolution stimulated by a shift in philosophic thought and by economic pressures; the American revolution as a revolt against England's attempt to arrest the political and economic freedom of her colony. Questions were raised concerning possible interrelationships of these social forces and the literature, art, music, and government of the time. Students were eager to explore so many lines of interest that committee study of specific aspects of the total problem seemed the only hope for achievement of their goals within reasonable time limits.

From this general setting of problems to be studied, the group considered sources of information and also methods of individual and group study and of sharing of committee findings with the class as a whole. Phases of the total problem were considered best treated by the class operating as a committee of the whole with the teacher as leader-chairman. Other phases called for students' individual and group use of primary and secondary source materials available in the Enoch Pratt Free Library, the Walters Art Gallery, the Museum of Art, the Peale Museum, and the Maryland Historical Society. Students consulted textbooks, fiction and non-fiction available in classroom and school libraries, and also sound-motion pictures and recordings procurable from the Central Office Audio-Visual Department. Use was made, in addition, of regularly scheduled and special radio programs, movies being exhibited in local theatres, *human* resources among the faculty, friends and relatives of students and also scientists, journalists, artists, and civic leaders in the community.

In connection with the exploration of sources of information, training was given in evaluating them, in intelligent note-taking with accurate bibliographic data, and in selecting appropriate and effective methods of sharing committee findings with the class as a whole. The variety of methods of presentation used by the students was evidence of the value of making communication arts reinforce each other.

Chalk talks were given by students talented in art; music was sung and played by students trained in music; dramatizations were created and presented by students for whom words were an effective medium of expression. Recordings which were made by individual pupils of radio programs were presented for discussion. Other boys and girls selected sound-motion pictures and gave interpretative talks to introduce the picture or to clinch impressions gained from seeing it. Editorials, letters, informal essays, long source papers, radio scripts, and original verse were outgrowths of reading, thinking, listening, and talking.

The individual personal needs for letters, for talking about school and home situations as they were experienced came in for their share of attention by teacher and students. Direct guidance and well-motivated practice plus evaluation were given in the techniques of effective writing and speaking in the many situations which occurred as the students and teacher worked together in the classroom, in the school library, at the public library, at the museum of art, and in field trips to places of significance in interpreting how the peoples of the past have left their imprint on Baltimore of today.

Both the students and their teacher are convinced that these experience-centered activities have increased the quality and quantity of speaking, listening, reading, and writing. Social understandings were developed in a richness of context as broad as life itself. Literature as life and life as literature were experienced by the group. All media of communication—words, art, music, discoveries and inventions, institutions, laws, and customs—were seen in relation to man's ongoing struggle for freedom.

The end of the first quarter came in November. At that time, the teacher was obliged "to grade" the students in *English four* and in *United States History.* This task was easy, for co-operatively with the pupils at the beginning of the semester, she had set up desired outcomes and methods of appraising pupils' accomplishments. Departmental and standardized tests were used along the way. The teacher had read and listened to thousands of words from each student. Recordings of panel discussions were available for restudy to discover needs and to measure growth.

Students themselves appraised the work of individuals on their own committees and of the committees on which they had not worked. Co-operatively, teacher and students weighed all evidence and recorded appraisals including the quality and quantity of participation in discussion; in reading; in creative expression in words, in music, and in art; and also in utilization of school and community resources.

The final *grade* given each student was recognized by him and by all his classmates as an adequate evaluation of his contribution and of his personal growth.

A Community Study

Karen Falk Johnson teaches an eighth grade, combination English, speech, social studies, and science, in the Wisconsin High School. Her class decided to study its own city —Madison. "The plan involved learning about the uniqueness of Madison as a capital city and university center, and as a growing industrial and service center in its geographic location among four lakes." Committees investigated these four areas of interest. Students read newspapers, texts, pamphlets released by the Chamber of Commerce, travel agencies, industries, and unions. By letter and telephone, committees secured appointments with leading citizens. They went to interviews equipped with tape recorders, and brought back information as first-hand listening experience for the rest of the class. The geography committee arranged for the entire class to fly over the Madison area. Maps were studied, and students planned the route of flight. Photography enthusiasts selected areas for "shooting."

When the flights were completed, the students in the class wrote freely of their experiences, reinforced their writing in water color and oil, and illustrated maps which were in turn used in talks and demonstrations by individuals who needed additional opportunity to share their tremendous experience. In the course of approximately four weeks, with community study as their center, the youngsters had interviewed, discussed and reported; listened to individuals, groups, transcriptions, and sound motion pictures; written letters and reports; read letters, brochures, advertisements, texts and stories; observed pictures, maps, and the beautiful expanse of the four-lake city; demonstrated with maps, photographs, painting, industrial products—and loved every minute of their activity.

Edythe Daniel, teaching sixth-, seventh-, and eighth-grade classes in the Training School of the State College of Platteville, Wisconsin, describes how students worked together to "study the ways in which the people of Platteville 'talk' to one another—particularly the ways through which the community 'speaks' to boys and girls themselves, and the ways through which they can communicate their responses."

Committees were formed to investigate the technical facilities—highways, railroads, air routes, and telephone lines—with "emphasis on the advertising and schedules through which they reach the minds of the public." Groups explored the "obvious mass media of radio, motion picture, and newspaper." Students interviewed local managers and studied printed material for their information. Three boys made "an exhaustive study (eight consecutive hours at one book-magazine stand) of the comic book offerings, and emerged with a very creditable classification of comic books into 'those we might read' and 'those we should not read.'"

As the project developed the class became aware of some more subtle aspects of communication. What kinds of letters do people write to one another in Platteville? What do the designs of houses and public buildings communicate to us? What does landscaping say? What is the effect of window decorations in stores? This last question led ultimately to a nearly city-wide window decorating contest in which merchants permitted the sixth-, seventh-, and eighth-graders to undertake the decorations.

The results of this study were drawn together into an illustrated 200-page book entitled "Communication in Platteville," with a running commentary on various aspects of life in Platteville.

Variations in a Local Program

In Bethlehem, Pennsylvania, English teachers in the four junior high schools and the senior high school with its academic and technical branches, have made concerted efforts to alert their students to the mutual reinforcement of many media and skills. Illustrations from Liberty High School and the technical high school show different approaches with the same common concept. Mary Crow, first co-ordinator of the program, describes a twelfth-grade Liberty High School project on "Use of Leisure Time."

Special-interest groups were formed and scheduled to present their findings at weekly meetings. One committee, using local newspapers, clipped and placed on the bulletin boards articles announcing the great variety of valuable leisure time activities provided by their community for any youth or adult. Reports of personal experiences or of interviews with participants in these activities followed, accompanied by photographs of people and events. Another group presented oral reports on their hobbies, bringing in finished work or demonstrating and frequently recommending magazines, books, etc., relating to individual hobbies. A panel of Protestant, Jewish, and Catholic pupils discussed the leisure time opportunities offered by their churches, and, as a result of their reading, recommended a local inter-faith council of teen-agers. Naturally, reading, moving pictures, radio, and TV as leisure time activities, were discussed. Further research on standards for judging, and sources, purposes and value of reviews resulted. Soon bulletin boards were covered with reviews, suggestions, and rating charts.

As a conclusion to the project, the classes jointly, in their own leisure time, made a two-reel, 8 mm. motion picture showing their own worth-while leisure-time activities during one week. When the developed film had been returned, a final committee wrote a carefully synchronized script to accompany the showing for their class, for the faculty, and for future classes.

Ninth-grade boys in the four-year technical branch, some coming from Bethlehem and some from outlying schools, undertook an orientation project suited to them and the needs in their school. Their classroom was the newly constructed library secured by Anna May Todd, second co-ordinator of the Bethlehem English program, developing the "laboratory practice" procedures recommended by the Citizenship Education Project [8] at Teachers College, Columbia University.

An extensive orientation-citizenship-education-communication arts project in a class of ninth-grade boys . . . transformed a library-classroom center into a communication workshop.

The boys toured the school, visited the shops to see demonstrations of the kind of training provided, and interviewed shop instructors as a basis for discussion periods and written reports in their English class, utilizing the skills of observing, listening, writing, and speaking. In their reports they were able to use (and spell correctly!) a newly acquired vocabulary of technical terms such as T-square, micrometer, French curve, vise, lathe, . . . and to draw sketches of these tools as they explained their use to their classmates. They found a new inter-

[8] Initiated by President Dwight D. Eisenhower of Columbia University and President William F. Russell of Teachers College, with a grant from the Carnegie Corporation of New York.

est in reading trade and related popular magazines as well as books, both fiction and non-fiction, with a vocational slant. Not highly skilled in verbal communication, they "discovered" their ability to communicate through displays and posters. From magazine advertisements they borrowed plans for lay-outs and learned the importance of the forceful slogan. Bulletin boards came to life as the students interpreted their school in pictures, models, and words. Finally, the production of a handbook for future ninth-grade boys created a real concern for effective written communication, highlighted by line drawings to aid in getting the information across. At this stage the opaque projector did extra duty as all materials were projected for final class criticism and approval before being included in the handbook.

Many of the students developed, for the first time, an awareness of the various skills and media of communication and of the interrelationships among these (e.g., observing a process in a shop for the purpose of describing it to others).

During the first six years of the English curriculum project, begun in 1946, the Bethlehem schools conducted a citywide Communication Arts Project in order to gain general understanding and reinforcement at all grade levels and in the community. It was described as follows by the coordinators after the first four years:

The theme for 1947–48, "To advance better community relations in Bethlehem," developed from a desire of the English teachers to do something about a conflict in interests . . . in the Bethlehem community. An excellent piece of work was done by a junior English class in preparing an assembly program based on . . . Thornton Wilder's *Our Town* and revealing what they had observed of developing community relations that made them proud to live in Bethlehem.

The following year the students chose as their topic the "Racial-Cultural Background of Bethlehem." Classrooms became veritable museums of folk art, costumes, family relics, and the like, as students became acquainted with the contributions of the various racial groups to the whole community. One of the junior high schools with a pupil population predominantly of foreign or mixed parentage presented over the local radio station a broadcast based on this theme, using autobiographical materials compiled by the students.

For the 1949–50 school term, the Communication Arts subject was "Bethlehem in the Future." Again a wide variety of purposeful activities resulted. A model airport was constructed; scrapbooks on Bethlehem were assembled; important civic leaders, including the mayor, were interviewed; a survey of vocational opportunities was made; welfare agencies were visited. In a junior high school assembly a panel discussion on "Bethlehem's Future Needs" with guest moderator met with such enthusiastic response from the pupil audience that it was only with difficulty that the moderator succeeded in bringing it to a close after a discussion lasting an hour and a half.

The next year, the theme was "Better Leisure-Time Activities."

The project was discontinued in 1953, having accomplished its initial purpose. Teachers did not want it to become routine and perfunctory. A city-wide literary publication was initiated in its stead.

A Symbol Centered Program

In California, James Squire uses a unit which he calls "Symbolism in Literature and Life." He writes, "Students have difficulty comprehending the concept of symbolism, and an understanding of symbolism as a literary technique is essential to an understanding of much literature that we read." He describes the sequence of procedures which have proved useful in "awakening perception of the problem." First, there is a discussion of the purpose of symbolism arising from the reading of literature. From this the class proceeds to an "analysis of symbolism in life, involving discussion of the purpose of such symbols as flags, national anthems, advertising trademarks, map symbols, flowers, military insignia, roadside signs, money, and animals (Easter bunny, Thanksgiving turkey, and the like)."

The class proceeds to an "analysis of symbolism in color and form." Such motion pictures as *The Moon's Necklace*, *Boundary Lines*, and *Fiddle Dee Dee* illustrate the use of form and color in symbolizing rhythm and emotion. The suggestive values of colors are investigated, for example, white for purity, light, joy; black for sorrow, death, despair. Students then put this knowledge of symbolism to work through "some graphic activity to enable themselves to interpret symbolically through color and form the themes and conflicts of the literature read." These compositions are evaluated and lead to "generalizations of the suggestive value of lines in art and architecture," . . . diagonal and curved lines for dynamic force and action; tall, vertical composition with high focal point for expression of elegance and dignity; tall, vertical composition with low focal point for expression of conflict, fight, struggle.

The class goes on to consider the "symbolism of words." Committees construct and present association tests "designed to indicate students' familiarity with common symbols not previously mentioned." The class analyzes the varying responses to these test words, leading to an "introduction to semantic problems in understanding verbal symbols." Finally, there is "an evaluation of students' understanding of the concept through analysis of symbols expressed in literature."

A High School Humanities Program

Kenneth McPhaden, an art teacher and audio-visual director at Vancouver, Washington, who in 1952–53 held a John Hay fellowship in humanities, has described a high school humanities course in which he uses five chronological divisions of history, relating to these periods the literature, drama, art, and music which they produced. "In this course I have used movies, slides, Balopticon, and considerable reference material on art. The music teacher has also been very helpful in taking the class over for periods when the discussion involved music." Commenting on the intense interest his students have shown in "the great world of literature, music, and art," Kenneth McPhaden adds: "In a public high school the problem seems to be one of relating their learning to the world around the students, of which the many media of communication are an important part." The one major medium which is omitted from the syllabus of this course is television, "as many parts of the United States do not have suitable TV programs for such a course."

PROBLEMS IN MULTIPLE REINFORCEMENT

How shall the wide range of practices by twenty-five teachers be appraised? What are their values? What are their limitations? Do they point to any leading principles and significant trends or tendencies in belief or concept on the part of English teachers?

Evaluation of Programs

Probably they testify first to the wide ranging interests, enthusiasms, imagination, and venturesomeness of English teachers—amply illustrated long before this in the correlations and reinforcements reported in such National Council of Teachers of English publications as *An Experience Curriculum* (1935), *A Correlated Curriculum* (1936), *Conducting Experiences in English* (1939), *Radio and English Teaching* (1941), *Evaluating Instruction in Secondary School English* (1941), *What Communication Means Today* (1944), *An Emerging Curriculum in English* (1946), and most recently *The English Language Arts* (1952) and *Language Arts for Today's Children* (1954). These factors of enthusiasm and venturesomeness can be prime values. For in any program emphasizing growth and development, a lively exploratory spirit must rank high, inviting spontaneity and appeal to the "amateur spirit" as well as to systematic study—from "incidental correlation" to systematic humanities programs.

Besides enthusiasm, the chief characteristic of all these practices is flexibility, essential at a time when new media, contexts and habits of communication, new insight into language, new conceptions of the role of literature and the other humanities, call for fluid inquiry rather than fixity and finality. In such new contexts, students and teachers must be learners together. Today's students, with their remarkable range of experience in the new media, have a great deal to

contribute. Given the chance, they can tell much, as illustrated by the replies of 200 seventh-graders (in New York in
1948) who were asked by Edward G. Bernard what media in
and out of school gave them most in connection with eleven
stated aims of the curriculum. Among the aims were character development, appreciation of the American heritage, emotional health, clear thinking, good social relationships, exploratory outlook, and breadth of culture. In free response
the most frequent sources listed by the students were (1)
Life magazine, (2) the novel *Tom Sawyer*, (3) the film
Gentleman's Agreement, and (4) the radio program "Gang
Busters." [9]

Varied Contextual Elements in the Programs

Given the values of exploratory enthusiasm and flexibility,
what then? Spontaneity has its limitations and may leave
random impressions. If teacher and students develop a bulletin board for organizing and focusing cumulative contributions, as Stanley Wagner and Peter Donchian have appropriately recommended, sooner or later there must be some
organizing concept. Illustrations in this chapter suggest
four main kinds of concepts or contexts: the *aesthetic*, dealing with matters of form in the arts; the *social-cultural*, dealing with language and art among other social phenomena in
a community; the *communication arts* context, dealing with
cultural-psychological-aesthetic processes and means of communication, including literature and art; the *humanities*
context, concerned with the most notable expressions of human values in literature, the arts, philosophy, religion, and
the history of the human spirit. These contexts are not mutually exclusive, but they differ enough in scope, focus, and
emphasis so that teachers and students need to give them
systematic thought. They offer varying measures of diffi-

[9] Edward G. Bernard, *Providing Materials for the Teaching of Literature in Junior High School English Classes in New York City*, Doctoral project (New York, Teachers College, Columbia University, 1949), pp. 129–135.

culty, also, for teachers and students. Probably the question should not be *which* of these to choose, but *in what order* to learn to work with each, according to need and opportunity. For the plain fact is that teachers and research workers and students are working in each of these contexts, according to their particular bents, and the well-prepared and growing teacher will become equipped to work in any of them.

Formidable as this may sound, there are very practical ways of accomplishing this end, first by way of "communication arts," then "social-cultural," then "aesthetic," and then "humanities."

At first glance, "communication arts" may appear to be the largest and least manageable context. In reality, it offers the readiest entry. Teacher and student are already active in it, knowing much about it from experience. It can be largely contemporary, although it has the perspective of one's own experience with changing media, including for most people the changes brought by television, and it calls finally for perspective on communication and the arts in various epochs. Its various aspects may be sampled quickly. Above all it throws into relief, often exaggerated relief, the basic substance of all human communication—the wide range of signs or symbols through which men have learned to communicate their experience and values in language, sound effect, musical suggestion, gesture, picture, trade mark. Linguists, psychologists, philosophers of art, anthropologists, propaganda analysts and workers in communication and the arts generally—all agree that the common substance of communication is the "symbol," with language symbols predominant. They do not mean by symbol only allegorical or literary "lion-stands-for-courage" abstractions, of course, but any sign used to convey a meaning, ranging from a numeral to a spoken word, to a drawing of a cat to the cross on a church tower. Man's ability to communicate depends on his ability to recognize, understand and use symbols of many kinds, at increasing stages of maturity.

Concern with Symbols

The fact that nearly half the teachers contributing to this chapter indicate a concern with "symbols" shows a growing awareness of something made more and more apparent in modern mass media, as well as in such reputable books as Ogden and Richards' *The Meaning of Meaning* (1923), A. N. Whitehead's *Symbolism: Its Meaning and Effect* (1927), G. H. Mead's *Mind, Self and Society* (1934), Suzanne K. Langer's *Philosophy in a New Key: A Study in the Symbolism of Art, Rite, and Reason* (1942) and her *Feeling and Form* (1953).

If the study of symbols is left merely as an ingenious exercise in perception and manipulation, it suffers, of course, from the same defects as Plato saw in persuasive rhetoric in his dialogue, *The Gorgias:* "The rhetorician need not know the truth about things; he has only to discover some way of persuading the ignorant. . . ." Teachers are rightly fearful of the same dangers in studies of communication, particularly if the studies stop with mere smatterings of findings from various sciences. Several years ago the editor of a PMLA journal warned against proposals to "*superimpose* on traditional instruction in English, *at all levels* of education (including graduate work), a medley of 'communication arts' involving necessarily small doses of psychology, sociology, semantics, politics, librarianship, radio-listening, television-viewing, and so forth," leading to a "brand-new department" with a "catch-all social-studies character." This is a sound warning, but if the communication arts are conceived of as contemporary applied humanities, concerned with symbols of value as they should be, they need not fall into such perils.

They may contribute, as contemporary applied humanities, to needs which the editor of PMLA has called attention to more recently in the humanities generally: [10]

[10] William Riley Parker, "For Members Only," *PMLA*, Vol. LXVIII (April, 1953), p. 1.

Anyone seen the Humanities lately? Yesterday, history tells us, they were strong, were clear and far-extending in their influence on men. Today, try to define their influence. For that matter, try to define the Humanities. Are we in the MLA included—literary historians, new critics, linguists, and all? By what definition? . . . Perhaps symptomatically, the director of the Division of the Humanities of the Rockefeller Foundation is a political scientist. . . . [observe that] there exists no national council of literary scholars and authors, of art historians and artists, of musicologists and musicians . . . [consider] the flourishing state of anthropology, psychology, sociology, and other studies that actively explore *the nature and behavior of man.* Have we students of literature been too little interested in this potential product of our own studies, which laymen sometimes expect of us? Have we been too little interested in learning something from current discoveries in these other allied fields? What do we mean by saying we are in the Humanities? If we do not redefine and rededicate our activities, humanity may tell us what we are and ask us please to excuse the expression.

If teachers of language, literature, communication, and the humanities are to take more than superficial account of these other "studies of man," attention must be focused on something of common concern to all. As Suzanne K. Langer has pointed out, there has developed an intense concern in many fields with the symbolic nature of thought and communication—"a new key."

Given such focus, teachers and students can penetrate to considerable depth into "symbols for communication," "symbols of culture," the aesthetics of "symbolism," and "symbols of value" central to the various contexts indicated earlier—with mutual reinforcement of one another.

Preparation of Teachers

The teacher with a substantial undergraduate English major can gain a good workable grasp of the communication arts concept in a year of graduate work, or in a year or two of systematic classroom projects with capable students, stressing literary values in various media. Such a grasp provides a firm hold also on one key factor in a social-cultural or community context, since communication is basic to *community*. It offers a good center for core programs, insuring more attention to communication skills than many core programs provide.

Developing a full-fledged *aesthetic* context or *humanities* context requires a longer time, at least two or three years of graduate work or a longer period with cumulative projects carried on by able groups in English classes. Both of these contexts require of the teacher considerable historical and philosophical background along with very extensive acquaintance with literature and arts of many peoples and periods.[11] If the works of literature and art are studied as major symbols of value, they can be kept related in their multiplicity. And the teacher who will plan his professional reading and seeing and listening for three or four years can guide students in several contexts.

There is no more ultimate easy magic in the word *symbol*, of course, than there is in the words *English*, or *communication*, or *humanities*. All of them require steady work. All symbolize important and varied contexts themselves. Like the communication arts and skills reported in this chapter, they too can reinforce one another in helping students to grow.

BIBLIOGRAPHY

Books

ADAMS, Charles, *Producing and Directing for Television* (New York, Henry Holt & Company, Inc., 1953).

BOARDMAN, Gail, *Oral Communication of Literature* (New York, Prentice-Hall, Inc., 1952).

BROWN, John Mason, *As They Appear* (New York, McGraw-Hill Book Company, Inc., 1952).

[11] For an exploratory project on values and difficulties in studying the humanities and gaining application to high school classes, see David S. Stevens, *Changing Humanities: Appraisal of Old Values and New Uses* (New York, Harper and Brothers, 1953) and Edward S. Evenden and R. Freeman Butts, eds., *Columbia University Co-operative Program for Preservice Education of Teachers; a Staff Report of a Three-year Demonstration Conducted by Barnard, Columbia, and Teachers College in Co-operation with the Commission on Teacher Education of the American Council of Education* (New York, Teachers College, Columbia University, 1942).

————, *Seeing More Things* (New York, McGraw-Hill Book Company, Inc., 1948).

————, *Still Seeing Things* (New York, McGraw-Hill Book Company, Inc., 1950).

CARROLL, John B., *The Study of Language* (Cambridge, Mass., Harvard University Press, 1953).

DALE, Edgar, *Audio-Visual Methods in Teaching* (New York, The Dryden Press, 1954).

D'AMICO, Victor, "Make Feeling and Seeing Pictures," in his *Art for the Family* (New York, Museum of Modern Art, 1954), pp. 11–16.

————, "The Child as Creative Inventor," in his *Creative Teaching in Art* (Scranton, Pa., International Textbook Company, 1953), pp. 185–209.

HAYAKAWA, S. I., *Language in Thought and Action* (New York, Harcourt, Brace & Company, Inc., 1949).

————, *Language, Meaning, and Maturity* (New York, Harper and Brothers, 1954).

LAIRD, Charlton, *Miracle of Language* (Cleveland, World Publishing Company, 1953).

LEE, Irving, *How to Talk with People* (New York, Harper and Brothers, 1952).

McGRATH, Earl, ed., *Communication in General Education* (Dubuque, Iowa, William C. Brown Co., 1949).

SHAYON, Robert Lewis, *Television and Our Children* (New York, Longmans, Green & Company, 1951).

SIEPMAN, Charles Arthur, *Radio, Television, and Society* (New York, Oxford University Press, 1950).

TRACY, Henry Chester, *English as Experience* (New York, E. P. Dutton & Co., Inc., 1928).

Periodicals

FAGAN, E. R., "To Literature via the Collage," *English Journal,* Vol. XL (December, 1951), pp. 562–566.

GREY, Lennox, "Co-ordinating the Communication Arts," *English Journal,* Vol. XXXIV (June, 1945), pp. 315–320.

————, "Test Case," *Teachers College Record,* Vol. 57 (November, 1955), pp. 129–135.

SHAYON, Robert Lewis, "Two Roads to Dilemma: Radio or Television," *Saturday Review,* Vol. 33 (November, 1950), p. 28.

SHOEMAKER, Francis, ed., "Communication and Communication Arts," *Teachers College Record,* Vol. 57 (November, 1955), pp. 59–149.

PREVIEW OF CHAPTER 12

Articulation, a Two-Way Process
   The Effect of Numbers
   The Movement toward Education for Life

Preparation in English—What the Colleges Want
   Variety and Change in Demands
   Relations between High School and College
   The Nature of Admissions Examinations
      and Placement Tests
      Examinations of the College Entrance
         Examination Board
      Subject A in California
      The New York Regents Examinations
      College placement tests
   The Need for Conference between the School
      and College
      On the relation of admission to success
         in English
      On the level of performance required
      On the specific requirements to be met
   The Puzzle of Flexibility
   Suggestions for Consideration

Secondary School and College Relationships

Conclusions

Bibliography

CHAPTER 12

Meeting College Entrance Requirements

THE SECONDARY SCHOOL and college are mutually concerned with establishing and meeting college entrance requirements. The problem is at the heart of their relations one with the other. Together they are earnestly engaged in studying the question of what may be done to make the transition both natural and assured.

Although the secondary schools of this country have never served college-bound students exclusively, the success at college of their students who go on to further training has always been a major element in judgments of the quality of their instruction. How to care adequately for those preparing for college, including the so-called "gifted," and at the same time meet the needs of those seeking a terminal education in high school is a problem confronting curriculum-makers. An equally perplexing task is how to prepare students for college and at the same time for life outside an academic environment. To many, there seems no antagonism between these two aspects of the program, inasmuch as power to communicate through reading and expression and ability to think are necessary for both. To some, special emphasis seems essential to preparation for college.

ARTICULATION, A TWO-WAY PROCESS

It is obvious that neither the college nor the high school can solve the problem of articulation alone. Each one from the point of view of its own philosophy and its experience with young people has a contribution to make to the solution. If the view [1] of the Commission on the English Curriculum is accepted—that a curriculum must grow, like the student himself, from the ground up—the problem of the college is to understand the elements which have gone into the background of the high school student and the particular stage of development he has attained. On the other hand, the colleges have had years of experience with students who represent for the most part the upper half of the high school population, and have, in general, given serious thought to the problem. High schools have equally serious problems to cope with in the interests of all the students of secondary school age. Articulation can never be a one-way process. It demands adjustments on the part of both high school and college and constant conference between their representatives. The question of preparation for college is not alone, What do the colleges want?, but What is the next step in the education of able young people if they are to reach their fullest potentialities and contribute to the welfare of their communities, their country, and their world?

The Effect of Numbers

Growth in attendance at secondary schools has been staggering. Estimates of the number of youth of high school age who attend secondary schools range from 7 per cent in 1890 to 75 or 85 per cent in 1950 or 1951.[2] If the percentage of all eighteen-year-olds in the population is used as a base, the number in 1950 was probably 20.7.[3]

[1] National Council of Teachers of English, Commission on the English Curriculum, *The English Language Arts*, NCTE Curriculum Series, Vol. I (New York, Appleton-Century-Crofts, Inc., 1952), Ch. 2.

[2] Harold A. Odell, "Admissions and the Secondary School," *College Admissions* (Princeton, N. J., College Entrance Examination Board, 1954), p. 63. Frances Dwane McGill, "The Public High School Intervenes," 2. *College Admissions. The Great Sorting* (Princeton, N. J., College Entrance Examination Board, 1955), pp. 17–18.

[3] R. Clyde White, "The Potential and Probable Supply of College Students," *College Admissions* (Princeton, N. J., College Entrance Examination Board, 1954), p. 16.

Predictions indicate still further and more rapid growth in college enrollments in the future. Paul H. Farrier estimates on the basis of studies in Cleveland, Ohio, in Virginia, and for the nation as a whole that from 1950 to 1970 the college population will increase by 100 per cent.[4] Samuel A. Stouffer, in his analysis of the social forces that produce the "great sorting," believes that by 1970 the numbers seeking college admission will be much greater than the 75 per cent increase represented by births.[5]

Numbers should swell not only because of increases in population but because of endeavors to recognize what has kept able students out of college and to prevent these factors from continuing to operate. Students may be without financial resources or without motivation. Half of the bright group of Minnesota high school seniors studied by Ralph F. Berdie were so little interested in college that they would not expect to go even if the money were made available to them.[6] Berdie also, in a study in Minnesota, found that 50 per cent of the boys in metropolitan areas were planning to go to college in comparison to 20 per cent of farm boys.[7] The higher the education of the parents the higher was the probability that their children would go to college.[8] A study by Horace Leonard Davis in Kentucky showed that about half of the best "college risks" did not enroll in college, whereas about a seventh of the poorest "college risks" did enroll.[9] Financial barriers will have to be overcome. So will barriers created by a lack of motivation.

[4] Paul H. Farrier, "The Population and College X," *College Admissions* (Princeton, N. J., College Entrance Examination Board, 1954), p. 35.

[5] Samuel A. Stouffer, "Social Forces That Produce the 'Great Sorting,'" 2. *College Admissions. The Great Sorting* (Princeton, N. J., College Entrance Examination Board, 1955), p. 2.

[6] Dael Wolfle, "Restrictions on the Supply of College Students," *College Admissions* (Princeton, N. J., College Entrance Examination Board, 1954), p. 27.

[7] Samuel A. Stouffer, *op. cit.*, p. 2.

[8] *Ibid.*, p. 3.

[9] Irving Lorge, "The Intellectual Sorting," 2. *College Admissions. The Great Sorting* (Princeton, N. J., College Entrance Examination Board, 1955), p. 29.

It is well to keep in mind that the problems of individual high schools vary greatly. Sixty per cent of the youth of America are in small high schools of two hundred or fewer, from which one or two pupils a year will go on to college. In contrast, the city of Newton, Massachusetts, sends 70 per cent of its seniors to institutions of higher learning, more than 60 per cent of them by the route of the College Entrance Examination Board tests.[10]

The Movement toward Education for Life

The trend in schools with a small staff and limited enrollments was for many years to let college entrance requirements dominate the high school program. The last two or three decades have seen significant efforts to consider the preparation of all students, whether bound for college or not, for the demands of the world outside the school. Many schools have made changes in this direction. Others have been untouched by the movement. In some schools the gifted pupil has been lost in the shuffle or allowed to drop to a mediocre level of achievement. Where this situation exists, it has aroused leaders in both high school and college to study the problem carefully, for the leadership of the country and of the world is at stake, to say nothing of the satisfaction which the individual boy or girl may gain from the full exercise of his own powers.

PREPARATION IN ENGLISH—
WHAT THE COLLEGES WANT

For many reasons, what the colleges at the present time want for admission is clear neither from the requirements nor from the policy of admission. Catalogue statements are vague; statements about policy are meager. It is also becoming evident that requirements as stated in the catalogue and admission policy, in some instances, are not consistent.

[10] Harold B. Gores and Leo Barry, "College-Level Courses in Secondary School," *College Board Review*, No. 28 (Winter, 1956), p. 4.

Variety and Change in Demands

The number of colleges is increasing, presenting a variety of opportunities because of differences in aims and offerings. At the same time, there are more high school graduates, representing a wide range of interests, capacities, and future goals, who are seeking admission to college. Under the circumstances, an admissions officer in any college, in reviewing an applicant's records, needs to ask: "Will it be good for *this* student, with *his* abilities and interests and deficiencies, to come to my college to try to carry out his plans for a life and a career?" [11]

General statements in regard to requirements for college admission indicate an absence of interest in the content of the subject of English—and in that of other subjects. B. Alden Thresher, Director of Admissions at the Massachusetts Institute of Technology, characterizes the era from 1900 to 1935 in the annals of the College Entrance Examination Board as one of exclusive emphasis on subject-matter requirements and essay-type examinations. From 1935 to the present, he terms the era one of aptitude tests and appraisal of intellectual promise on a basis at least partially divorced from achievement in specific subject matter. He believes a third era opened in 1955 with the inauguration of the Scholarship Service of the Board, the era of socialized admissions. [12]

Questions of admission to college have veered from specific requirements in specific subjects to a combination of kinds of evidence of fitness for college: the high school record, the record of extracurricular activities, a letter of recommendation from the principal, interviews, and test records of all kinds, including those of standardized tests

[11] Norman O. Fredericksen, "The Evaluation of Personal and Social Qualities," *College Admissions* (Princeton, N. J., College Entrance Examination Board, 1954), p. 105.

[12] B. Alden Thresher, "The College Intervenes," 2. *College Admissions. The Great Sorting* (Princeton, N. J., College Entrance Examination Board, 1955), p. 14.

given in the school as well as those given outside the school for admission to college. An excellent account of standardized tests is John E. Dobbin's discussion [13] of the admissions officer as a consumer of guidance. Various aspects of these kinds of evidence are under scrutiny. Paul Burnham, for example, found the average of grades along with the Scholastic Aptitude Test more accurate than the commonly used record of the rank in class.[14] The extent to which the various kinds of evidence or even of "hidden factors" affect the acceptance or the rejection of a candidate has not been defined. It is hoped that colleges will reveal figures indicating the relative importance of each kind of evidence and also the actual scores and records of students they have admitted.

Relations between High School and College

In 1950 Pattillo and Stout summarized discussions which had appeared in print during the previous six years concerning causes of dissatisfaction in the relations between high schools and colleges.[15] Among the causes from the point of view of the high school were that "colleges do not provide high schools with adequate information about college programs, admission requirements and procedures, and the level of ability of students in particular higher institutions." Those from the point of view of the colleges were that high schools failed to recognize the diversity of purposes existing among colleges and the right of private institutions to preserve their autonomy by selecting those students who best qualify for their particular programs. The colleges also complained that

---

[13] John E. Dobbin, "The Admissions Officer as a Consumer of Guidance," 2. *College Admissions. The Great Sorting* (Princeton, N. J., College Entrance Examinations Board, 1955), pp. 32–42.

[14] Paul S. Burnham, "The Evaluation of Academic Ability," *College Admissions* (Princeton, N. J., College Entrance Examination Board, 1954), p. 77.

[15] Manning M. Pattillo, Jr., and Lorence Stout, "Co-operation between Secondary Schools and Colleges," *North Central Quarterly*, Vol. 25 (January, 1951), pp. 313–345.

many students coming from the high school today lack the basic skills in reading, writing, and thinking necessary for serious intellectual activity. They believed the lack of continuity between the high school and the college was due to failure in continuity within the high school program itself in setting more and more mature tasks and in making increasingly greater intellectual demands upon all students in general and upon the more able in particular. Growth in habits of study and in powers of a distinctly intellectual character was emphasized in contrast to the old concern for specific content to be covered. The high school and the college each complained that the other had not revised its curriculum and methods of instruction in accordance with modern research in education.

Constantly reiterated complaints about the inability of many high school graduates to express ideas clearly and logically and to comprehend and examine critically ideas to be found through reading make the problem of preparation for college particularly acute for English teachers. What the colleges feel their students should have, therefore, for admission, for success in college, and for success in English classes is a matter of serious concern to high school teachers everywhere.

The Nature of Admissions Examinations and Placement Tests

One means of determining some aspects of what the colleges want is to study the examinations they require of students for admission and placement. This study is important even though a high school diploma is sufficient in many state supported colleges and universities; and high grades in academic subjects without a diploma are, under certain conditions, acceptable in both privately endowed and state institutions.

There follows a discussion, in turn, of the tests of the College Entrance Examination Board, the Subject A Examination in California, the New York Regents Examinations, and locally constructed or standardized tests such as those developed by the Educational Testing Service.

Examinations of the College Entrance Examination Board. The largest and most influential agency for testing students for admission to college is the College Entrance Examination Board, of which 171 [16] colleges—including the United States Air Force Academy and the United States Military Academy—were members in the winter of 1956. In addition, 15 nonmember colleges participated in the College Scholarship Service. The growth of the College Entrance Examination Board (C.E.E.B.) has been rapid in recent years. In 1951, candidates taking the examinations prepared by the C.E.E.B. numbered 75,000. From 10 per cent of all final [17] candidates for admission to college in 1951, the number rose to 15 per cent in 1955. The estimate for 1962 is 300,000 final candidates, 37 per cent of all college entrants predicted for that year.[18] This number will increase with the use of these tests in scholarship programs such as those of the General Motors Corporation and the National Merit Scholarship Corporation.[19]

The College Entrance Examination Board offers the Scholastic Aptitude Test, with a Verbal and a Mathematical section. Many member institutions require this test and no other. In 1954–55 it was taken by 155,191 candidates, an increase of 37,122 over 1953–54.[20] Although the Verbal Aptitude Test is

[16] For list of colleges, see inside back cover *College Board Review*, No. 28 (Winter, 1956).

[17] Those who apply for admission to a particular college and complete all aspects of the admission requirements of that institution.

[18] Frank H. Bowles, "New Goals for College Admissions: Social Demands on Schools and Colleges," *College Board Review*, No. 26 (Spring, 1955), pp. 7–8.

[19] The College Entrance Examination Board, *54th Report of the Director* (Princeton, N. J., The College Entrance Examination Board, 1955), pp. 11–12.

[20] The College Entrance Examination Board, *53rd Report of the Director* (Princeton, N. J., The College Entrance Examination Board, 1954), p. 62.

not specifically a test of English, since it measures a candidate's verbal equipment for any field of study, it appears to be a better predictor of success in English than any other test. So far, studies have indicated that coaching does not help in preparing for the test,[21] which does not undertake to determine the extent to which abilities have been developed through instruction.[22]

Final candidates often take three Achievement Tests prepared by the C.E.E.B. The English Composition Test [23] continues to be taken by the majority of all candidates who take any of the Achievement Tests. Its popularity was not affected when the General Composition Test was also available.

Copies of the English Composition Test (ECT), a one-hour test, are not released, but a clue to its nature is given in a booklet, *Bulletin of Information*, sent candidates for the examination. The 1955–56 issue describes the test as "designed to measure the candidate's ability to organize ideas coherently and to express them clearly and well. This ability, normally developed in schools both by practice in writing and by the study of literature, will be tested by a variety of means." Examples in the pamphlet, *English Composition*,[24] give a fair indication of some of the kinds of questions that may be used. Three types of questions are illustrated. One aims to test the student's ability to arrange materials in logical and coherent order. The second asks the student to improve a poorly written passage, approximating a common school situation in which a student must revise a first draft of a composition before handing it in, or a classroom situation in which a class is asked to improve portions of a

[21] John W. French, "An Answer to Test Coaching, Public School Experiment with the SAT," *College Board Review*, No. 27 (Fall, 1955), p. 5.

[22] *53rd Report of the Director, op. cit.,* p. 23.

[23] *Ibid.,* p. 57. In 1955–56, 59,761 candidates took ECT, an increase of 13,356 over 1953–54 (*54th Report of the Director, op. cit.,* p. 62).

[24] College Entrance Examination Board, *English Composition* (Princeton, N. J., The College Entrance Examination Board, June, 1954), pp. 8–27.

student essay. The essay is triple-spaced so that he may insert changes into the text. No errors are indicated for him. The third type tests the student's appreciation of style, tone, rhythm, and meaning in short passages of poetry. In some instances, for example, he is to choose from four possible final lines of a four-line stanza, one which is appropriate and others which are inappropriate in (1) rhythm or meter, (2) style or tone, and (3) meaning. Similar techniques may test feeling for fitness of language in tone, imagery, or rhythm, such as choosing from a list of five figures of speech or five descriptive passages the one which best fits the tone of the passage or the general atmosphere created in it. The ability to discriminate these passages seems to be closely related to abilities the student must use in reading and writing. At the end, the Bulletin offers a key to answers.[25]

Another question that has been used is a passage from S. E. Morison's *The Young Man Washington*. Lines are numbered. The student is told that Mr. Morison names or implies several qualities Washington gained from the discipline of the wilderness. In not more than three connected sentences the student is asked to identify four such qualities and show how they are illustrated or suggested in the text. Those sentences must answer three specific questions: one on the point made in lines 6–7 by repetition of the word *crowded*, one on the ways the sea is like a tough old nurse, and one explaining the connection of the comparison of *nurse* and *sea* with the main idea of the paragraph. Such a task resembles free writing, involving many of the qualities of good composition.

Types of questions may change as experiments reveal a variety of techniques. Some experimental material now being tried out calls for comparing and contrasting the theme and method of approach in one stanza from each of two poems,

[25] College Entrance Examination Board, *College Board Tests* (*1955–56*) *Bulletin of Information* (Princeton, N. J., College Entrance Examination Board, 1956).

rewriting a passage combining choppy sentences, and revising sentences to avoid repetition and haziness of meaning.

The nature of the English Composition Test is well summarized in *English Composition,* in which the writers say: [26]

> What is most important for the student taking the English Composition Test is the ability to handle language, to know when ideas are well or badly expressed, when a clause, or a sentence, or a paragraph performs its function effectively and when it does not. This ability is almost native to a few, apparently; but, in general, those who must develop it do so in two ways: they read a lot and they write a lot. They do not read just anything, any more than they write in just any manner. They read good literature of all kinds, and they write about all kinds of things. They are helped in their choice of reading, of course, and they are guided in the development of their writing ability. But they are not helped to choose any specific reading, nor are they guided in any particular way. Familiarity with the good that has been written brings with it a feeling for a better as opposed to a worse way of saying things; and practice in trying to say things well increases the facility with which they can be said. The teacher who wants a formula for preparing his students for the English Composition Test must be disappointed unless he will accept the very general one: See that your students do a lot of reading and writing; help them with both.

It is difficult to see how such a program can be accused of "regimenting" the high school course. Even the small school with no desire and no facilities for "segregating" the college-bound student has equal chances of success in such a scheme.

There has been some question among the users and readers of the College Board tests as to whether the ability to write, "which is a creative aspect of the human personality," can be measured by objective techniques or whether the only adequate way to test a student's ability to write is to have him write.[27]

The English Composition Test according to its makers, provides an *indirect* measure of the ability to write English in the sense that "It does not require the student to write an

[26] *Ibid.,* pp. 27–28.
[27] "Should the General Composition Test Be Continued?" *College Board Review,* No. 25 (Winter, 1955), pp. 2–13.

essay," but "to do a number of things which, when taken together, show reasonably well whether he has the power to do so."

Furthermore, experience has shown that the writing of a one-hour essay provides a poorer basis for measuring a student's writing ability than does the indirect approach of the English Composition Test, which also takes an hour. [One reason is that] readers do not agree very well in their marking of essays. . . .

. . . the examiners believe that the student who has had much practice in writing will be able to do better on the test than one who has had little practice. Furthermore, it is known that students with high scores on the test tend to write better essays in college than do those who have low scores. . . . it does get at the underlying abilities which are necessary to good writing and which are developed by actual practice in writing. . . .

[It is the intention of the Board in offering] no specific subject matter for the English Composition Test [that there should] be no incentive for cramming certain material into students' heads just before test time.[28]

The construction of such a test as the English Composition Test requires ingenuity and strategy. A single item is planned to test many qualities. The total test is a subtle and inclusive measure of the elements involved in competence in writing. By comparison, using an hour to write a single long theme as a measurement device may seem a wasteful way of probing a very complex problem.

Also of interest in connection with the English Composition Test is the fact that studies suggest "that *if* the English Composition Test is a valid index of writing ability, as has been assumed, then extensive reading may have more to do with the development of writing ability than the writing of class themes. It may mean, however, that the ECT is, in fact, less a composition test than it is a reading test. It is also conceivable but less likely that extensive theme writing tends to increase SAT-Verbal scores more than it does ECT scores."[29]

[28] *English Composition, op. cit.*, pp. 5–6 and 27.
[29] *College Board Scores, Their Use and Interpretation*, No. 2 (Princeton, N. J., College Entrance Examination Board, 1955), p. 66.

An outstanding study that indicates the merit of indirect means of measuring the ability to write is Edith Huddleston's doctoral dissertation, "Measurement of Writing Ability at the College-Entrance Level." [30]

Because of deep and serious interest in writing, the College Entrance Examination Board offered experimentally in May, 1954–55–56, the General Composition Test (GCT), a two-hour writing examination, not an English test but "an essay in writing English of any kind." Literary material was not emphasized.[31] An essay topic of wide interest suggested a problem: Should women be given the same educational and professional opportunities as men? Or, is there a conflict between science and human values? Reading material was provided for a background. The student was to outline his essay, write it, and summarize the theme briefly. Impartial judging was to be on the basis of five qualities, each of which was defined: mechanics, style, organization, reasoning, and content.[32] Each of these was given a separate score, and the candidate's score appeared as a two-dimensional graph.

The General Composition Test was dropped from the Board program after May, 1956, but it demonstrated a need for essay material in the Board program. At this time the study of essay material will be continued in the Advanced Placement Program and the Developed Abilities Program.[33]

Other tests involving English are Tests of Advanced Placement, developed by representatives of the School and College Study of Admission with Advanced Standing and continued by the College Board as the Advanced Placement Program. This program retains the flexible and responsive character of the exploratory project, supported in 1952 to

---

[30] "Measurement of Writing Ability at the College Entrance Level: Objective vs. Subjective Testing Techniques," *Journal of Experimental Education*, Vol. 22 (March, 1954), pp. 165–213.

[31] "The GCT Experiment: Final Report," *College Board Review*, No. 29 (Spring, 1956), pp. 31–32.

[32] *College Board Tests* (*1955–56*), *Bulletin of Information, op. cit.*, p. 38.

[33] "The GCT Experiment: Final Report," *op. cit.*, p. 32.

1955 by the Fund for the Advancement of Education, to help gifted students during their high school years to complete work equivalent to college freshman English and other freshman courses.[34]

The description of the requirements in English Composition are thought-provoking both for teachers of regular classes and for those whose pupils seek Advanced Standing: [35]

The aim of any course in composition is to teach students to write well about something important. The essential core of training in composition is therefore the frequent writing and careful revision of substantial themes on subjects sufficiently mature to challenge both thought and linguistic powers. Theme-writing should not be regarded as merely a means to an end, but as an intrinsically valuable process of mental self-exploration and orientation. The student writer the Advanced Placement Program wishes to encourage must be capable of grasping a given subject, comprehending and becoming involved in it, developing ideas from it, and presenting judgments supported by ready reference. . . . His papers must be distinguished by superior command of *substance*, thoughtfully and interestingly presented.

The student, the bulletin further suggests, must demonstrate proficiency in organization, in writing of well-rounded, self-contained paragraphs with clear sentence structure. Sound and compelling logic is expected, a feeling for style revealed in both precision and fluency, and mastery of the mechanics of writing.

The Advanced Placement Examination in English Composition was set up to require three hours, offering wide variety in topic and treatment, subjects to be drawn from social sciences, behavior, literature, the fine arts, and theoretical and natural science. A possibility is an argument based on memory and general knowledge, addressed to the general reader. It has a fixed short length with time allowed for revision. Another is an argument of uncon-

[34] College Entrance Examination Board, *Advanced Placement Program*, 1956, p. 7. See also *Advanced Placement Tests, Bulletin of Information*, 1955–56 (Princeton, N. J., College Entrance Examination Board). The Advanced Placement Tests are constructed by the College Entrance Examination Board and administered, scored, and reported by the Educational Testing Service.

[35] *Advanced Placement Program, op. cit.*, p. 16.

trolled length based on a "springboard" quotation or simple data, and addressed to a special reader. The third is an exposition based on a brief passage, "structured" by three or four questions to promote rapid and extensive writing.

It is noteworthy here, as in the other examinations, that the colleges are interested strictly in *expository* writing, the development and treatment of *ideas;* at least that is the skill in which they examine. The Committee on Advanced Standing specifies certain organizational patterns of presenting ideas which are important for passing the examinations: spacial and/or chronological order; development by comparison, contrast, or analogy; definition by genus and differentiae; reasoning by cause and effect, by conclusions derived from particulars or consequences resulting from basic principles. All inductive and deductive patterns are significant.[36]

Teachers were given some specific suggestions for advanced or college-level composition courses in high school, the outcomes of which can be measured by these tests. Classes of students with high native ability and consistent interest in thought and writing should have a membership under twenty. Each teacher should have a limited pupil-load, seventy-five or less. Each week the teacher should read at least one composition by each student and supervise its revision. It was not considered desirable to teach composition without literature or literature without composition.

In preparation for the literature examination, the student's goal should be power rather than fact. Preparation should be intensive rather than superficial and extensive, with the "full" reading of works of all the main types of literature. Intensive study should include unity, paradox, the progression of plot, style, and backgrounds. The aim should be not to produce precocious young critics, but students who can read works as wholes and who have enough critical vocabulary, not jargon, to talk communicatively about them. The texts,

[36] The School and College Study of Admission with Advanced Standing, Gordon K. Chalmers, Chairman, *College Admission with Advanced Standing, Announcement and Bulletin of Information* (Gambier, Ohio, Kenyon College, January, 1954), pp. 7–9.

chosen for their literary value from the literature of any age, should be imaginative, permanent, and of moderate complexity. The work should be a whole work.[37]

In short, the Committee on Advanced Standing declares: [38]

Books are too often replaced by books about books. Lists of titles and dates, biographical information about writers, and historical surveys are no substitute for the books themselves in the development of that reading skill which is the objective of the course . . . As a rule of thumb, it may be suggested that no biographical or historical information should be introduced by the teacher if it can be omitted without definite loss of understanding or enjoyment by the student.

An account of the reading as revealed in the examination administered in May, 1954, gives insight into secondary school literary experiences for advanced standing.[39]

A test that is planned by the C.E.E.B. and that should have influence on preparation in English is the "Test of Developed Ability." These tests are designed to appraise the specific abilities of college applicants and the extent to which the specific abilities have been developed, enlarged, and disciplined through instruction.[40] These tests, which may become the core of the testing program of the College Entrance Examination Board, aim to define the kinds of abilities teachers should develop in their college-bound students. The point of view of the new test would minimize memorization and emphasize all the various kinds of mental operations which constitute the ability to think. The test focuses on mental operations, what students are supposed to do with their minds whether inside or outside a classroom.[41] In all probability a promising student prepared in English in the

[37] *Ibid.*, pp. 9–14.

[38] College Entrance Examination Board, *Advanced Placement Program* (Princeton, N. J., The Educational Testing Service, 1956), p. 23.

[39] Albert B. Friedman, "The Literary Experience of High School Seniors and College Freshmen," *The English Journal*, Vol. XLIV (December, 1955), pp. 521–524.

[40] *53rd Report of the Director, op. cit.*, p. 23.

[41] Henry S. Dyer, "Can College Admissions Be Part of Education?" 2. *College Admissions. The Great Sorting* (Princeton, N. J., College Entrance Examination Board, 1955), pp. 48–49.

direction suggested by the College Entrance Examination Board should not have difficulty in meeting any college entrance requirements in that subject.

It is interesting to note that power of thought and expression and also ability to read intelligently are outcomes likewise sought in the other major examination systems.

Subject A in California. The Subject A Examination is required by a number of colleges in California for placing students in English classes but not as a device for admitting or rejecting applicants. It is usually in two parts: one, an objective test of at least sentence structure, reading, and punctuation (grammatical usage is not included); and the other, a theme of at least four hundred words on one of many topics of a general nature, suitable for most high school seniors.

The question on sentence structure may ask students to place a plus sign after sentences (in running discourse) which are acceptable and a minus sign after those which are ambiguous, meaningless, muddled, or structurally incorrect. Reading ability is tested by a multiple-choice vocabulary and comprehension test based on several paragraphs of a selection (usually expository) of a high level of maturity. The punctuation test requires the insertion of marks other than periods into a passage of connected discourse.

The 1953 statement by Stanford University, the University of California, and other colleges of the Bay Area is typical of all such statements made by college groups within the last two or three years. They deplore the fact that "teachers of high school English are constrained to provide the candidates for college with a cram course, a last gasp stagger through English grammar—largely drills upon detailed aspects of grammar as presented in workbooks and textbooks— ironically, at the expense of frequent practice in writing." [42] They say that the purpose of the Subject A Examination is

[42] Alfred H. Grommon, "Preparing High School Students for College Composition," *California Journal of Secondary Education,* Vol. 28 (February, 1953), p. 113.

to provide "some immediate evidence of how well the entering student can write sentences and paragraphs." [43] It asks for the writing of a theme and the passing of an objective test on sentence structure, syntax, punctuation, spelling, and vocabulary. The theme "is the crucial test, the ability to write the language rather than knowledge about particular grammatical aspects of it." [44] Greater weight is given to the theme than to the more objective part of the test.

Such aims, they maintain, are important for all students, not only for those going to college. Major emphasis, they believe, of the high school program in composition should be upon learning to think and to express one's thoughts.

The New York Regents Examinations. The Regents examinations in English are also tests of power-to-do much more than of fact or information. The Fourth Year Regents Examination gives major emphasis to a composition of 250 to 300 words on any one of a wide variety of topics from areas of personal and public concern. Next in emphasis are questions which test power in the reading of expository material and breadth of reading or personal reaction to books each pupil has read. The test in reading comprehension is objective, calling for a choice among five responses. The literature questions present alternatives. One is writing about literary selections of the student's own choosing related to a theme to be considered. An example of such a question is this one:

> The possession of moral or spiritual values helps people face the problems of living. The lack of such values often leads to unhappiness or tragedy. From the novels, full-length plays, and full-length biographies you have read, choose *two* books and in *each* case show by definite references how a person in the book was helped or hindered by the possession or lack of such values. Give titles and authors. (Source: *English-Four years,* June 15, 1956.)

The alternative, designed for a student who does not choose to write interpretatively on what he has read, offers multiple-choice questions on forty books from both classic and contemporary literature frequently used for extensive

[43] *Ibid.,* p. 114.
[44] *Ibid.,* p. 114.

reading. The student is asked to identify twenty. These three questions—the essay, the test of reading comprehension, and the literature question—make up 70 per cent of the examination. The other 30 per cent tests briefly such fields as general vocabulary, spelling, pronunciation, usage (not grammatical terminology), abbreviations, library skills, and knowledge of magazines.

A statement to Superintendents and Principals of Secondary Schools (June 1, 1950) indicates that the Regents examinations in New York State were recommended for general supervisory purposes and as partial measures of achievement for pupils of average and above average ability who take courses of study upon which Regents examinations are based.[45] These tests are said to be useful devices for measuring success in further study.

College placement tests. To place freshmen in English courses, many colleges utilize tests other than those of the College Entrance Examination Board, the Regents, or Subject A in California. In 1954, David Litsey [46] examined the various placement tests used in 194 colleges in forty-four states and in the District of Columbia. His study was a repetition of an analysis made in 1933 on the basis of which he could discuss the trends in the last twenty years. Forty-seven of the colleges reporting were large, state-supported universities, nineteen were state teachers colleges, and the rest were smaller private and state institutions varying in size from a few hundred to several thousand students. Returns were best from New York, California, and the member states of the North Central and Southern Associations. They were smallest from New England. In the latter section, also, numbers of colleges replying used only essay-type tests. Six used for placement the College Entrance Examination Board tests, copies of which were not available for tabulation.

[45] Sherman N. Tinkelman, Supervisor of Test Development, New York State Department of Education, *Regents Examinations,* University of the State of New York, Bulletin No. 1424 (October, 1953), p. 6.

[46] David M. Litsey, "Trends in College Placement Tests in Freshman English," *The English Journal,* Vol. XLV (May, 1956), pp. 250–256.

Of the nine categories of test items, the two most important were punctuation and capitalization, which rose from an emphasis of 21 per cent in 1933 to 32 per cent in 1954, and grammatical usage, which increased in emphasis from 24 per cent to 30 per cent. The next two, spelling and vocabulary, dropped from 23 per cent and 19 per cent to 18 and 13 per cent respectively. Sentence structure decreased from 7 to 4 per cent. Knowledge of technical grammar, which was tested in 4 per cent of the items in 1933, dropped to 2 per cent in 1954. The last two, pronunciation and miscellaneous items, made up fewer than 1 per cent of the items. Punctuation rules were not called for.

Some of these differences may not be significant. The important conclusion to be drawn from the results is that these colleges, too, support the underlying principle of the examination already discussed, namely, that ability to use language, not ability to label and underline forms, is the major concern of the colleges.

Litsey notes also that knowledge of word meanings plays an important part in the examinations. There is likewise evidence of less concern with "niceties of diction and purisms in expression" than there was twenty years ago. "Many present-day tests have drawn upon scientific studies by Leonard, Marckwardt and Walcott, Fries, and others to arrive at modern usage for test items," although they still contain certain items repudiated by the linguists.[47]

The study also indicated that many smaller colleges required the writing of an essay. Larger colleges frequently said they would prefer an essay-type examination, but numbers would not permit the use of it.

The Need for Conference between the School and College

It is obvious that there is no set array of authors, no listing of periods of English or American Literature, and no items of technical grammar required for entrance to college or

[47] *Ibid.*, p. 256.

university under the major systems of examinations in the United States. When individual colleges or individual high schools set up requirements that run counter to the general emphasis upon power-to-do, it would be well for all concerned to meet together to answer the question, "Why?"

On the relation of admission to success in English. It must not be overlooked that the preparation of a student for college is judged not alone by those in admissions offices but also by college teachers confronted by students who have already been admitted. The conclusion of the teachers may be totally different from that of the admissions officer; it is likely to be far more exacting in a particular subject. Students prepared for college should be able to meet both standards.

On the level of performance required. The question at issue today is not one of the content tested so much as it is whether the level of performance required in some examinations is unattainable by many students if time is to be available for other aspects of the language arts program which may be as important for individual pupils as ability to write and to read material demanding a very high level of competence. How to reconcile the various objectives of the secondary school with such requirements may well be the subject of discussion at conferences involving the staffs of both high school and college.

On the specific requirements to be met. The following standards prepared at the University of Syracuse and mimeographed for distribution to the high schools of New York State are typical of those arrived at through close co-operation between university and high school departments.

HIGH SCHOOL PREPARATION FOR COLLEGE WORK IN ENGLISH

The Department of English of Syracuse University has received many inquiries from high school teachers as to what preparation it would like entering freshmen to have. It has presumed therefore to draw up the present statement.

READING

Capacity. Ability to read easy materials rapidly and more difficult ones closely with adequate understanding and appreciation of both.

Content. Experience in reading literature of various types and on various levels from the very simple to the moderately complex and in analysis of the complex under the guidance of the teacher. Coverage of particular works or particular periods in English and American literature is neither required nor expected.

WRITING

Spelling. Accuracy with respect to common words and the habit of consulting the dictionary for less common ones.

Diction. Sensitivity to the meaning and color of everyday words and skill in consulting the dictionary for others. Our freshmen tend to use "big words" for effect without knowing precisely what they mean.

Sentence construction and punctuation. Ability at least to handle sentences of moderate length. Also desirable, ability to diversify sentence patterns for variety and exact communication of logical relationships. A simple style, however, is preferable to an affected one.

Paragraph construction. Ability to construct a unified and progressive paragraph, with topic sentence and the necessary transitional elements.

Theme construction. Ability to turn out a well-organized theme of at least several pages. Practice in outlining is desirable.

Library method. Habituation to consulting the library, with elementary practice, if feasible, in note-taking and in bibliography and footnote form.

SPEAKING

Classroom discussion. The habit of participating in informal discussion and the ability to do so with cogency and reasonable correctness.

The Puzzle of Flexibility

When requirements were inflexible, teachers hoped for flexibility and freedom. Now that requirements are flexible, freedom is difficult to handle. Meeting flexible requirements may be either stimulating or frustrating. The situation offers a teacher many opportunities to do the wrong things in preparation. Emphasis should not be on preparation for the Verbal Section of the Scholastic Aptitude Test. The tests do not call for long lists of words memorized or defined without close scrutiny of the context. The emphasis should not be on spelling, grammatical terminology, mechanics, drill, "correctness," but rather on power in communicating with human beings. A knowledge of specific works of literature is not demanded, nor is knowledge *about* language unaccompanied by power *with* language. The emphasis is not on facts to be memorized—whether facts associated with literature or a definition of metaphor. Students are not required to do superficial, random, extensive reading of easy material without regard to its intrinsic merit or the unity of the whole work. Reading and literature should not monopolize all English instruction, nor should aspects of composition; the reading of literature is important; so is constant, thoughtful, logical perceptive writing. In reading bulletins setting forth college entrance requirements, students should be helped to see hidden requirements within brief statements—not interpreting as maximum goals what are actually minimum requirements.[48]

Suggestions for Consideration

Periodicals are full of suggestions for slanting high school curricula toward preparation for college. All of them are fairly obvious. High schools should provide instruction in note-taking, typewriting, library research, the use of the dictionary, and preparation for examinations. They should give increased emphasis to fast reading (likewise slow reading when occasion demands) and to opportunities for practice in writing.[49] They should require expository writing and make clear the place of current usage.[50] Listening and speaking are important, though they are not specifically tested. High schools should revamp their courses [51] in the emphasis on powers to be attained. They should maintain high standards and insist on superior teachers. The gifted should be

[48] Frances Dwane McGill, *op. cit.*, p. 21.

[49] Harold Odell, *op. cit.*, p. 67.

[50] J. E. Graves, "College-Prep Composition," *The English Journal*, Vol. XLIV (December, 1955), pp. 534–535.

[51] Maurice L. Pettit, "Should We Give Up on High School English?" *Bulletin of the National Association of Secondary-School Principals*, No. 39 (November, 1955), pp. 133–137.

identified, where possible, and preparation for college anticipated at least as far back as the eighth grade.

Both academic and nonacademic factors have bearing upon college success. The need for creative imagination is great.[52] The search for leaders (not to mention the emphasis in the entrance examinations) may tend to overlook those individuals whose lives will be devoted to fine arts, drama, music, literature, and teaching. It may be that a student has a neurotic personality. Some such students do badly; some are among the most creative and the best citizens. One writer warns against accepting boy heroes who "have everything" and against accepting only emotionally stable, charming, dependable, conforming—useless characters.[53]

Qualities which may make a difference in a student's so-called success in college are "industry, a willingness to work, determination, perseverance, persistency, or however we may describe students who are willing to work up to their capacity in spite of any obstacles placed in their way by forces in our environment; adaptability . . . the minimum of emotional stability that will enable a student to perform effectively in college; intellectual curiosity . . . ; growability. . . ." [54]

Case studies indicate very clearly how difficult it may be to forecast success in college. Student performance cannot be charted infallibly.[55] Probably the most famous example of the unpredictable nature of success in relation to formal schooling is Winston Churchill, described by Dr. F. Cyril James in a program on the topic—"Society—the Chief Examiner." [56]

[52] R. Alden Thresher, *op. cit.*, p. 9.

[53] J. Roswell Gallagher, "The Role of the Emotions in Academic Success," *College Admissions* (Princeton, N. J., College Entrance Examination Board, 1954), p. 108.

[54] Eugene S. Wilson, Jr., "Sorting by Personal Factors," 2. *College Admissions. The Great Sorting* (Princeton, N. J., College Entrance Examination Board, 1955), p. 59.

[55] Henry S. Dyer, "The Evaluation of Case Histories," *College Admissions* (Princeton, N. J., College Entrance Examination Board, 1954), pp. 109–121.

[56] *53rd Report of the Director, op. cit.*, p. 30.

SECONDARY SCHOOL AND COLLEGE
RELATIONSHIPS

Mutual understanding by the schools and colleges of the aims and programs of their respective institutions has always been desirable. Such understanding seems increasingly urgent in these days of (1) flexibility in course requirements and (2) the use of examinations prepared by testing agencies which protect the reliability of the tests by releasing only general information in regard to them.

Many secondary school teachers have been successful in promoting articulation between schools and colleges. Through series of conferences and visits to secondary schools, college teachers have become acquainted with the program, the pupils, and the staffs in the secondary schools. Where reciprocal arrangements have been developed, secondary teachers have visited colleges to observe the adjustment of their students to the freshman English program and to gain first-hand information concerning the personal characteristics and linguistic competencies which are likely to contribute to success in that college.

The trend, as shown in Chapter 3, is toward systematic attempts to improve articulation. English clubs and regional accreditation associations sponsor conferences and provide representatives from both levels on committees engaged in secondary and college curriculum study.

As early as 1925, the School and College Conference on English was established "to study and discuss the teaching of English in secondary schools and the freshman year of college and to consider such related problems as the kind of examination in English most useful in testing fitness for college." [57] The Conference has played an important part in molding the policies of the College Entrance Examination Board in English. It defined power in reading and writing in

[57] A three-page statement prepared by the School and College Conference.

The Report of the Language Committee, April, 1940, and *The Report of the Literature Committee,* April, 1942.[58] *General Education in School and College* has an acknowledgment of indebtedness to both pamphlets.[59]

Another factor making for mutual understanding of the problems involved in articulation is the informal exchange of ideas between high school and college teachers in the scoring of free-response answers to questions in the English Composition Test, the General Composition Test, and the Advanced Placement Tests in Composition and Literature of the College Entrance Examination Board.

Understanding between high school and college teachers may come through committees organized for that purpose. Though there are many other examples, two such groups may be found in the Northwest and in New Jersey. The Interstate Committee on High School–College Relations, more than 20 years old, represents the state universities and colleges, privately endowed colleges, and the high schools of Oregon and Washington.[60] A New Jersey committee is more youthful. In October, 1955, at the meeting of the New Jersey Education Association there was a joint meeting of the New Jersey Association of Teachers of English with the New Jersey Secondary School Principals Association, and the Association of Colleges and Universities. Involved in the "Presentation and Discussion of the Report of the Subcommittee for the New Jersey State Committee on Articulation between School and College" were a representative of a public school, an independent school, a teachers college, and a privately endowed university. Speakers reported on a questionnaire on English composition, on the teaching of

[58] Copies may be secured from the Secretary-Treasurer, Douglas A. Shepardson, Choate School, Wallingford, Connecticut.

[59] A Committee Report by Members of the Faculties of Andover, Exeter, Lawrenceville, Harvard, Princeton, and Yale (Cambridge, Mass., Harvard University Press, 1952).

[60] Frances Dwane McGill, *op. cit.,* p. 23.

composition in New Jersey schools, and on the recommendations of the committee on English literature and composition. It is clear that there is co-operative planning and that there should be understanding.

The program set up for advanced placement varies considerably in certain respects from recent offerings, for example, in the field of communication instituted in many colleges and universities. It contains elements of strength recognized in the chapters in this volume on composition and literature and on speech and listening, but it also differs from them. Frank discussion of the peculiar values and limitations of each program would be helpful in meetings arranged jointly by college and secondary school teachers.

Colleges through bulletins, conferences, and workshops are now striving to promote understanding. Only a few of the possible examples are given here. The February, 1956, *Bulletin of Education* of the School of Education of the University of Kansas reported in some detail the Third Annual Kansas University Conference on Composition and Literature in High School and College.[61] *Purdue English Notes,* October, 1955, devoted almost half its eight pages to " 'Passing the Buck'—But Who Has the Buck?" a reply to an article by the Assistant Superintendent of Public Instruction, State House, Indianapolis, Indiana. This reply in the bulletin seeking "to promote better understanding and greater co-operation between the high school teachers and the college teachers of English" in Indiana was signed by the Committee on Composition Courses, Committee on High School Relations, Department of English, Purdue University. Other items in the bulletin concerned the Fourth English Language Arts Conference at Indiana University and an account of the 89 graduates of Indiana high schools who received extra English credit at Purdue.[62] Stanford University has

[61] Oscar M. Haugh, editor, Lawrence, Kansas, 64 pages.
[62] Department of English, Purdue University, Lafayette, Indiana.

had successful conferences.[63] Two conferences have been held at Yale University, sponsored by the Master of Arts in Teaching Program of the Graduate School.[64]

The National Council of Teachers of English, with its membership drawn from all levels of education, over the years has been bringing about improvement in understanding between schools and colleges. This has been accomplished not only through its conventions and committees, but also through its curriculum series,[65] prepared by a commission broadly representative of all levels, and its periodicals, *Elementary English, The English Journal, College English,* and *College Composition and Communication.*

English clubs throughout the country, affiliates of the National Council, have also helped to bridge the gap between secondary schools and colleges. Many of these clubs have membership from all levels. Among such groups are sections of the California Association of Teachers of English, the California Council of English Associations, the Illinois Association of Teachers of English,[66] the Michigan Council of Teachers of English, the New York State English Council, the New Jersey Education Association, and the New England Association of Teachers of English.

Wherever and whenever the teachers of secondary schools and colleges get to know each other as persons and to share information concerning the adjustment of their students, a smoother transition from school to college is effected.[67]

[63] Communicate with Alfred H. Grommon, English Department, Stanford University.

[64] Reports and speeches of the conferences may be secured by writing Professor Edward S. Noyes, Director of the Master of Arts in Teaching Program.

[65] *The English Language Arts* (1952), *Language Arts for Today's Children* (1954); *The English Language Arts in the Secondary School* (1956); *College Teaching of English* (in preparation); *Preparation of Teachers of the English Language Arts* (in preparation), the whole series published by Appleton-Century-Crofts, Inc., New York.

[66] J. N. Hook, ed., "Evaluating Twelfth-Grade Themes," *Illinois English Bulletin,* Vol. 40 (April, 1953).

[67] Cf. Chapter 3.

CONCLUSIONS

Establishing and meeting college requirements today are complex problems which must be faced on a broad scale by high school and college. Articulation is a two-way process demanding adjustments by both institutions. The question is one of determining, on the basis of a scientific study of the present status of the students, what is the next step in preparing them to perform life's tasks at a level of intellectual competence commensurate with their abilities.

The complexity of the admission problem is due in part to social forces which prevent some able students from entering college, while favoring others with less ability. Students who can profit by a college education should be admitted to college. Sufficient information concerning the standards, offerings, and character of the student body of different colleges should be made available to those who guide individual students toward the colleges most appropriate for them. The breadth of the field of English adds to the complexity. So, too, does recent research in test construction. With growing flexibility of course requirements for college entrance, it becomes increasingly necessary to develop valid testing instruments which will measure reliably, in the shortest possible length of time, the competencies needed for success in college.

Constant research is imperative. Continuous changes in admission requirements and policies are to be expected on the basis of due consultation among all concerned. After conference upon their implications for the program of the secondary school and college, the changes should be duly reflected in both.

All English teachers at the secondary level must be aware of the nature and the breadth of college entrance requirements. Awareness will come from working with students, even several years in advance of their admission to college, to discover strengths and weaknesses in their preparation. It will come from a study of the experimentation and policy decisions of individual colleges and of regional associations of colleges and secondary schools. It will come from the cooperation of secondary schools and colleges in utilizing research through informal, as well as formal, conferences and curriculum workshops sponsored locally, regionally, and by national groups which, like the National Council of Teachers of English, represent all levels of the educational system.

Emphasis in the major examination systems of the country all point to a definite shift from specific ground to be covered to mental processes and skills to be developed. Clarity of thinking, the disciplined use of language, and perceptive, appreciative, and critical reading are among the most important of these.

Ability to comprehend and to judge critically and appreciatively *as wholes* literary works of a high level of maturity is more important than a knowledge of periods of literary history or the biographies of authors.

Ability to use language effectively should be the aim rather than knowledge about language. Regular weekly essays with real substance and on mentally challenging topics should be a part of the students' preparation for college. Classes should be small enough to make careful evaluation and supervised revision possible.

Since ability in English is one of the important factors in admission and in success after admission, English teachers of high caliber are required, not members of the staff transferred to the English Department because they are not needed any longer to teach the subject in which they majored. They should be those broadly trained in the English language arts, who can think, express themselves effectively in speech and in writing, who can read appreciatively and analytically, and who can teach others to reach their highest powers.

Throughout this volume, it has been assumed that a major responsibility of secondary teachers of the English language arts is to assist in identifying those students who are likely to benefit from a college education and to become leaders in the adult world. No other member of the faculty has richer opportunities for knowing students than does the language arts teacher. The program outlined in this volume aims to emphasize those powers and skills important both for preparation for college and for life outside the school.

BIBLIOGRAPHY

Books

College Entrance Examination Board, 2. *College Admissions, The Great Sorting* (Princeton, N. J., The College Entrance Examination Board, 1955).

————, *Advanced Placement Program* (Princeton, N. J., The Educational Testing Service, 1956).

————, *Advanced Placement Tests, Bulletin of Information, 1955–56* (Princeton, N. J., The College Entrance Examination Board, 1956).

————, *College Admissions* (Princeton, N. J., The College Entrance Examination Board, 1954).

————, *College Board Scores, Their Use and Interpretation*, No. 2 (Princeton, N. J., The Educational Testing Service, 1955).

————, *College Board Tests (1955–56) Bulletin of Information* (Princeton, N. J., The College Entrance Examination Board, 1956).

————, *English Composition* (Princeton, N. J., The College Entrance Examination Board, June, 1954).

————, *54th Report of the Director* (Princeton, N. J., The College Entrance Examination Board, 1955).

————, *53rd Report of the Director* (Princeton, N. J., The College Entrance Examination Board, 1954).

FUESS, Claude M., *The College Board, Its First Fifty Years* (New York, Columbia University Press, 1950).

The Fund for the Advancement of Education, Evaluation Report No. 1, *Bridging the Gap between School and College* (New York 22, Fund for the Advancement of Education, 575 Madison Avenue, June, 1953).

General Education in School and College, A Committee Report by Members of the Faculty of Andover, Exeter, Lawrenceville, Harvard, Princeton, and Yale (Cambridge, Mass., Harvard University Press, 1952), language, pp. 40–47; literature, pp. 78–94; integration of school and college, pp. 84–86.

Litsey, David M., *An Analysis of English Placement Tests in Use in Major Colleges and Universities in 1955* (University of Minnesota Study in Education), briefly reported in "Trends in College Placement Tests in Freshman English," *The English Journal,* Vol. XLV (May, 1956), pp. 250–256.

President's Commission on Higher Education, *Higher Education for American Democracy,* Vol. I, *Establishing the Goals* (Washington, D. C., U. S. Government Printing Office, December, 1947).

The School and College Study of Admission with Advanced Standing, Gordon K. Chalmers, Chairman, *College Admission with Advanced Standing Announcement and Bulletin Information* (Gambier, Ohio, Kenyon College, January, 1954).

Smith, Dora V., *Evaluation of Secondary School English, A Report of the Division of the New York Regents' Inquiry into the Character and Cost of Education in New York State,* Monograph No. 11, National Council of Teachers of English (Champaign, Ill., The Council, 1939), o.p.

Periodicals and Bulletins

College Board Review, No. 25 (Winter, 1955), No. 26 (Spring, 1955), No. 27 (Fall, 1955), No. 28 (Winter, 1956).

Friedman, Albert B., "The Literary Experience of High School Seniors and College Freshmen," *The English Journal,* Vol. XLV (December, 1955), pp. 521–524.

Grommon, Alfred H., "Preparing High School Students for College Composition," *California Journal of Secondary Education,* Vol. 28 (February, 1953), pp. 113–118.

Hook, J. N., ed., "Evaluating Twelfth-Grade Themes," *Illinois English Bulletin,* Vol. 40 (April, 1953).

Huddleston, Edith, "Measurement of Writing Ability at the College Entrance Level," *Journal of Experimental Education,* Vol. 22 (March, 1954), pp. 165–213.

Pattillo, Manning M., Jr., and Stout, Lorence, "Co-operation between Secondary Schools and Colleges," *North Central Association Quarterly,* Vol. 25 (January, 1951), pp. 313–345.

Pettit, Maurice L., "Should We Give Up on High School English?" *Bulletin of the National Association of Secondary-School Principals,* No. 39 (November, 1955), pp. 133–137.

Tinkelman, Sherman N., *Regents Examinations,* University of the State of New York, Bulletin No. 1424 (October, 1953), p. 6.

Ward, W. S., "High School–College Co-operation in English," *College Composition and Communication,* Vol. VII (May, 1956), pp. 93–96.

For the latest available information at any time on changes in college entrance requirements and examinations, the reader may consult current issues of the following publications:

College Board Review, published three times a year by the College Entrance Examination Board, Princeton, N. J.

College Composition and Communication, the Official Bulletin of the Conference on College Composition and Communication, published quarterly by the Conference on College Composition and Communication (Champaign, Ill., The National Council of Teachers of English).

College English, published monthly except June, July, August, September by the National Council of Teachers of English (Champaign, Ill., The Council).

The English Journal, published September–June by the National Council of Teachers of English (Champaign, Ill., The Council).

North Central Association Quarterly, North Central Association of Colleges and Secondary Schools (University High School, Ann Arbor, Michigan).

Index

Achievement Tests, CEEB, 447
Achieving Objectives of Education,
  Minneapolis Public Schools, 58
Adamic, Louis, 293
Administrators and the speech program, 243-244
  teachers for college preparatory
  students, 468
Admissions examinations, college,
  445-458
Adolescents, growing anonymity
  faced by, 6
  approaches to understanding, 14-
  15
  books read by, 21-24
  books which portray, 21-24
  conflicting purposes and traditions,
  9
  growing up of, as unit of study,
  114-115
  language characteristics, 16-20
  physical, mental, and emotional
  characteristics, 16-20
  poem about, 12
  tensions caused by submergence
  of individual, 6-9
  world background for, *see* World
  characteristics
Advanced Placement Program,
  CEEB, 451
Advanced Standing Examinations,
  451-454
  in composition and literature, 452,
  464
Advertising art, use in teaching, 415
Aesthetic context, communication
  arts and, 432-436
Age of students, increasing differences and, 127
Agreement, in grammar, 372-373
Ainsworth School, Portland, 343
Allport, Gordon, 217
All-school responsibility, listening,
  257-269

reading, 176-179
Alphabet, as reference tool, 392
Altick, Richard, 334
American English, 357-358; *see also*
  English language
American literature, 145-148
American Magazine, 101
Articulation, 52, 439-440
  education-for-life movement, 442
  effect of numbers, 440-442
  between elementary and second-
  ary, 52, 257-258
  between high school and college,
  439-440, 458-460, 463-466, 467
  listening program, 132-133
  problems of, 52
  study of problems of, 52-53
Assemblies, in listening program,
  264-267
Assignments, in writing, 319-321
Association of Colleges and Universities, 464
Atkinson, George, School, Portland,
  342
Atlanta, Georgia, unit guides, 114n
Atlantic Monthly, 149
Audio-visual equipment, 223-226
  in study of literature, 149-152
Automation, 4
Ayer, Fred, 389

Back-Country America, unit of study
  on, 70-112, 229, 318, 339
Baker, Franklin T., 411
Baltimore Public Schools, 53n
  history and communication arts integrated, 422-424
  listening, study in, 269
  remedial reading in, 197-198
  unit guides in, 114n
  workshops in, 49
Barlow, Elizabeth R., 209-210
Barzun, Jacques, 296

473